# ROUTLEDGE LIBRARY EDITIONS: SOCIOLINGUISTICS

Volume 3

# RECENT ADVANCES IN LANGUAGE, COMMUNICATION, AND SOCIAL PSYCHOLOGY

# RECENT ADVANCES IN LANGUAGE, COMMUNICATION, AND SOCIAL PSYCHOLOGY

Edited by
HOWARD GILES AND ROBERT N. ST. CLAIR

LONDON AND NEW YORK

First published in 1985 by Lawrence Erlbaum Associates

This edition first published in 2019
by Routledge
2 Park Square, Milton Park, Abingdon, Oxon OX14 4RN

and by Routledge
52 Vanderbilt Avenue, New York, NY 10017

*Routledge is an imprint of the Taylor & Francis Group, an informa business*

© 1985 Lawrence Erlbaum Associates

All rights reserved. No part of this book may be reprinted or reproduced or utilised in any form or by any electronic, mechanical, or other means, now known or hereafter invented, including photocopying and recording, or in any information storage or retrieval system, without permission in writing from the publishers.

*Trademark notice*: Product or corporate names may be trademarks or registered trademarks, and are used only for identification and explanation without intent to infringe.

*British Library Cataloguing in Publication Data*
A catalogue record for this book is available from the British Library

ISBN: 978-1-138-34952-0 (Set)
ISBN: 978-0-429-43466-2 (Set) (ebk)
ISBN: 978-1-138-35002-1 (Volume 3) (hbk)
ISBN: 978-1-138-35286-5 (Volume 3) (pbk)
ISBN: 978-0-429-43617-8 (Volume 3) (ebk)

**Publisher's Note**
The publisher has gone to great lengths to ensure the quality of this reprint but points out that some imperfections in the original copies may be apparent.

**Disclaimer**
The publisher has made every effort to trace copyright holders and would welcome correspondence from those they have been unable to trace.

# RECENT ADVANCES IN LANGUAGE, COMMUNICATION, AND SOCIAL PSYCHOLOGY

edited by
**Howard Giles**
*University of Bristol, U.K.*

**Robert N. St. Clair**
*University of Louisville, U.S.A.*

Copyright © 1985 by Lawrence Erlbaum Associates Ltd.
All rights reserved. No part of this book may be reproduced in any form, by photostat, microform, retrieval system, or any other means, without the prior written permission of the publisher.

Lawrence Erlbaum Associates Ltd., Publishers
Chancery House
319 City Road
London EC1V 1LJ

**British Library Cataloguing in Publication Data**

Recent advances in language, communication and social psychology.
1. Psycholinguistics   2. Sociolinguistics
I. Giles, Howard    II. St. Clair, Robert
401'.9    P37

ISBN 0-86377-000-2

Typset by Blackmore Press, Shaftesbury
Printed and bound by A. Wheaton & Co. Ltd., Exeter

# Contents

**List of Contributors** viii

1. **Introduction** 1
   *Howard Giles*

2. **Towards a Theory of Communication in Terms of Preconditions: A Conceptual Framework and Some Empirical Explorations** 10
   *Rolv M. Blakar*

   Introduction 10
   The Explanatory Value of Current Communication Theory 15
   Explications of a Social-Developmental Framework of Communication Oriented Research 21
   Towards More Fruitful Communication-Oriented Research on Schizophrenia 32

3. **Psychological and Interactional Dimensions of Communicative Development** 41
   *Barbara J. O'Keefe and Jesse G. Delia*

   Introduction 41
   Linguistic Competence, Communicative Competence, and the Resources of Communication 42
   Symbolic Interactionism and the Outline of an Interpretive Concept of Communication 48
   The Constructivist Analysis of Interpretive Processes and Human Communication 55

An Overview of Constructivist Research on Interpersonal Construal
　　　Processes and Communicative Behaviour　68
　　A Concluding Note　80

4. **Acquiring Social Variation in Speech　86**
   *Jean Berko Gleason and Rivka Y. Perlmann*

   Introduction　86
   Speech to Children　87
   The Acquisition of Communicative Competence　94
   Variation in Child Language　96
   The Acquisition of Politeness Routines　102
   Conclusions　107

5. **Speech Cues and Social Evaluation: Markers of Ethnicity, Social Class, and Age　112**
   *Richard J. Sebastian and Ellen Bouchard Ryan*

   Introduction　112
   The Effects of Nonstandard Speech on Social Evaluation and
       Behaviour　114
   Age Estimates and Age-related Inferences　132
   Future Research Directions　136
   Summary and Conclusions　138

6. **Towards a Social Psychology of Voice Variations　144**
   *Bruce L. Brown and Jeffrey M. Bradshaw*

   Introduction　144
   Personality and Vocal Patterns　145
   Emotion and Vocal Patterns　169

7. **Temporal Patterns of Speech and Gaze in Social and Intellectual Conversation　182**
   *James M. Dabbs, Jr.*

   Social and Intellectual Functions　182
   The "Look" of a Conversation　186
   Probable Differences Between Social and Intellectual Form　190
   Conclusions　196

8. **An Expectancy Interpretation of Language and Persuasion　199**
   *Michael Burgoon and Gerald R. Miller*

   Introduction　199

Passive Message Reception Paradigm　　203
　　　The Active Participation Paradigm　　213
　　　Resistance to Persuasion Paradigm　　216
　　　Some Concluding Comments　　225

9. **Pragmatics Versus Reinforcers: An Experimental Analysis of Verbal Accommodation**　　230
   *Howard M. Rosenfeld and Pamela K. Gunnell*

   Introduction　　230
   Perspectives on Verbal Behaviour　　232
   Mands and Illocutionary Acts　　234
   A Serendipitous Opportunity: The Double Agent Revisited　　236
   Empirical Evidence　　244
   Discussion　　258

10. **Interpersonal Accommodation and Situational Construals: An Integrative Formalisation**　　263
    *Peter Ball, Howard Giles and Miles Hewstone*

    Introduction　　263
    Social Psychology and Social Situations　　264
    Social Psychology and Language　　267
    A Catastrophe Theory Formalization　　270
    Communication Within Groups and Code-elaboration　　278
    Conclusions　　282

**Index**　　287

## EDITORS

**Howard Giles,** Psychology Department, University of Bristol, Bristol, U.K.
**Robert N. St. Clair,** English Department, University of Louisville, Kentucky, U.S.A.

## LIST OF CONTRIBUTORS

**Peter Ball,** Psychology Department, University of Tasmania, Hobart, Tasmania, Australia
**Rolv M. Blakar,** Institute of Psychology, University of Oslo, Norway
**Jeffrey M. Bradshaw,** Psychology Department, Brigham Young University, Provo, Utah, U.S.A.
**Bruce L. Brown,** Psychology Department, Brigham Young University, Provo, Utah, U.S.A.
**Michael Burgoon,** University of Arizona, Tucson, Arizona, U.S.A.
**James M. Dabbs, Jr.,** Psychology Department, Georgia State University, Atlanta, Georgia, U.S.A.
**Jesse G. Delia,** Speech Communication Department, University of Illinois at Urbana-Champaign, Urbana, Illinois, U.S.A.
**Jean Berko Gleason,** Psychology Department, Boston University, Boston, Massachusetts, U.S.A.
**Pamela K. Gunnell,** Management Department, University of Hartford, West Hartford, Connecticut, U.S.A.
**Miles Hewstone,** Institute of Psychology, University of Tübingen, Tübingen, F.R.G.
**Gerald R. Miller,** Communication Department, Michigan State University, East Lansing, Michigan, U.S.A.
**Barbara O'Keefe,** Speech Communication Department, University of Illinois at Urbana-Champaign, Urbana, Illinois, U.S.A.
**Rivka Y. Perlmann,** Psychology Department, Boston University, Boston, Massachusetts, U.S.A.
**Howard M. Rosenfeld,** Psychology Department, University of Kansas, Lawrence, Kansas, U.S.A.
**Ellen Bouchard Ryan,** Psychiatry Department, McMaster University, Hamilton, Ontario, Canada
**Richard J. Sebastian,** Management and Finance Department, St. Cloud State University, St. Cloud, Minnesota, U.S.A.

# 1 Introduction

**Howard Giles**
*University of Bristol*

Those fascinated by the importance and complexities of language in social life might look to social psychology for some insights. After all, much of an individual's behaviour occurs in a social context, is manifest linguistically, mediated by cognitive processes, and was afforded central focus of attention by the pioneers of social psychology (see Farr, 1980). While language studies figure prominently in many areas of psychological inquiry such as in cognition, psycholinguistics and in development (albeit asocial and non-communicative in the former cases), detailed explorations of the dynamics of language within social psychology have been conspicuous by their absence over the last couple of decades, as has been argued elsewhere (Giles, 1979). Admittedly there were certain individuals who were important exceptions (e.g., Michael Argyle, Roger Brown and Wallace Lambert), and also a few books and research topics (such as nonverbal communication, persuasion, and group interactional analysis), but an examination of mainstream journals and influential texts in social psychology in the early 1970s suggested that language held at the most a peripheral status within that discipline. Correspondingly, a perusal at this time of the multidisciplinary endeavour, sociolinguistics, demonstrated a comparable neglect in its journals and texts of a coherent social psychological approach. Important exceptions were again apparent with regard to the study of bilingualism and forms of address, and it is true that some sociolinguists (e.g., William Labov, Lesley Milroy and Carol Scotton) have emphasized the role of social-psychological constructs, such as attitudes, identities, and motivations, in their analyses.

The complex reasons why a "social psychology of language" has never really gelled historically (apart from in Canada, see for example Gardner

& Kalin, 1981) have been the topic of some debate in the literature (e.g., Fraser & Scherer, 1982a). As yet, unfortunately, such speculations appear incomplete and unconvincing. Suffice it to say, however, that there are many indications that it has *arrived* as a distinctive, complementary approach to those of the sociology of language, anthropological linguistics, sociolinguistics, and so forth. In the forthcoming *Social Science Encyclopaedia* (Routledge & Kegan Paul), there will be a separate entry for the "social psychology of language". Indeed, research activity since 1977 has grown enormously and, as will be seen from the plethora of theoretical models and ideas conveyed in this present volume, blossomed considerably in recent years. Indications of the sudden outgrowth are evident in the advent of numerous edited books in the discipline (e.g., Fraser & Scherer, 1982b; Markova, 1978; Rommetveit & Blakar, 1979; St. Clair & Giles, 1980), the appearance in 1982 of an international series of monographs devoted to it (published by Edward Arnold), the emergence of two international Conferences on this perspective at Bristol in 1979 and 1983 attracting enthusiastic participation world-wide, as well as the establishment of the *Journal of Language and Social Psychology* as a coherent forum for this speciality in 1982. Interestingly, an active "interpersonal communication" branch of the International Communications Association has developed with an implicit social psychological bias.

Given an overlap on many topics by both sociolinguists and social psychologists (e.g., relationships between language and social situations, sex roles, ethnicity), what then *is* the social psychology of language? It lies essentially in two domains, theoretical and methodological. Theoretically, researchers are interested in the ways in which the production and reception of language behaviours are mediated by *cognitive organizational* processes. Aspects of cognitive organization which appear in the ensuing chapters of this book include perceived goal structures, situational construals, cognitive monitoring, causal attributions, etc., and the interactive roles they play in determining, for instance, speaking and listening strategies. Given that social-psychological theories are mostly about the complexities and dynamics of cognitive organization and the representation of the social world and social structure, this perspective broadens the *explanatory* scope of language study. For example, social identity theory (Tajfel & Turner, 1979) proposes that we desire to belong to social categories which afford us a positive social identity. It articulates the conditions under which group members will search for, or even create, dimensions (linguistic and nonlinguistic) along which they are positively differentiated from relevant outgroups. This, then, enables us to help explain why some groups maintain their own language, dialects, and nonverbal styles while other lose them and assimilate towards the communicative patterns of a more powerful group (Giles & Johnson, 1981).

Methodologically, the social psychology of language utilizes, for the most part, the experimental method characteristic of general psychology (see Giles, 1983). Such a procedure is extremely useful in its potential for replication and rigorous control of extraneous variables as well as in its capacity to allow more exact specifications of the conditions under which certain language patterns are emitted, and the types of responses people afford particular language behaviours in specific contexts. This methodology is, of course, complemented by case study and naturalistic observation techniques, as can be seen later in this volume, not to mention ethogenic analyses (Harré & Secord, 1972) all of which are openly encouraged as an eclectic means of extending our data base (Robinson, Giles, & Smith, 1980). In addition, the discipline, as again will become apparent, has techniques (electronic and questionnaire format) for measuring complex psychological states and dispositions (e.g., ideologies, personalities), attitudes, attributions, cognitive structures, and representations, etc.

Moving beyond the conceptual concerns and boundaries of a social-psychological perspective, the present volume is a further articulation of this emerging approach with respect to a wide range of language behaviours (e.g., eye gaze, language intensity, politeness routines), social processes (e.g., aggression, persuasion, stereotyping), methodological and analytical procedures (e.g., case studies, naturalistic observations, electronic measurements under laboratory conditions), and theoretical formulations (e.g., constructivist, expectancy, speech act approaches). Our guiding theme is to study the crucial and creative role of cognitive structures in elucidating how communication between individuals develops in childhood and beyond (Chapters 3 & 4), functions in and defines social situations (Chapters 7 & 10), expresses feelings and values (Chapter 6), influences others (Chapters 8 & 9), evokes social categorizations, inferences and behavioural reactions (Chapter 5), and how it can break down (Chapter 2).

We make no pretence whatsoever at covering all major areas important to the future development of a social psychology of language; that has been attempted in large measure by us elsewhere (Giles, Robinson & Smith, 1980; Robinson, 1983; Scherer & Giles, 1979). Our intention here has been, somewhat akin to the *Advances* edited by Fraser and Scherer (1982b), to provide a forum for some of what we believe to be the most innovative and interesting scholars in the field to introduce and discuss their most recent findings and theoretical orientations in more or less extended fashions. A further *Advances* to that of Fraser and Scherer was deemed necessary and fruitful for a variety of reasons. First, there is, happily, a proliferation of group research traditions which scientific articles can rarely do justice to within the confines of single journal issues.

Second, and relatedly, whilst pursuing the developmental, socioclinical, situational, conversation structural, and interpersonal accommodation themes inherent in the Fraser and Scherer volume further, and in ways which draw somewhat more furtively from areas of mainstream social psychology (see McKirnan, 1983; Taylor, 1982), we wish to cast our net even more diversely into other areas as well, including for example the relationships between language and attitude change, the elderly, emotions, intergroup behaviour, reinforcement and communication breakdown. Third, we wish, by means of a large number of the chapters herein as well as the volume title, to underline the fact that significant advances in this area could not maintain their impressive momentum if devoid of explicit and detailed recourse to the complex relationships between language and *communication* processes. Finally, Fraser and Scherer (1982a) imply that the study of language is a more integral and accepted component of European social psychology compared to its peripheral status in the United States. While this may well be true, a subordinate aim of the present volume is to underscore the view that a social psychology of language is alive and thriving beyond the confines of Europe too.

Without further ado, let us provide a flavour of what is to follow in this volume. Rolv Blakar (Chapter 2) provides a useful scene-setter by arguing for the fundamental importance of a communication perspective for understanding human behaviour which is on a par with historical, economic, sociological analyses. He also underlines the need, so often unappreciated by researchers, to define communication operationally, and to provide a conceptual framework in terms of the preconditions necessary for it to occur successfully. Prime attention amongst the preconditions is given to the desire to negotiate shared meanings and to take into account the perspective of the other. His so-called "social developmental" model, and the empirical research deriving from it, is extremely interesting because of its implications for handling communication failure in general, and the use of language in schizophrenic families in particular. Indeed, the examination of "abnormal" patterns of communication in the socioclinical sphere is not only a welcome advent in the social psychology of language in its own right but is also important with respect to its implications for "normal" language functioning.

Barbara O'Keefe and Jesse Delia (Chapter 3) continue the focus on the importance of creating and maintaining *shared meaning* in the analysis of communication, and pay particular attention to the developmental-interactional processes by which children and adults learn to acquire the formal codes of language. They argue cogently that communication must invoke more than a knowledge of the linguistic code and the sociocultural rules for its use. It must deal with the ongoing processes of interpretation and social coordination as well as the development of behavioural strategies to fulfil the perceived goals of the encounter. They deal with these issues within their own constructivist model of communication and report some of their most recent findings in this vein. As with the previous chapter, they highlight lucidly the negotiative character of interaction and the need to take into account the role and identity needs of the other, as well as certain dimensions of complexity in cognitive structures.

Jean Berko Gleason and Rivka Perlmann (Chapter 4) also focus upon the development of communication as a social phenomenon. However, they pay attention to the environments that surround children learning to talk and particularly to the ways in which children acquire social variation in speech. These scholars provide an in-depth discussion of the roles of speech interactions between children and their mothers and fathers in the *acquisition* of communicative competence. Their research, naturalistic and laboratory oriented, provides much needed insight into how children structure their linguistic environments, identify social markers, cope with politeness routines, and resolve various cognitive burdens characteristically associated with the acquisition of language.

Richard Sebastian and Ellen Ryan (Chapter 5) discuss how the various speech cues of ethnicity, social class, and age (the emphasis here being not on children but on the other, quite unexplored end of the life span) affect attitudes and can lead to certain types of discriminatory behaviour. On this basis of their extensive empirical research, they propose two distinct mechanisms which may explain evaluative responses of individuals to speech. The negative affect mechanism postulates that speaker denigration stems directly from the discomfort aroused by the unintelligibility of various speech sounds and sequences. The other mechanism involves the use of voice cues to make (usually negative) inferences about the membership of a speaker in one or *more* (outgroup) categories. This chapter provides a timely breakthrough into the complex process whereby listeners make *multiple* classification of speakers from voice cues and highlights the possible processes involved (unlike most of the descriptive, atheoretical work in this area).

Bruce Brown and Jeffrey Bradshaw (Chapter 6) continue the focus on interpersonal perception from voice cues with particular emphasis on how such features can be instrumental in uncovering information about personality and emotions. Not only have they conducted an extensive review of the literature—with even *re*-analyses of some of the data conducted with exemplary statistical rigour—but they have also added to their paralinguistic quest by providing useful commentaries on the need for an integrated theory of emotions as expressed through voice (yet another underdeveloped topic). Their emerging research paradigm which is highly sophisticated methodologically is not only allowing them access now to naturally occurring communications in highly sensitive social arenas but also inducing them to explore the intriguing domain of self-deception theory.

Patterns of speech and their relationships with visual interaction is the theme which James Dabbs concentrates upon (Chapter 7). A conversation, he argues, may have both social and intellectual functions. The former deals with the establishment and maintenance of social bonds whilst the latter deals with information about the world. In conversing, both the social and intellectual parameters of speech are interwoven within the pragmatic contexts of communicative use. What is significant however is Dabbs's findings regarding how these patterns of visual and vocal information are sequenced and temporally intercalated. Hence, the way in which words are strung together with interludes of sound and silence and changing facial expression provides functional insight into how communication goes far beyond a mere structural focus on verbal forms.

Michael Burgoon and Gerald Miller (Chapter 8) are particularly concerned with how norms and expectations of usage are developed through language in different contexts. In this contribution, they have summarized their extensive empirical researches and placed them informatively in the context of numerous propositions and corollaries on the interpretation of expectancy in the language of persuasion. For example, they propose (and have data to suggest) that the use of language variables in a message, which conform more closely than expected to what is considered to be communicatively appropriate, facilitates that message's persuasive impact. Their theoretical framework is important as it makes sense of a large body of attitude change research which has been more or less renowned for its welter of contradictory findings. This chapter is an example, *par excellence*, not only of the way in which social psychology has been blinkered in its sensitivity to language variables but also in the great potential that studying the latter can have for the development of social psychology *per se*.

The context of verbal influence is taken up again in the penultimate contribution by Howard Rosenfeld and Pamela Gunfield (Chapter 9). They have concentrated upon how language problems as envisaged by other disciplines, in this case learning and speech act theories, can contribute to a more effective social psychology of language and communication by an incorporation of "mand" and "illocutionary act" into the framework. Since each discipline interprets speech within its own conceptual domain, these perspectives can and do lead to encroachments (so-called) on epistemological domains and result in paradigmatic conflicts such as the famous controversy between Chomsky and Skinner. This chapter reviews the literature on these issues which not only points to an enrichment of the social psychology of language but leads into their empirical investigations of "double agents" in verbal conditioning situations, underlining the crucial methodological value of the case-study approach. Thus, these authors do not "throw out the baby with the bathwater"—a syndrome all too common in some areas of contemporary psychology when considering traditional learning theories—but they incorporate with insight meaningful and pervasive aspects of reinforcement principles into their theoretical and methodological stances.

The final chapter by Peter Ball and associates attempts to bring together a number of different sociolinguistic topics within a cognitive social-psychological framework which depicts participants as jointly theorizing about their social encounters as they proceed, testing and revising them, and using them to organize their behaviour so as to approach their situational goals. The passive and active roles of speech markers are described and previous taxonomic progress on speech and social situations is noted as specifying potential components for participants' situational models. Hence, Chapter 10 brings us round implicitly to where this volume started. The authors proceed to tighten existing links between speech accommodation theory and the social psychology of intergroup relations, employing the mathematic cusp catastrophe theory to derive the conclusion that speech accommodation processes are accentuated by the extent to which speakers perceive encounters as being intergroup, rather than interindividual, in nature. Finally, the theory of elaborated and restricted sociolinguistic codes is linked to the foregoing, arguing that the former is primarily the code of interindividual communication and the latter primarily that of within-group communication when group membership is salient.

The contributors to this volume share the superordinate concern that a vibrant social-psychological perspective should be fostered in order to promote, coalesce, and develop further the ideas of those like-minded scholars who share our conceptual inclinations. But more than that we share the belief that a vital and cohesive social psychological approach can do much to enhance our understanding of communicative phenomena and processes in a concrete manner that other subdisciplines cannot illuminate, at least at present. While we are obviously very committed to the development of this perspective, we are not, as we have stated often before, so blinkered as to think it is a panacea for all communication problems and issues; no one approach could possibly unravel all the important biological, sociological, linguistic, historical, and so forth, complexities involved in communication. Indeed, contributors to this volume have drawn directly upon other approaches in order to expand their descriptive and explanatory powers and horizons. We can only hope, despite the fact that social psychologists have really only recently begun to explore the field, that other language-hyphenated disciplines will also find us in turn fruitful complements from which they may draw freely. At the sametime, we would wish that language and communication processes may once again be appreciated as being at the heart of mainstream social psychology everywhere.

## ACKNOWLEDGEMENT

The author acknowledges some material provided by the coeditor of the volume for an earlier draft of this Introduction, certain parts of which have been used in modified form in the present version.

## REFERENCES

Farr, R. Homo loquens in social psychological perspective. In H. Giles, W. P. Robinson & P. M. Smith (Eds.), *Language: social psychological perspectives:* Oxford: Pergamon, 1980.

Fraser, C., & Scherer, K. R. Introduction: Social psychological contributions to the study of language. In C. Fraser & K. R. Scherer (Eds.), *Advances in the social psychology of language.* Cambridge: Cambridge University Press, 1982.(a)

Fraser, C., & Scherer, K. R. (Eds.) *Advances in the social psychology of language.* Cambridge: Cambridge University Press, 1982.(b)

Gardner, R. C., & Kalin, R. (Eds.) *A Canadian social psychology of ethnic relations.* Toronto: Methuen, 1981.

Giles, H. Sociolinguistics and social psychology: An introductory essay. In H. Giles & R. N. St. Clair (Eds.), *Language and social psychology.* Oxford & Baltimore: Blackwell & University Park Press, 1979.

Giles, H. The second Bristol conference: A personal assessment. *Journal of Language & Social Psychology,* 1983, *2,* 301-314.

Giles, H., & Johnson, P. The role of language in ethnic group relations. In J. C. Turner & H. Giles (Eds.), *Intergroup behaviour.* Oxford & Chicago: Blackwell & Chicago University Press, 1981.

Giles, H., Robinson, W. P. & Smith, P. M. (Eds.) *Language: social psychological perspectives.* Oxford: Pergamon, 1980.

Harré, R., & Secord, P. *The explanation of social behaviour.* Oxford: Blackwell, 1972.

McKirnan, D. Review of "Advances in the social psychology of language." In C. Fraser & K. R. Scherer (Eds.), *Journal of Applied Psycholinguistics,* 1983, *4,* 93-98.

Markova, I. *Language in its social context.* London: Wiley, 1978.

Robinson, W. P. (Ed.) Special triple issue of Invited Papers at the 2nd International Conference on Social Psychology and Language, Bristol. *Journal of Language & Social Psychology,* 1983, *2* (2,3 & 4).

Robinson, W. P., Giles, H., & Smith, P. M. Epilogue. In H. Giles, W. P. Robinson & P. M. Smith (Eds.), *Language: Social psychological perspectives:* Oxford: Pergamon, 1980.

Rommetveit, R., & Blakar, R. (Eds.) *Studies in language, thought and communication.* London & New York: Academic Press, 1979.

St. Clair, R. N., & Giles, H. (Eds.) *The social and psychological contexts of language.* Hillsdale, N.J.: Lawrence Erlbaum Associates, 1980.

Scherer, K. R., & Giles, H. (Eds.) *Social markers in speech*. Cambridge: Cambridge University Press, 1979.

Tajfel, H., & Turner, J. C. An integrative theory of intergroup conflict. In W. C. Austin & S. Worchel (Eds.), *The social psychology of intergroup relations*. Monterey, Cal.: Brooks/Cole, 1979.

Taylor, D. M. Review of "Advances in the Social Psychology of Language." In C. Fraser & K. R. Scherer (Eds.), *Journal of Language & Social Psychology,* 1982, *1,* 77-80.

# 2
# Towards a Theory of Communication in Terms of Preconditions: A Conceptual Framework and Some Empirical Explorations

Rolv M. Blakar
*University of Oslo*

## INTRODUCTION

This chapter begins with arguments and illustrations of how communication theory represents a basic perspective in the understanding of human activities on a par with, for example, the historic and the economic perspectives. From this viewpoint, two somewhat paradoxical observations will be presented and discussed. First, representing such a fundamental and general perspective, it is surprising how relatively little effort has traditionally been invested in research and conceptual clarification specifically within the field of communication. This state of affairs becomes even more paradoxical because we argue that an adequate understanding of language and language processing *presupposes* the adoption of an explicit communication perspective. Secondly, when the communication perspective ultimately became popular as an integrated aspect of the general trend of the last two or three decades to adopt social perspectives, the use of vague, diffuse and implicit concepts of communication produced confusions rather than clarifications. The conclusion from this analysis is evident: there is at present an urgent need for explication and clarification of the concept of communication and communication theory.

The substantial body of this chapter concentrates on presenting an *explicit* approach to communication proper. The problems of what is to constitute a fruitful *definition* of communication are addressed, and a definition is proposed. Then the *conceptual framework* for what may be called a social-developmental theory of communication is presented and a method devised for further empirical explorations of communication according to this conceptual framework is advocated. Finally, a series of *empirical studies* exploiting this particular method are presented to show how this alternative theoretical approach may enable us to grasp and analyze acts of communication in their total social, developmental and dynamic complexities.

## Communication: A Fundamental Perspective on Man

Communication constitutes a basic precondition for all social intercourse. No social system, organization or society can be established and maintained, or changed, *without* communication. Only through participation in communicative activities does Man become a truly social being. This can easily be demonstrated in various ways. First, if we utilize all our imagination and try to conceive of Man as completely lacking communicative abilities, we immediately realize the absurdity of this autistic being—unable to participate and unqualified for membership in any social organization. Secondly, if we try to define concepts such as, "social fellowship," "social system" or "society," we discover that one decisive factor is whether members or participants have developed, or have at their disposal, a communication system. And, in making decisions with respect to whether a person is a member of a particular society, social system or group, a fundamental criterion is whether or not the person focused upon knows the relevant communicative system that enables him or her to engage in communicative activities with other members.

The implications of these observations are far-reaching. In order to gain insight into and understand ourselves and our fellow Man (*qua* individuals) as well as the society surrounding us (*qua* social system), it is absolutely necessary to adopt a communicative perspective and develop communication theory.

Historical theories are basic to our understanding of society because society is not static but develops and changes over time; economic theories are essential for understanding society because society comprises economic relations. This seems to be generally accepted. Similarly, the communication perspective and theories of communication are necessary in order to understand society because society is based upon communication and interaction. Historical, economic, communicational and other relevant perspectives *supplement* each other. They are *not* mutually exclusive or competitive. The historian understands history precisely by attempting to reconstruct and understand communication and interaction systems which existed in the past in different societies. The object of historical change in a society is, among other things, its communication systems. The development of a written language, the art of printing, as well as television, all illustrate how changes in communicative systems may promote revolutionary social changes. Society cannot, of course, be understood from the point of view of communication alone, but neglect of this perspective will necessarily result in an inadequate understanding.

On a par with the historical perspective, the communication perspective is also a *general* one. A historical perspective can facilitate our understanding of an individual's life situation as well as the situation of a family, a local community, a town or city, an organization, a corporation, a nation or culture, etc. In a similar manner, we may conceive of an individual as a member of various communication systems and as a participant in various acts of communication. We may analyse a family in terms of the patterns of communication existing within the family as well as between family and environment. A society can be described by means of the communication systems it has developed. A particularly relevant criterion for evaluating the degree of democratic development within a given society is whether, and to what extent, members have equal access to and control over communication facilities (cf. Blakar, 1979). Moreover, the relations between superpowers cannot be completely understood without a communication perspective. The recent addition of China (to the Soviet Union and the USA) as a superpower has necessarily made communication patterns more complex.

Under these circumstances, it is really surprising to observe that the communication perspective has not been more frequently exploited *within* the various disciplines, and that theories of communication have not been elaborated and refined to a greater extent. It is difficult to identify the reason(s) for this relative neglect, apart from the fact that communication represents a very complex phenomenon—but then so do most social phenomena and processes. Within the discipline of psychology, for example, much more effort has traditionally been invested in understanding the related phenomena of language, language processing and thinking than communication proper. This relative lack of studies on communication, empirical as well as theoretical, is to our contention, the more surprising as an adequate understanding of language and language processing *presupposes* the adoption of a communication perspective.

Communication and the Study of Language

Language can be studied from various perspectives and various conceptual frameworks and models can be exploited for this purpose. Several *choices* therefore confront the student of language. Language can be studied from the perspective(s) of linguistics, philosophy, mathematics, information theory, biology, sociology, anthropology, psychology, etc. A psychologist and a linguist will obviously consider *dissimilar* issues, utilize *dissimilar* conceptual frameworks and base their efforts on *dissimilar* models. This multitude of perspectives is productive and indeed necessary in order to achieve a total understanding of "the most human of all human phenomena", language. On the other hand, there are several choices with regard to general and basic perspectives on the study of language which have to be made *regardless* of whether the researcher is committed by training to the framework of sociology or linguistics, of psychology or mathematics. This Chapter considers some of the more important of these choices and presents what I consider to be the most favourable position. It should be mentioned that the dominant research traditions in language are based on what I consider to be faulty choices with regard to the basic perspectives on language study.

First, language must be studied *in use*. Although this may at first glance seem obvious, the dominant approaches to the study of language have nevertheless favoured the opposite position, that before one attempts to investigate language in use one has to answer the questions concerning what language *is*. For example, the leading contemporary linguist, Noam Chomsky (1968), programmatically states: "If we hope to understand human language ... *we must ask what it is, not how or for what purpose it is used* (p. 62)." This position may seem equally sound, but for Chomsky the problem becomes *how* language is to be studied if not in use. If not *in use,* how then is language manifested for Chomsky and other linguists? They naturally have in mind types of common everyday language-use situations, and within these (rather special) limits they analyze *what* language *is*. However, as Rommetveit (1972a, p. 5), expressing his doubts concerning Chomsky's position on this issue, puts it: "But how is it possible, in view of Wittgenstein's (1968) thorough analysis of these issues to disentangle *meaning* from *use*? Will not any statement pretending to maintain something about what language *is* include *concealed assumptions concerning use*?" The only way to avoid such concealed assumptions (which may very well prove faulty) is explicitly to study language *in use*.

Second, language must be studied embedded *in its (social) contexts*. Again, this is an apparently obvious assertion, and once again we discover that only a minority of the students of language support this position. Common practice within the dominant traditions in the study of language continues to be analysis of the individual element (be it the phoneme/word, or the sentence/utterance) in isolation, detached from the more inclusive (social) contexts.[1] In defence, it is maintained that a

---

[1]Sociolinguistics can be seen as a reaction to the study of language *in vacuo*. However, within modern sociolinguistics there has been a strong tendency to shift to the other extreme and to map *abstract relations* between language and society detached from the actual social situation within which the use of language takes place (cf. Blakar, 1979).

"division of labour" is necessary, that a reasonable goal is the description of purely linguistic elements and structures, and that the task of "putting language back in its natural social contexts" has to be carried out by others or at some time in the future. For example, the semantic theory developed by Katz and Fodor (1963) is explicitly in accordance with this scheme. The difficulties of putting language back in context is not my only objection to such approaches; such analyses *in vacuo*, severed from context, will easily result in some odd conclusions. For example, when Katz and Fodor (1963) conclude that the sentence, "My spinster aunt is an infant," is a linguistic anomaly, they do so because they fail to analyse the sentence *as embedded in contexts*. One can easily imagine various (social) contexts in which this sentence is highly acceptable (Rommetveit, 1968; Rommetveit & Blakar, 1979; Uhlenbeck, 1967).

Third, language must be studied from a *communication perspective*. Here, again, we find ourselves as exponents of a minority position among students of language. However, use of language almost by definition involves something being made known (that is, *communication*) in a particular social context (that is, a *communication setting*).[2] Hence, the perspective of communication represents the vital and integral perspective if the *use* of language, as embedded *in (social) contexts*, is to be systematically investigated. Basically, language *cannot* be adequately understood as a means to promote, establish, and maintain social contact, if the perspective of communication is ignored. This does not imply that only problems connected with language and communication are worth studying. Of course, studies related to language and thinking, language and memory, language and peception, language and development, language and social class, language and social reality, just to mention but a few key issues, are important in order to achieve a total understanding of language and language processing. It does imply, however, that in the study of these and other relevant issues concerning language and language processing, it should always be kept *explicitly* in mind that the use of language involves *that something is being made known*. For example, a subject's memory of verbal material can only be adequately assessed and understood in terms of what is being made known to the subject by the presentation of the verbal stimulus material (cf. Blakar & Rommetveit, 1975; Rommetveit et al., 1971; Wold, 1978). Once again, the problem is not only that studies of language and language processing which ignore the communication perspective are bound to give incomplete information, but that such studies are most likely to give *misleading* information.[3]

---

[2]The definition of communication will be discussed on pp.23-25.

Before returning to examine communication theory it is worth mentioning a further choice of perspective. While the three perspectives considered so far express *fundamental choices*, the fourth one indicates a *strategic position* within a multidisciplinary field. Every discipline, be it psychology, linguistics, sociology, biology, etc., must study language *on its own premises*. By this, we do not prescribe disciplinary isolationism. Interdisciplinary efforts are definitely necessary if the riddles of language are ever to be resolved. We are sceptical, however, of the tendency to split language up into "pieces," to assume that a given discipline is the ultimate authority on each "piece" and to regard the other disciplines as subservient in relation to this authority with regard to that particular "piece." Ervin-Tripp and Slobin (1966), for example, ascribe psychology such a *subservient* position in relation to linguistics when they maintain that the task of psychology is to identify "the processes by which *the competence described by the linguists* is acquired by children and is reflected in performance under a variety of conditions [p. 436, our italics]." In the late 1950s and early 1960s, psychologists who identified the "psychological processes and mechanisms" underlying Chomsky's (1957) generative model, were left betrayed when Chomsky later (1965 and 1972) extensively revised his model. (A new generation of optimistic psychologists naturally undertook the task to identify the "psychological processes and mechanisms" underlying this *revised* model.) Similarly, linguists have looked towards the "authorities", i.e., psychology and sociology, in order to learn about language in use under varying social conditions. Our conclusion is simple. Each discipline must be responsible for posing its *own* problems of inquiry within its *own* conceptual framework and on the basis of its *own* perspectives, but each of these should be open to continual reassessment and the adoption of "authoritativeness" and "master-slave" relations should be avoided.

## THE EXPLANATORY VALUE OF CURRENT COMMUNICATION THEORY

The foregoing analysis should have made clear the potential explanatory value of communication theory and the potential fruitfulness of adopting a communication perspective in the study of human behaviour. Under

---

[3]Here we have only briefly outlined our paradigmatical positions that language should be studied: (1) in use; (2) as embedded in (social) contexts; and (3) from a communication perspective. For further theoretical elaborations of and empirical support on these issues, the reader is recommended to Rommetveit & Blakar, 1979. (Cf. also Blakar, 1980c, in press-a; Rommetveit, 1968, 1972a, 1972b, 1972c, 1974).

these circumstances, particularly when taking into account the general trend of our time (*Zeitgeist*) to adopt a *social perspective* in the study of an ever growing number of issues and phenomena (cf. Blakar, 1981a, in press-a), it is not at all surprising that during the last two or three decades communication theory has gained increasing popularity and has been adopted over a wide range of different issues and utilized within a large number of different fields. Phenomena varying from sex and children's play to psychopathology and schizophrenia, to mention but a few key examples, have been analysed *in terms of* communication. It follows from the discussion above that the adoption of a communication perspective on these and other phenomena should add considerably to our understanding. On the other hand, it is my contention that communication theory as it is developed and exploited *at present* within various fields of research has *not* contributed to any such clarification. On the contrary, much so-called "communication-oriented" research has actually been characterized by the fact that one "mystery" (for example, schizophrenia) has been "explained" by another "mystery" (communication, or more adequately, deviant communication). We have elsewhere (Blakar, 1980a, in press-a) argued that in the eagerness to redefine, for example, schizophrenia *in terms of* communication, one has almost forgotten and totally ignored the problems with regard to defining communication itself. Hence, we are here forced to undertake a critical examination of communication-oriented research.

This critical examination of the status and quality of current communication-oriented research might have been pursued and explored in various manners. For example, current communication-oriented research might have been reviewed systematically in order to expose cases of such ignorances over a wide range of topics and fields. Or, one single field might have been chosen as a target field and presented in quite some detail to demonstrate how the various conceptual and methodological short-comings within it have hindered progress. Whereas the first strategy would add to the generality of our argument, the latter would give an opportunity to corroborate it. At present, the latter strategy is preferable. The validity of the argument should be convincingly established before its representativeness is questioned.

### The Case of Communication-Oriented Research on Schizophrenia

For various reasons, we have chosen the field of communication-oriented research on psychopathology (in particular schizophrenia) as the target field for our analysis. First and foremost, the study of deviant or pathological communication may actually make essential additions to the knowledge about "normal" communication. But alas, hitherto, the study of familial communication in connection with psychopathology (schizophrenia) has been an almost totally ignored topic within the disciplines of sociolinguistics and the social psychology of language. Second, the family represents a key unit within, and offers considerable problems to, social psychology in general. The family too has not yet received the attention it deserves as a crucial unit within the fields of sociolinguistics and the social psychology of language. In our society, the family constitutes the communicative system within which the individual (the child) to a great extent acquires communicative abilities and style. Moreover, within the field of communication-oriented research on psychotherapy, the communication perspective has been adopted by a number of different research groups for a considerable time. (Almost 30 years represents a long time within our young disciplines.) However, the various clinically-oriented research groups have had no, or little, contact with the more traditionally academic disciplines devoted to the study of language and communication, such as sociolinguistics and the social psychology of language (cf. Blakar, 1980c, in press-a; Riskin & Faunce, 1972). Finally, family research is one of the fields within which social psychological theory (in this case, communication theory) has been put seriously to the test from the point of view of applied psychology (cf. Blakar, in press-a; Blakar & Nafstad, 1981, 1982).

Although the family communication and systems perspective can be said to have evolved gradually within the study of psychopathology, it may even be argued that it was implicit in some of Freud's writings (cf. Ackerman, Beatman & Sherman, 1961; Blakar, 1980c), but it was not before the late forties/early fifties that this perspectve was *explicitly* adopted as an alternative paradigm in the study of psychopathology. Haley, himself one of the pioneers of the field, in retrospect (1959) described the change of perspective that took place in the study of schizophrenia in the following way: "A transition would seem to have taken place in the study of schizophrenia; from the early idea that the difficulty in these families was caused by the schizophrenic member, to the idea that they contained a pathogenic mother, to the discovery that the father was inadequate, to the current emphasis upon all three family members involved in *a pathological system of interaction*. [p. 358, my italics]."

This radical shift in perspective was not produced by any compelling findings nor promoted by any new observations. On the contrary, it reflected the general trend and the willingness to *re-interpret* earlier observations from a social perspective. This is clearly seen from Ruesch and Bateson's (1951) arguments in support of their programmatically stated position to conceive of psychopathology *"in terms of* disturbances of communication":

> Psychopathology is defined in terms of disturbances of communication. This statement may come as a surprise, but if the reader cares to open a textbook on psychiatry and to read about the manic-depressive or the schizophrenic psychosis, for example, he is likely to find terms such as "illusions", "delusions", "hallucinations", "flight of ideas", "disassociation", "mental retardation", "elation", "withdrawal", and many others, *which refer specifically to disturbances of communication*; they imply either that perception is distorted or that expression–that is, transmission—is unintelligible. [pp. 79-80, our italics.]

What is offered, then is *an alternative perspective*. (Cf. Kuhn's (1970) general descriptions of "the structure of scientific revolutions" in terms of shifts of paradigms.) Two reasons for this change of perspective at this particular time, can easily be identified. In addition to the general trend to adopt a social perspective, the widespread frustration with regard to the lack of efficiency of traditional, individually-oriented therapy, definitely represented a motivational impetus for a (any) shift. As would be expected, this shift of theoretical perspective posed a series of conceptual and methodological problems to the field. Again, Haley (1971) in retrospect has described the situation: "Once the hypothesis was posed that schizophrenia was a product of a certain kind of relationship, a problem became apparent. *There were no languages for describing relationships, no theoretical models, and no means of testing the relationship between two people.* Previous research had tested a person [p. 274, my italics]."

One might have expected that in adopting a communication perspective, the various traditional social disciplines (social psychology, in particular) would have been turned to in order to resolve the problems related to the adoption of a social perspective. Surprisingly enough, this did *not* happen. As Riskin and Faunce (1972) observed in their extensive and systematic overview of the field: "interdisciplinary isolation is striking [p. 369]."[4]

After the breakthrough of the social perspective in the early fifties, the field can be said to have developed over three (or four) more or less distinct phases. That the adoption of the social perspective really represented a "breakthrough", is reflected for example in the fact that Weakland (1974, p. 269) in "a self-reflexive hindsight" characterized the launching of the double-bind theory as representing almost a "scientific

---

[4]Elsewhere (Blakar, 1981b), I have analyzed more systematically the pervading tendency to ignore social psychological theory and knowledge in general.

earth-quake." The first phase, from the beginning to the mid or late fifties, was characterized by the launching of "the great theories". A variety of theoretical models and conceptual frameworks were introduced aiming at an understanding of psychopathology (in particular schizophrenia) *in terms of* the communication patterns of the family. Among the variety of models and theories outlined, the highly different theories of Bateson, Jackson, Haley, and Weakland (1956), Lidz, Cornelison, Terry, and Fleck (1957), Wynne, Rykoff, Day, and Hirsch (1958) have gained a somewhat special status. Due in part to the authoritative review of various theories and models of the field by Mishler and Waxler (1965), the theoretical positions of these three research groups have been canonized.

The next phase, partly overlapping the first one and fading away gradually in the early seventies, was characterized by an intense empirical research activity, where literally hundreds of studies were conducted for (or against) the various theories launched in the first phase; for a review, see for example Riskin and Faunce (1972), Blakar (1980a, 1980b), and Helmersen (1983). Taken together, the above phases may be called the "optimistic period" of family and communication research on psychopathology. It was testified to, for example, by all the researchers appearing within this young field. In the seventies, this optimism has been replaced by a more pessimistic and critical attitude. A series of reviews and analytical papers identifying methodological and conceptual weaknesses hindering the progress of all this empirical work appeared (Blakar, 1980a, c; Haley, 1972; Helmersen, 1983; Jacob, 1975; Riskin & Faunce, 1972). Recently, attempts have been observed to proceed beyond this criticism and to approach the identified problems of the field by more general and coherent theoretical models and frameworks, developed, for example, within general social psychology (Blaker, 1980b, in press-a; Blakar & Nafstad, 1982; Doane, 1978). Towards the end of this chapter I return to these alternative approaches. Initially, the problems and shortcomings claimed to hinder progress in the field of family communication research on psychopathology have to be examined in some more detail to attempt to gain support for the hypothesis that these hindrances could possibly be surmounted if one relied on general social (in this case, communication) theory.

First, when reviewing the empirical research in the field of family interaction Haley (1972) was forced to conclude that: "The evidence for a difference between the normal family and a family containing a patient member is *no more than indicative* [p. 35, my italics]." At the present stage, what is of particular interest is Haley's explanation of *why* this is the case. From this conclusion, Haley (1972) starts analysing the underlying problems of any research into family interaction and concludes by ascribing the lack of progress directly to a lack of adequate methods:

"This does not mean that schizophrenia is not produced by a type of family, nor does it mean that a family with a schizophrenic is grossly different from the average family. It means *that sufficient reliable evidence of a difference has yet to be provided. The methodology for providing that evidence is still being devised* [p. 35, my italics]."

Second, in their comprehensive critical oveview of the field, Riskin and Faunce (1972) identified various conceptual and methodological shortcomings. The major problem, according to their analysis, seems to be a lack of "intermediate concepts" connecting observable phenomena to the superordinate concepts used in theorizing about the pattern of communication in families containing deviant members. They point out that family research involves abstract, theoretical concepts (such as double-bind, pseudo-mutuality, marital schism and marital skew), while, at the same time, a number of relatively simple phenomena, which can easily be measured (for example, "Who speaks to whom?"), are in operation. The connection between these abstract concepts and the readily operational phenomena is, however, lacking. Moreover, the following quotation is telling with regard to Riskin and Faunce's (1972) criticism of the lack of conceptual clarity in the field generally:

> Many terms in today's research are often used in a formulalike, ritualistic or ambiguous manner, and this tends to interfere with, or substitute for, clear thinking. *An instance of ambiguous usage is "communication"*, which sometimes seems to refer specifically to verbal messages. And "interaction" is used in exceedingly variable ways. One wonders, if these expressions were stricken from the vocabulary, would hard thinking be encouraged, or would other terms immediately fill the vacuum? [p. 37, my italics].

In addition, the research of the field has been seriously criticized for more specifically technical reasons, for example, that the experimenter often has not been "blind", that "clinical" rather than "statistical" assessments have been used, etc. (cf. Jacob, 1975; Riskin & Faunce, 1972).

We agree with Haley's (1972) and Riskin and Faunce's (1972) observations respectively. However, we hesitate to characterize either of these factors as *the* cause of the lack of progress in the field. To be sure, if one wants to study the communication patterns of families with and without psychopathological members, it will of course be critical that one has *(a)* adequate methods for investigating the process of communication, and *(b)* intermediate concepts connecting the observations made to the superordinate concepts used in theorizing. However, the lack of adequate methods and intermediate concepts are "symptoms" only. These identified factors are related to a more fundamental deficiency, namely, that the concept of communication used in family-oriented research is vague and left undefined (see Blakar, 1980c, in press-a; Sølvberg & Blakar, 1975). An explicated and clarified concept of X (in this case, communication) should by logic represent a *prerequisite* for developing methods for studying *X*. Or, how could one even hope to construct adequate methods for studying a process so vaguely defined as is the concept of communication in the field? A theory of communication, for example, elaborated in terms of preconditions for (successful) communication, would represent guidelines and give ideas in method development with respect to variables to be manipulated and conditions to be controlled. Thus, to surmount the obvious problems and shortcomings with respect to adequate methods in the study of family communication, one has to start by defining and explicating the concept of communication. Moreover, with regard to the lack of intermediate concepts, the lack of an adequate *theory* of communication in general, is even more striking.

In conclusion, instead of throwing oneself into time-consuming empirical research on communication patterns in various categories of families (cf. the optimistic period described on p.19), much more work should have been, and will need to be, invested in clarifying the conceptual framework of communication theory. For, in general, if the adoption of a communication perspective in any specific field is going to be productive and beneficial, and not only represent a popular programmatic position, *the communication theory of that particular field* has to be worked out in quite some detail. On this point, there are no short cuts. The communication perspective is *not* a magic wand that can be exploited by everyone everywhere. On the contrary, the adoption of a communication perspective *presupposes* a thorough understanding of the multiple social realities involved. Ignorance of these problems, that is, to adopt a communication perspective *without* bothering about exploring the corresponding communication theory, is bound to result in conditions of absurdity where one mystery (e.g., psychopathology) is being *explained* by means of another mystery (e.g., familial communication, or more accurately, deviant familial communication). Although we do not subscribe to his position in detail, we cannot but join Smedslund (1978, 1979) in his vigorous plea for an aprioristic psychology. The present target field, i.e. family communication research on psychopathology constitutes a sad demonstration of how an enormous amount of empirical research is most likely to have represented a futile waste of effort, because the aprioristic, conceptual problems of this field have not been taken seriously.

## EXPLICATIONS OF A SOCIAL-DEVELOPMENTAL FRAMEWORK OF COMMUNICATION-ORIENTED RESEARCH

From the foregoing analysis, it can be seen that the challenge to social psychology in general, and communication theorists in particular, should have been made explicit, viz., to transform communication theory from a programmatic but vague and diffuse perspective into a specific and refined tool of analysis in the study of human behaviour. To enable us to conduct studies (for example, on schizophrenia[5]) that could possibly add to our understanding, as a minimum, the following issues must be seriously attended to and no longer ignored.

First, there is now the well-rehearsed, major problem of an adequate *definition* of communication. Second, a *conceptual framework* by which the process of communication can be adequately grasped and conceived has to be developed. Perhaps, at this point it should be stressed that there is no criticism of the lack of progress and success of communication-oriented research in the various fields *per se,* for the development of an adequate theory of human communication represents an enormously complex task. At present, there is no fully elaborated theory of communication available. The criticism, therefore, refers to the predominant tendency to *pretend* that problems are being solved by means of vague and too-extensive definitions. Furthermore, there is a strong tendency to employ the existing concepts *as if* they were unproblematic and everyone would know and agree about what, for example, "communication" or "normal family communication" is or implies. Third, *methods* explicitly anchored in communication theory have to be designed. Fourth, the *empirical knowledge* about human communication in general under varying social and situational conditions has to be considerably enlarged. For example, our knowledge at present of what is the variation of "normal familial communication patterns" across different socio-cultural backgrounds is much too restricted to allow any safe conclusions with regard to what are (are not) deviant (familial) communication patterns. By logic, the latter two enterprises *presuppose* a certain degree of progress with regard to the first two. However, here a word of warning is needed. If communication-oriented empirical work should be postponed *until* a refined and fully satisfying theory of human communication in general is developed, we are afraid that one would never get involved in empirical work, and communication-oriented studies of schizophrenia, or of any other phenomenon, would never be conducted. Moreover, there is a dialectical relation between empirical studies and theoretical clarifications, so that empirical studies in connection with, for example, familial communication may promote the development of general communication theory (cf. Blakar, in press-a). Consequently, the rest of this chapter is devoted to an outline of an alternative approach to human communica-

---

[5]As I have pointed out elsewhere (Blakar, 1980a, 1980c, in press-b), communication-oriented research on schizophrenia has been characterized by the researchers knowing a lot more about schizophrenia (the phenomenon to be explained) than about communication (the conceptual framework within which the explanation is to be offered).

tion which explictly tries to take the issues discussed so far into consideration.

## Towards a Definition of Communication

Our criticism of the concept of communication as it is employed in current research can be summarized as follows: (1) to the extent that attempts have been made towards presenting definitions of "communication", they are much too general and extensive, almost all-inclusive: (2) in most studies in the field, the operationalizations of "communication" represent trivial oversimplifications which fail to grasp essential aspects of communication. The almost paradoxical co-occurrence of (1) and (2) only adds to our criticism.

With regard to the too-extensive definitions (usually the "definitions" are left implicit), they can be classified as of two types. First and foremost, communication is often conceived of as almost synonymous with *behaviour* (see also the quotation by Riskin & Faunce on p.20). Watzlawick, Beavin and Jackson (1967) provided a classic and, in many respects, "authoritative" example when they claimed that: ". . . all behaviour, not only speech, is communication and all communication–even the communicational clues in an impersonal context–affects behaviour [p. 22]." Second, communication is often vaguely characterized as *"the flow of information"*. This type of definition is usually only reflected indirectly in the scoring of categories such as "information exchange" (Ferreira & Winther, 1968a, 1968b), "information giving" (Goldstein et al., 1968), "informing" (McPherson, 1970), etc. The underlying concept of communication, however, appears to be as all-embracing as the definition put forward by Athanassiades (1974): "Verbal and non-verbal communication, i.e., *the flow of information, impressions, and understanding from one individual to others*. [p. 195, my italics]."

One might ask sarcastically *why* a concept of communication is needed at all, and, in particular, *why* it is such an essential concept when *all* behaviour is communication? It seems instead that what one would need is a more specified concept of behaviour. Similarly, one could pose analogous questions to those who conceive of communication as "the flow of information." Ideally, definitions should prove useful in revealing and specifying the subject matter. Vague and extensive definitions of this type only serve to disguise and veil fundamental distinctions. That this is actually so, can only be realized by briefly juxtaposing the above definitions of communication with the following quotation by Rommetveit (1968, p. 41): "The communicative medium is related to the message it conveys only via an intentional act of encoding". Without taking a definite stand on Rommetveit's general theoretical position, it is immediately obvious that a number of crucial issues, which are ignored in the above definitions, are exposed. To be of any use, a definition of communication must make explicit issues such as: Does it make sense to speak about "not-intended (non-intended) communication"? Are there any fundamental differences between "receiving messages" and "getting information"? (For a more detailed exposition of the crucial issues which definitions of communication should explicitly incorporate, see Blakar, 1980c, in press-a).

Our second point of criticism was that the operational elements of communication in most studies involve trivial oversimplifications. Variables of the type: Who speaks? Who speaks to whom? How long (much) does each of the participants speak? The number of interruptions? Who interrupts? Who is interrupted by whom? How long and/or how complex are the sentences used? etc. We do not say that these aspects of communication are of no interest. However, the *interpretation* of each one of these observations depends on one's theory of communication (which may involve vague definitions, or none at all). For example, an interruption may reflect a power struggle, but it may also reflect perfect mutual understanding between the participants ("I have already understood/anticipated what you are going to say"). Nothing much, therefore, can be learned by an atheoretical counting of interruptions. Correspondingly, incomplete sentences may reflect lack of verbal or communicative competence, they may also reflect perfect mutual understanding (ellipsis) where elaborated sentences would not be needed, and they could also create an impression of alienation.

In defining "communication", the main problem is to capture the essential aspects of this common and universal human activity, while at the same time distinguishing it from processes and activities carrying fundamental resemblances to communication. To reiterate, the most essential characteristic of communication is that something is being made known to somebody. It follows from this that an act of communication is *social* and *directional* (from a sender to a receiver). A crucial characteristic distinguishing communication from the general flow of information is that the sender has an intention to make something known to the (particular) receiver. (The intentionality in acts of communication is reflected, for example, in the attainment of the same ends (equifinality) by different means of communication). When communication is defined as an intentional act (sender's) to make something (the message) known to others (the receiver(s)), then the behavioural, as well as the informational, aspects of the definitions discussed above become integrated, *at the same time* as we manage to distinguish communication from behaviour and information processing in general. Two comments may be warranted in connection with the launching of a definition of this kind. First, that if a particular act of communication is not classified as communication (i.e., is excluded by the definition), it does not, of course, imply that it is of no interest to our analysis of human interaction and behaviour. It implies only that it has to be grasped and handled by means of *other* concepts. Second, acts of communication are part of, and must be analyzed within, wider behavioural settings and contexts of social interaction. Hence, whereas the above definition gives us a more refined analytical tool, it does not exclude any relevant aspects, for example, non-intentional or unconscious behaviour, from our total integral analysis. We are forced, however, to develop or refine our conceptual framework in order to grasp all the various aspects and nuances of human interaction by means of adequate notions. To exploit a vague and extensive concept of communication only conceals distinctions which may prove fundamental to our understanding. (A comprehensive exposition of a conceptual framework developed along these lines is given by Blakar, 1980c, in press-a; Rommetveit, 1974; Rommetveit & Blakar, 1979). From the above definition, methods for studying and concepts for analyzing processes of communication can be derived (cf. Blakar, 1973, 1980c) and a whole series of intriguing enquiries and corresponding strategies for research to gain insight into the riddles of human communication readily offer themselves.

Outline and Explication of a Conceptual Framework

What has so far been guiding and integrating our enquiries and our attempts at the construction of theory within the field of human communication, is the following fundamental question: *What are the prerequisites for (successful) communication, i.e., under what conditions will somebody succeed (to a reasonable degree) in making something known to somebody else?* To (clinically-oriented) psychologists, the counter-part of this enquiry may be even more intriguing. Which of the preconditions have *not* been satisfied when communication fails? An important aim of research, with obvious theoretical as well as practical implications, is, therefore, an identification and systematic description of the various prerequisites for (successful) communication. Such a research programme needs to encompass individual and situational, as well as social, variables (Blakar, 1974, in press-a). Consequently, a theory of communication should involve a specification of the *individual, social* and *situational* preconditions for (successful) communication and a description of the *interplay* beteen these preconditions.

In an effort to identify and describe some of these prerequisites of communication, we developed a particular experimental method (Blakar, 1973). The method was directly derived from our general conceptual framework, and it was further inspired by various studies of communication breakdowns, especially those typical for children (for example, Piagetian studies on egocentrism), and also by analyses of everyday misunderstandings and how they occur (for example, Garfinkel, 1972; Ichheiser, 1979).

The general idea of the method was very simple, but in practice it proved very difficult to realize. The aim was to try to create a communication situation where one of the preconditions for (successful) communication was *not* satisfied. If one were able to create such a situation, one would be able to study at least: (1) the impact of that particular variable on communication; (2) the potential "missing" requirements or preconditions to which the subjects would attribute the resultant communication difficulties; and (3) what the subjects actually do in order to try to "improve" their communication when it goes astray.

The hypothesis can be that the most basic precondition for successful communication, i.e., in order for it to take place at all, is that the participants have established *"a shared social reality"* (see Chapter 3), a common "here-and-now" within which an exchange of messages can take place (Blakar, 1973; Blakar & Rommetveit, 1975; Rommetveit, 1972c, 1974). An ideal experimental situation would thus be one where two (or more) participants communicate with each other *under the belief* that they are "in the same situation" (i.e., have a common definition of the "here" and "now" situation), but where they are in fact in different situations. In other words, we tried to create a situation where each participant speaks and understands what is said on the basis of his or her own particular interpretation of the situation and falsely believes that the other (others) speaks and understands on the basis of that same interpretation (as in everyday quarrels and misunderstandings).

The problems that we encountered in developing an experimental situation that "worked", i.e., a situation where the subjects would communicate for a reasonable period of time without suspecting anything awry, will not be dealt with here (see Blakar, 1973). The final design, however, was simple and seemed quite natural. Two persons, $A$ and $B$, are each given a map of a relatively complicated network of roads and streets in a town centre. On $A$'s map two routes are marked with arrows, one short and straightforward (the practice route), and another longer and more complicated (the experimental route). On $B$'s map no route is marked. $A$'s task is then to explain to $B$ the two routes, first the simple one, then the longer and more complicated one. $B$ will then, with the help of $A$'s explanations, try to find the way through the town to the predetermined end point. $B$ may ask questions, for example, ask $A$ to repeat the explanations, or to explain in other ways, and so on. The experimental manipulation is simply that the two maps are not identical. An extra street is added on $B$'s map–a street is lacking on $A$'s map. Therefore, no matter how adequately $A$ explains, and no matter how carefully $B$ carries out $A$'s instructions, $B$ is bound to go wrong. The difference between the two maps causes problems for the complicated route only, since the practice route is straightforward on both maps.[6]

The practice route was included for three reasons: (1) to get the subjects used to the situation; (2) to strengthen their confidence in the maps; and (3) to obtain a sample of their communication in the same kind of situation, but *unaffected* by our experimental manipulation (a "before-after" design). The two participants sit at opposite ends of a table, with two low screens shielding their maps from each other. The screens are low enough for them to see each other and allow natural eye contact (Argyle, 1973; Moscovici, 1967). Everything said is tape-recorded, and for certain analyses the tape is subsequently transcribed; for more detailed presentations of the method and its theoretical background, see Blakar, 1973 and 1980c.

A study where students served as subjects convinced us that the experimental manipulation was successful (Blakar, 1973). Blakar (1981b) summarized the most interesting findings from this first exploratory study as follows:

1. It took an average of 18 minutes from the start on the experimental route before any doubt concerning the credibility of the maps was expressed. During this time, the subjects communicated under the false assumption that they were sharing the *same* situation (the same "here").
2. Moreover, the situation proved successful in demonstrating how the subjects "diagnosed" their communication difficulties, and what kinds of "tools" they had at their disposal in order to remedy and improve their communication. The experimental situation seemed to make great demands on the subjects' powers of flexibility and ability to modify their communication patterns, and also on their capacity to decentre and see things from the other's perspective [p. 200].

The latter involves actually a tentative specification of prerequisites for (successful) communication. Therefore, let us take, for example, "capacity to decentre and see things from the other's perspective" as an illustrative example in a further exposition of our conceptual framework.

The ability and/or willingness to decentre (at least to some extent) and to take the perspective of the other(s), is a fundamental prerequisite for successful communication, and extreme egocentrism may strongly hinder

---

[6]In presenting the standardized communication situation, we have been strictly descriptive. Blakar & Pedersen (1980a, 1980b) have shown how core social variables such as *control* and *self-confidence* are involved.

communication. In particular, when problems are encountered in the communication process, a minimum of decentration is required in order to re-establish shared premises for further communication. Decentration in communication is characterized by the fact that the sender anticipates the receiver's decoding, takes the receiver's perspective into account and encodes on the receiver's premises. Similarly, decentration on behalf of the receiver is reflected in the receiver's listening and decoding on the premises of the sender. The following statement where the sender in the above communication conflict situation tries to describe a point on the map, is an example: "... then you come to a cross, there *you* are in the upper left-hand corner of a rectangle which is to *your* right under the cross...."

Egocentrism, on the contrary, is characterized by the fact that the participants do not take each other's perspective, and do not speak and listen, respectively, on each other's premises. In a situation resembling the one just mentioned in the above example, an egocentric statement would be "... and then you go down *here* and across *there*, and then you come to a cross..."

Our use of the concept of egocentrism is inspired by Piaget's (1926) analysis of children's language, but the concept's more social flavour is influenced by Mead's (1934) "the generalized other". Closley related to these concepts is Rommetveit's (1968) notion that "encoding involves anticipated decoding". Only by the communicants taking the perspective of the other(s) into account, so that they (sender and receiver) may establish commonality, is communication rendered possible.

In addition to the actual lack of sharing of perspectives, there is another important aspect of egocentric communication, i.e., that this lack is constantly covered up so that the communicants act *as if* their communication were not egocentric. This is noted in Rommetveit (1972c): "Egocentrism ... is characterized by an underlying postulate that the other always sees and keeps the same thing in mind as oneself, i.e., by an unreflected presupposed convergence of memory and attention between speaker and listener [pp. 49–49, our translation]."

The concept of egocentrism/decentration may thus be applied to characterize *both* the persons involved (he/she is egocentric) *and* the communication process itself (the communication is egocentric, cf. Blakar, 1974, in press-a). That these two levels do not necessarily coincide, may be seen from the following example. If a person (sender) is egocentric in his or her way of speaking, this can be compensated for by a particularly decentred receiver, so that the communication may nevertheless flow tolerably well. This is, for example, often the case in child-adult interactions.

Before we continue to amplify our conceptual framework by specifying a few more preconditions for (successful) communication, some general theoretical-methodological issues should be commented explicitly upon. First, the relationship between the various prerequisites, on the one hand, and the process of communication, on the other, is of a *logical* type. For example, it can be concluded on the basis of logical analysis of the involved concepts that a greater capacity to decentre and to take the perspective of the other will make communication run more smoothly, and that extreme egocentrism will hinder communication. Nevertheless, when undertaking systematic identification and specification of the various preconditions and analysis of the subtle interplay between them, illustrative empirical material of the kind envisaged in the communication-conflict situation above is almost indispensable (cf. Blakar, 1980a, in press-a). Moreover, when it is reported (Blakar, 1981a; Blakar, Paulsen, & Sølvberg, 1978; Mossige, Pettersen, & Blakar, 1979; Sølvberg & Blakar, 1975) that the pattern of communication in families containing schizophrenic members is characterized by more (extreme) egocentrism than comparable control families, this represents empirical findings which could *not* be derived by logical analysis of the concepts involved (Blakar, 1980c). Second, the concept of a scale of egocentrism/decentration illustrates the openness in models of communication with regard to aspects of social processes as well as of individual capacities. Third, the foregoing analysis of egocentrism/decentration in communication highlights the problems of studying human communication (i.e., the communicant's establishment and maintenance of intersubjectivity) from the perspective of an outside observer in various ways. In assessing an utterance as being egocentric/decentred, the wider context and the communication process as such has to be taken into account. Only on the basis of what the participants at a certain point in time have established as a shared social reality, (cf. Blakar & Rommetveit, 1975; Rommetveit, 1974) can anything uttered be assessed as egocentric/decentred. Hence, the observer has to follow the communication process carefully *over time* in order to "know" at each moment *what* the participants may tacitly take for granted. However, the *outside* observer to the communication process has no immediate access to the participants' experiences. A particularly salient fallacy for such an outside observer is to judge as egocentric a sequence of communication which actually is characterized by ellipsis (Blakar, in press-a; Rommetveit, 1974) and thus in a way reflects almost perfect commonality on behalf of the participants. Consequently, analyses of the process of communication ideally enforce some sort of oscillation between the "from-within-perspective" of the communicants and the "from-outside-perspective" of the observer (Blakar, 1980c).

Finally, the above analysis should have given clues as to why we have coined our approach *social developmental*. The individual communicant's capacity to decentre and take the perspective of the other, i.e., an essential prerequisite for (successful) communication, can only be assessed within the framework of developmental psychology. In an earlier section, we refuted the models of individual psychology and sociology respectively, and a model integrating individual, social and situational preconditions for communication was envisaged. A "social-individual" model open to situational variation thus seems optimal. The most obvious and only general perspective from which to conceive of the *individual communicant* is definitely the developmental perspective.[7]

On the basis of the foregoing general theoretical-methodological considerations, we now briefly exemplify a few more of the prerequisites for communication. In so doing, we exploit the foremonetioned standardized communication-conflict situation, and refer to some of the studies conducted with this particular method for two reasons. First, this will constitute a somewhat standardized observational framework which will hopefully highlight the subtle and extensive interplay between the various preconditions. Second, due to the experimental manipulations, we are granted systematic contextual variation (the simple versus the conflict situation).

The *directional* and the *social* character of acts of communication were underlined in the above explication of the concept of communication. Another essential aspect of human communication is the *contractual* aspect (Blakar, 1980c, in press-a; Rommetveit, 1972a, 1972c, 1974). In various respects, the process of communication and the premises for intersubjectivity, are fundamentally negotiable (Rommetveit, 1979). The communicants continually face critical moments of choice at which their underlying premises have to be coordinated in order to render communication possible. For example, in the situation described earlier the critical concepts "right" and "left" can be meaningfully exploited from the perspective of the driver as well as from the perspective of the participants seated at the table. In order to make the routes common (i.e., communicate), they to *endorse* contracts of behaviour, which then guide their process of communication, with regard to this particular aspect of communication. The communicants' ability to endorse contracts guiding the process of communication thus constitutes an essential prerequisite for communication. In the present standardized communication-conflict

---

[7]In earlier writings, we have often referred to our approach as "social-cognitive." Although essential in describing and analyzing the individual communicant (in the functions of sender and receiver respectively), cognition represents but *one* aspect. Only from a general developmental perspective can we manage to grasp and describe the individual communicant in full complexity (cf. Blakar & Nafstad, 1982; Nafstad & Gaarder, 1979).

situation, it has been shown that the communicants endorse contracts concerning topic, perspective, categorization, orientation, roles and strategy, as well as meta-contracts (Blakar, 1973), and schemes for analyzing the process of communication in terms of contracts have been developed (Blakar, in press-a). A finding worth reporting here is that on the basis of the quality of the contracts endorsed in the simple situation, relatively good predictions concerning the communicants' degree of success and failure with regard to unravelling the induced conflict could be made (Blakar, 1980c).

Communication conflicts, misunderstandings and situations involving lack of mutual understanding are inevitable in any human intercourse. When communication runs into more or less serious trouble, it is essential, in order to re-establish commonality, that the difficulties are adequately identified and so *attributed* (Heider, 1958). The induced communication conflict offers an almost optimal opportunity to study patterns of attribution during the process of communication. Schemes for assessing patterns of attribution have been developed, (Hultberg, Alve, & Blakar, 1980) and Brisendal (see Blakar, in press-a) has enquired more systematically into the communicants' creative hypotheses concerning "the cause" underlying the communication conflict in which they found themselves. Exploiting the prediction procedure mentioned above, Teigre (see Blakar, in press-a) analysed the influence of another fundamental precondition for communication, i.e., the communicants' *confidence* in him or herself and the other person. To a certain extent, it was possible to predict married couples' degree of success and failure with regard to unravelling the induced conflict on the basis of the patterns of confidence assessed in the simple situation.

In the above section, we have outlined singular concepts (for example, contract, attribution of communication difficulties, confidence, egocentrism vs. decentration). Obviously, these concepts are *interconnected*; they are all derived from the same conceptual framework. The existence of such interrelations may be illustrated as follows. The egocentrism of one of the communicants may result in him or her tacitly taking for granted (as free information) something which could not possibly be known by the others. This may result in communication difficulties, either directly or indirectly. In order to re-establish commonality, the communication difficulty experienced has to be identified (attribution of communication difficulties). As a consequence of the (adequate or inadequate) attribution of communication difficulties, the underlying contracts are frequently modified or new contracts are endorsed to prevent further tangles of the same kind (Blakar, in press-a). Naturally, this brief exposition can give only a vague idea of the conceptual framework in terms of preconditions for communication.

## TOWARDS MORE FRUITFUL COMMUNICATION-ORIENTED RESEARCH ON SCHIZOPHRENIA

To assess the explanatory value of current communication theory, the field of communication-oriented research on schizophrenia was reviewed critically. A reasonable test of the social-developmental alternative advocated above would be to determine whether this conceptual framework enables us to promote a sensible understanding of schizophrenia from the perspective of communication. In this context, it should be kept in mind that the lack of progress of all the efforts invested in communication-oriented research on schizophrenia was attributed in particular to a lack of adequate methods (for example by Haley, 1972), whereas we, on the contrary, argue that the lack of methods was a "symptom" only reflecting the lack of explicit communication theory. It is therefore essential to underline that this particular communication conflict situation offers a method of approach grounded in the aforementioned general conceptual framework (Blakar 1973). Of the first observations made in connection with the use of this method, the following made by Blakar (1981b) particularly led to the idea that it could possibly be used to illuminate communication deficiencies in families with schizophrenic members:[8]

> Moreover, the situation proved successful in demonstrating how the subjects "diagnosed" their communication difficulties, and what kinds of "tools" they had at their disposal in order to remedy and improve their communication. The experimental situation seemed to make great demands on the subjects' powers of flexibility and ability to modify their communication patterns, and also on their capacity to decentre and see things from the other's perspective [p. 201].

These observations go well together with core aspects of recent research as summarized by Haley (1972):

> Abnormal families appear to have more conflict, to have different coalition patterns, and to show more inflexibility in repeating patterns, and behaviour. *The most sound findings would seem to be in the outcome area: When faced with a task on which they must cooperate, abnormal family members seem to communicate their preferences less successfully, require more activity and take longer to get the task done.* [p. 35, my italics].

The present standardized communication-conflict situation was designed precisely to make possible more detailed analyses and descriptions in "the outcome area." In this situation, difficulties are bound to emerge. Con-

---

[8]For a presentation of the more general theoretical rationale for the clinical applicaiton of this method, see Blakar, 1980a, 1980c, in press-a,-b &-c.

cepts such as *attribution* (how and to which cause the induced communication difficulties are attributed), the ability to *decentre* and *take the perspective of the other*, the capacity to endorse, maintain and modify interactional *contracts*, and so on, consequently become of central significance in the analysis. Our method thus enabled us to draw upon theorists within general social and developmental psychology such as Heider (1958), Mead (1934), Piaget (1926), Rommetveit (1972b, 1974) and others in the description of deviant patterns of communication in abnormal families.

In the first exploratory study (Sølvberg & Blakar, 1975), we chose, both for theoretical and practical reasons, to concentrate on the parent dyad. Obviously, this is the core dyad in the milieu into which the child is born and within which she/he later matures into a healthy or pathological person. Moreover, we did not want to include patients in this very first study in which the method and conceptual framework itself was to be tried out. Since the communication task given to each couple was in principle unsolvable, we had to decide beforehand the criteria for terminating the experiment:[9]

1. The task would be considered finished successfully as soon as the error was correctly localized and identified.
2. The task would also be considered resolved when the route was correctly reconstructed to the location of the error and when one or both of the subjects insisted that the maps were not identical and, hence, that it was pointless to go on. In this context, it must be mentioned that the experimenter was instructed to neglect all suggestions that something might be wrong and give the impression, for as long as possible, that everything was as it should be (Blakar, 1973 p. 418).
3. If no solution according to criteria one or two was reached within 40 minutes, the communication task would be brought to an end. The subjects would then be shown the discrepancy between the maps and told that the task was actually unsolvable. The 40-minute limit was based on findings of earlier experiments (Blakar, 1973) and pre-tests.
4. Finally, it was decided that if the task should upset the couple too much, the experimenter would stop and reveal the true nature of the experiment.

In order to simplify comparisons between the various couples, the distribution of the two different maps among the spouses had to be standardized. To counteract potential culturally-determined male domi-

---

[9]Additional research has forced us to refine these termination criteria in the light of a more explicit theory concerning the solution of communication conflicts (Blakar, 1980c, in press-a).

nance, we gave the map with the routes drawn in to the wives so that the husbands had to follow the directives and explanations of their wives.

A very important issue in this exploratory study was to establish two comparable groups, one consisting of parents *with* schizophrenic offspring (*Group S*) and one matched control *without* (*Group N*). During this research, we chose to limit ourselves to small but strictly controlled and matched groups. We concentrated on establishing *Group S* first. We decided to accept the definition of schizophrenia generally held in Norwegian psychiatry, i.e., according to Kraepelin.[10] Our point of departure was that the "index" person (i.e., the diagnosed person according to whom we classify the family) in *Group S* had been diagnosed as being schizophrenic at a psychiatric institution. The use of the diagnostic category ensured that all reference persons would be over 15 years of age. We put the upper age limit at 30, and, within this range, we sought the youngest possible reference persons to ensure that they had not been separated from their families for too long. Establishing *Group S* was a long and laborious process (Sølvberg & Blakar, 1975). Having established *Group S*, much effort was put into assembling a matching *Group N*. Variables such as age, number of years of marriage, education, employment, social group, annual income, domicile, living condition, number of children and their sex and age, were all matched satisfactorily (for details of the matching, see Sølvberg & Blakar, 1975). *Group N* represented a "normal group" in the sense that it included ordinary couples *without* problems that had led themselves or their children into contact with treatment or penal institutions. Nothing else is implied by "normality" in this context.

Since the primary purpose of this exploratory study was methodological, our hypotheses bearing upon the differences between *Group S* and *Group N* couples were not very refined. The following rather general hypotheses may in fact be considered tentative conclusions based upon reviews of the literature:

1. Couples from *Group S* will communicate less efficiently than these from *Group N if* the cooperation situation is vague and complicated, requiring critical evaluation and change in patterns of communication. In other words, the *Group S* couples will have *more problems* and will require *more time* in solving the experimental route where the communication conflict is induced.

2. Couples from *Group S* will manage as well as couples from *Group N if*

---

[10]For a detailed discussion of problems encountered in communication-oriented research when applying the traditional nosological categories in selecting subjects, see Blakar & Nafstad (1982).

the cooperation situation is plain and simple in the sense that no readjustment is required from their usual pattern of communication and cooperation. In other words, no difference in time spent on the simple task (the practice route) is expected.
3. Qualitative differences in the communication between *Group S* and *Group N* couples will be revealed, and such differences are expected regardless of whether the communication situation is simple or complex. In addition, it is expected that such qualitative differences observed in communication in the simple and straightforward situation will shed some light on why *Group S* communication fails when the communication situation is more demanding.

All couples became involved in the task. The experimenter had no particular problems getting them to grasp the instructions and start on the practice route, although some of the couples put some pressure on the experimenter to structure the situation more explicitly. None of the couples seemed to experience serious problems with the practice route. The actual time spent, however, ranging from 2 minutes 2 seconds to 9 minutes 56 seconds, indicates that the task and communication situation were not equally easy for all of them. If we compare the two experimental groups, we find that *Group S* used 4 minutes 50 seconds in mean (ranging from 2 minutes 9 seconds to 9 minutes 56 seconds), while *Group N* used 4 minutes 57 seconds in mean (ranging from 2 minutes 2 seconds to 8 minutes 52 seconds). Actually, this is very close to the student dyads, with a mean of 4 minutes 27 seconds on the simple situation (Blakar, 1973). Until then, the student dyads we had run had solved the induced communication conflict according to criteria one or two above, and *within* the 40-minute limit. However, only six of the ten parent couples managed to solve the communication conflict according to criteria one or two. Four of the ten couples went on for more than forty minutes, and were consequently stopped and shown the discrepancy between the maps. In dealing with the conflict situation, therefore, the ten couples formed two subgroups: six solvers and four non-solvers, and the crucial question is how the *Group S* and the *Group N* couples were distributed over these subgroups. While all five *Group N* couples solved the induced communication conflict, only one of the *Group S* couples managed to do so. All the four non-solvers were thus *Group S* couples.

As regards the simple situation, where no conflict was induced and hence no critical evaluation and readjustment of communication strategy was required, *Group S* parents performed as well as *Group N* parents, and actually similarly to the younger and more highly educated student dyads. However, *when a discrepancy with respect to premises* was induced, most *Group S* parents failed. Detailed analysis of the patterns of communication in the simple and conflict-free situation, moreover, indicated subtle qualitative differences. These differences did not influence communication efficiency in the plain and simple situation, but they proved critical in the more demanding communication-conflict situation.

In the present context, a tenable conclusion seems to be that a standardized communication-conflict situation which is really *sensitive* with respect to the participants' abilities/inabilities to unravel underlying conflicts, has been established. From the perspective of social psychology in general and communication theory in particular, this should come as no surprise. In the present method such fundamental preconditions for (successful) communication are systematically manipulated (see pp. 25-31), so that *if* there is any reality to the idea that families containing schizophrenic members demonstrate deviant communication patterns, this *should* indeed be revealed under these conditions of communication. Moreover, the conceptual framework explicated in the present experimental design allows for specifications of situational conditions *under which* the differences will be salient (cf. the hypotheses); for a more detailed presentation of the present study, see Blakar, 1980c; Sølvberg & Blakar, 1975.

The success of the above study does not imply that all the conceptual and methodological problems in communication-oriented research on schizophrenia are settled. On the contrary, we have elsewhere (Blakar, 1980a, 1980c, 1981b) claimed that in retrospect the Sølvberg & Blakar study "may be conceived of as a lucky shot", and that the study posed more issues than it settled. However, the social-developmental framework outlined above constitutes a theoretical framework within which all these problems and questions can be meaningfully conceived.

Although at present, we have corroborated these findings in various ways,[11] we find it an apt conclusion here to quote a section from the Sølvberg & Blakar (1975) paper stating the most significant questions which then emerged from their exploratory study. This may serve the dual function of demonstrating the potential contributions of our alternative conceptual approach and at the same time representing an invitation to joint efforts in further explorations and elaborations:

1. Do *Group S* couples use a more egocentric and less decentred form of communication? In other words, are *Group S* spouses less able and/or will-

---

[11]In a series of replications and follow-up studies conducted within this conceptual framework and integrated in a systematic research programme (cf. Blakar, 1980c, 1981b; Blakar & Nafstad, 1981, 1982), the findings from the exploratory Sølvberg and Blakar study have been corroborated in various ways (Blakar, 1981b; in press a, c; Hultberg et al., 1980; Mossige et al., 1979; Stockstad, Lagerløv, & Blakar, 1979); for overview presentations, see Blakar, in press-a, -b.

ing to take the perspective of, and speak on the premises of, the other? For instance, utterances such as ". . . and then you go up *there*," ". . . and from *here* you take a right," when "here" and "there" could, obviously, not be known to the other, were frequently observed in communication of the *Group S* couples.

2. Are *Group S* couples less able and/or willing to endorse (and adhere to) contracts that regulate and monitor the various aspects of their communication (for example, role distribution, perspective, strategy of explanation)? Only a few contractual proposals were found (regarding, for example, categorization and explanation strategy). Furthermore, many cases were observed in which implicitly or explicitly endorsed contracts were broken or ignored.

3. Do *Group S* couples show less ability and/or willingness to attribute their communication difficulties (adequately or inadequately) to any potential causes? The *Group S* couples could apparently return to the starting point again and again without any (overt, explicit) attempt to attribute their communication difficulties to anything [p. 531].

These were some of the most significant questions that emerged from this very first exploratory study. All these questions were formulated *within a conceptual framework* dissimilar to that usually employed in the study of schizophrenia. The formulations were inspired by the theoretical work of people such as Heider, Mead, Piaget, Rommetveit, and others, as outlined above. The mere stating of these questions represents a contribution towards describing (and hence in part explaining) schizophrenia within the framework of a general social-developmental theory.

## ACKNOWLEDGEMENTS

The author is indebted to Jeri Doane, Howard Giles, Hilde Eileen Nafstad, Ragnar Rommetveit, Olav Skårdal and Jan Smedslund for valuable comments on an earlier draft of this chapter. The work reported has been supported by the Norwegian Council for Social Science and the Humanities.

## REFERENCES

Ackerman, N. W., Beatman, F. L., & Sherman, S. N. (Eds.) *Exploring the base for family therapy.* New York: Family Service Association of America, 1961.
Argyle, M. (Ed.) *Social encounters.* Hammondsworth: Penguin Books, 1973.
Athanassiades, J. C. An investigation of some communication patterns of female subordinates in hierarchical organisations. *Human Relations,* 1974, *27,* 195-209.
Bateson, G., Jackson, D. D., Haley, J., & Weakland, J. H. Towards a theory of schizophrenia. *Behavioural Sciences,* 1956, *1,* 251-264.

Blakar, R. M. *Communication: A social perspective on clinical issues.* Oslo: Universitetsforlaget. Distributed in the United States by Columbia University Press and in Great Britain by Global Book Resources, in press. (a)
Blakar, R.M. Communication in the family and psychopathology: A social-developmental approach to deviant behaviour. In H. Tajfel (Ed.), *The social dimension: European developments in social psychology.* Cambridge: Cambridge University Press, in press. (b)
Blakar, R. M. Distinguishing social and individual psychology. *Scandinavian Journal of Psychology,* 1974, *15,* 241-243.
Blakar, R. M. An experimental method for inquiring into communication. *European Journal of Social Psychology,* 1973, *3,* 415-425.
Blakar, R. M. Language as a means of social power: Theoretical-empirical explorations of language and language use as embedded in a social matrix. In J. L. Mey (Ed.), *Pragmalinguistics: Theory and practice.* The Hague: Mouton, 1979, 131-169.
Blakar, R. M. Psychopathology and familial communication. In M. Brenner (Ed.), *The structure of action.* Oxford: Basil Blackwell, 1980. (a)
Blakar, R. M. Schizophrenia and communication: A paradox of theory and research. *International Journal of Family Psychiatry,* in press. (c)
Blakar, R. M. Schizophrenia and familial communication: A brief note on follow-up studies and replications. *Family Process,* 1981, *20,* 109-112. (a)
Blakar, R. M. The social sensivity of theory and method. In M. Brenner (Ed.), *Social method and social life.* London: Academic Press, 1981. (b)
Blakar, R. M. Statistical significances versus theoretical clarification: A comment on the Doane-Jacob & Grounds dispute. *Family Process,* 1980, *19,* 291-294. (b)
Blakar, R. M. *Studies of familial communication and psychopathology. A social-developmental approach to deviant behaviour.* Oslo: Universitetsforlaget. Distributed in the United States by Columbia University Press, and in Great Britain by Global Books Resources, 1980.(c)
Blakar, R. M., & Nafstad, H. E. The family as a unit in the study of psychopathology and deviant behaviour: Conceptual and methodological issues. Paper presented at the conference *Discovery strategies in the psychology of action,* Bad Homburg, 1981, *19,* 1-24.
Blakar, R. M., & Nafstad, H. E. The family: A social-developmental framework for understanding psychopathology and deviant behaviour. *Psychiatry and Social Science,* 1982, *2,* 23-34.
Blakar, R. M., Paulsen, O. G., & Sølvberg, H. A. Schizophrenia and communication efficiency: A modified replication taking ecological variation into consideration. *Acta Psychiatrica Scandinavia,* 1978, *58,* 315-326.
Blakar, R. M., & Pedersen, T. B. Control and self-confidence as reflected in sex-bound patterns in communication: An experimental approach. *Acta Sociologica,* 1980, *23,* 33-53. (a)
Blakar, R. M., & Pedersen, T. B. *Sex-bound patterns of control in verbal communication.* Paper presented at the conference "Language and Power" at Bellagio, Italy, April 4th-8th, 1980. (b)
Blakar, R. M., & Rommetveit, R. Utterances *in vacuo* and in contexts: An experimental and theoretical exploration of some interrelationships between what is said and what is seen or imagined. *International Journal of Psycholinguistics, 4,* 5-32, and in *Linguistics,* 1975, *153,* 5-32.
Chomsky, N. *Aspects of the theory of syntax.* Cambridge, Mass.: M.I.T. Press, 1965.
Chomsky, N. *Language and mind.* New York: Harcourt Brace Jovanovich, 1968.
Chomsky, N. *Studies on semantics in generative grammar.* The Hague: Mouton, 1972.
Chomsky, N. *Syntactic structures.* The Hague: Mouton, 1957.

Doane, J. A. Family interaction and communication deviance in disturbed and normal families: A review of research. *Family Process*, 1978, *17*, 357-376.

Ervin-Tripp, S. M., & Slobin, D. Psycholinguistics. *Annual Review of Psychology*, 1966, *17*, 435-474.

Ferreira, A. J., & Winther, W. D. Decision-making in normal and abnormal two-child families. *Family Process*, 1968, *7*, 17-36. (a)

Ferreira, A. J., & Winther, W. D. Information exchange and silence in normal and abnormal families. *Family Process*, 1968, *7*, 251-276. (b)

Garfinkel, H. Studies of the routine grounds of everyday activities. In D. Sudnow (Ed.), *Studies in social interaction*. New York: The Free Press, 1972.

Goldstein, M. J., Gould, E., Alkire, A., Rodnick, E. H., & Judd, L. L. A method for studying social influence and coping patterns within families of disturbed adolescents. *Journal of Nervous Mental Disorders*, 1968, *147*, 233-251.

Haley, J. Critical overview of present status of family interaction research. In J. L. Framo (Ed.), *A dialogue between family researchers and family therapists*. New York: Springer Publishing Company, 1972.

Haley, J. The family of the schizophrenic: A model system. *Journal of Nervous Mental Disorders*, 1959, *129*, 357-374.

Haley, J. Family therapy: A radical change. In J. Haley (Ed.), *Changing families*. New York: Grune & Stratton, 1971.

Helmersen, P. *Family interaction and communication in psychopathology: An evaluation of recent perspectives*. London: Academic Press, 1983.

Heider, F. *The psychology of interpersonal relations*. New York: Wiley, 1958.

Hultberg, M., Alve, S., & Blakar, R. M. Patterns of attribution of communicative difficulties in couples having a "schizophrenic," a "borderline" or a "normal" offspring. In R. M. Blakar (Ed.), *Studies of familial communication and psychopathology*, Oslo: Universitetsforlaget, 1980.

Ichheiser, G. *Appearances and realities. Misunderstandings in human relations*. San Francisco: Jossey-Bass, 1979.

Jacob, T. Family interaction in disturbed and normal families: A methodological and substantive review. *Psychological Bulletin*, 1975, *82*, 33-65.

Katz, J. J., & Fodor, F. A. The structure of a semantic theory. *Language*, 1963, *39*, 170-210.

Kuhn, T. S. *The structure of scientific revolutions*. Chicago: University of Chicago Press, 1970.

Lidz, T., Cornelison, A., Terry, O., & Fleck, S. The intra-familial environment of the schizophrenic patient: Marital schism and marital skew. *American Journal of Psychiatry*, 1957, *114*, 241-248.

McPherson, S. Communication of intents among parents and their disturbed adolescent child. *Journal of Abnormal Psychology*, 1970, *76*, 98-105.

Mead, G. H. *Mind, self and society*. Chicago: University of Chicago Press, 1934.

Mishler, E. G., & Waxler, N. E. Family interaction processes and schizophrenia: A review of current theories. Merrill-Palmer Quarterly, *Journal of Behaviour and Development*, 1965, *11*, 269-315.

Moscovici, S. Communication processing and the properties of language. In L. Berkowitz. (Ed.), *Advances in experimental social psychology*, (Vol. 3), New York: Academic Press, 1967.

Mossige, S., Pettersen, R. B., & Blakar, R. M. Egocentrism and inefficiency in the communication of families containing schizophrenic members. *Family Process*, 1979, *18*, 405-425.

Nafstad, H. E., & Gaarder, S. *Barn—utvikling og miljø*. Oslo: Tiden, 1979.
Piaget, J. *The language and thought of the child*. New York: Harcourt Brace Jovanovich, 1926.
Riskin, J., & Faunce, E. E. An evaluative review of family interaction research. *Family Process*, 1972, *11*, 365-455.
Rommetveit, R. Deep structure of sentence versus message structure: Some critical remarks to current paradigms, and suggestions for an alternative approach. *Norwegian Journal of Linguistics*, 1972, *26*, 3-22. (a)
Rommetveit, R. Language games, deep syntactic structures and hermeneutic circles. In J. Israel & H. Tajfel (Eds.), *The context of social psychology: A critical assessment*. London: Academic Press, 1972. (b)
Rommetveit, R. On "meanings" of situations and social control of such meaning in human communication. Paper presented at The Symposium on the Situation in Psychological Theory and Research, Stockholm, June, 1979, 17-22.
Rommetveit, R. *On message structure*. London: Wiley, 1974.
Rommetveit, R. *Språk, tanke og kommunikasjon*. Oslo: Universitetsforlaget, 1972. (c)
Rommetveit, R. *Words, meanings and messages*. New York: Academic Press and Oslo: Universitetsforlaget, 1968.
Rommetveit, R., & Blakar, R. M. (Eds.) *Studies of language, thought, and verbal communication*. London: Academic Press, 1979.
Rommetveit, R., Cook. M., Havelka, N., Henry, P., Herkner, W., Pecheux, M., & Peters, G. Processing of utterances in context. In E. Carswell & R. Rommetveit (Eds.), *Social contexts of messages*. London: Academic Press, 1971.
Ruesch, J., & Bateson, G. *Communication: The social matrix of psychiatry*. New York: Norton, 1951.
Smedslund, J. Bandura's theory of self-efficacy: A set of common sense theorems. *Scandinavian Journal of Psychology*, 1978, *19*, 1-14.
Smedslund, J. Between the analytic and the arbitrary: A case study of psychological research. *Scandinavian Journal of Psychology*, 1979, *20*, 129-140.
Sølvberg, H. A., & Blakar, R. M. Communication efficiency in couples with and without a schizophrenic offspring. *Family Process*, 1975, *14*, 515-534.
Stokstad, S. J., Lagerløv, T., & Blakar, R. M. Anxiety, rigidity and communication: An experimental approach. In R. Rommetveit & R. M. Blakar (Eds.), *Studies of language, thought, and verbal communication*. London: Academic Press, 1979, 441-456.
Uhlenbeck, E. M. Some further remarks on transformational grammar. *Lingua*, 1967, *17*, 263-316.
Watzlawick, P., Beavin, J. H., & Jackson, D. D. *Pragmatics of human communication*. New York: Norton, 1967.
Weakland, J. H. The double-bind theory by self-reflexive hindsight. *Family Process*, 1974, *13*, 269-277.
Wittgenstein, L. *Philosophical investigations*. Oxford: Blackwell, 1968.
Wold, A. H. *Decoding oral language*. London: Academic Press, 1978.
Wynne, L., Rykoff, I., Day, J., & Hirsch, S. Pseudomutuality in the family relations of schizophrenics. *Psychiatry*, 1958, *21*, 205-220.

# 3 Psychological and Interactional Dimensions of Communicative Development

Barbara J. O'Keefe and Jesse G. Delia
*University of Illinois*

## INTRODUCTION

For the past decade, the concept of meaning has been moving slowly towards its rightful central place in the understanding of communication. In this chapter, we aim to give that movement a boost via an analysis of communicative development across childhood, stressing some of the processes through which meaning is generated and sustained in human discourse. It should, perhaps, be made clear at the outset that we see meaning as a ubiquitous feature of human existence. Any philosophical anthropology must, in our view, begin with some conception of Man-the-symbol-user or Man-the-interpreter. For us, therefore, it is an oversimplification to define communication as coterminous with the processes involved in the creation of meaning. Rather, the problem of communication is creating and sustaining social or shared meaning; its work is in making personal and subjective meanings public and intersubjective. Hence, any analysis of communicative development must give centrality to those processes through which personal meanings are made common. At the same time, however, we argue that socially shared processes such as language are, alone, inadequate to understand communication and its development. Our aim, as will become clear, is to provide a framework for incorporating the role of individual cognitive processes (particularly social perception processes) into a developmental-interactional theory of communication (in this regard also see Applegate & Delia, 1980; Delia & B. O'Keefe, 1979; Delia, B. O'Keefe, & D. O'Keefe, 1982).

Our discussion is divided into four parts. We first briefly discuss mainstream linguistic and sociolinguistic conceptions of communicative competence to which our analysis is offered as an extension. Then, in the second section we sketch the outline of interpretive conception of communication through a discussion of the perspective of the Chicago school of symbolic interactionists. The third section recasts aspects of the symbolic interactionist perspective by developing our own constructivist (organismic-developmental) approach to the analysis of social-cognitive processes and communication. The final section then briefly overviews recent research carried out within our framework.

## LINGUISTIC COMPETENCE, COMMUNICATIVE COMPETENCE, AND THE RESOURCES OF COMMUNICATION

While it seems obvious that communicative abilities must involve more than knowledge of a linguistic code, such a view has been suggested by the considerable emphasis contemporary theorists have given to language acquisition apart from the context of ongoing interaction between children and their care-givers and peers. The emphasis upon language acquisition as a social process has led to the formulation of communicative competence as code competence. When communication is viewed as a process in which encoded ideas are transmitted from a sender to a receiver, the only necessary competence required for interaction is code competence. Utterances are given structure only in terms of the code; and meanings are seen as transmitted via the coded message, rather than created in an ongoing process of interpretation. This view is represented by DeVito (1970), who explains that "the code . . . refers to the rules or grammar of communication which override or govern the form of the various messages. In the case where source and receiver are native speakers of English and communicating orally, the code is the grammar of English [p. 86]." Under this view, communication will be successful to the extent that the codes of the interactants overlap. When the rules of the code are violated or when interactants employ different codes, miscommunication and misunderstanding occur (see Chapter 2).

The difficulties in viewing communicative competence as code competence have been exacerbated by many contemporary theorists' reliance on the narrow conception of linguistic competence forwarded by Chomsky (although Chomsky, himself, never took his theory of linguistic competence to apply to communicative competence). As is well known, in his conception of linguistic competence, Chomsky (1965) seeks to isolate purely linguistic factors from what he terms "performance factors" by arguing that the linguistic knowledge of the idealized speaker-hearer of a language, consists primarily of the grammatical knowledge which allows him or her to link underlying semantic representations with phonological representations.

Applied to the problem of development, this view results in a focus upon language acquisition. The considerable attention given to language acquisition since the early 1960s has been due mainly to the promise of Chomskyian theory as a framework for research. Not surprisingly, researchers within this tradition (as Smith [1975] states) have studied "language acquisition without serious consideration of the development of other faculties [p. 303]." During the 1960s, primary attention was given to stages in the acquisition of grammatical knowledge (linguistic rules) against the backdrop of the adult language system as described in Chomskyian theory. A variety of perspectives were pursued (e.g., Brown's view of the child's language as telegraphic in its omission of various grammatical constituents, open-pivot grammar, case grammars), all of which proved inadequate for accounting for the child's linguistic performance. The particulars of these various efforts need not concern us here, as they have been thoroughly reviewed and critiqued elsewhere (e.g., Bowerman, 1973; Brown, 1973; Greenfield & Smith, 1976). Suffice it to say that by the early 1970s there was a growing awareness among those working in language acquisition that a purely linguistic analysis of the processes involved in language development would be inadequate.

The major shift in language acquisition research has been in the direction of considering the dependency of language acquisition upon general cognitive developments (e.g. Hayes, 1970; Moore, 1973). As Wells (1974) suggests, researchers came to see "the child's task . . . as being to match the organization of language with the cognitive organization that he has already imposed upon his experience [p. 243]." Hence, initially acquired linguistic structures more and more frequently came to be seen as reflecting fundamental cognitive operations (e.g., Sinclair-de-Zwart, 1969; Wells, 1974). In this view, with the development of new modes of conceptualizing experience, the child is seen as forced to master more complex and varied syntactic and semantic processes in order to actualize his or her meanings and intentions. Many theorists have argued, further, that once language is initially acquired the relationship between cognitive and linguistic development becomes a reciprocal one. For instance, Clark (1974) claims: "Just as the acquisition of linguistic structure is affected by psychological processes, so is the efficiency of these processes affected in turn by the child's growing linguistic knowledge [p. 1]." Indeed, Brewer (1974) argues that interrelations of all the higher mental processes must be considered in the analysis of meaning.

Simultaneous with, and in some instances related to, the recognition of the role of cognitive factors in language acquisition, a number of sociolinguists have raised serious objections to the traditional view of linguistic competence. First, it has been argued that the narrow sense of linguistic competence oversimplifies the nature of language by ignoring linguistic diversity (e.g., Hymes, 1972). In any language community, many varieties of that language are employed systematically according to situation of participants. Systematic variations in the use of language are characteristic of the everyday use of language. A speaker may use one dialect at work and another at home; speak formally in some situations and informally in others; respond to status and role with changes in forms of address. Many sociolinguists have argued that linguistic theory must, in order to describe linguistic competence adequately, explicate the knowledge allowing speakers to vary their linguistic choices.

A second sociolinguistic objection to the narrow view of linguistic competence is based on the fact that speaking involves more than formulating sentences. In fact, it has been argued that Chomsky's ideal speaker-hearer would be a conversational monster, since such an individual lacks the everyday knowledge that any competent member of a speech community possesses: Namely, how to structure a speech act and coordinate it within a larger interaction situation (Fillmore, 1973). Interaction is governed by community understandings regarding how to begin speaking, how to gain or retain the floor, when to speak and when to remain silent, and so on. Becoming a competent member of a speech community requires the acquisition of rules of interaction as well as rules of syntax, since language is of little value unless one knows how to use it. As Hymes (1968) says, "development of the child's ability to communicate is influenced as much by his sensitivity to communicative demands of the speech situation as by his increasing linguistic knowledge [p. 1]."

A third objection to the narrow view of linguistic competence raised by sociolinguists and others centres on the fact that speaking is always a situated activity. A speaker must know not only how to form sentences, but also how to construct utterances taking account of the preceding interaction. Indeed, Rommetveit (1974) argues that the essential character of all communication is reflected in the actualization of semantic potentialities within a contextually fabricated architecture of intersubjectivity binding the interlocutors together; linguistic structures can only be understood, he argues, within the architecture of intersubjectivity, and then only as messages, not as propositional or formal structures. In short, communication involves messages, and messages are always only socially meaningful within a system of intersubjectively shared understandings.

Although there have been other critiques of linguistic competence models by sociolinguists, the kinds of objections sketched here have pointed to a broader view of linguistic competence. This broader view holds that a speaker's competence includes social and discourse knowledge (knowledge of linguistic variation, knowledge of the structure of speaking situations, knowledge of turn-taking rules and rules of discourse sequencing, etc.). Hymes (1968, 1971) and other sociolinguists have called this broad view of linguistic competence "communicative competence."

The kinds of arguments raised by sociolinguists and by those emphasizing the role of cognitive development in language acquisition have served, in part, as the impetus for theoretical interest in analyses of speech acts and speech events (e.g., Cole & Morgan, 1975; Dore, 1975). This general shift in linguistic theory has been accompanied by theoretical statements pointing to the role of the child's communicative efforts in the emergence and development of linguistic and communicative competence. In fact, in recent years a rising chorus of theorists have called for viewing the child's acquisition of control over language primarily as a communicative process (e.g., Bruner, 1975; Halliday, 1975; Lewis & Rosenblum, 1977; Lock, 1977; Ryan, 1974). While there is considerable diversity among the views of these theorists, they share the conviction that language comes to be controlled in order to accomplish specific communicative aims, and that analysis of the child's developing linguistic ability cannot be separated from the functions language usage fulfils within the contexts of the child's ongoing social interactions.

Such an approach reflects a conception of language as a mode of action rather than as a countersign of thought. This general line of argument has been most forcefully advanced by Bruner (1975). He suggests that rather than seeing communication as emerging from the acquisition of language, we see language as acquired within the context of an already existing prelinguistic structure of communication binding together the child and his or her care-givers. He argues that the inference of communicative intent, early reference, the use of language in the regulation of joint action, early forms of prediction, and grammar itself can be seen as emergents out of a process of prelinguistic communication. Language acquisition is embedded within the development of speech acts which are, themselves, acquired within the structure of prelinguistic social acts. Thus, for Bruner, in learning language, children must learn to articulate meaningful speech acts within the parameters opened up by their culture for achieving interpersonal aims.

Although we subscribe to the kind of view articulated by Bruner, we would emphasize three other features in the development of communication: The extent to which language must also be treated as an organized system to be mastered by the child, the cultural definition of speech acts, and the development of elaborated functional control over the interpretive, sociocultural, and behavioural resources of communication.

Although we agree that language learning ought to be studied within the structure of the child's pragmatic communicative aims, it seems to us, in the first place, that the kind of stance taken by Bruner does not emphasize adequately the "grammaticalization" of utterances. We have argued, as he has, that language cannot be decontextualized and treated as a formal system, but it must be recognized at the same time that language is characterized by strong regularity. Children do not simply learn to achieve pragmatic social ends through communication; they also learn to achieve this through the grammatical system used within their speech community. Language is historically preserved as an organized system; children confront this system and must accommodate to it; hence, an essential part of communicative ability must be understood as the development of purely linguistic knowledge.

There is also a second sense in which Bruner's analysis of the development of communication appears unrealistically narrow. This is in his conception of speech acts. We think it is important in considering communicative development to recognize, as Bruner emphasizes, that the child, in learning to communicate, articulates speech acts. However, in Bruner's conceptualization, a speech act is taken to be an intentional, personally functional utterance. Such a conception underemphasizes the extent to which speaking is a form of action with its own mode of organization within the social world. The child, in learning to communicate, not only faces an historically preserved linguistic system, but also an historically preserved system which specifies parameters for any speech event—what forms it is to take, when it is appropriate, with whom, in what way, on what topics. That is, in learning to give expression to a speech act, the child not only learns to express his or her semantic and pragmatic intentions through the grammatical and conventional system of language, but also learns to articulate those intentions within the cultural constraints upon the event of communication. Learning to articulate a speech act is but a part of learning to communicate, to participate in the culturally-framed process of creating or altering the architecture of intersubjectivity. Any speech act simultaneously actualizes both the speaker's personal intentions and aims, and sociocultural definitions of the event of communication (Silverstein, 1976). Hence, analyses of communicative development must encompass a developmental ethnography of communication, for the overt aims and intentions of speech acts are formulated within cultural frames which define the forms and functions of language usage.

Finally, it should be emphasized that functional strategic control over communication is acquired at increasingly abstract levels throughout the course of development and that such strategic control over communication is intertwined with interpretive processes, particularly social perception processes. This has been argued indirectly by Weinstein (1969) in his claim that competence for interaction implies not simply knowledge of a code, but also the ability to employ interpersonal strategies to accomplish interpersonal tasks. In any interaction situation, competent actors adapt their behaviour strategically in order to elicit desired responses from each other. The actors' strategies are guided by their definition of the situation, their best guess as to the nature of the reality with which they are currently engaged, their answer to the question, "What's going on here?" From the definition of the situation, each actor can draw inferences concerning the other's probable behaviour and the other's expectations. They can formulate strategies for self-presentation and strategies for casting the other into a desired role. Such actions involve the deployment of elaborated verbal strategies through which communication is adapted to the perspective of the other interactant so as to manage the situation toward personally defined goals. All this obviously depends upon the ability to tacitly recognize exactly what the socioculturally common understandings in a given situation are (so that interaction may proceed smoothly) and the ability to anticipate the other's reactions to alternative tactics (so that strategies designed to manipulate the other's view of the situation or self may be selected). The sociocultural constraints upon speaking and the social-cognitive ability to take the other's perspective on the situation are thus obviously essential parts of strategic competence (see Chapter 2). In learning to organize and articulate complex strategies directed towards particular other persons, the child must learn to coordinate all his or her communicative choices within a given speech event (or set of speech events) and organize them toward some end or ends. In order to do this, the child must both tacitly understand the shared cultural constraints upon communication, and also have the ability to erect, sustain, and adapt his or her cognitive assessment of the other across interaction sequences.

The analysis and extension of current work converging on the problem of communicative development thus reveals that such development involves a complex nexus of cognitive, linguistic, sociocultural, and behavioural achievements. Communicative development clearly must be understood to involve more than mastery of the linguistic code and the sociocultural rules for its use in situated interaction. In addition, as we have seen, communication is dependent as well upon the development of interpretive processes (particularly those involved in social perception) and behavioural strategies for the accomplishment of interpersonal goals. Any adequate treatment of how language subserves communicative objectives, must account for the individual and social processes by which interactants recognize, create, sustain, and manipulate various aspects of the reciprocal structure of intersubjectivity which forms the grounds of social communication. Thus, we argue that a child, in coming to control communication, must become adept at making interpretive assessments of the world (including, especially, the perspectives of other persons) and that this is true at nonverbal and paralinguistic, linguistic, sociolinguistic (sociocultural), and tactical/strategic levels. In developing this viewpoint, in the next section, we outline the basic commitments of an interpretive approach to communication; then we present our own constructivist version of an interpretive perspective in the subsequent section.

## SYMBOLIC INTERACTIONISM AND THE OUTLINE OF AN INTERPRETIVE CONCEPT OF COMMUNICATION

### On Interpretive Views of Communication

Our approach to communication builds upon an interpretive view of human interaction. Such a view is premised upon the assumption that there is more to communicating than mere behaviour exchange and the transmission of messages in some code. While alternative interpretive approaches vary in their central concepts and details, all accept that communication is an emergent, creative activity through which human social reality is constituted. As Delia and Grossberg (1977) observe, "within interpretive social theories, persons are agents of action, not mere responders to events. Actors are capable of originative action, and, consequently, communication is not completely bound by its past, but involves an emergent process in which social, that is to say intersubjective, reality is constituted [p. 36]."

While emphasizing the creative aspect of communication, most interpretive orientations also recognize that communication is accomplished within sociohistorical constraints. In fact, Grossberg (1976) defines the essential structure of interpretive understandings of communication in terms of the dialectic of creativity and tradition—the social reconstruction of reality is seen to involve an interplay of individual and socially constituted processes and contexts. Delia and Grossberg (1977) put it this way:

> While the individual's approach to reality is defined within ongoing processes of interpretation, the everyday world with which he or she is confronted is already meaningful. Social reality is predefined, presented as an already-meaningful whole. Thus, the individual, in the process of socialization, does more than simply coordinate his or her idiosyncratic beliefs about the world with those of the larger sociocultural group . . . ; one embraces an entire universe of shared meaning and acquires a range of socially and historically constituted vehicles (a common language, shared cultural understandings, typical modes of interpreting expressions and experiences) for interpretation and communication. However, communication always involves individuals with their own personal interpretive perspectives and projects acting in concrete situations [p. 36].

Hence the polar terms: constraint and creativity, culture and individuality, language and thought.

The Symbolic Interactionist Perspective

The significance of such an orientation for an understanding of communication and its development can be shown by our briefly summarizing in this section the key terms in one particular interpretive theory, the so-called Chicago school of symbolic interactionism (see Meltzer, Petras & Reynolds, 1975). Taking as its touchstone the approach to social interaction offered by George Herbert Mead (1934), this orientation has been developed by such sociologists as Blumer (1969), Strauss (1969) and Denzin (1977). In the following treatment, our aim is not to summarize the symbolic interactionist programme, but rather to construct a set of terms with which to approach the problem of communicative development. In this regard, we find it most useful to divide the major concepts populating symbolic interactionist writings into two categories: Those concerning basic social processes and those concerning issues in the social construction of reality. While reflecting the view of no single symbolic interactionist, such a segmentation serves to provide a framework suited to the present task.

*Fundamental Social Processes.* For symbolic interactionists, as for Mead, Blumer (1969) states that society is "to be seen as consisting of acting people, and the life of the society is to be seen as consisting of their actions [p. 85]." Furthermore, he emphasizes, "under the perspective of symbolic interaction, social action is lodged in acting individuals who fit their respective lines of action to one another through a process of interpretation [p. 84]." Thus Chicago school symbolic interactionists place processes of interpretation at the centre of their analysis of social action. Society is composed of units of acting individuals; individuals' actions are governed by their interpretations of the world around them.

This analysis of interaction is built upon an understanding of a series of concepts, the most fundamental of which is the "reflexive self." Mead (1934) argued that in internalizing social meanings, the actor acquired a reflexive self constituted as an ongoing process rather than as a configuration of traits, drives, or needs. Indeed, to say that the human being has a self is to say that he is capable of becoming an object to him/her self. As Blumer (1969) explains:

> . . . this reflexive process takes the form of the person making indications to himself, that is to say, noting things and determining their significance for his line of action. To indicate something is to stand over against it and to put

> oneself in the position of acting toward it instead of automatically responding to it. In the face of something which one indicates, one can withhold action toward it instead of automatically responding to it. With the mechanism of self-interaction the human being . . . acts toward his world, interpreting what confronts him and organizing his action on the basis of the interpretation. [p. 64].

Thus, human action takes on a radically different character from that of other life forms because it is a process of self-interaction; individuals make indications to themselves, interpret what they indicate, and create lines of action to accomplish their goals.

According to Mead and the symbolic interactionists, the acquisition of self and meaning both rest on existence in a social world, since it is recognition that behaviour calls forth the same response in self and others that allows the creation of symbols; the internalization of symbols allows the individual to take the perspective of others and to understand the responses that his or her projected acts will call out. The ability to take a generalized perspective on him/her self similarly allows the individual to make indications to him/her self, and thus to assess the importance of objects and events for his or her projected acts.

The ability to take the perspectives of others also underlies the human ability to engage in joint action. In joint action between two or more individuals, participants coordinate their respective lines of action. Each individual, in confronting the situation, acts on his or her own definitions and interpretations of that situation; but in order to construct acts which express the joint orientation and goals shared with a coparticipant, the individual must be sensitive to the other's definitions and interpretations. Together, participants must forge some consensual definition of the situation and each other. In this process of coordination, the ability to take the perspective of the other, "role-taking" in Mead's terminology, is central. As Blumer (1969) explains: "to indicate to another what he is to do, one has to make the indication from the standpoint of the other [p. 9]."

We thus find that for symbolic interactionists the two fundamental processes underlying social interaction are interpretation (including self-indication and role-taking) and strategy. As Blumer (1969) emphasizes:

> . . . in symbolic interaction . . . individuals . . . are necessarily required to take account of the actions of one another as they form their own action. They do this by a dual process of indicating to others how to act and of interpreting the indications made by others. Human group life is a vast process of such defining to others what to do and of interpreting their definitions; through this process people come to fit their activities to one another and to form their own individual conduct. Both such joint activity

and individual conduct are formed *in* and *through* this ongoing process; they are not mere expressions or products of what people bring to their interaction or of conditions that are antecedent to their interaction . . . [p. 10].

Since society is seen to be constructed in ongoing interaction, acts are directed at defining aspects of this reality; social reality is constructed and reconstructed through a process of negotiation in which strategies are reciprocally advanced and interpreted.

For the symbolic interactionist, every communication involves a strategic aspect, for every act represents an attempt to define or redefine several aspects of social reality. Since action is based on the actors' beliefs about the reality in which they are engaged, their action can be seen as an attempt to forward their conception of reality. Their view is proffered as an hypothesis in their actions, which may be accepted or rejected by the others with whom they interact. The actors express their own view of reality via strategies which represent the adaptation of their beliefs and intentions to the pre-existing conditions of the interactional situation.

It is important to emphasize, however, that all strategies are not self-consciously advanced. Symbolic interactionists have emphasized that routines represent an important subcategory of strategies. As aspects of social reality come to be defined and reaffirmed, these aspects are taken for granted. No longer at issue, the beliefs thus generated form the basis for routinized joint strategies for handling recurring situations in ongoing or socially formalized relationships. These recurring joint strategies are set apart as a unique set by the extent to which they are organized towards tacitly held background understandings, rather than current interactional issues.

Thus, with the concept of routines as a special subclass of strategies, symbolic interactionists implicitly recognize communication to involve the constraint of tradition upon creativity. This is an important point, for as we saw earlier it is a mistaken view that sees communication as involving only the capacity to formulate overt lines of action. Within any cultural group an "implicit communication theory" is acquired; this tacit system of beliefs defines the functions talk may serve and the forms it may take. "Having a conversation," "making a speech," "rhyming while skipping" "talking like a man," "joking," and an endless variety of other potential communicative events are defined with particular forms and functions by various cultures and groups (e.g., see Bauman & Sherzer, 1974). Communication involves an organized system of activities in which alternative episodes are framed by deeply tacit expectations and beliefs acquired in acculturation (see Goffman, 1974). It is in just this sense that, as Malinowski recognized, language usage is bound up with "the context of culture."

*Issues in the Social Construction of Reality.* Although no symbolic interactionist has treated the following concepts exactly the way we do, the remaining terms in their analysis of social interaction can be seen to represent the issues involved in the social construction of reality. Since social reality is constituted in the ongoing process of interpretation and interaction, various aspects of that reality may be addressed and re-negotiated.

Most fundamentally, interaction involves the negotiation of a definition of the situation. Participants in an interaction must generate some shared conception of the interaction situation and the norms governing conduct in that situation. These understandings take the form of beliefs about what the situation is and beliefs which form general constraints on action conducted within that situation. All aspects of the situation facing the participants in interaction are subject to negotiation; hence, in the course of an interaction, a number of more specific issues may arise. Acceptable solutions to these issues must be generated in order for joint action to proceed smoothly.

The first of these more specific issues is the question of the identities of the individuals involved in the situation. Actors generate strategies for self-presentation and alter-casting, representing respectively their solutions to the problems of their own and the other's situational identity. Given their identities, participants also must construct an acceptable definition of their relationship. Their understanding of their relationship takes the form of beliefs about how their identities are related and beliefs about how action is to be conducted within their relationship ("relational rules"—additional constraints within which actions are formulated). In addition, issues may arise over the focus of interaction, those aspects of reality toward which attention is jointly and explicitly directed. Of course, at times the overt focus of interaction may be upon some aspect of the definition of the situation or the identities and relationship of the interlocutors. However, most often these aspects of the reality will simply be assumed and taken for granted. In such cases, the focus of interaction will involve whatever is the overt subject of talk. Importantly, even the most mundane and pedestrian subjects are open to negotiation, as can be seen in the existence of routine strategies for introducing and switching topics in conversation. It is only the focus of interaction which serves as the subject for the explicit negotiation of social reality.

These, then, are the fundamental and implicit issues in every interaction, because in the process of constituting social reality, interactants must constitute the interaction situation itself. Only the focus of interaction is directly and explicitly defined by participants; the other issues (situations, identities and relationships) typically are negotiated implicitly, because it is the interactant's beliefs about these aspects of the interaction that constrain his or her choice of strategies.

Hence, we find that the creative, emergent process of interpretive interaction is worked out not only within a set of sociohistorically inherited constraints (sociolinguistic rules, definitions of prototypical situations and contexts, etc.) but also within a set of situationally emergent constraints. Individuals must create strategies which actualize their intentions, but which do so within the constraints imposed by the contextually-constituted definitions given to situation, self, other relationships, and the focus of interaction. They must introduce their projects into the interactional agenda, securing focused attention for their concerns. The strategies generated thus must not only actualize their intentions, but also must be appropriate within the constantly emerging definition given to reality in interaction.

## Role-taking and Communication

For the symbolic interactionists, then, the fundamental processes underlying interpersonal interaction are interpretation and strategies. Individuals interpret one another's actions, making indications to the self from the standpoint of the other (role-taking), and set out strategic lines of action based upon their respective interpretations. For Mead, the capability to engage in such symbolic interaction arises with the emergence of the ability to take the perspectives of others, and this ability arises directly from the internalization of anticipated responses in the acquisition of social meanings. Internalizing a system of shared symbols allows the inidividual to produce responses incipiently in formulating an action. The intention to act reveals the implicit response the other is expected to make. Because the response of the other is contained in the act-as-contemplated, the meaning of the act for the other is thrust on the individual. Role-taking is thus implied by the acquisition of language and the perspective of a cultural, or generalized, other.

The basis for more differentiated role-taking lies in the history of relationships. As individuals interact within a social group, they develop a system of terms and gestures unique to that group. Thus, they internalize understandings shared with specific individuals; these shared meanings form the basis for more individuated role-taking.

This conception of role-taking is fundamental to the symbolic-interactionist view. In our estimation, however, there are a number of difficulties with this approach. In the first place, as is discussed in detail by B. O'Keefe (1976), the analysis is dependent upon Mead's faulty analysis of the relationship between language and thought, in which thought (and hence all interpretive processes such as role-taking) is seen as identical with language. More importantly for the present discussion, however, additional difficulties stem from the fact that for symbolic interactionists, role-taking is act- and situation-specific. Symbolic interactionism argues explicitly that society is created not in terms of pre-existing structure, independent of the acts of individuals, but rather in terms of the ongoing activity of individuals in fitting together their lines of action. Thus, interaction takes form only in the ongoing coordination of actions by individuals. Moreover, since actors are seen to construct acts only in terms of the history of the social group in which they act, only the content of that history, a collection of shared beliefs, is seen to structure interaction. Furthermore, every history is seen to be unique and unrepeatable. The result of this analysis is an inability to generate cross-situational understanding of interaction. Interaction is not seen to be structured in terms of either external social processes or individual psychological processes; thus general characterizations of interaction cannot be couched in these terms. Since history itself is unique to a group or relationship, it is difficult to generate characterizations of interaction transcending the particular features of any interaction.

Thus, symbolic interactionist research often represents little more than an illumination of the particular in terms of a general set of categories. Of course, one would not want to reject symbolic interactionism just because it is inconvenient. The argument that social processes can only be understood in terms of the ongoing activity of individuals is, in our opinion, largely justified. On the other hand, the failure to recognize the importance of individual psychological structure is a serious defect in symbolic interaction theory, for, as we discuss later, there are important continuities in an individual's social perceptions across situations and also continuities in underlying changes in social perception processes which occur across the span of the individual's development. The consequent failure of symbolic interactionists to recognize the extent to which social interaction is structured by the stabilities in the interpretive and behavioural practices of individuals represents an additional inadequacy in their approach. Within the constructivist framework, which we elaborate later, one can characterize the effect of qualitative differences in psychological processes on communicative strategies, and thereby transcend the particulars of any specific situation. A constructivist approach, therefore, unlike symbolic interactionism, provides a basis for analysis of the relationship between social perception processes and behavioural aspects of communication, and not merely a set of categories for the description of situated interactions.

Before turning to our elaboration of the constructivist framework, however, two further observations concerning role-taking and communication are in order. Since both these points have been made elsewhere (Delia &

Clark, 1977; Delia & B. O'Keefe, 1979), we need merely to reiterate them here. First, it must be realized that role-taking or perspective-taking is only one aspect of social perception. Realization of this is important since most researchers seem to assume that only changes in social perceptions which reflect increases in role-taking are relevant to increases in communicative effectiveness. However, the child can be seen to obtain a potential basis for communicative adaptation whenever any attribution is made concerning another's action, role, character, intention, emotional state, or knowledge. Given the relevance of such perceptions to communication, it becomes important to realize (as we discuss later) that interpersonal understanding can be conceptualized as developing along a variety of axes, and not just in terms of increasing knowledge of the perspectives of others.

A final difficulty in attempts to relate developments in role-taking and communicative abilities is the seemingly universal presumption that perception is related directly to behaviour. Theorists and researchers alike apparently expect that if an interactant takes another's perspective, the interactant's perceptions will be translated directly into adaptations in messages, and lines of action directed towards the other. However, as Delia and Clark (1977) have shown, this assumption is both conceptually and empirically unjustified. Perceptions do not bear a one-to-one relationship to behaviour; rather a complex of processes operates between perceptions and behaviour (see the general theoretical argument advanced by B. O'Keefe & Delia, 1982).

## THE CONSTRUCTIVIST ANALYSIS OF INTERPRETIVE PROCESSES AND HUMAN COMMUNICATION

In this section, we elaborate our analysis of social perception processes; our principal aim is to develop a framework within which to conceptualize and operationalize stable aspects of social perception processes which have implications for developmental and individual differences in communication. We find it most useful to work within a general constructivist framework. Constructivism as an approach to communication study builds upon the orientation of symbolic interactionism, but modifies the interactionist emphasis upon act- and situation-specific processes by giving attention to individual stabilities in social-cognitive and behavioural aspects of communication. This is achieved through the integration of George Kelly's (1955) theory of personal constructs with aspects of Werner's (1957; Wapner, Kaplan, & Cohen, 1973) organismic-developmental theory as the basis for analysis of social construal processes. In this section, we first treat some general aspects of our framework and its contrast with that found in symbolic interactionism and then consider developmental differences in social construal processes.

### Interpersonal Constructs, Interpretive Schemas, and Interpersonal Perception

*A Constructivist Approach to Interpersonal Perception.* Both Crockett (1965) and Delia (1976) have outlined similar accounts of impression formation processes within the framework of Kelly's (1955) cognitive theory and Heider's (1958) conception of social inference processes. In their view, impressions are erected within the cognitive structures the perceiver brings to interpersonal situations. Thus, in contrast to the treatment of interpretive processes within symbolic interactionism, within constructivism, social perception is seen not as fluid but as channelled through the re-application of stable interpretive schemas. With Kelly's theory, these cognitive structures are conceptualized as personal constructs—dimensions of classification within which events, objects, or persons are interpreted or given meaning. Kelly's framework can be extended, however, to take account of more complex interpretive schemas that involve the integration and organization of a variety of elements and which guide the interpretation and remembering of person-relevant information over the temporal courses of interaction (e.g., see Cantor & Mischel, 1979; Crockett, 1977; B. O'Keefe & Delia, 1982). Moreover, as we detail later when discussing our reformulation of symbolic interactionism, it must also be recognized that cognitive schemas relevant to the organization of social situations and interaction are acquired as well and that they are integrated with schemas and constructs for understanding persons. Thus, within the constructivist perspective, stability and regularity in social construal processes are located in the character of the constructs and schemas making up the individual's interpersonal construct system. As we show later, analysis of the qualitative and organizational characteristics of interpersonal cognitive systems can be approached through considering developmental differences in construct systems and social construal processes.

*Individuality and Commonality of Constructs.* Although primarily concerned with individuality of construction processes, Kelly's personal construct theory also gives attention to construct commonality across individuals. By elaborating upon this aspect of Kelly's theory, we seek to encompass within an individualist-cognitive framework the processes emphasized by symbolic interactionists and others for whom interpretive processes emerge from a pre-existent social process. However, by conceptualizing shared construal processes within Kelly's framework, we are sensitized to the need to treat shared constructs (and other supra-individual concepts such as norms, role, and culture) not simply as social products but as similar elements of individual cognitive systems which are acquired within, and sustained through, historically preserved forms of interaction.

In the constructivist perspective, the individual is recognized as acquiring in the process of socialization the view of reality held within his or her social group. In the context of interaction, and throughout his interactive career, socializing agents force differentiation in the child's world view. Moreover, this differentiation is channelled by the ways in which others, by their actions, indicate objects within the social world, their similarities and differences, and their functions. It is through such a process and in this sense that constructs come to be shared.

Thus, in the process of socialization individuals come to share a common view of reality with other members of their culture. This socialization to a cultural reality begins even before the child starts to acquire language. One phenomenon illustrating this socializing process has been discussed by Brown (1970), who points to a mother's expansions of an infant's utterances as a case of cultural socialization. He argues that this expansion serves a significant role in socialization:

> The mother's expansion encodes aspects of reality that seem to be nothing less than the basic terms in which we construe reality: the time of an action, whether it is ongoing or completed, whether it is presently relevant or not; the concept of possession and such relational concepts as are coded by *in*, *on*, *up*, *down*, and the like; the difference between a particular instance of a class ("Has anybody seen *the* paper?") and any instance of a class ("Has anybody seen *a* paper?"); the difference between extended substances given shape and size by an "accidental" container (*sand*, *water*, *syrup*, etc.) and countable "things" having a characteristic fixed shape and size (*a cup, a man, a tree*, etc.). It seems to us that a mother in expanding speech may be teaching more than grammar; she may be teaching something like a world view [pp. 88-89].

In other words, part of the very acquisition of language—the child's conduit to the world of social meanings—itself depends upon the simultaneous acquisition of a system of constructs segmenting and organizing reality. In large measure, the shared referential quality of language can be understood to depend upon the child's acquisition of those dimensions for organizing experience which are historically sustained within his or her speech community.

Following the acquisition of language, constructs further differentiating diverse aspects of the social world (including other persons) are developed in the context of communication. Dimensions and schemas of interpretation employed by others provide ways of segmenting the social world that are taken over and integrated in idiosyncratic ways within the system of constructs elaborated through direct experience. The ways in which this cultural world view is presented are subtle and rooted in concrete events of interaction; but there is no question that the individual comes, through the process of communication itself, to employ socially common, though not identical, dimensions to construe the physical and social worlds. The result of the process, albeit subtly, is a construct system that is a curious and complex, and always unique, mix of individuality and cultural commonality.

*Individual and Situational Consistency in Social Construals.* Given the foregoing discussion, it should be evident that the major issues emerging from the juxtaposition of symbolic interactionist and constructivist treatments of interpretive processes concern the possibility of generating structures for identifying trans-situational consistencies in social perception and interaction processes. We are proposing, of course, that such trans-contextual structures are rooted in stable developmental differences in the individual's system of interpersonal constructs and schemas and in commonalities among individuals' constructs for understanding other people and social situations. Rather than constructing every situation anew from the ground up, the individual's perceptions are channelled through the re-application of stable interpretive schemas. These constructs and schemas represent the psychological structures through which the individual generates beliefs about other people and social situations. As we show below, these cognitive structures change with development in number, organization, quality, and content. In establishing a framework for approaching communicative development in terms of stabilities in individual social-cognitive organization, we argue later:

1. That stable differences in individual's social construals are in part a function of developmental characteristics of interpersonal construct systems.

2. That situational variations in an individual's level of cognitive and social functioning (for example, in utilizing advanced modes of construal with most persons while utilizing quite primitive modes in understanding those with whom one is intensely involved) can be understood within our framework through reference to the relationship of cognitive structure and environmental and task complexity (see the general analysis of Chandler, 1982).

In addition, however, it is also important that we do not overlook the fact that individuals employ different frames for structuring alternative kinds of social encounters (e.g., a business meeting, a date, a classroom discussion, or a casual conversation). It is also apparent that frequently a common definition of the situation is spontaneously arrived at by all participants in an episode (see Goffman, 1974). As we emphasized earlier, it is essential that we do not lose sight of the fact that individuals who have been influenced by similar cultural processes of social organization and interpretation share schemes of reference within which alternative kinds of communicative situations are structured and their activities organized. However, such construal processes can be accommodated within an individualist position if it is recognized that particular constructs are applicable to differing situations and objects and that many such constructs are acquired in similar form by members of a culture.

*The Developmental Analysis of Social Construal Process.* It is important from our point of view, however, that a perspective also be found for dealing with regularities explictly reflecting individual stabilities and competencies in interpretive and interaction processes. Towards such an end, we propose that such individual differences be approached through analysis of developmental characteristics of individuals' interpersonal construct systems. In providing the framework for such an analysis, we briefly review the premises of Wernerian organismic-developmental theory (see Wapner, Kaplan, & Cohen, 1973); we give particular attention to the developmental axis of egocentrism-perspectivism which in many ways parallels the idea of role-taking in symbolic interaction theory. Within the context of organismic-developmental theory, we then offer an orientation to the developmental analysis of construct systems and construal processes which can serve as the basis for relating stabilities in individual social perception processes to interactional competencies.

The heart of Werner's (1957) conception of development is stated succinctly in his Orthogenetic Principle: "Whenever development occurs, it proceeds from a state of relative globality and lack of differentiation to a state of increasing differentiation, articulation, and hierarchic integration [p. 126]." Werner sketched out the implications of this principle as follows:

> According to this principle, a state involving a relative lack of differentiation between subject and object is developmentally prior to one in which there is polarity of subject and object . . . this freedom from the domination of the immediate situation also permits a more accurate assessment of others. The adult is more able than the child to distinguish between the motivational dynamics and overt behaviour of personalities. At developmentally higher levels, therefore, there is less tendency for the world to be interpreted solely in terms of one's own needs and an increasing appreciation of the needs of others and of group goals [p. 127].

It should be noted that the Orthogenetic Principle provides a definition of development independent of chronological age. Moreover, in certain circumstances—for instance, under conditions of intense stress or emotional involvement—Werner predicted a kind of "regression" characterized by processes of "de-differentiation and de-hierarchization." Research has shown, in fact, that stress and emotional involvement are accompanied by the adoption of lower-level cognitive processes in social perception (e.g., Rosenbach, Crockett, & Wapner, 1973).

A central developmental axis derived from the Orthogenetic Principle is egocentrism-perspectivism. Egocentrism here in no way refers to selfishness or an inordinate concern with one's personal well being. Rather, as Looft (1972) has noted in discussing egocentrism-perspectivism in the context of Piaget's more widely known cognitive-developmental theory, the developmental axis refers to a process in which the child gradually comes "to differentiate cognitively among several aspects of an event and between his own and others' points of view [p. 74]." As with all development, the movement from egocentrism to perspectivism is conceptualized as a sequence of qualitative transformation; egocentrism at each level of development is characterized by its own unique qualities. Hence, as Elkind (1970) observes:

> The transition from one form of egocentrism to another takes place in a dialectic fashion such that the mental structures which free the child from a lower form of egocentrism are the same structures which ensnare him in a higher form of egocentrism. From the developmental point of view, therefore, egocentrism can be regarded as a negative by-product of any emergent mental system in the sense that it corresponds to the fresh cognitive problems engendered by that system [p. 50].

It should be noted that some, including symbolic interactionists such as Lindesmith, Strauss, and Denzin (1977) have claimed that the young child is not egocentric, but is, from birth, "socio-centric" or other-directed. This dispute is in large measure premised upon the mistaken assumption that egocentrism as elaborated in cognitive-developmental theories represents a single stage of development. Hence, these critics have argued, quite rightly, that even very young children are capable to some extent of taking account of others' viewpoints. While Piaget (1926/1955) initially referred to egocentrism as a stage of development between the autistic and social, in his later view and in the Wernerian system, egocentrism refers not to a particular stage or level of development but to a developmental axis. Egocentrism is present in qualitatively different forms all across the span of development.

Moreover, egocentrism is only one of a number of axes in terms of which developmental changes in cognitive processes can be conceptualized. In addition to changing from egocentric to perspectivistic, children's social perceptions have been shown to change with age in their differentiation, stability across situations, abstractness and sensitivity to motivations and psychological states, integration and organization, and in a host of other ways. Within organismic-developmental theory, such changes are seen to represent changes along interrelated developmental axes—egocentrism-perspectivism, concreteness-abstractness, lability-stability, diffuseness-integration, and globality-differentiation, to name the most important. Thus, taken alone, such concepts as role-taking and egocentrism are too general to be of great utility in understanding either the development of social perception or the relationship of social perception to communication.

Following the Orthogenetic Principle and its derivative axes the development of interpersonal constructs and schemas can be conceived as proceeding in the direction of increasing differentiation, articulation, abstractness, and hierarchic integration. Considerable research has, in fact, provided support for all of these expected developmental changes in children's impressions of others (e.g., Delia, Burleson, & Kline, in press; Scarlett, Press, & Crockett, 1971). Such observations of developmental changes in the number, quality, and organization of interpersonal constructs are consistent with research on the development of role-taking and social perspective-taking, the development of emphatic awareness of others' affective states, the development of social attribution processes, and the development of aspects of moral and interpersonal reasoning. This work is summarized in various forms in Livesley and Bromley (1973), Shantz (1975), and Damon (1977, 1979).

Importantly, parallel differences in differentiation, organization, abstractness, and egocentrism are found to distinguish impressions formed by young adults with highly differentiated (as compared to less differentiated) sets of personal constructs. As a result of varying social experiences, the variety of individual reactions to interpersonal conflicts, and a host of other factors that are, at best, poorly understood, any group of adults will contain some individuals with highly differentiated, hierarchically integrated, psychologically centred sets of interpersonal constructs and others with sparse, globally organized, relatively concrete sets of constructs. A number of studies have supported the hypothesis that interpersonal cognitive differentiation is associated with more complex and flexible ways of construing others and their perspectives (see D. O'Keefe and Sypher, 1981).

Interaction and Communication

*A Constructivist Conception of Human Action and Interaction.* Our view of human action and interaction is based upon a general interpretive view and can be seen as a cognitive-organismic reformulation of the symbolic interactionist perspective. Like the interactionists, we see human action as structured and guided by interpretive processes, while offering an alternative formulation of these processes. We have expressed our viewpoint elsewhere (B. O'Keefe, Delia, & D. O'Keefe, 1980) in discussing our conception of "interpretive schemes":

> By "interpretive scheme" we refer to any classification device persons employ in making sense of their world. These interpretive schemes channel behaviour: an individual acts on the basis of his or her conception of what the situation is, contains, and demands; that conception is created through the application of interpretive schemes; and as a result, the interpretive scheme outlines a set of alternative courses of action an individual may follow. The act of interpretation both limits and indicates choices for action [p. 26].

Some of the construals of situations result in conscious beliefs and subserve specific intentions; however, most construals remain tacit and guide behaviour implicitly. Whether conscious or tacit, however, construals of situations and intentions are seen as organizing action. Since action is always organized simultaneously at multiple levels, even much of intentional conduct reflects deeply (and tacitly) held, schemes for organizing aspects of behaviour (schemes organizing phonological and syntactic levels of language use, schemes organizing action within prototypical social situations and social roles, etc.) However, the application of constructs and interpretive schemes also forms the basis for the individual's selection of intended courses of action since they are the source of beliefs (whether tacit or conscious) about situations. The relationship between implicit construals of situations, conscious beliefs about situations, and intentions generating behavioural strategies towards situations accordingly will be seen as a subtle and developmentally changing one. Behaviour always is action in that it is always organized by cognitive processes, though only certain aspects of action are strategic in being organized by conscious beliefs, intentions, and behavioural choices.

One other aspect of the view of human action underlying the later review of communicative development concerns the situated, emergent nature of human action. Because persons act on the basis of context-specific intentions and context-relevant beliefs, and because their strategic choices to a large extent depend on beliefs about the situations in which they act, human action is always situated. And because actions are seen to reflect a people's beliefs about an unfolding situation, actions are seen as characterized by emergence. Any choice of action is based on the immediate beliefs held by individuals, which originate in their interpretation of their own history. The act is projected into the future, for it is designed to accomplish the individuals' intentions. The choice of strategy rests on the individuals' predictions about the future from events in the past, and their strategically organized behaviour serves as an implicit test for those predictions. Present action permits validation or modification of interpretive understandings; future choices will reflect the success or failure of the present choice. In this way, every act collapses past, present, and future; and thus every act emerges from a new past into a new future (see Blumer, 1969).

The view of human action just outlined results in a view of human interaction as a process in which persons coordinate their respective lines of action through schemes for the organization and interpretation of action. Individuals coordinate their behaviour through reliance on a variety of interpretive schemes which exist just "to classify acts in relation to other acts, to fit together lines of action of independent persons [B. O'Keefe, Delia, & D. O'Keefe, 1980, p. 26]." That is, interaction is organized through reliance on a set of socially shared interpretive schemes "which allow one person to produce acts with recognizable implications for another person's behaviour and permit persons to respond coherently and appropriately to acts which have been produced [p. 26]."

There are two important kinds of interpretive schemes that serve the process of interactional coordination. On the one hand, persons rely upon a general set of interpretive assumptions that allow discourse to be produced as coherent in any instance. One description of such general interpretive principles is presented by Grice (1975) who argues that talk is structured around the principle "Be Cooperative" and its corollaries. Alternatively, Cicourel (1974) has discussed a number of "deep interpretive practices" relied upon by persons in connecting their knowledge of social structure and rules to situated utterances: The assumption that there is a reciprocity between the perspectives of interactants, the assumption that future events and utterances will clarify present ambiguities, etc. At the same time, interactants rely upon interpretive schemes that are specifically relevant to making connections among particular kinds of acts. Elsewhere, we have called these more specific interpretive devices "organizing schemes"; for us (B. O'Keefe et al., 1980), that term:

> ... covers a variety of interactional classification devices: general plans for speech events (e.g., the typical form of a committee meeting), adjacency pairs (sequentially linked pairs of acts, e.g., question-answer), routine procedures for accomplishing particular tasks or goals (e.g., the standard procedure a family follows in getting up and dressed in the morning), general

knowledge about the organization of behaviour in institutional settings (e.g., as Schank and Abelson [1977] have described it, a general script that customers follow in restuarants), and so on [p. 27].

The fact that individuals share general interpretive principles and organizing schemes is what permits them to coordinate their behaviour and activities. However, to say that such schemes are shared by members of a social group in no way implies that members' processes are identical or that coordination can only be accomplished when schemes are identical. Persons can coordinate their behaviour even though their interpretive schemes may be dissimilar in some respects; there must, however, be sufficient similarity for the purposes of a particular interaction. For example, while an adult and a very young child have (because of differences in development) qualitatively different understandings of social interaction, they can coordinate their actions for some (but obviously not all) purposes. Two persons can engage in a form of social activity even though each is unaware of the details of the other's role or even of much beyond his own limited role, provided that their understandings and actions interlock within some very general shared scheme (as in my putting a letter in a postbox and its being picked up by some postal worker unknown to me). Shared interpretive principles and organizing schemes thus serve the coordination of behaviour because they are available as resources to interactional participants. They serve as frames into which persons can fit their actions and as ways of implicitly anticipating the behavioural choices of others. Persons achieve the coordination of behaviour and meaning through establishing and fitting action to such jointly understood schemes. Thus interactional coordination is not straightforwardly given in interpretive practices and organizing schemes, but is achieved through establishing and relying on such practices and schemes. Interaction, therefore, is a process of implicit negotiation in which the very understanding through which it is accomplished is refined and elaborated (see the more general discussion of this point in Delia et al., 1982; B. O'Keefe, 1978; B. O'Keefe et al., 1980).

*The Constructivist Conception of Human Communication.* Building upon the foregoing analysis of human interaction, we take communication to be a process of interaction in which the communicative intentions of participants are a focus of coordination. In communication, action is mobilized to serve the needs of expression and interpretation and is guided by the attribution of the intention to express. Thus, although many different intentions direct communicative action (e.g., to persuade or to sooth distressed feelings), at base communication originates in the attempt to make publicly available some private state and the organization of behaviour towards that end.

It should be stressed that in saying that communicative intentions are a focus of interactional coordination, we do not mean to imply that intentions are unambiguously manifest in behaviour or that individuals need necessarily to establish their intentions for communication to proceed. Communication is always interaction and thus shares the characteristics of interaction in general. Communication is a situated activity; it is a process in which persons coordinate their behaviour through the application of shared interpretive schemes; it is a process of implicit negotiation. What is involved in communication is the process of taking communicative intentions as the implicit or explicit focus of interpretation and negotiation. Communication is grounded in coordination, but the occurrence of communication depends on the attempt to coordinate, not on the product of that process of coordination.

Communication as a process of coordination may result in "correct" or "incorrect" interpretations of intentions, in understanding or misunderstanding. It is the organization of interpretation and behaviour around the attribution of the intent to communicate that sustains communication. Few behaviours or utterances implicate only a single unambiguous intention; most utterances can be responded to appropriately in a variety of ways. Indeed, Jacobs (1977) has shown that in normal communicative interaction, it is not essential that interactants actually understand one another at all if they are able to respond to one another's utterances so as to sustain the dialogue. Social meanings do not emerge straightforwardly from the expression of communicative intentions, but from the interactional negotiation of imputed intentions. Hence, the meaning of the first utterance in an utterance/response response-to-response sequence is an emergent social product of the interactional sequence, not a property of the isolated act (this point also has been made by Goffman, 1976; and Rommetveit, 1978). What is fundamental to communication is the process of reciprocally imputing and negotiating intentions and meaning, not the results of that process. As Rommetveit (1978) has emphasized, the product of the process of communication in normal discourse is always a partial rather than a complete shared understanding.

*Foundations of a Social, Psychological, and Contextual Framework for the Analysis of Communicative Development.* It should be clear from the foregoing discussion that within the constructivist perspective communication is viewed as simultaneously social and psychological. Indeed, representing this duality is a major part of the general project of this chapter. Accordingly, in the foregoing discussion emphasis was given to the fact that communication always involves psychological processes of individual communicators; rather than being simply an exchange of behaviour or information, communication is grounded in processes of perception, interpretation, and memory. Persons create the meanings of the messages they encounter through the application of interpersonal constructs and interpretive schemes. However, it was also stressed that communication is not simply a psychological process of interpretation; it is also a process of social coordination. Although communication is always grounded in individual processes of interpretation, the aim of communication is to create socially shared meaning. To this end, as was noted, persons make their meaning accessible to others through organizing behaviour and actively seek out the communicative intentions of others through the application of interpretive schemes.

Interpretive processes make possible both the meaningful organization of behaviour and inferences about the communicative intentions of others. The ability to select a behavioural strategy that will contribute to interactional coordination and be meaningful to another depends on the ability to predict, at least on conventionalized bases, the likely response of the other to alternative modes of action. The ability to infer the meaning and intentions of another depends on similar conventionalized and individuated structures for conceptualizing that person's psychological processes. It is the ability to anticipate the other's actions and to conceptualize the covert psychological processes of others which make social coordination possible.

It should be noted, however, that the interpretive understanding of the other's behaviour and psychological processes need be neither conscious, complete, or very sophisticated. In the sense in which the term is being used here, interpretive understanding refers to all of the cognitive processes by which we make sense of other persons and their actions. This includes a variety of processes not involving complicated or abstract forms of social inference. For example, interpretive understanding may be based in institutional social norms governing the (unconscious) display of certain intentions and meanings. Moreover, as we noted earlier, persons' psychological processes change qualitatively with development. The interpretations of perspectives made by very young communicators, for instance, are likely to be exceedingly concrete and closely tied to behaviour, while more developmentally advanced communicators will be better able to go beyond immediate surface behaviour in making abstract inferences about the psychological processes of others.

Interpersonal constructs and interpretive schemes of a given quality will permit the individual to handle some communicative tasks, but not others. Thus, the organismic-developmental perspective leads to a need for revising prevailing conceptions of "communicative competence." There is not a set of linguistic, socio-cultural, or cognitive processes that provide "competence" for dealing with all interactional situations and contexts. Any individual, regardless of his or her social experience, will have developed the resources for adaptively managing interaction at some levels, but not at others. Hence, for example, even severely retarded children are likely to acquire the interpretive schemes for recognizing and managing turn-taking in routine interaction (e.g., Price-Williams & Sabsay, 1979), and hence are "communicatively competent" in organizing certain aspects of their interactions. Similarly, while an adult and a very young child have (because of differences in development) qualitatively different understandings of social interaction, they can co-ordinate their actions for some (but obviously not all) purposes. Hence, rather than thinking about "communicative competence," we believe a more useful orientation is provided by considering individuals' levels of "communicative development." For the idea of development implies the presence of sets of structures that are evolving and which provide the means of organizing interpretation and behaviour at particular levels (see also the discussion by Shatz, 1978).

The constructivist analysis of communicative development thus places emphasis upon the content and quality of the communication-relevant interpretive processes which the individual has developed and the levels at which these processes provide control over interpretation and behaviour. With social experience, individuals come to develop constructs and schemes allowing them to recognize and attribute an increasing range of communication-relevant characteristics to others and to control their behaviour at progressively more complex levels in expressing their intentions and in channelling the interpretations of others. Behaviour is interpreted and organized at several levels, including the nonverbal (behavioural and paralinguistic), the linguistic (lexical and grammatical), the sociolinguistic or socio-cultural, and the tactical or strategic. All these levels are interrelated (hence, for example, social rules may be strategically exploited; syntactic structures may subserve clarity of expression or ambiguity; paralinguistic aspects of speech associated with a particular "accent" may be purposely adopted; etc.).

The important questions to ask of a theory of communication concern the processes and modes of understanding and behaviour the person has developed and whether these processes and modes are adequate to the communicative task at hand. Schizophrenics have been shown to do as well as normals on an easy referential communication task, but to do much poorer when the task is difficult (Cohen, 1978; see Chapter 2). Likewise, a typical social actor may be perfectly "competent" to carry on normal discourse, but have inadequate control over the strategic resources of communication at the sociolinguistic level to "pass" as a member of a particular social group (e.g., see the analysis of Goffman, 1969). Moreover, the organization of given communicative resources may not be actualized within some contexts, while they can be purposefully controlled in others. It is a commonplace observation (given theoretical status within the Wernerian framework) that emotional arousal, tension, and the like, have a disorganizing effect upon communicative performance. The ability of an individual to organize interpretation and action cannot be separated in the final analysis from a contextual analysis, for all behaviours are situated within particular contexts. The idea of an organismic-developmental or constructivist approach to communication thus points toward a genuinely social, psychological, and contextual perspective in which attention is given to:

1. The character of the interpretive schemes the interactants have developed.
2. The modes of behavioural organization and control over the resources of communication those schemes provide.
3. The situated and emergently negotiated character of understandings and interpersonal tasks that are achieved through the interpretive and behavioural resources of communication.

## AN OVERVIEW OF CONSTRUCTIVIST RESEARCH ON INTERPERSONAL CONSTRUAL PROCESSES AND COMMUNICATIVE BEHAVIOUR

In building upon a symbolic interactionist approach to communication, we have sought to emphasize that communication is not a process that is accomplished straightforwardly through a shared linguistic or discourse system. Rather, like many other theorists and researchers, we have underscored the extent to which intersubjective meaning is dependent upon a momentary, partially shared interpretive frame. Thus, with others, we give emphasis in our analysis of communicative intelligibility to the contextual character of meaning. However, in most of our research we have focused not on the contextual character of shared meaning, but on what purpose the contextual character of the function messages is meant to serve. We have stressed throughout the foregoing discussion that communicative action is part of social action and that messages subserve many functions other than the purely communicative (i.e., messages subserve not only intelligibility but also instrumental, relational, identity, and related functions). In particular, our research has focused upon the ways in which developments in the quality of one's interpersonal cognitive schemes channel communicative intentions and behaviour. In this section, recent research on functional communication conducted within our framework is summarized in reference to three topics: interpersonal cognition and the development of receiver-focused communicative strategies, the definition of the situation and interactional objectives, and the social context of interpersonal cognitive and communicative development.

## Interpersonal Constructs and Receiver-Focused Communicative Strategies

The relationship of interpersonal cognition to communication has been most often studied through assessing the role of perspective-taking ability in making listener-adapted message choices (e.g., Flavell et al., 1968; see also Delia & Clark, 1977; Delia & B. OKeefe, 1979; and B. O'Keefe & Delia, 1979, for our own similar analysis of the social cognition-message strategy relationship). We have argued recently for considering other roles that developments in interpersonal cognition might play in communicative behaviour, including, in particular, the role of social cognition in generating the intentions that organize receiver-focused message production (B. O'Keefe & Delia, 1982). Specifically, we advance the thesis that variations in social cognitive development (construct differentiation) lead to differences in the perception of obstacles and subsidiary objectives that must be addressed in the pursuit of a dominant situational goal.

The line of research we interpret as supporting this conclusion is based on the hierarchic ordering of message structures in terms of the degree to which multiple dimensions (obstacles and aims) of complex communication situations are recognized and reconciled in messages. Most of this research involves coding schemes derived from the work of Clark and Delia (1976) and Applegate and Delia (1980).

Clark and Delia's (1976) message classification system defines general types of messages that might be produced when a child is asked to make a request of a listener. Each message type reflects one possible response to an influence situation in which the persuadee is presumed to be reluctant to grant the request. Clark and Delia identified four basic message strategies: simple request; elaborated requests (in which the needs of the persuader are stressed): counterarguing (in which the objections of the persuadee are anticipated and refuted); and advantage to other (in which the advantages of compliance to the persuadee are stressed). In research on the development of persuasive message production, Clark and Delia (1976) and Delia, Kline, & Burleson, (1979) have shown that these four message types appear to be developmentally ordered: as children develop, they first produce simple requests, then elaborated requests, then counterarguments, and finally messages emphasizing advantages to the persuadee. Moreover, in both developmental research (e.g., Delia, Kline, & Burleson, 1979) and research with adults (e.g., Applegate, 1982b; Burke 1979), the production of strategies higher in this hierarchy has been found to be positively correlated with individual differences in interpersonal construct differentiation in both role-play situations where there is no physically present listener and in actual interaction.

In interpreting these results the relationship of the message hierarchy to the structural character of the persuasion situation should be considered. Persuasion occurs when one person wants something from another person who is presumably unwilling to satisfy the want. Thus, the essential structure of a persuasion situation implies two people, persuader and persuadee, with competing agendas (see Chapter 8). Approached in this way, the ordering of Clark and Delia's four message strategies can be explained as a function of increasing success in reconciling the needs of persuader and persuadee in the message—from emphasizing one's own agenda, to denying the validity of the persuadee's agenda, to manufacturing a common agenda. Clark and Delia's message strategies thus represent four alternative actions that comprise a set of generalized options for dealing with the competing wants of persuader and persuadee. The strategies are not simply ways of adapting messages to listeners, nor are the strategies ordered by increasing listener-adaptedness, although individual differences in social cognitive schemes clearly are implicated as playing a central role in the perception of situational obstacles and issues.

Research on situations requiring regulative and comforting communication even more clearly demonstrate the role of social cognitive developments in the recognition of obstacles and the possession of multiple aims and the reconciliation of primary aims with perceived obstacles and with subsidiary aims. For example, the message analysis system used to categorize regulative messages (in which the communicator must modify another's behaviour) involves a set of nine hierarchically ordered categories which can be seen as reflecting variations in attempts to accomplish multiple aims in messages (see Applegate, 1980a, 1980b; Applegate & Delia, 1980; Husband, 1981; Kline & Ceropski, in press; also see B. O'Keefe & Delia's (1982) discussion of the coding system). The first three categories (physical punishment, commands, and rule-giving) all involve messages produced with a single aim, the primary aim of the subject's assigned task: modify the message recipient's behaviour. The next three categories involve messages which address the obstacle of gaining the message recipient's compliance (offering reasons for rules, discussing consequences of noncompliance, and discussing general principles behind appropriate behaviour). The final three categories involve messages in which the communicator simultaneously corrects the behaviour, offers reasons for compliance, and encourages the message recipient to be empathic in his or her social conduct (describing feelings produced by inappropriate behaviour, encouraging the message recipient to see multiple aspects of the situation in terms of feelings, helping the message recipient to make an empathic response through analogy, leading the message recipient to reason through the situation, etc.)

Messages produced in response to comforting situations (in which conflicts in feelings figure prominently) have been classified using a coding system that essentially reflects the degree to which a communicator increasingly deals with multiple dimensions of interpersonal conflicts, including hurt feelings, the reasons for and consequences of hurt feelings, and the message recipient's ability to understand and empathize in conflict situations (see Applegate, 1980a, 1980b; Applegate & Delia, 1980; Borden, 1979; Burleson, 1981, 1982, in press-a & -b; Burleson & Samter, 1983; Husband, 1981). Thus the lowest level strategies deal with the immediate situation without regard to the message recipient's need for support; strategies at the intermediate levels deal with the situation through acknowledging feelings and providing psychological support; strategies coded at the highest levels deal with the immediate situation, provide psychological support, and help the message recipient to reason through the situation and to learn from it.

The finding of this series of investigations parallel those of investigations of persuasive communication skills using Clark and Delia's message analysis system: For both role-played and realistic interaction situations within age-homogenous groups of adults and children, and across the age span from early childhood to young adulthood, interpersonal construct differentiation is significantly related to performance on message construction tasks. Taken as a whole, this research suggests that interpersonal construct system development plays a central role in the perception of communication-relevant objectives and obstacles and in the use of communicative strategies to organize dominant and subsidary intentions in situations.

We want to emphasize one striking implication of the foregoing results given our interest in reformulating the symbolic interactionist analysis of social processes within an elaborated cognitive-developmental social psychology. Specifically, from the standpoint of the concept of the definition of the situation, it seems plain that the communicative task was construed quite differently by groups of participants in our studies. For example, it appears that some communicators saw as genuinely "regulative" those situations in which there was a normative basis for action; that is, a legitimate and sufficient basis for controlling the message recipient's behaviour evidently was attributed by some communicators to be inherent in such role relationships as a mother addressing a child or a manager addressing an employee. However, other communicators appeared implicitly to have represented these role-defined situations as requiring persuasion, not regulation, since the message recipient was treated as a free and autonomous agent of action responsible for his or her own conduct. Free and responsible agents are not to be controlled. Rather, they act on the basis of their own autonomous beliefs. Hence, control or regulation must be accomplished by "persuasion," i.e., by leading the other to see the implications of his action so that he or she will be led to "choose" to act responsibly. In terms of Kelman's (1961) classic analysis of social influence, some communicators appear implicitly to represent control situations as involving individuals who can and should be influenced by compliance structures, while others appear to represent situations as involving individuals who can and should only be influenced by internalization structures. Applegate's (1980a, 1980b; Applegate, Burke, Burleson, Delia, & Kline, in press) research with mothers and teachers, Husband's (1981) work with residence hall supervisors, and Kline and Ceropski's (in press) and Kasch's (in preparation) work with medical practitioners, all reveal this distinction in control situations as a function of differences in interpersonal construct differentiation. In the following section, we summarize our recent research that directly extends our analysis of personal goal structures in complex communication situations within a framework emphasizing the concept of the definition of situation.

### The Definition of the Situation and Subsidiary Interactional Aims

In the symbolic interactionist framework, the definition of the situation is the symbolic representation of the social situation in the minds of interactants: their conceptions of the activity in which they are engaged, of the roles of interactants within that activity, and of the spatio-temporal setting in which the activity occurs. The definition of the situation is the source from which interactants derive their sense of relevance and appropriateness; it is the set of beliefs about a situation which shape and channel conduct and supply the context for interpreting the conduct of others. As a result, a joint (mutually imputed) definition of the situation is critical to the efforts of interactants to coordinate their behaviour. It is for this reason that symbolic interactionists have devoted considerable attention to the processes through which interactants come to a shared definition of the situation and cope with the misunderstandings and conflicts that threaten the "working consensus" they have achieved.

A number of theorists (e.g., Goffman, 1959; Strauss, 1969; Weinstein, 1969) have noted that a central element in the definition of any social situation is the identities of the participants, and Goffman (1959), in particular, has argued that in all social situations, "face (the positive social value one claims for oneself)" is the centrally relevant feature of one's identity. Moreover, face is one element of the definition of a situation which is necessarily called into question in a wide range of activities and under a wide range of circumstances. As a consequence, social systems develop routine procedures and strategies for managing recurring situations in which the definition of the situation is threatened by the conflict between the need to protect face and the need to pursue some activity (e.g., making a request, regulating another person's conduct), or deal with some untoward occurrence that reflects badly on the identity of one or more interactants (e.g., someone knocking over a lamp, someone being caught in a lie).

There is a considerable literature on the conversational strategies people employ in attempting to avoid or repair damage to face. Much of this research describes and classifies interactional tactics commonly used in dealing with particular problems of identity management (e.g., Gross & Stone's [1964] analysis of embarrassment; Scott & Lyman's [1968] analysis of accounts). By contrast, Brown and Levinson's (1978) analysis of universal structures in politeness offers a deeper and more systematic analysis of the forms discourse may take as it is shaped to meet the needs of face protection. They argue that "face" actually consists of two wants: the want that one's wants be valued by others (positive face); and the want not to be impeded by others (negative face wants). There are a large number of actions which are intrinsically threatening to the face wants of either actors or their interactional partners—for example, requests are intrinsically threatening to the negative face wants of the target of the request, since a request necessarily involves some degree of imposition.

Brown and Levinson point out that, confronted with the possibility of performing a face-threatening action (FTA), actors may elect one of four generalized options: (1) do the FTA, baldly; (2) do the FTA, but with redress; (3) do the FTA off record; and (4) do not do the FTA. Doing the FTA "baldly" involves performing the face threatening action in a recognizably direct and unambiguous fashion ("on record"). Doing the FTA "with redress" is accomplished through adding features designed to satisfy face wants (such as compliments, hedges, apologies) to on-record FTAs. Doing the FTA "off record" involves performing the FTA with some degree of indirectness (by boldly performing some nonthreatening action which logically or conventionally implies the FTA). One thing Brown and Levinson point to is the fact that these four options all represent different ways of resolving the conflict between efficient communication (saying clearly what one wants or means) and face wants. They go on to show how, across a variety of cultures, politeness is instantiated in the form of indirectness and types of redress.

What Brown and Levinson's work represents is a move away from the standard symbolic interactionist practice of analyzing discourse strategies, which is to identify some recurring interactional problem and identify the strategies people commonly use in dealing with that problem. This practice is attributed to two features of symbolic interactionism we mentioned earlier: a persistent failure to recognize and take into account the stable, internal structures of discourse systems that generate utterances; and a failure to develop more than a rudimentary conception of individual cognitive systems. As a consequence of these two failings, the only basis for generalization available to the analyst is the identification of specific conditions in situations that tend to recur; a symbolic interactionist would be unlikely to develop the kind of analysis Brown and Levinson have offered, in which discourse strategies available for protecting face are shown to involve the rational exploitation of a structured system of discourse options in the pursuit of goals.

However, in all the work on strategies for pursuing identity-relevant objectives (including that of Brown & Levinson) there has been a common focus on describing the shared repertoire of strategies available to members of a social group for handling identity-related problems within face-threatening situations. All this work has involved the assumption that the interactants involved have the goal of protecting face. Virtually no attention has been given to the question of how people use their strategic repertoires. An individual's use of the shared repertoire of face-protection strategies should, of course, depend on that person having face-protection as a goal and being able to recognize the identity-relevant implications of actions.

Recent lines of research within our framework have explicitly addressed the question of how individuals use the strategic repertoire available to them for face protection. One of these lines of work, undertaken by Kline (1981a, 1981b, 1982, 1983), has been concerned with determining how individual differences in social cognition influence the use of strategies for face protection. In this research, subjects were asked to consider themselves in a position of authority and facing the task of getting a subordinate to mend his or her ways. This is, of course, a situation which intrinsically threatens both the positive and negative face wants of the subordinate, since both an imposition (negative face) and a negative evaluation of the subordinate's current behaviour (positive face) are inherent to the action to be taken by the superordinate. Subjects were asked to write what they would say to the erring subordinate, and their responses were coded along two dimensions. The first dimension along which responses were classified concerned the degree to which the response assigned a negative identity versus a positive identity to the subordinate (e.g., in describing the offence, did the subject cast it as a wrongful or defective act characteristic of the subordinate, or in some more positive light). The second dimension along which responses were classified concerned the degree to which the strategy for regulating conduct involved imposition of authority versus some attempt to grant autonomy to the subordinate (e.g., simply giving an order as opposed to engaging to persuade the subordinate—persuasion being an act which intrinsically presupposes and therefore implies some degree of autonomy for the persuadee). Kline explicitly grounds her work in Brown and Levinson's analysis of face, so these two dimensions correspond to what they would describe as positive and negative face.

In an initial study using this paradigm, Kline (1981a; also see Kline, 1981b and 1983) found that there were considerable individual differences in the use of strategies for protecting positive and negative face, and that both the sex of the subject and the subject's degree of construct differentiation were significantly related to strategy use. More often than men, women used face protecting strategies and were particularly more likely than men to use strategies granting greater autonomy to the subordinate. Subjects who were relatively high as opposed to low in construct differentiation produced responses which were both more likely to grant autonomy to the subordinate and to preserve a positive social identity for the subordinate. This construct differentiation/face support relationship has been replicated among children and adolescents (Burleson, 1982) and adults (Applegate, 1982a).

In a second study, Kline, (1982) sought to determine whether these differences among individuals were attributable to differential knowledge of available discourse strategies or differences in goals. The failure to use a face protecting strategy could result from either not having a strategy available or from not having the goal (face protection) which the strategy is designed to achieve. In this second investigation, Kline attempted to make her earlier findings less ambiguous employing an experimental manipulation designed to induce subjects to have the goal of face protection if they failed to have it spontaneously. Half the subjects were simply given the standard regulative communication task; the other half were given the regulative communication task and explicitly told that they were to seek to protect the face of the partner. Her findings suggest that the inattention to face wants displayed by low differentiation subjects is primarily attributable to their failure to have spontaneously the goal of face protection, because when low differentiation subjects were told to protect face wants, their performance did not differ from that of subjects high in construct differentiation. Thus, while the discourse system available to everyone contains a set of options for designing messages to protect face, individuals differ in their exploitation of that system, and it appears that this difference is attributable to differences in the goals they set for themselves in interactions. Moreover, these differences in goals appear to be related in a regular fashion to the cognitive structures individuals have for interpreting social situations and behaviour (and thus to individual differences in such cognitive structures).

What Kline's work suggests is a model of social conduct in which individual differences in structures for social cognition lead individuals to have fundamentally different ways of defining social situations. Some people apparently are simply less likely to represent social situations in such a way that face implications and face protection become part of the scheme of relevance defining the concrete situation. This model is given further support in recent work by B. O'Keefe and Shepherd (1983a, 1983b).

B. O'Keefe and Shepherd analyzed the strategies people use to protect the face wants of self and partner and maintain interaction in an interpersonal conflict situation. They asked pairs of subjects who were known to disagree strongly about a policy issue to discuss that issue; each interactant was instructed to try to persuade the other to accept his or her own position on the issue. These dyadic persuasive interactions were videotaped and the behaviour of interactants was classified as to the degree to which behaviour was organized in such a way as to deal with the face-threatening features of the situation and to at least maintain the appearance of a coherent dialogue on the assigned topic.

Given that subjects were told explicitly that they disagreed strongly on the assigned topic and that they were assigned the task of persuasion, every behavioural option available to participants involved some potential threat to own or partner's face wants or to the maintenance of continued and coherent discussion or both. In displaying this feature of their experimental situation, B. O'Keefe and Shepherd argued that there are four basic categories or "modes" of action available to interactants in the situation as publicly defined. These four modes are generated by two decisions interactants must repeatedly make as they organize their actions in relation to the situation as defined. First, they must decide whether to convey acceptance (to some degree) or rejection (to some degree) of the position advocated by the partner—and this decision necessarily involves an orientation to one's own position as well, since own and partner's position are opposite on the issue. Second, they must decide whether or not to explicitly and overtly acknowledge the conflict between the two positions. These two choices, taken together, generate four general classes of action that may be performed in this situation: (1) avoidance and simple agreement (implicit acceptance); (2) explanations (implicit disagreement); (3) arguing (explicit disagreement); and (4) compromise (explicit agreement).

The decision simply to agree with the partner (or at least not to disagree) and the decision not to explicitly acknowledge the conflict between positions generates a basic posture of avoidance: people try to avoid discussing the topic and in particular try to avoid expressions of opinions on the topic. Subjects acting within this mode denied having the positions attributed to them by the experimenter (they are known to have lied); introduced topics other than the one assigned; simply agreed with what their partners said while at the same time closing off discussion; said they did not care about the issue (they are known to have lied) and would take any position on it. While actions falling within this mode involve no direct threat to the partner's face wants, they all create identity problems for the actor (by intrinsically involving a very questionable characterization of one's own position, or publicly devaluing one's own beliefs, or simply accepting the imposition of alter's beliefs), and they all create problems for interaction maintenance (it is hard to have a discussion if one interactant refuses to discuss; it is hard to be responsive to the partner in this situation if one refuses to express opinions about the assigned issue or encourage the partner's expression of opinion).

The decision to express rejection of the partner's views combined with a desire to avoid explicit acknowledgement of the conflict between positions generates a mode of behaviour that B. O'Keefe and Shepherd label "explanation." Subjects acting within this mode simply explain their own position on the issue and the reasons why they personally hold their positions, without criticizing the positions of the partner or engaging in any act which is conventionally recognizable as urging their position on the partner. Thus, while subjects acting within this mode do express a point of view at odds with the view of the partner, they explain their positions in such a way as to avoid explicitly acknowledging or implying that they see a conflict between their own and the partner's positions. As mentioned earlier, actions that refuse to explicitly acknowledge the existence of conflict make interaction maintenance difficult—this is true of action within the mode of implicit rejection as well. Holding to a posture of simply explaining one's own point of view makes it difficult to sustain interaction past a few turns and to be responsive to the partner's conversational contributions. Moreover, even though adopting a posture of explanation reduces the face threat to the partner that is intrinsic to any rejecting action, nonetheless there is some residual threat to the partner's positive face wants in the failure to accept the partner's viewpoint and the expression of one's own conflicting position.

The decisions to reject the partner's position and to do so in a way that explicitly and overtly acknowledges the existence of conflict result in a posture of arguing. Subjects acting within this mode actively urged their positions on the partner and criticized the partner's viewpoint. Obviously, the primary interactional problems created by this mode of behaviour are face-related: In explicitly and unambiguously rejecting the position of the partner, one necessarily threatens both the partner's positive and negative face wants and risks creating a negative identity for oneself (by appearing inconsiderate, unfriendly, and impolite).

The decisions to explicitly acknowledge the existence of a conflict and to express some degree of willingness to accept the partner's position generate a posture of compromise. Subjects acting within this mode offered compromise positions to their partners or acknowledged having been persuaded by arguments made by the partner. Action within this mode poses few problems for interaction maintenance but does pose a direct threat to face. Action within this mode intrinsically trades off one's own face wants against the partner's face wants—to the degree that one repudiates one's own position, one threatens one's own positive and negative face wants; to the degree that one qualifies or limits one's acceptance of the partner's position, one refuses the partner's face wants.

Thus, each of the four modes within which subjects could act in this situation potentially involved some threat to the definition of the situation, either through creating difficulties for interaction maintenance or through threatening face or both. The questions that interested B. O'Keefe and Shepherd were:

1. How might interactants organize their behaviour to avoid or deal with these potential problems as they acted within these four modes?
2. In what ways might individuals differ in dealing with the conflict among the assigned objectives they were given in the situation, the potential goal of maintaining interaction, and the potential goal of maintaining face?

B. O'Keefe and Shepherd argue that subjects have available three basic ways of dealing with the distinctive problems created by action within each of the four modes (also see B. O'Keefe & Delia, 1982). Subjects can fail to recognize or can ignore the interactional maintenance and face problems of the mode within which they are acting, and simply perform some baldly produced action. Subjects can recognize and deal with the interactional problems created by their actions through redressive or mitigating embellishments of the basic act they are performing (e.g., through accounts, hedges, compliments to the partner, and so on). Or subjects can avoid the potential problems created by the mode of action by actively redefining some element of the situation so as to create a new situation in which the conflict among objectives does not exist (e.g., by redefining the assigned task as simply having a conversation, or getting to know the other person's position so as to become better acquainted; by redefining the participants' roles as detached—but not personally involved—analysts of social policy, or as teacher and student). Subjects pursuing this third strategy must adopt roles or methods of approaching the task which are at variance with the definition of the situation supplied by the experimenter, but which legitimize the mode of action being performed and minimize or eliminate the potential interactional problems of a given mode.

B. O'Keefe and Shepherd used their analysis of modes of action available in conflict situations, and strategies for managing interactional problems associated with the modes, to develop a coding system for classifying the behaviour that interactants produced in the discussions they had. Interactions were segmented into their discrete, pragmatically and semantically coherent units (the unit of analysis corresponded roughly to a subtopic of the assigned topic—for a more specific description, see B. O'Keefe & Shepherd, 1983b). The behaviour of each participant within each unit was classified as to the mode of action it instantiated and the strategy for managing interactional problems it reflected.

B. O'Keefe and Shepherd found that there was considerable individual variation in the use of strategies for dealing with interaction maintenance and face threats, and that individual differences in strategy use were related to the individual's degree of construct differentiation. Subjects relatively high in construct differentiation, as opposed to those low in construct differentiation, were more likely to engage in redressive action and more likely to undertake redefinition of the situation to resolve the conflict among objectives. The relationship between construct differentiation and the use of situation-redefining strategies were particularly strong ($r = .61$, $p < .001$). In short, consistent with Kline's previous findings, high differentiation communicators appear more likely to design their behaviour in such a way as to avoid or redress threats to face and interaction maintenance. Again, it appears that for high differentiation communicators, but to a much lesser extent for low differentiation communicators, these potential features of the situation are incorporated as dimensions of their definition of the situation and are pursued as interactional goals. In the following section, the implications of these differences for socialization and communicative development are considered briefly.

## Receiver-Focused Communication and the Social Context of Development

Earlier we noted that individuals acquire many of their interpretive schemes in common with others in the context of socialization. In interaction itself, socializing agents force particular differentiations on the child's world view by the ways in which they make manifest in their actions and speech particular domains of experience. This idea has served as the basis for socialization studies in which we have attempted to investigate the influence of receiver-focused communication of mothers on their children (see Applegate et al., in press; Applegate & Delia, 1980; Delia, Burleson, & Kline, 1979; and Jones, Delia, & Clark, 1981).

In undertaking these studies we reasoned that mothers who control their children's behaviour and deal with their interpersonal problems through discussing consequences, giving reasons, and elaborating upon perspectives (as opposed to using commands, rules, etc.) present to the child a social world that includes the psychological domain of experience as a manifest feature of reality. Over time, children raised by a mother using highly receiver-focused strategies should come to develop a more differentiated and abstract (psychologically-centred) set of constructs for understanding persons and social situations. In representing communicative situations within such constructs, the wants, needs, and perspectives of others should be a more salient aspect of the relevance structure defining the situation. Moreover, since the psychological domain of experience should be more manifest in the child's world, the child of such a parent gradually should be led to develop communicative strategies taking the wants, needs, and interests of the listeners into account.

Our research has directly supported this expectation. Jones, Delia, & Clark, (1981) found greater receiver focus in maternal communication to be a significant predictor of both the children's interpersonal construct system development and of their use of more receiver-focused persuasive appeals. Interestingly, this relationship was stronger among seventh-grade than second-grade children. In a longitudinal study, a similar pattern of results has been obtained showing that person-centred maternal communication becomes an increasingly strong force in shaping the child's interpersonal construct system and communicative strategies from early into middle childhood (see Applegate & Delia, 1980; and Delia, Burleson, & Kline, 1979 for initial reports of this work; also see Applegate et al., in press, for our analysis of "reflection-enhancing" maternal communication).

## A CONCLUDING NOTE

The point we wish to end on is to suggest the need, in studies of communication and communicative development, for the recognition of the complexity of the psychological and interactional processes organizing communicative behaviour and of the complexity of the pragmatic tasks that are accomplished in and through communication. Only when these complexities are recognized will we be able to begin to develop adequate systems for analysis of communicative interaction.

## REFERENCES

Applegate, J. L. Adaptive communication in educational contexts: a study of teachers' communicative strategies. *Communication Education,* 1980, *29,* 158-170. (a)

Applegate, J. L. *Construct system development and identity-management skills in persuasive contexts.* Paper presented at the annual meeting of the Western Speech Communication Association, Denver, Col. 1982. (a)

Applegate, J. L. The impact of construct system development on communication and impression formation in persuasive contexts. *Communication Monographs,* 1982, *49,* 277-289. (b)

Applegate, J. L. Person- and position-centred teacher communication in a day-care center. In N. K. Denzin (Ed.), *Studies in symbolic interaction* (Vol. 3). Greenwich, CT: JAI Press, 1980. (b)

Applegate, J. L. Burke, J. A., Burleson, B. R., Delia, J. G., & Kline S. L. Reflection-enhancing parental communication. In I. E. Sigel (Ed.), *Parents' constructions of child development.* Hillsdale, N.J.: Lawrence Erlbaum Associates, in press.

Applegate, J. L., & Delia, J. G. Person-centred speech, psychological development, and the contexts of language usage. In R. St. Clair & H. Giles, (Eds.), *The social and psychological contexts of language.* Hillsdale, N.J.: Lawrence Erlbaum Associates, 1980.

Bauman, R., & Sherzer, J. (Eds.), *Explorations in the ethnography of speaking.* Cambridge: Cambridge University Press, 1974.

Blumer, H. *Symbolic interactionism: perspective and method.* Englewood Cliffs, N.J.: Prentice-Hall, 1969.

Borden, A. W. *An investigation of the relationships among indices of social cognition, motivation, and communicative performance.* Unpublished Ph.D. dissertation, University of Illinois at Urbana-Champaign, 1979.

Bowerman, M. *Early syntactic development: a cross-linguistic study with special reference to Finnish.* Cambridge: Cambridge University Press, 1973.

Brewer, W. F. The problem of meaning and the interrelations of the higher mental processes. In W. B. Weimer & D. S. Palermo (Eds.), *Cognition and symbolic processes.* Hillsdale; N. J.: Lawrence Erlbaum Associates Inc., 1974.

Brown, P., & Levinson, S. Universals in language usage: Politeness phenomena. In E. N. Goody (Ed.), *Questions and politeness.* Cambridge: Cambridge University Press, 1978.

Brown, R. *Psycholinguistics.* New York: Free Press, 1970.

Brown, R. *A first language: the early stages.* Cambridge, Mass.: Harvard University Press, 1973.

Bruner, J. S. From communication to language—a psychological perspective. *Cognition,* 1975, *3,* 253-286.

Burke, J. A. *The relationship of interpersonal cognitive development to the adaptation of persuasive strategies in adults.* Paper presented at the annual convention of the Central States Speech Association, St. Louis, Mo., 1979.

Burleson, B. R. Comforting communication. In H. E. Sypher & J. L. Applegate (Eds.), *Understanding interpersonal communication: social cognitive and strategic processes in children and adults.* Beverley Hills, Cal.: Sage, in press. (a)

Burleson, B. R. The development of comfort-intending communication skills in childhood and adolescence. *Child Development,* 1982, *53,* 1578-1588.

Burleson, B. R. Effects of social cognition and empathic motivation on adults' comforting strategies. *Human Communication Research,* in press. (b)

Burleson, B. R. *The influence of age, construct system developments, and affective perspective-taking on the development of comforting message strategies: a hierarchical regression analysis.* Paper presented at the annual meeting of the International Communication Association, Minneapolis, Minn., 1981.

Burleson, B. R., & Samter, W. *Social cognitive and personality influence on prosocial behaviour: a model of comforting determinants and an empirical test.* A Paper presented at the University of Kansas Conference on Social Cognition and Interpersonal Behavior, Lawrence, Kan., 1983.

Cantor, N., & Mischel, W. Prototypes in person perception. In L. Berkowitz (Ed.), *Advances in experimental social psychology, Vol. 12.* New York: Academic Press, 1979.

Chandler, M. J. Social cognition and social structure. In F. C. Serafica (Ed.), *Social-cognitive development in context.* New York: Guildford Press, 1982.

Chomsky, N. *Aspects of the theory of syntax.* Cambridge, Mass.: MIT Press, 1965.

Cicourel, A. V. The acquisition of social structure: Towards a developmental sociology of language and meaning. In A. V. Cicourel, *Cognitive sociology.* New York: Free Press, 1974.

Clark, R. A., & Delia, J. G. Cognitive complexity, social perspective-taking, and functional persuasive skills in second- to ninth- grade children. *Human Communication Research,* 1977, *3,* 128–134.

Clark, R. A., & Delia, J. G. The development of functional persuasive skills in childhood and early adolescence. *Child Development,* 1976, *47,* 1008–1014.

Cohen, B. D. Referent communication disturbances in schizophrenia. In S. Schwartz (Ed.), *Language and cognition in schizophrenia.* Hillsdale, N.J.: Lawrence Erlbaum Associates, 1978.

Cole, P., & Morgan, J. L. (Eds.) *Syntax and semantics: vol. 3: Speech acts.* New York: Academic Press, 1975.

Crockett, W. H. Cognitive complexity and impression formation. In B. A. Maher (Ed.), *Progress in experimental personality research* (Vol 2). New York: Academic Press, 1965.

Crockett, W. H. *Impressions and attributions: Nature, organization, and implications for action.* Paper presented at the annual convention of the American Psychological Association, 1977.

Damon, W. (Ed.), *Social cognition.* San Francisco: Jossey-Bass, 1979.

Damon, W. *The social world of the child.* San Francisco: Jossey-Bass, 1977.

Delia, J. G. A constructivist analysis of the concept of credibility. *Quarterly Journal of Speech,* 1976, *62,* 361–375.

Delia, J. G., Burleson, B. R., & Kline, S. L. Developmental differences in interpersonal impression in childhood and adolescence. *Journal of Genetic Psychology,* in press.

Delia, J. G. Burleson, B. R., & Kline, S. L. *The development of interpersonal cognition and communicative abilities: a longitudinal analysis.* Paper presented at the annual convention of the Central States Speech Association, St. Louis, Mo., 1979.

Delia, J. G., & Clark, R. A. Cognitive complexity, social perception, and the development of listener-adapted communication in six-, eight-, ten-, and twelve-year-old boys. *Communication Monographs,* 1977, *44,* 326–345.

Delia, J. G., & Grossberg, L. Interpretation and evidence. *Western Journal of Speech Communication,* 1977, *41,* 32–42.

Delia, J. G., Kline, S. L., & Burleson, B. R. The development of persuasive communication strategies in kindergarteners through twelfth-graders. *Communication Monographs,* 1979, *46,* 241–256.

Delia, J. G. & O'Keefe, B. J. Constructivism: the development of communication in children. In E. Wartella (Ed.), *Children communicating.* Beverley Hills, Cal.: Sage, 1979.

Delia, J. G., O'Keefe, B. J., & O'Keefe, D. J. The constructivist approach to communication. In F.E.X. Dance (Ed.), *Comparative human communication theory.* New York: Harper & Row, 1982.

Denzin, N. K. *Childhood socialization.* San Francisco: Jossey-Bass, 1977.

DeVito, J. *The psychology of speech and language.* New York: Random House, 1970.

Dore, J. Holophases, speech acts and language universals. *Journal of Child Language,* 1975, *2,* 21-40.

Elkind, D. *Childhood and adolescence.* New York: Oxford University Press, 1970.

Fillmore, C. J. A grammarian looks to sociolinguistics. In R. W. Shuy (Ed.), *Report of the twenty-third annual round table meeting on linguistics and language studies: sociolinguistics.* Washington: Georgetown University Press, 1973.

Flavell, J. H., in collaboration with Botkin, P. T., Fry, C. L., Wright, J. W., & Jarvis, P. E. *Role-taking and communication skills in children.* New York: Wiley, 1968.

Goffman, E. *Frame analysis.* Boston: Houghton-Mifflin, 1974.

Goffman, E. *The presentation of self in everyday life.* New York: Doubleday, 1959.

Goffman, E. Replies and responses. *Language in society,* 1976, *5,* 257-313.

Goffman, E. *Strategies interaction.* Philadelphia: University of Pennsylvania Press, 1969.

Greenfield, P. M., & Smith, J. H. *The structure of communication in early language development.* New York: Academic Press, 1976.

Grice, P. Logic and conversation. In P. Cole & J. L. Morgan (Eds.), *Syntax and semantics, vol. 3: speech acts.* New York: Academic Press, 1975.

Gross, E., & Stone, G. P. Embarrassment and the analysis of role requirements. *The American Journal of Sociology,* 1964, *70,* 1-15.

Grossberg, L. *Imminent and transcendent aspects of meaning.* Unpublished manuscript, Department of Speech Communication, University of Illinois at Urbana-Champaign, 1976.

Halliday, M. A. K. *Learning how to mean.* London: Edward Arnold, 1975.

Hayes, J. R. (Ed.), *Cognition and the development of language.* New York: Wiley, 1970.

Heider, F. *The psychology of interpersonal relationships.* New York: Wiley, 1958.

Husband, R. L. *Leadership phenomenology: A case study and social cognitive correlates.* Unpublished doctoral dissertation, University of Illinois at Urbana-Champaign, 1981.

Hymes, D. Models of the interaction of language and social life. In J. J. Gumperz & D. Hymes (Eds.), *Directions in sociolinguistics: The ethnography of communication.* New York: Holt, 1972.

Hymes, D. *On communicative competence.* Unpublished manuscript, Department of Anthropology, University of Pennsylvania, 1968.

Hymes, D. On linguistic theory, communicative competence, and the education of disadvantaged children. In M. L. Max, S. Diamond, & F. O. Gearing (Eds.), *Anthropological perspectives on education.* New York: Basic Books, 1971.

Jacobs, C. S. *The practical management of conversational meanings: Notes on the dynamics of social understanding and interactional emergence.* Paper presented at the annual convention of the Speech Communication Association, Boston, Mass., 1977.

Jones, J., Delia, J. G., & Clark, R. A. *Person-centred parental communication and the development of communication in children.* Paper presented at the annual convention of the International Communication Association, Minneapolis, Minn., 1981.

Kasch, C. R. *Person-centred communication and its correlates among nurses in long-term chronic renal care.* Unpublished Ph.D. dissertation, University of Illinois at Urbana-Champaign, in preparation.

Kelly, G. A. *The psychology of personal constructs* (2 vols.). New York: W. W. Norton, 1955.

Kelman, H. C. Processes of opinion change. *Public Opinion Quarterly,* 1961, *25,* 57-78.

Kline, S. L. *Construct system development and face support in persuasive messages: two empirical investigations.* Paper presented at the annual meeting of the International Communication Association, Minneapolis, Minn., 1981. (a)

Kline, S. L. *Construct system development, empathic motivation, and the accomplishment of face support in persuasive messages.* Paper presented at the annual meeting of the Speech Communication Association, Anaheim, Cal., 1981. (b)

Kline, S. L. *The effect of instructional set on the provision of face-support by persons differing in construct system development.* Paper presented at the annual convention of the Speech Communication Association, Louisville, Ky., 1982.

Kline, S. L. *Social cognition, mental cognition, and the provision of face-support in persuasive communication.* Paper presented at the annual convention of the Southern State Speech Association, Orlando, Fla., 1983.

Kline, S. L., & Ceropski, J. M. Person-centred communication in medical practice. In J. T. Wood & G. M. Phillips (Eds.), *Human decision-making.* Carbondale, Ill.: Southern Illinois University Press, in press.

Lewis, M., & Rosenblum, L. A. (Eds.) *Interaction, conversation, and the development of language.* New York: Wiley, 1977.

Lindesmith, A. R., Strauss, A. L., & Denzin, N. K. *Social psychology.* (5th ed.) New York: Holt, Rinehart, and Winston, 1977.

Livesley, W. J., & Bromley, D. B. *Person-perception in childhood and adolescence.* New York: Wiley, 1973.

Lock, A. *From gesture to symbol.* New York: Academic Press, 1977.

Looft, W. R. Egocentrism and social interaction across the lifespan. *Psychological Bulletin,* 1972, *78,* 75–92.

Mead, G. H. *Mind, self and society.* Chicago: University of Chicago Press, 1934.

Meltzer, B. N., Petras, J. W., & Reynolds, L. T. *Symbolic interactionism: genesis, varieties, criticism.* London: Routledge and Kegan Paul, 1975.

Moore, T. E. (Ed.) *Cognitive development and the acquisition of language.* New York: Academic Press, 1973.

O'Keefe, B. J. *A constructivist approach to human interaction.* Unpublished doctoral dissertation, University of Illinois at Urbana-Champaign, 1976.

O'Keefe, B. J. *The theoretical commitments of constructivism.* Paper presented at the annual meeting of the Speech Communication Association, Minneapolis, Minn., 1978.

O'Keefe, B. J., & Delia, J. G. Construct comprehensiveness and cognitive complexity as predictors of the number and strategic adaptation of arguments and appeals in a persuasive message. *Communication Monographs,* 1979, *46,* 231–240.

O'Keefe, B. J., & Delia, J. G. Impression formation and message production. In M. E. Roloff & C. R. Berger (Eds.), *Social cognition and communication.* Beverly Hills, Cal.: Sage, 1982.

O'Keefe, B. J., Delia, J. G. & O'Keefe, D. J. Interaction analysis and the analysis of interactional organization. In N. K. Denzin (Ed.), *Studies in symbolic interaction.* Greenwich, Conn.: JAI Press, 1980.

O'Keefe, B. J., & Shepherd, G. J. *The effects of construct differentiation on behaviour and interpretations in persuasive interactions.* Unpublished raw data, University of Illinois, Urbana-Champaign, 1983. (a).

O'Keefe, B. J., & Shepherd, G. J. *A system for classifying actions produced in persuasive interactions.* Unpublished manuscript, University of Illinois, Urbana-Champaign, 1983. (b).

O'Keefe, D. J. The attitude-behaviour problem: a constructivist analysis. In D. P. Cushman & R. D. McPhee (Eds.), *The message-attitude-behaviour relationship: theory, methodology, and application.* New York: Academic Press, 1980.

O'Keefe, D. J., & Sypher, H. E. Cognitive complexity measures and the relationship of cognitive complexity to communication: A critical review. *Human Communication Research,* 1981, *8,* 72–92.

Piaget, J. *The language and thought of the child.* Trans. Marjorie Gabain. New York: World Publishing, 1955. Originally published, 1926.

Price-Williams, D., & Sabsay, S. Communicative competence among severely retarded persons. *Semiotica,* 1979, *26,* 33–63.

Rommetveit, R. *On message structure.* New York: Wiley, 1974.

Rommetveit, R. On negative nationalism in scholarly studies of verbal communication and dynamic residuals in the construction of human intersubjectivity. In M. Brenner, P. Marsh, & M. Brenner (Eds.), *The social contexts of method.* London: Croom Helm, 1978.

Rosenbach, D., Crockett, W. J., & Wapner, S. Developmental level, emotional involvement, and the resolution of inconsistency in impression formation. *Developmental Psychology,* 1973, *8,* 120–130.

Ryan, J. Early language development: towards a communicatorial analysis. In M. P. M. Richards (Ed.), *The integration of a child into a social world.* Cambridge: Cambridge University Press, 1974.

Scarlett, H. H., Press, A. N., & Crockett, W. H. Children's descriptions of peers: A Wernerian developmental analysis. *Child Development,* 1971, *42,* 439–453.

Schank, R., and Abelson, R. *Scripts, plans, goals and understanding: An inquiry in human knowledge structures.* Hillsdale, N.J.: Lawrence Erlbaum Associates, 1977.

Scott, M. B., & Lyman, S. M. Accounts. *American Sociological Reviews,* 1968, *33,* 46–62.

Shantz, C. U. The development of social cognition. In E. M. Hetherington (Ed.), *Review of child development research* (Vol. 5). Chicago: University of Chicago Press, 1975.

Shatz, M. The relationship between cognitive processes and the development of communication skills. In B. Keasey (Ed.), *Nebraska Symposium on motivation, 1977.* Lincoln: University of Nebraska Press, 1978.

Silverstein, M. Shifters, linguistic categories, and cultural description. In K. H. Basso and H. A. Selby (Eds.), *Meaning in anthropology.* Albuquerque: University of New Mexico Press, 1976.

Sinclair-de-Zwart, H. Developmental psycholinguistics. In D. Ellind & J. H. Flavell (Eds.), *Studies in cognitive development.* London: Oxford University Press, 1969.

Smith, C. S. Review of T. Moore, *Cognitive development and the acquisition of language. Journal of Child Language,* 1975, *2,* 303–304.

Strauss, A. L. *Mirrors and masks: The search for identity.* San Francisco: The Sociology Press, 1969.

Wapner, S., Kaplan, B., & Cohen, S. B. An organismic-developmental perspective for understanding transactions of men and environments. *Environment and Behaviour,* 1973, *5,* 255–289.

Weinstein, E. A. The development of interpersonal competence. In D. A. Goslin (Ed.), *Handbook of socialization theory and research.* Chicago: Rand McNally, 1969.

Wells, G. Learning to code experience through language. *Journal of Child Language,* 1974, *1,* 243–253.

Werner, H. The concept of development from a comparative and organismic point of view. In D. B. Harris (Ed.), *The concept of development.* Minneapolis: University of Minnesota Press, 1957.

# 4 Acquiring Social Variation in Speech

Jean Berko Gleason and Rivka Y. Perlmann
*Boston University*

### INTRODUCTION

Language is a social phenomenon. It does not develop spontaneously in children who are isolated from all human contact. Children, when they acquire language, acquire, along with the basic grammatical and lexical features, many special social markers that indicate such things as their sex, status and social class. In addition, early in life, every child must learn to use language appropriately in a variety of social situations. Learning to make conversation, to talk to babies and older people, to be as polite as the occasion demands, are social as well as linguistic accomplishments.

In studying language development in children from an interactive and social psychological perspective, we can focus on two broad areas of concern: the first is the environment that surrounds the child learning to speak, with special emphasis on input language or the special kinds of language adults use when speaking to children; the second area of investigation centres on the development of language by children, with special emphasis on how children acquire social variation in their speech. We might ask, for instance, when young children first begin to be identifiable through linguistic markers as boys or girls, how they first learn to vary the politeness of their requests, to simplify their speech when talking to babies, and so on. Ultimately, this kind of investigation asks not so much how all children acquire the universal features of language, which are features common to all speakers, but rather how each individual comes to speak as a representative of a particular family, sex, ethnic or regional group, in a variety of speech situations. In general, we shall refer to this ability to use language appropriately in the social context as *communicative competence* (Hymes, 1971).

The study of the acquisition of communicative competence entails investigating the ways in which children acquire society's rules for the use of language in a variety of social situations, rather than simply in the mother-child interaction at home, which has been the focus of most traditional studies that have centred on the acquisition of grammar or vocabulary. Social features can vary with the speech situation, with the topic, or according to the person one is addressing. Children have to learn to talk on the telephone as well as face-to-face, and to talk to teachers and babies as well as their mothers. While children are learning to vary their speech along these dimensions, they are also learning to use language to mark their own individuality—to acquire markers for sex, regional origin, and social class, that will ultimately constitute their own idiolect, or individual way of speaking.

In this chapter, we will consider first speech to children and then turn to children's learning of linguistic variation. Our understanding of these subjects is based partly on the work of others, but primarily stems from data collected over the past several years by our own research group. In our research, we have collected naturalistic data in the homes of 24 families with preschool children aged 2–5 years. The home observations occurred during the dinner hour, and were all tape-recorded and transcribed for analysis. The families were also seen in the laboratory; in this portion of the study, each of the children (12 boys and 12 girls) came to the university twice, once with each parent. Parent and child were videotaped while engaging in three semi-structured activities: playing "store" with a toy cash register and other appropriate items; reading or making up a story from a picture book; and playing with a toy automobile that could be taken apart. The transcripts of these sessions have provided many insights into the nature of parent-child interaction, and they have enabled us to examine linguistic variation in the children's speech under several conditions.

## SPEECH TO CHILDREN

Anyone who has ever listened to mothers and fathers talking to their babies must have been struck by the fact that what one says to a twelve-month-old does not sound in the least like what one say to colleagues at work. Imagine attempting to borrow a pencil from the woman at the next desk by saying in a high, musical voice, "Give me a pencil. Give me a pencil. That's right, give it to me," and, if she should comply, exclaiming loudly, "*Good* girl!" Such speech might be amusing, or insulting, when addressed to an adult, but it is an absolutely standard way of talking to infants in English. While the fact that adults have special ways of talking to infants has been known for some time, it is only recently that researchers have begun to believe that the form and content of adult utterances actually have an important effect on children's language acquisition. At present, there is little agreement among linguists about how much importance to ascribe to input language. Among those who discount the influence of the linguistic environment are innatists (e.g. Chomsky, 1965), who believe that children are born preprogrammed to learn language, and that all they need to do to become competent speakers is to be exposed to adult language. According to this view, overhearing adults speaking with one another (i.e. *exposure*), suffices to set in motion the child's innate language abilities, and one need postulate no special features in the speech of adults that may facilitate children's language development. At the other end of the spectrum are those who believe that mother's speech contains everything necessary to explain language development (Moerk, 1975).

While it seems clear to us that the ability to acquire language partly depends on a number of innate linguistic and cognitive capacities that are unique to the human brain, it is also clear that communicative competence develops only after a protracted period during which the child not only interacts with adults, but is also spoken to in a very special way. Adults are typically unaware of the many ways they modify their ordinary pattern of speaking when they talk to children. Baby talk vocabulary, words like *tum tum* and *beddy bye*, may be the only particularly marked feature that adults notice. This has a historical parallel in the literature on speech to children: the presence of "nursery words" has long been noted by anthropologists in their ethnographies of diverse languages (Casagrande, 1948; Crawford, 1970; Ferguson, 1964). Only in the past decade have researchers turned their attention to the other features that distinguish input language from the speech adults address to other adults.

### Mothers' Speech

By now a considerable literature on mothers' speech in many languages has accrued (Broen, 1972; Farwell, 1973; Remick, 1971; Snow & Ferguson, 1977; Waterson & Snow, 1978; etc.). The first wave of these studies sought primarily to describe mothers' speech, rather than determine its effect on children's language development. In general, mothers' speech to children learning language was found to be simpler, clearer, more redundant and more grammatical than speech to adults. A mother talking to her 2-year-old tends to speak in a higher tone of voice, to speak about half as quickly as she does to adults, and to use clear, short phrases. She repeats herself quite frequently, and transcriptions of what she says look rather like language lessons. We often note sequences of the following type:

Look at the book, Donnie
See the book.
It's a nice book.
It's Donnie's book.

Mothers' speech is simplified not only in its form, but in its subject matter as well: it is limited to the here and now and to the kinds of things that might be of interest to young children. Typically, it is the child who sets the topic and maintains it by paying selective attention to what the mother says; if the mother begins to talk about things that are not of interest to the child, the child simply ignores her. Learning to pretend to pay attention to something that one finds intrinsically boring is a skill that is acquired much later in life.

We might ask at this point in what other ways mothers' speech is the product of interactive forces. In the first place, it is important to note that input language is not a static phenomenon; it changes over time as children grow older, and speech to 1-year-olds is not the same as speech to 2-year-olds, or 4-, or 5-year-olds (Bellinger, 1980). We can describe some general characteristics of speech to children who are at different developmental levels. Speech to prelinguistic infants, those less than one year old, tends to be quite highly pitched and musical but not necessarily grammatically simple. As children approach their first birthday and appear to begin to comprehend speech, mothers slow down and their speech takes on the characteristics that have been described above. Once children begin to speak themselves, these simplified features gradually drop out of mothers' speech and the speech takes on other kinds of characteristics. Speech to 5-year-olds, for instance, emphasizes not so much linguistic rules as the rules of the world. Listening to mothers talking to their young children, we frequently hear them say things like, "Look both ways before you cross the street," or "Say *thank you* to Mrs. Robinson," or "Why don't you eat your peas now?"

Input language, therefore, has a natural history of its own that appears to mesh with the child's needs and capabilities at each stage of the child's development (Penman, Cross, Milgram-Friedman, & Meares, 1983). Speech to pre-linguistic infants is highly pitched, musical, and of a nature to attract the infant's attention. Mothers talk to their babies in this way while caring for them, and we can postulate that this helps set the motivational base for babies' learning to talk: language has become a good and attractive thing, associated with a nurturant person. When babies first begin to coo and babble, mothers coo and babble back at them. In this way, babies begin to have experience at turn taking and other conversational interactions many months before they actually begin to speak. As infants approach their first birthday and begin to show signs of understanding, mothers begin to enunciate clearly and to speak slowly and simply. In both of these cases it is clear that the mother is regulated by the baby. When they are given the choice, young infants will choose to listen to high-pitched voices (Sachs, 1977) and they are thus more likely to listen to mothers speaking in this way. Signals from the baby indicate the beginning of comprehension; for instance, when the baby learns to look where the mother is pointing rather than at the mother's face or finger, the mother begins to label objects in the environment. The simplified speech we have described continues until such time as the child gives clear evidence of being in control of the linguistic system by producing well formed utterances and appropriate feedback signals or back channels. Few people would continue to say "Look at the book. See the book," etc. to a child who nods and says, "Yes, it's very interesting." Once the child has progressed to this point, emphases in the input language switch to the social rather than the linguistic realm. Since it takes many years before children appear socially and intellectually competent, we see this "language of socialization" persisting in parents' speech in one way or another for a number of years. The fact that parents do speak this way is a source of contention in many families with adolescents, who ultimately produce many negative signals when told such things as "Do your homework now," or "Be in by 11."

### Fathers' Speech

While most of the research on input language has been on mothers' speech, the few studies that have been done on fathers' have found basically the same set of simplifying and clarifying features described earlier (Bellinger & Gleason, 1982; Giattino & Hogan, 1975; Gleason, 1975; Gleason & Greif, 1983; Greif & Gleason, 1980; Masur & Gleason, 1980; Rondal, 1980). In a recent study, Jacobson, Boersma, and Olson (1983) demonstrated through spectrographic analysis that fathers, like mothers, raise the fundamental frequency of their voices and speak in a higher pitch when they address infants and small children. Fathers' speech is not, however, the same as mothers' speech, any more than men's speech is exactly like women's speech. The major differences are associated with the father's role within the family and with the ways in which men and women's cognitive styles may find different expression. At home and in the laboratory fathers use more direct imperative constructions than mothers. They are more likely to say, "Take your plate off the table," where a mother would express the same intent in a more polite form, "Would you like to take your plate off the table?" In the laboratory, we also found that fathers are more likely to express some of their directives in a rather obscure form; to a child assembling a toy car, the father might say, "The wheel is going to fall off," when his intention is to get the child to take the wrench and tighten the nut that holds the wheel on. This kind of language places a greater cognitive burden on the child than either the typical mother's directive, "Why don't you tighten the nut?" or the other form fathers use, "Tighten the nut." While mothers appear to be warmer and more sensitive to their children, fathers are more demanding both in terms of the way they request action and in the kinds of intellectual striving they encourage.

These mother-father differences can be seen in other areas as well. Fathers, for instance, use more difficult vocabulary than mothers. One father we saw told his 3-year-old son about a "construction site." In playing with the toy car, which came with a screwdriver and wrench for removing such components as the wheels, engine, and steering wheel, fathers were more likely than mothers to use the actual names of the parts. For example, a father might ask the child to get the "screwdriver," while the mother would instead refer to the "thing you use to loosen screws" (Masur & Gleason, 1980). Fathers were also more likely than mothers to ask the child to name the object.

Fathers do not adjust their language to the child's level to the same degree that mothers do (McLaughlin, White, McDevitt, & Raskin, 1983). Engle (1980) found that fathers' speech to their 2-year-old sons did not differ in complexity from their speech to 3-year-olds. Mothers, on the other hand, do modulate the complexity of their utterances in accordance with the child's age, thereby demonstrating greater sensitivity than fathers to their child's developmental level.

The sex of the child also has some effect on the speech of the parent, although the differences are not as great as one might suppose. In our home samples, fathers not only used more imperatives with their sons than with their daughters, they also tended to use more jocular, but insulting, terms of address with sons. While little girls were called "honey" and "sweetie," little boys received appellations like "dingaling" and "nutcake." Finally, in a study of interruptions in the laboratory, Greif (1980) showed that fathers interrupt more than mothers, and that both fathers and mothers interrupt daughters more frequently than sons.

These studies have shown that speech to children is very special speech indeed. Parents react to the age and the sex of the child with speech that contains a number of interactive markers. While the general features that might enhance language acquisition are present in fathers' and mothers' speech to young children, there are some differences as well. Fathers' speech is both less polite and more demanding than mothers' speech. Mothers appear to be more sensitively tuned to their children, and, since they know so well what their children intend, they demand less of them. The fathers we have seen are avid testers and consolidators of their children's knowledge. Thus, mothers and fathers are not providing identical linguistic and cognitive input to their children; and they do not always treat boys and girls in the same way.

Through their speech to their children, parents delineate their own roles and their perceptions of the children's roles. Our research and the research of others (e.g. Engle, 1980) highlights the complementarity of roles within the traditional family, each parent aiding their child's development in different ways. While fathers are less polite and more insensitive than mothers, nevertheless the style of their interaction can be seen to have a positive effect on children. In fact, by being less sensitively tuned to their children, they are forcing the children to extend themselves and stretch their cognitive abilities in order to communicate. In this way fathers can be seen as bridges to the outside world, helping children to express themselves more clearly.

A question still open to research concerns the implications that such role complementarity as exists within the traditional family has for the development of children who are raised in non-traditional family settings, with single parents, for example. Research on father absence has shown that children, especially boys, who are raised without a father have more trouble developing an appropriate sex-role identity, and their cognitive profile also tends to differ from that of children who are raised in intact homes (Biller & Bamm, 1971; Carlsmith, 1970). These effects of father absence may well be related to the lack of the type of input we described above as characteristic of fathers. Since we are speaking here about role-related speech styles suited to the needs of children, presumably any other member of the family or society who could fulfil the role would aid in the child's development. Thus, the mother may be able to assume both roles, or the child may find males outside the home to provide an appropriate model of male speech. Otherwise, the child's linguistic development may indeed be hampered in certain ways.

Cross-cultural comparisons are also relevant here. There are societies in which children are raised by various family members and generally spend most of their time with peers (Ochs, 1982). In some societies children acquire language primarily from interaction with other children. While older children may provide adequate samples of linguistic input to help younger children acquire speech, they may not do as well for the child as a father or mother. Harkness (1977), for example, analysed the verbal environment of children acquiring language in the Kipsigis tribe of Western Kenya. Kipsigis children spend most of their time with peers, and the language of older to younger children does contain some of the simplifying characteristics typical of baby-talk. However, the factor which correlates most highly with linguistic sophistication in Harkness' sample was the amount of time the child spent talking to adults rather than to other children. This suggests that, while children as young as 4 years old simplify their speech when talking to younger children, these modifications may not have the same implications for language acquisition as do the modifications in adult-child language.

Also relevant here are findings in our own culture, reported by McCarthy (1954) concerning the linguistic development of children from different size families. A number of studies reviewed by McCarthy have shown that in their linguistic development only-children far outstrip children who have many brothers and sisters. However twins, who spend the most time with a peer, are the most disadvantaged. A more recent study (Nichols & Broman, 1974) reports that language retardation is six times as frequent in twins as in singletons. Of course, families with many children also tend to be from low income groups, and so the linguistic effects of coming from a large family may be confounded with socioeconomic status in some of the older demographic studies reported by McCarthy. Twins are also known to be more at risk in all respects than singletons. Nevertheless, the contemporary evidence concerning the cognitive advantages of being an only child (or a first-born) is fairly conclusive, and there is good reason to assume that it would apply to linguistic development as well.

That input from parents or from others, who are consistently available and nurturing adults, is critical for development has been shown by McCarthy who also reviewed studies of children in orphanages and other institutions. Even controlling for I.Q. and socio-economic status, there are significant differences in language development in favour of children from intact homes. This is hardly surprising, of course. But it is important to regard peer influences in a broader sociolinguistic framework. Communicative competence includes the ability to play, to swear, to joke, to interact with peers and other groups in appropriate ways. And there are certain ways of speaking which are only acquired from peers and cannot be obtained from parents. Parents, for instance, cannot provide the child with current slang or idiomatic expressions, do not know the current sound effect noises and have different words for labelling "good" or "bad." In fact, using words such as "swell," "neat," "keen," or "cool" immediately marks a person as belonging to a particular generation.

Opie and Opie (1969) have catalogued the enormous variety of games children of different ages engage in and their descriptions make apparent how diverse and specialized peer *registers*, or styles of speaking, can be.

The child who does not master the register current in his or her peer group may be rejected, and this may clearly have psychological consequences. This point highlights how closely intertwined linguistic and social development can be and, also, how purely linguistic factors (such as mastery of appropriate peer registers) can have ramifications in non-linguistic spheres.

## THE ACQUISITION OF COMMUNICATIVE COMPETENCE

A social-psychological perspective on child language is espcially useful for a number of reasons. First, by focusing upon the study of parent-child interaction, it illuminates the children's contribution to structuring the linguistic environment. Their own responses are seen as helping to set the pace and pattern of development and, in this sense, the approach is interactive. Second, by merging the traditional distinction between competence and performance a social perspective broadens the range of abilities the child is assumed to be acquiring on the road to becoming a fluent speaker. In acquiring language, it is not sufficient that children master the rules of phonology, of grammar and lexicon, competence in the traditional sense, they must also master the rules and conventions of what has come to be called communicative competence. How to address different listeners in different situations; how to use routines and politeness formulas; how to use language to organize and direct non-verbal activities; how to speak like a member of one's familial and social group. In a language like English, contextual phenomena do not constitute separate, obligatory parts of the grammar. As compared with French, German or Spanish, English speakers do not have to draw on their social knowledge and judgement in order to select the correct second-person pronoun, for example. Thus, sociolinguistic variations do not appear in a traditional grammar book and in fact cannot be easily described in the form of rules. Rather, such variations (registers, codes or styles) consist simply of constellations of linguistic features which correlate with particular situations (Ure & Ellis, 1972). Stylistic contrasts become intuitively apparent to a native speaker of English who would, for example, immediately distinguish between the ways of speaking typical of a telephone operator, an elementary school teacher, a mother to her young children, a judge in a courtroom or a car mechanic. Speech in one situation may be formal and complex and produced with an even intonation. In another, it may be syntactically simpler and marked by a wide range of pitch variations. By making use of different kinds of register patterns, speakers show that they are implicitly aware of the social situation in which the speech is taking place. Competence in the use of language includes the ability to shift from one variety to another as circumstances require, and the sensitivity to detect violations in the conventions for use of any particular variety (see Chapter 8).

Finally, a social-psychological perspective aims not only at describing how language is used for appropriate communication in different social situations, but also at understanding how language which is appropriately used aids in establishing and defining one's personality characteristics. Language may both *form* and *represent* one's personality. The differences we see in language usage are not simply surface differences, various linguistic forms used in one situation or another, but they also reflect the fact that individuals have different underlying psychological makeups. Reflecting the different social roles that one assumes during a lifetime, one's speaking style evolves as part of one's social and psychological identity. In this sense there is a psychological reality to a variable such as sex, for example. In coming to talk like a man, one takes on certain feelings and attitudes that constitute part of a male identity in the society. This identity may itself get reinforced by judgements and attitudes that others form about one on the basis of one's speaking style. While attempts to relate psychological characteristics to sociolinguistic variables have recently become the focus of a number of investigations of adult speech (see, for example, the collection of chapters edited by Scherer and Giles, 1979), these questions have barely begun to be asked by developmental psychologists. Developmental sociolinguistics itself does not have a long history and most studies have initially aimed at describing variation in child speech. Understanding the psychological determinants for sociolinguistic variation will, hopefully, be part of future research agendas. Reflecting this state of the art in the field, we will provide, in the next section, a selective survey of work on children's sociolinguistic skills. We will focus on a few of the more salient dimensions of the social context, examining how young children come to incorporate them into their speech. More specifically, our review will be directed to answering—sometimes only partially—the following questions:

How early do children become sensitive to different aspects of the social context, and when do they learn that it is possible (in fact, sometimes necessary) to mark such awareness in their speech?

Which dimensions of the social situation do young children attend to? Are they aware of different listeners' communicative needs? Are they aware of subtle differences in the pragmatic functions of situations?

How do registers unique to children develop? For example, the language of pretending games?

Is the child's awareness of contextual modifications manifested at the same time in all aspects of the language system? In phonology before syntax, for example?

When do children begin to form social judgements based on their interlocutor's speaking style? How do children generally reflect awareness of social role memberships in their speech?

## VARIATION IN CHILD LANGUAGE

One of the first kinds of contextual signals to which children become sensitive involves characteristics of the person with whom they are speaking. Earlier research on children's sensitivity to listener needs had found that children, up to about 8 years of age, were quite lacking in this ability (Alvy, 1968; Flavell, 1968). At the time, this research appeared to confirm Piagetian notions about children's cognitive egocentrism. More recent work, however, has challenged the earlier studies on the grounds that they tested children's knowledge in highly contrived experimental settings and gave them tasks which were beyond their cognitive capacity. In studies of this sort, for instance, young children were required to describe a picture of an abstract geometric design with sufficient accuracy and explicitness to allow their listeners (whom they could not see) to select that picture from an array of pictures containing similarly abstract designs. It is now acknowledged that these referential communication tasks were not adequate tests of children's communicative abilities. Nor were they fair measures of children's sensitivity to listener needs. The social, communicative function of language has to be more broadly defined to include skills other than the ability to convey obscure information to invisible listeners.

When more natural tasks are devised, and when the cognitive burden placed on the child is not beyond his or her capacity, it turns out that children as young as 2 years *can* take account of listener needs and modify characteristics of their speech accordingly—for example, when speaking with younger children as opposed to peers and adults (Dunn & Kendrick, 1982; Gleason, 1973; Sachs & Devin, 1976; Shatz & Gelman, 1973). When speaking with younger children they reduce the length of their utterances to make them simpler, they raise the fundamental frequency of their voices and often repeat themselves to catch and hold the attention of their younger listeners. They perform these modifications at least in part in response to cues they perceive in their younger listeners. Although at that age they have not yet mastered the entire range of baby-talk features, they nevertheless exhibit a sufficient degree of flexibility to carry on meaningful interactions. We see here how the interactive component of language is evident in the speech used by children as young as two.

Children's sensitivity to listener's influence has been documented especially forcefully in much of the literature on social class differences in language use. When speaking to an adult whom they perceive as an intimidating authority figure, especially when the adult is of a different race or class from them, children's language performance typically drops dramatically. In such asymmetrical situations, children often speak in monosyllables, giving the impression of having nothing to say about anything, thus leading some to drastically underestimate their overall language competence (Labov, 1970). What sociolinguists like Labov and others were able to show is the necessity of taking situational variability into account when assessing children's linguistic abilities. (See Cazden, 1970 for a fuller discussion of the issue.)

A related question is; how do individuals' ways of speaking serve as a basis for judgement by interlocutors, not of their linguistic competence, but of their intellectual, social and personality attributes? It has been shown, for example, that many teachers are prone to making unfavourable evaluations of pupils' intelligence and scholastic abilities simply on the basis of speech characteristics—a non-standard accent, for instance (Edwards, 1979; Williams, 1970; see Chapter 5). A fruitful area for study would be to determine when children begin to use their interlocutor's style of speech as a criterion for making value judgements about his or her personal worth. Why do they do it and where do they learn it? From their parents, peers, or perhaps from teachers? Rosenthal (1977) is the only study to our knowledge that has begun to look at certain aspects of these questions. Rosenthal's study was concerned with the acquisition of sociolinguistic awareness in very young children. On the basis of findings from her study of 136 preschool children, Rosenthal suggests that social awareness of language and dialect differences develops between the ages of 4 and 5, although its beginnings could already be detected as early as age 3. Rosenthal further suggests that preschool children are not only able to discriminate between two linguistic varieties, but also form specific attitudes towards each variety. They expressed, for example, a higher evaluation of the standard American English variety as compared with Black English. These issues, of considerable relevance to a social-psychological perspective in language acquisition, should be explored more extensively.

Most of the social class literature is concerned with children of elementary school age and beyond. It implies that children's sensitivity to the social status of their interlocutors emerges in conjunction with the beginning of school attendance. More recent studies of children's sociolinguistic skills have shown that preschool children may begin to respond to subtle differences in role and status which may exist at home, between fathers and mothers, for example. In a review of studies on how children learn to formulate requests, Ervin-Tripp (1977) cites a dramatic example of a 3-year-old girl who made a sharp differentiation between her mother and father. She regularly used repetition and politeness modifiers with her father, much more so than with her mother. Thus to her mother she said, quite bluntly: "*Mommy, I want milk.*" But to her father: "*Daddy, I want some, please? Please, Daddy, huh?*" Requests, or directives, are generally a sensitive area for detecting children's perceptions of the social meanings conveyed by different types of utterances.

Sex differences in language use have long been noted for adults in different societies. For example, Labov's studies in the U.S. (Labov, 1972) and Trudgill's studies of British adults (Trudgill, 1975) all found women's speech to be marked by a more careful and formal pronunciation style. Similarly, Lakoff's work (Lakoff, 1973) has characterized women's speech style as less direct and less assertive than men's, and containing certain lexical and intonation patterns which mark it as typically feminine. Few studies so far have systematically explored the developmental origins of such sex differences. An early study by Fischer (1958) found sex differences in sociolinguistic features in 3- to 10-year-old children in a semirural New England village. Boys' speech contained more contractions and deletions, and generally was more colloquial than girls'. Thus, for example, boys said *fishin'* and *swimmin'*, while girls said *fishing* and *swimming*. Sachs (1977) showed that the voices of boys and girls between the ages of 5 and 12 years typically sound different from one another even though there is no evidence for the existence of anatomical differences in the size of their vocal tracts (see Chapter 6). She suggests that at least part of the reason why prepubertal boys and girls sound different is that very early on they learn to use the voice and speech style that is viewed as appropriate for their sex in the culture.

Pragmatic considerations may also affect the way speech is structured. It is necessary to determine the communicative intent of a particular interaction before selecting the appropriate linguistic devices. Speech variations potentially caused by changes in the setting, for example, may not occur if the function of the interaction in the different settings is construed by the participants as being the same, (see Chapter 3). Similarly, the same setting may elicit different speech styles on two different occasions if the communicative intent has changed (see Chapter 10). Thus an adult-child interaction which is meant to test the child's knowledge will be differently structured from a similar interaction—in the same setting and on the same topic—if the latter serves as an occasion for mutual sharing of knowledge. In the testing situation, adults' speech would be replete with questions and directives and that of the children would consist of many short, single-word responses. In the situation in which the children are not being tested, the children would be more talkative and their speech patterns would resemble those of the adults (Hall & Cole, 1978).

Our own observations of parent-child interaction in a semistructured laboratory setting also illuminate the relationship between situational and linguistic variations. From these interactions, we gain insight into how situational variations in the speech patterns of young children change over time. As described earlier in the chapter, our studies involve 24 boys and girls aged 2 to 5 in separate interaction sessions with their mothers and fathers. All families were asked to engage in three tasks: taking apart a wooden toy car; playing "store"; and telling a story from a wordless picture book. Each of these tasks was designed to represent a different underlying function. The "car" situation was intended to reflect the directive function of language (Luria, 1959). The "store" situation was intended to represent the social function of language in a pretend play context. And, finally, the "book" situation represented the referential function. Analyses of the parents' speech in these three situations indicated that they were highly responsive to the different requirements of each task and varied their speech accordingly (Weintraub, 1978). We are now beginning to look at the ways in which the children are learning to vary their speech in these same situations. Two observations stand out from preliminary analyses of the children's protocols.

We believe, first, that there is a developmental progression in the children's awareness of the function of the situation. And, second, that there is also a developmental progression in the children's ability to realize this awareness in speech. These observations can be illustrated by focusing on the "store" situation as an example. In this situation, a shelf stocked with some real and toy food containers, dishes and a toy cash register served as the "store," and the parents were simply asked to "play store" with their children. The children's behaviour in this situation varied a great deal, depending on their age and to some extent their sex as well.

The youngest 2- year-olds, boys and girls alike, did not evidence any awareness of the function of the task at hand. They played with the available objects in an appropriate but literal fashion, counting money, opening and closing containers, all the while recounting their ongoing activities. Their style of playing and speaking did not exhibit any features allowing us to infer that they knew they were supposed to construct a "play store" situation. More likely, they did not possess the linguistic and, possibly also, the cognitive abilities to behave in a make-believe mode in this particular context.

The next level of response to the situation included a group of children whose play was similar to that of the youngest children in all respects but one. The children (about 2½ to 3½) "announced" that they were "playing store" and sometimes even claimed to assume a role (that of "customer", for example), but they gave no evidence in their speech that would attest to such claims. They had no make-believe markers in their speech whatsoever.

The next level appears to us to be a transitional phase and it begins at about 3½. Like the previous group, these children were clearly aware of the purpose for which the situation was intended, but they exhibited considerably more sociolinguistic knowledge, although their sociolinguistic skills were still at a fairly elementary level. Their speech had a mixed pattern. They were not able to sustain speaking in a role as long as older children. Even when they did, some of their utterances contained a few appropriate speech modifications, while others would have struck any observers as odd. There are also changes in mid-course, as the following utterance from one 3½-year-old boy illustrates. Playing in the role of "customer," and pointing to a make-believe milk bottle, he said to the "shopkeeper": "I want" [then pauses before rephrasing] "I would like milk." This child is seen here groping for the right way to make a request. He is aware that there is more than one way of doing it and is attempting to select the correct variant. He succeeds in this case in picking an appropriate *syntactic* form for phrasing a polite request. But his voice quality, on the other hand, did not contain the dramatic phonological markers which would indicate the pretend-play situation. This group of children, then, have begun to master some, but by no means all, of the registral features required in this situation.

The speech of the oldest group of children in our sample (the oldest being 5) is considerably more diversified, and that of the oldest girls more so than the boys. They are capable of sustaining speech in a role for much longer stretches. Their speech in this situation contains a range of lexical, phonetic and syntactic speech modifications, marking this situation as stylistically distinct from the other two situations.

In these 2- to 5-year-old children, we have seen the gradual development of sensitivity to the requirements of a particular situation and the concomitant development of the ability to use language to meet these requirements. In a laboratory study of children in roughly this same age range (2½ to 3½ years), Bock and Hornsby (1981) showed that as children grow older they become increasingly aware of the polite dimensions embodied in the words *ask* and *tell*, and increasingly able to produce appropriately polite requests. Sensitivity to the social requirements of situations has important implications. A speaker who is aware of the range of functions and uses to which language can be put, and who has available a diversified stylistic repertoire is clearly at an advantage over a speaker whose code switching ability is narrower. A richer repertoire of speech styles gives the speaker access to a wider range of contexts and enables him to operate more effectively in a wider range of social roles. (The interested reader should refer to Basil Bernstein's work for a controversial discussion of the implications of one's social class background for one's linguistic development. e.g., Bernstein, 1972 and Chapter 10).

It is clear that as children get older their stylistic repertoire widens, reflecting their accumulated social experiences. Andersen (1977), for example, studied 5- to 10-year-olds' ability to assume different social roles by asking them, in an experimental situation, to "talk like different people": a mother, father, baby, teacher, and foreigner. She found considerable developmental changes with age, both in the capacity to assume different role memberships and in the ability to express them in speech characteristics.

Most of what we know about stylistic variation in child speech comes from studies in which children are asked to *act out* different social roles. They thus give us a clue as to what children may know about social role *stereotypes*, which is certainly itself a type of social knowledge. But few studies have explored the development of stylistic variations in a real life, naturalistic setting. When, for example, do children become aware that they must speak differently to their teacher as compared with another adult? When do they learn that you must speak with deference when addressing a policeman? That you do not curse a doctor even when he is hurting you? In short, at what point in development do children begin to realize that different ways of saying things have different communicative effects? How do they come to know all of these things?

As we noted already, the role played by the environment in language acquisition has generally been a matter of theoretical debate for some time. The empirical evidence concerning the contribution of parental input to the child's learning of syntax remains equivocal despite a number of relevant studies on this question (see Nelson, Carskaddon, & Bonvillian, 1973; Newport, Gleitman & Gleitman, 1977; and, most recently, Furrow, Nelson, & Benedict, 1979).

The relationship between the parents' phonology and the phonological system acquired by children has hardly been studied at all. A provocative paper by the American linguist, Charles Hockett, speaks of the influence of peers (in contrast with parents) on the child's acquisition of accent in his native language. In this paper, Hockett (1950) asserts "the importance of other children among the environmental forces which condition the emerging dialect of a child" (p. 451). A study of accent patterns within Black middle-class families in Washington D.C. lends some support to Hockett's assertive speculation (see Stewart, 1970). The evidence in general, however, is far from conclusive, with many anecdotes pointing in different directions. Which particular variety of local accent children will adopt may, in fact, depend on personality and social-psychological factors which, at the moment, are ill understood.

It may be precisely that the interactive and social components of language are most amenable to input effects from parents. We now turn to one such area of language, that of routines and politeness formulas, describing studies which show how the adult influence on the child is most apparent in this area.

## THE ACQUISITION OF POLITENESS ROUTINES

Many of the modifications that speakers have to make in order to sound appropriate have to do with the politeness rules of the language. A speaker does have a certain amount of leeway in deciding whether or not to use a particular register in a particular situation. Deviations in the application of registral conventions may well sound odd to most people, but it is our guess that they would not be judged as severely as violations of those sociolinguistic conventions that have to do with politeness. It may be possible to talk about degrees of sociolinguistic appropriateness, akin to the linguist's notion of degree of grammaticality. Accordingly, it would appear that violations of politeness rules might indeed be judged most harshly. Perhaps because of that, the pressure on children to speak politely starts early on. Unlike the acquisition of syntax, semantics, and even some sociolinguistic rules, when it comes to speaking politely adults do not leave it to the child to construct the rules on his or her own. Here, they take an active, even energetic, part in directly instructing their children in the use of the various politeness devices.

A polite speaking style can be achieved in some instances by modifying the syntactic form of the sentence (as from *I want* to *I would like*). Social routines are also very common markers of polite speech. We use the term *routines* loosely to refer to formula-based, ritualized speech that children must learn to produce on particular social occasions, such expressions as *Treat or Trick* at Hallowe'en, *Hi* as a greeting, *Thanks, Please* and *Goodbye*, and so on. Routines are components of the language which, unlike less ritualized speech, have little internal structure or variability and little in the way of intrinsic cognitive meaning. A child who is forced to say *Thank you* for a birthday present she hates, clearly does not feel thankful. The kind of cognition required by the child here involves the ability to recognize a particular social situation and apply the appropriate formula. Whereas in the production of referential speech adults are concerned with the truth value of the utterance, here they only care about the performance of the routine. Children are expected early on to learn to say the polite thing, regardless of the mismatch between their feelings and the words. The acquisition of social routines involves a different sort of process from the acquisition of the rest of language since they are explicitly taught by parents. Parents have been observed drilling routines into their children, consistently asking them to rehearse such speech formulas in an invariable, almost mechanical fashion.

Routines can be studied naturalistically and in the laboratory. We chose to study the American Hallowe'en ritual in the field, and the politeness formulas *Hi, Thanks,* and *Goodbye* were studied in the laboratory. In addition, we are currently engaged in extending the study of routines to the setting of the child's home.

The Hallowe'en study was particularly difficult to conduct because it is a study that can be carried out during a period of only about four hours a year. On only one night a year do American children dressed in costume go from door to door, ringing the bell and asking for candy by saying *Trick or Treat*, and this was the focus of our research. In our study (Gleason & Weintraub, 1976), we tape-recorded this ritual on three successive Hallowe'ens in two different households. We also followed a pair of young children and their mothers from door to door and recorded these children, their mothers, and the candy-giving householders. In all, we collected data on 115 children in this study, our only intervention being to stop the children as they left and ask them their ages.

In a typical Hallowe'en scenario, the child first rings the bell. The adult then opens the door, and the child immediately says *Trick or Treat*. (No other greeting is appropriate, except perhaps to say *Good Evening* in a Transylvanian accent if one is costumed as Dracula; one could not, however, say *Hello, Trick or Treat*, or anything similar.) The adult typically responds to the child by producing a rather routinized expression of mock surprise or fear, and an invitation to partake of the treat (e.g. *Oh, my goodness; come on in; where's your bag?,* etc.). In those rare instances where an adult responds to the actual meaning of the child's threat by choosing the *trick*, the child is confused and unable to decide what to do. The child, having received the candy, says *Thank you*, and turns to go. The adult then says *Goodbye,* and the child, on leaving, says Goodbye.

The child's portion of the routine contains three basic utterances: *Trick or treat, thank you* and *goodbye*, the last two of which are, of course, common politeness formulae. We examined the children's production of these rituals, and found that in general the child's age predicted what would be produced. Children younger than 3 years old simply stood silently with their bags open, waiting expectantly. Children aged 4 to 5 said only *Trick or Treat* and *Thank you*, while children over 11 added *Goodbye* as well.

Adults accompanying the younger children from door to door typically remained on the sidewalk while the children went to ring the bell. They urged them ahead of time to remember to say *Trick or treat* and *Thank you*, and frequently checked with them when they returned to make sure they had performed correctly. Even children dressed as horrible monsters were expected to say *Thank you*, as parents often called out *Thank you* themselves when their child was given candy. This adult pressure appears to be successful, since the incidence of *Thank you* among the children rose from 21% in the group under 6 years old to 88% in the group over 11. We were struck by the emphasis on thanks, and by the fact that adults consistently used the word *say* in attempting to elicit the routines from these children: *what do you say?* or *say Thank you* occurred most frequently.

After the Hallowe'en study, we had the opportunity to study two of the routines, *Thank you* and *goodbye,* as well as *Hi* or *Hello* in the laboratory (Greif & Gleason, 1980). As part of our videotaped study on parent-child interaction, 22 children between the ages of 2 and 5 were studied. Each child came to the laboratory twice, once with the mother and once with the father. The parent and child first engaged in some structured play, which was described earlier, for about half an hour. At what appeared to be the end of the session, an assistant entered the room with a gift for the child, which was presented according to a script designed to elicit the routines *Hi, Thanks,* and *Goodbye*. Basically, the assistant greeted the child and waited for a response, presented the gift, giving the child the opportunity to say *Thanks*, and left saying *Goodbye* to the child, who, once again was looked at expectantly and given the time to answer.

By structuring the interaction in this way, we could look at some of the variables that the Hallowe'en study had not dealt with in detail. Here, for instance, sex differences in the children's speech could be observed, as could mother-father differences, since the laboratory had equal numbers of boys and girls, mother and fathers. Analysis was aimed at determining if there were differences in the behaviour of boys and girls or differences in the way that boys and girls were treated by their parents; if mothers and fathers differ; and if there is typical behaviour that occurs when children fail to produce politeness routines. We were also interested in finding out if some of these routines are more obligatory than others, since we had found parents so insistent earlier on that their children say *Thank you*, even when costumed as vicious pirates or creatures from outer space.

Results indicated that these children were unlikely to produce routines of their own accord. Only about 7% said *Thank you* spontaneously, and about a quarter of them spontaneously said *Hi* and *Goodbye*. Prompting by parents was very common; if the child did not say the right thing, the parent typically said something like *What do you say?* or *say Thank you*.

The word *say* appeared in 95% of parent prompts. Parents were much more likely to prompt the child to say *Thank you* than to produce either of the other two routines. *Thank you* is therefore least likely to be produced spontaneously and most likely to be prompted; it is also most likely to be produced after a prompt. After being told to say *thank you* fully 86% of children complied.

The only sex difference that emerged in the children's speech was that boys were much more likely to say *Hi* to the assistant than were the girls: 41% of boys and only 18% of girls did so. Otherwise, boys and girls were equally likely to produce the routines and equally likely to be prompted for not producing them by mothers and fathers. Parents did not, for instance, insist that girls be more polite than boys.

The parents' speech, on the other hand, did show a differential use of politeness markers; parents also had the opportunity to greet the assistant, to comment on the gift, and to say farewell. Essentially all of the parents greeted the assistant, but mothers were much more likely to thank the assistant for the child's gift and to say *Goodbye*. Thus, of the 15 parents who thanked the assistant, 11 were mothers; and of the 18 parents who said *Goodbye,* 13 were mothers. Therefore, while girls and boys were treated in similar fashion by parents, parents themselves provided different models of politeness behaviour, with mothers exceeding fathers in the production of two of the three formulae. The study confirms speculation that women are more polite than men, and indicates a mechanism whereby young children learn sex-appropriate speech patterns. It would appear that modelling, or imitation of the same sex parent, has a greater influence on developing speech patterns than differential treatment of boys and girls.

Some additional observations were made on the use of politeness formulae in the homes of some of the families that had also participated in the laboratory study. (For an interesting cross-cultural view of politeness at mealtime among Cakchiquel speakers, see Wilhite, 1983). Dinner table conversations were recorded in the homes of 24 of these families. A tape recorder was placed in an unobtrusive corner of the room and no outside observer was present during the taping, which lasted approximately half an hour to 45 minutes. The entire conversation, carried on around the table, was transcribed and the transcripts were searched for politeness routines used by all members of the family. It was evident that the use of routines as part of dinner table talk was pervasive. Each family used politeness routines in one form or another. Interestingly, it was actually the child who uttered more politeness routines than any other member of the family, thereby helping to mark his or her lower status within the family. The pressure on both the boys and the girls to produce the appropriate formulas was considerable, with fathers and mothers serving both as models and tutors. In fact, the prompts for politeness which the parents directed to their children were themselves couched in the form of routines. The routines for eliciting routines included forms like: *What's the magic word?* and *What do you say?*. Furthermore, some of the routines the parents prompted their children to say are routines they themselves never use. (*May I be excused?*, for example).

In addition to learning about their own social roles and about social interaction, children gained *linguistic* insight from these interchanges with their parents. In a number of instances, the parents' prompts led the children to reformulate their requests in an increasingly polite manner, thus providing children with explicit instruction in stylistic variation. One child-parent exchange concerned a request for milk, for example:

*C*: Mommy, I want more milk.
*M*: Is that the way you ask?
*C*: Please.
*M*: Please *what*, Helen?
*C*: Please gimme milky.
*M*: No.
*C*: Please gimme milk.
*M*: No.
*C*: Please . . .
*M*: Please may I have more milk?
*C*: Pl . . . please may I have more milk?

Here the child began with an intention (i.e., to obtain more milk) which she expressed first in a blunt statement. *I want more milk*. The mother rejected the request, whereupon the child attempted an imperative with an appended politeness marker (*please*). This also was rejected. Ultimately the parent led the child through several steps until she produced an elaborately polite request. At the same time that the child was learning to use a specific politeness formula, she was also learning how to express her intention in several varying linguistic forms. Moreover, the syntactic structure of the utterance *Please may I have more milk*? may itself be acquired as a routine as well. Complex utterances of this type are never produced by this child spontaneously either at home or in the laboratory. While earlier work had shown that politeness formulae serve an important social function, in this study we have shown that they serve an important linguistic function as well.

## CONCLUSIONS

In this chapter, we have tried to point out that a fuller understanding of language acquisition requires a model of language competence which is broader than the one traditionally held by linguists. The linguist conceptualizes an ideal speaker-hearer in terms of his or her ability to construct formally correct utterances. A theory of communicative competence, in addition, envisages an individual who is capable of perceiving and expressing in speech all of the subtleties conveyed by the settings in which social interaction takes place. Whether competence of this kind should be included within linguistic competence *per se* may be a moot point. Lyons (1977) convincingly argues that for methodological reasons linguists have excluded many factors involved in communicative behaviour from analyses and models of the language system and have thus defined these factors as non-linguistic. The broad notion of communicative competence subsumes specifically linguistic competence within it. We have pointed out that developmental investigations which take this view of competence have so far focused on the acquisition of sociolinguistic variation in child speech. On the way to becoming a competent language user, a child must acquire many different registers and must learn to be sufficiently flexible in knowing when and how to use them. Since mastery of linguistic variation can be said to facilitate social interaction, individuals who lack this skill risk social ostracism and a host of other practical and psychological consequences (not obtaining a desirable job, for example). We are far from being able to spell out all the components of communicative competence. At this point, we can provide some descriptions of the linguistic units which go along with a range of different social contexts. But what remains to be delineated is a model of what *social* knowledge speakers must possess in order to map their linguistic skills into social contexts. Might it be possible to construct a hierarchical model of the acquisition of social functions akin to the model of cognitive functions of the type espoused by Piagetian psychologists?

The difficulties of establishing the validity of such a model might exceed those existing in the cognitive model of development. Considerations concerning the legitimacy of ordering social functions—class and culture-bound as they tend to be—according to some sort of hierarchy, may make construction of such an ideal model extremely problematic. Are there variations in language which all speakers must acquire? In what order, then, would the different varieties of language be acquired, and what would be the determinants of the acquisition order? Does the order reflect a larger social psychological reality in the society? Without a coherent theoretical framework, the empirical work in this area will continue to be largely descriptive and somewhat fragmented. At the same time, research in this field is still in its infancy. Our current theories of how children acquire purely linguistic competence were derived only after a large body of descriptive studies of the acquisition of phonology and grammar was amassed. By the same token, a comprehensive theory that accounts for the interactive and social-psychological components of language must await the accumulation of a data base that includes such things as children's acquisition of linguistic variation and their awareness of the social-psychological consequences that such knowledge entails.

## ACKNOWLEDGEMENT

This research was supported in part by Grant BNS 75-21909 AO1 from the National Science Foundation.

## REFERENCES

Alvy, K. The relation of age to children's egocentric and cooperative communication. *Journal of Genetic Psychology* 1968, *112*, 275-286.

Andersen, E. *Young children's knowledge of role-related speech difference: A mommy is not a daddy is not a baby.* Paper presented at the Ninth Annual Child Language Research Forum, Stanford University, 1977.

Bellinger, D. Consistency in the pattern of change in mothers' speech: Some discriminant analyses. *Journal of Child Language,* 1980, *7*, 3, 469-488.

Bellinger, D., & Gleason, J. B. Sex differences in parental directives to young children. *Sex Roles,* 1982, *8*, 1123-1139.

Bernstein, B. Language and socialization. In N. Minnis (Ed.) *Linguistics at large,* New York: The Viking Press, 1971.

Biller, H. B., & Bamm, R. M. Father-absence, perceived maternal behaviour, and masculinity of self-concept among Junior High School boys. *Developmental Psychology,* 1971, *4*, 178-181.

Bock, J. K., & Hornsby, M. E. The development of directives: How children ask and tell. *Journal of Child Language,* 1981 *8*, 1, 151-164.

Broen, P. The verbal environment of the language learning child. *American Speech and Learning Association Monograph,* 1972, *17*. Washington, D.C.

Carlsmith, L. The effects of early father absence on scholastic aptitude. In L. Hudson (Ed.), *The ecology of human intelligence.* Harmondsworth, England: Penguin, 1970.

Casagrande, J. B. Comanche baby language. *International Journal of American Linguistics,* 1948, *14*, 11-14.

Cazden, C. The situation: A neglected source of social class differences in language use. *Journal of Social Issues,* 1970, *26*, 2, 35-60.

Chomsky, N. *Aspects of the theory of syntax.* Cambridge, Mass.: M.I.T. Press, 1965.

Crawford, J. M. Cocopa baby talk. *International Journal of American Linguistics,* 1970, *36*, 9-13.

Dunn, J., & Kendrick, C. The speech of two and three year-olds to infant siblings: 'Baby talk' and the context of communication. *Journal of Child Language,* 1982, *9,* 3, 579–595.

Edwards, J. *Language and disadvantage.* New York: Elsevier, 1979.

Engle, M. *Do fathers speak motherese? An analysis of the language development of young children.* Paper presented at the International Conference on Social Psychology and Language. University of Bristol, Bristol, U.K., 1979.

Ervin-Tripp, S. Wait for me, roller skate. In S. Ervin-Tripp, & C. Mitchell-Kernan (Eds.), *Child Discourse.* New York: Academic Press, 1977.

Farwell, C. The language spoken to children. *Papers and reports on child language development,* Vols. 5 and 6. Stanford University, 1973.

Ferguson, C. Baby talk in six languages. *American Anthropologist,* 1964, *66* (6 part 2), 103–114.

Fischer, J. Social influence in the choice of a linguistic variant. *Word,* 1958, *14,* 47–56.

Flavell, J. *The Development of Role-taking and Communication Skills in Children.* New York: Wiley, 1968.

Furrow, D. Nelson, K. & Benedict, H. Mothers' speech to children and syntactic development: some simple relationships. *Journal of Child Language,* 1979, *6,* 423–442.

Giattino, J., & Hogan, J. G. Analysis of a father's speech to his language-learning child. *Journal of Speech and Hearing Disorders,* 1975, *40,* 524–537.

Gleason, J. B. Code switching in children's language. In T. E. Moore, (Ed.) *Cognitive development and the acquisition of language.* New York: Academic Press, 1973.

Gleason, J. B. Fathers and other strangers: Men's speech to young children. In P. Dato (Ed.), *Georgetown University roundtable on language and linguistics.* Washington, D.C.: Georgetown University Press, 1975.

Gleason, J. B., & Greif, E. B. Men's speech to young children. In B. Thorne, C. Kramerae & N. Henley (Eds.), *Language, gender and society.* Rowley, Mass.: Newbury House, 1983.

Gleason, J. B., & Weintraub, S. The acquisition of routines in child language. *Language in Society,* 1976, *5,* 129–136.

Greif, E. B. Sex differences in parent-child conversations. *Women's Studies International Quarterly,* 1980, *3,* 253–258.

Greif, E. B., & Gleason, J. B. Hi, thanks, and goodbye: More routine information. *Language in Society,* 1980, *9,* 159–166.

Hall, W. & Cole, M. On participants' shaping of discourse through their understanding of the task. In K. F. Nelson (Ed.), *Children's Language,* Vol. I., New York: Gardner Press, 1978.

Harkness, S. Aspects of social environment and first language acquisition in rural Africa. In C. Snow & C. Ferguson (Eds.), *Talking to Children.* Cambridge, U.K.: Cambridge University Press, 1977.

Hockett, C. Age grading and linguistic continuity. *Language,* 1950, *26,* 449–457.

Hymes, D. Competence and performance in linguistic theory. In R. Huxley, & E. Ingram (Eds.), *Language acquisition: Models and methods.* New York: Academic Press, 1971.

Jacobson, J. L., Boersma, R. F., & Olson, K. L. Paralinguistic features of adult speech to infants and small children. *Child Development,* 1983, *54,* 436–442.

Labov, W. The logic of non-standard English. In F. Williams (Ed.), *Language and poverty.* C. Markham Publishing Company, 1970.

Labov, W. *Sociolinguistic patterns.* Philadelphia: University of Pennsylvania Press, 1972.

Lakoff, R. Language and women's place. *Language in Society,* 1973, *2,* 45–79.

Luria, A. The directive function of speech in development and dissolution, I, II. *Word,* 1959, *15,* 341–352; 453–464.

Lyons, J. *Semantics: 2.* Cambridge: Cambridge University Press, 1977.
McCarthy, D. Research in language development. In L. Carmichael (Ed.), *Manual of Child Psychology,* 1954.
McLaughlin, B., White, B., McDevitt, T., & Raskin, R. Mothers' and fathers' speech to their young children: Similar or different? *Journal of Child Language,* 1983, *10,* 1, 245–252.
Masur, E., & Gleason, J. B. Parent-child interaction and the acquisition of lexical information during play. *Developmental Psychology,* 1980, *16,* 404–409.
Moerk, E. Changes in verbal child-mother interactions with increasing language skills of the child. *Journal of Psycholinguistic Research,* 1974, *3,* 101–116.
Nelson, K. E., Carskaddon, G., & Bonvillian, J. D. Syntax acquisition: Impact of experimental variation in adult verbal interaction with the child. *Child Development,* 1973, *44,* 497–504.
Newport, E., Gleitman, L., & Gleitman, H. Mother, I'd rather do it myself: Some effects and non-effects of maternal speech style. In C. Snow & C. Ferguson (Eds.), *Talking to children: Language input and acquisition.* Cambridge: Cambridge University Press, 1977.
Nichols, P., & Broman, S. Familial resemblance in infant mental development. *Developmental Psychology,* 1974, *10,* 3, 442–446.
Ochs, E. Talking to children in Western Samoa. *Language in Society,* 1982, *11,* 1, 77–104.
Opie, I., & Opie A. *Children's games in street and playground.* Oxford: Clarendon Press, 1969.
Penman, R., Cross, T., Milgram-Friedman, J., & Meares, R. Mothers' speech to prelingual infants: A pragmatic analysis. *Journal of Child Language,* 1983, *10,* 1, 17–34.
Remick, L. *The maternal environment of linguistic development.* Doctoral dissertation. University of California, Davis, 1971.
Rondal, J. A. Fathers' and mothers' speech in early language development. *Journal of Child Language,* 1980, *7,* 2, 353–370.
Rosenthal, M. The magic boxes: Pre-school children's attitudes toward black and standard English. *Florida FL Reporter,* 1974, *12,* 55–62, 92–93.
Sachs, J. Clues to identification of sex in children's speech. In B. Thorne & N. Henley (Eds.), *Language and sex: Difference and dominance.* Rowley, Mass.: Newbury House Publishers, 1975.
Sachs, J. The adaptive significance of linguistic input to prelinguistic infants. In C. Snow & C. Ferguson (Eds.), *Talking to children.* Cambridge: Cambridge University Press, 1977.
Sachs, J., & Devin, J. Young children's use of age-appropriate speech styles in social interaction and role-playing. *Journal of Child Language,* 1976, *3,* 1, 81–98.
Scherer, K., & Giles, H. *Social markers in speech.* Cambridge, England: Cambridge University Press, 1979.
Shatz, M., & Gelman, R. The development of communication skills: Modifications in the speech of young children as a function of listener. *Monograph of the Society for Research in Child Development,* 1973. No. 153.
Snow, C., & Ferguson, C. (Eds.). *Talking to children.* Cambridge: Cambridge University Press, 1977.
Stewart, W. Toward a history of American Negro dialect. In F. Williams (Ed.), *Language and Poverty.* Chicago: Markham Publishing Company, 1970.
Trudgill, P. Sex, covert prestige, and linguistic change in the urban British English of Norwich. In B. Thorne & N. Henley (Eds.), *Language and sex: Difference and dominance.* Rowley, Mass.: Newbury House Publishers, 1975.
Ure, E., & Ellis, J. Register in descriptive linguistics and linguistic sociology. In O. Uribe Villegas (Ed.), *Las problemas y concepciones actuales de la sociolinguistica.* Mexico City: University of Mexico Press, 1972.

Waterson, N., & Snow, C. (Eds.). *The Development of communication.* London: Wiley, 1978.
Weintraub, S. *Parents' speech to children: Some situational and sex differences.* Ph.D dissertation, Boston University, 1978.
Wilhite, M. Children's acquisition of language routines: The end-of-meal routine in Cakchiquel. *Language in Society,* 1983, 13, 1, 47-64.
Williams, F. *Language and Poverty.* Chicago: Markham Publishing Company, 1970.

# 5 Speech Cues and Social Evaluation: Markers of Ethnicity, Social Class, and Age

Richard J. Sebastian
*St. Cloud State University*

Ellen Bouchard Ryan
*McMaster University*

### INTRODUCTION

Upon first meeting others, a number of sources of information about them are relatively immediately accessible. An individual's sex, race or ethnicity, age and physical attractiveness are some of the more salient personal characteristics which are available for immediate processing. Despite the fact that objectively these various cues provide little information about specific individuals, these sources of minimal knowledge do, nonetheless, readily, substantially, and frequently influence a variety of responses towards them. For example, these cues affect inferences about personality characteristics (Karlins, Coffman, & Walters, 1969; Katz & Braly, 1933), expectations about future life experiences (Dion, Berscheid, & Walster, 1972), and judgements of likeability (Byrne, 1971). Interpersonal behaviours, such as helping and aggression, may also be affected by these minimal sources of information about others (Donnerstein & Donnerstein, 1976; West & Brown, 1975). Social perception, evaluation and behaviour are also significantly influenced by speech markers, which are easily perceived stimuli through which speakers provide important biological, social, and psychological information about themselves both voluntarily and otherwise (Giles, Scherer, & Taylor, 1979). Recently, increasing attention has been directed to investigating and understanding the influence of speech and language variables on social behaviour (see Giles & Powesland, 1975; Giles & St. Clair, 1979; Ryan & Giles, 1982). The research and theorizing up to the present have clearly demonstrated how the fields of social psychology and language study can mutually benefit one another.

The pioneering work on speech style and social evaluation was conducted by Lambert (see 1967) who clearly demonstrated that an individual's language and accent were important determinants of others' reactions. Similar research has been carried out subsequently in England, Canada, the United States, and elsewhere. The thorough review of this work by Giles and Powesland (1975) reveals that variations in listeners' judgements of a person's status and personality are commonly associated with the speaker's accent (as characterized by pronunciation features). In other words, style of speech and other speech markers, just like race or ethnicity, can be sources of minimal information about others which, nonetheless, can strongly influence social responses.

In the absence of any other information about a person, the individual's style of speech may lead to inferences about the social categories to which the person belongs. Thus, speech characteristics may affect assumptions about an individual's race or ethnicity, age, and social class. These responses, in turn, may then influence other reactions to the speaker. Exposing listeners to individuals whose style of speech systematically varies is consequently an indirect method of studying sterotyping and prejudice toward different social groups (see Lambert, 1967). A person's style of speech may also influence social reactions through other processes which do not involve the postulation of intervening assumptions about the speaker's membership in various social categories. For example, the speaker's style of speech may cause listeners to feel uncomfortable because it is difficult to understand. Negative evaluations of the speaker may then reflect the listeners' uncomfortable feelings rather than their stereotypes regarding social groups.

In this chapter, the influences of speech markers related to ethnicity, social class, and age are examined. Listeners' responses to individuals who speak Spanish-accented English or to persons whose speech marks them as elderly are the focus. The elderly and individuals of Spanish ethnicity represent United States' minority groups which are growing fast and receiving much social and scientific attention. The perceptions of and attitudes towards members of each group and towards individuals who belong to both groups can be assessed by exposing listeners to samples of speech. In addition to determining the nature of the reactions to these individuals, special attention is directed toward understanding the different social-psychological processes which may be involved. In particular, the roles of social inferences and the generalized negative affect of the downgrading of minority group speakers are analysed. These processes and issues concerning the elicitation of sterotypes by voice cues are of significance to the burgeoning interdisciplinary field of "language and social psychology". Even though the specific findings reported relate directly to our research with Spanish speakers and the elderly in the United States, the underlying processes with which we are concerned definitely play a greater or lesser role in social evaluations of speech across other cultural and intergroup settings.

## THE EFFECTS OF NONSTANDARD SPEECH ON SOCIAL EVALUATION AND BEHAVIOUR

### Evaluative Reactions: Inferences Concerning Ethnic Identity and Social Class

As mentioned above, research carried out in various countries indicates that the judgements of a speaker's status and personality are influenced by the person's style of speech. In some countries where there exists a widely recognized standard or high prestige style of speech, such as received pronunication (RP) in England, individuals who speak a nonstandard or less prestigious variety of the language are often downgraded (Giles & Powesland, 1975). In the United States, identifying a standard style of spoken English is quite difficult, but singling out nonstandard varieties is a much simpler task. In the past 15 years, for example, variants of Black English have been the subject of numerous sociolinguistic investigations, several of which have concerned attitudes (Shuy, 1969; Tucker & Lambert, 1969; Williams, 1976). Another variety, Spanish-accented English, has been the focus of our research. Specifically, we have asked under what conditions and for what reasons speakers of Spanish-accented English are responded to less favourably than speakers of standard English.

In several studies conducted by Ryan and her associates, the evaluative reactions of Midwest American listeners to speakers of Spanish-accented and standard English have been compared (Brennan & Brennan, 1981a, b; Ryan & Carranza, 1975; Ryan, Carranza, & Moffie, 1977). Speakers of Spanish-accented English were viewed as lower in status and sometimes less friendly than their standard counterparts. These findings have been obtained from white, black, and even Mexican-American listeners. The simplest explanation for these findings essentially involves a process of ethnic identification and stereotyping. Once the individual is categorized as a person of Spanish ethnicity, he or she assumes the evaluative content of this category (Allport, 1954). The beliefs and feelings associated with the category are evidently negative and consequently the individual speaker is similarly evaluated.

Although this ethnic stereotyping account is appealing because of its simplicity, these studies were conducted to illustrate its inadequacy for completely explaining reactions toward speakers of contrasting language varieties. First of all, differential evaluations have been obtained toward Spanish speakers with varying levels of accentedness in their English. Untrained listeners, at both secondary and university levels, have been able to distinguish reliably between as many as eight degrees of Spanish-accented English, and their accentedness ratings have been in agreement with both overall impressions and detailed phonological analyses of linguists (Brennan & Brennan, 1981b; Brennan, Ryan & Dawson, 1975). Furthermore, the degree to which speakers of Spanish-accented English have been downgraded is associated with their perceived *degree* of accentedness (Brennan & Brennan, 1981a; Ryan et al., 1977). That is, speakers who are judged to have stronger accents are also evaluated more negatively. If it is assumed that all objects classified in the same category are evaluated in basically the same way, then these findings fail to support the assumption. However, it may plausibly be argued that individuals assume the content of the category to the extent that their attributes match the defining or criterial attributes of the class or to the extent that they are prototypical (Cantor & Mischel, 1979). If accentedness is the cue for classification, which it presumably is, then its judged magnitude may affect the degree to which other category characteristics are assigned to a speaker.

The context in which the Spanish-accented English occurs has also been found to influence evaluative reactions to its speakers (Ryan & Carranza, 1975). Speakers of Spanish-accented English were less negatively evaluated when the setting for their speech was the home rather than school. An ethnic stereotyping explanation has considerable difficulty in incorporating these results. Minimally, one needs to posit that the standards used for evaluating speakers vary across contexts (Giles & Powesland, 1975) and that the appropriateness of the speech for the context is also a determinant of reactions to speakers.

That speakers of Spanish-accented English are evaluated negatively by blacks as well as whites is *not* especially problematic for the ethnic stereotyping explanation. It has been found that minority groups within a society tend to evaluate other minority groups, usually with the exception of their own, in the same way as the majority group (Ehrlich, 1973). The majority group essentially constitutes a reference group for the minority. The downgrading of speakers of Spanish-accented English by Mexican Americans indicates that minority group members may sometimes also accept the majority's view of their own group, a finding previously reported by others (e.g., Allport, 1954; Lambert, 1967).

A more fundamental question concerns whether the downgrading of speakers of Spanish-accented English is predominantly due to ethnic categorization or to the placement of the speakers in some other evaluatively significant social category, such as social class, or to both classifications. In the absence of other information, it is likely that speakers of Spanish-accented English are not only assumed to be Mexican American but also members of the lower class. Similarly, speakers of standard English are more likely to be viewed as middle class persons. Some evidence for these ideas is available in several studies with employment interviewers which showed that standard English speakers are favoured for supervisory and executive positions while semiskilled and unskilled positions are viewed as more appropriate for Spanish-accented speakers (de la Zerda & Hopper, 1979; Rey, 1977). In general, social class information has been found to be an important determinant of social judgements and evaluations, with lower class persons being judged less favourably than middle class ones (Smedley & Bayton, 1978; Triandis & Triandis, 1960). The observed responses to speakers with varying degrees of accentedness can therefore be predicted from the hypothesis that the more a particular individual's accent differs from the standard, the lower his or her presumed social class will be. The proposition that a speaker with an ethnic accent may be downgraded largely because of social class assumptions extends the notion of the class-related standard, which was developed by Giles and Powesland (1975) to account for evaluations of different regional accents, to a cross-cultural context.

Social class assumptions, such as those suggested here, can easily and directly account for the findings obtained on status measures. Furthermore, the results obtained for solidarity ratings (friendliness, trustworthiness, likeableness) can also be quite satisfactorily explained by a social class stereotyping process. To the extent that the category "lower social class" is a negatively evaluated one, persons placed in it can be expected to be derogated on such general affective measures as likeability. Even more specifically, Dienstbier (1972) has shown that social class information influences assumptions about belief similarity, such that middle class subjects perceive themselves to be more similar in beliefs to middle class than lower class stimulus persons. Since belief and attitude similarity are well documented determinants of liking or evaluative reactions (Byrne, 1971; Rokeach, 1980), information affecting inferences about attitude/belief similarity should directly infuence other evaluative reactions, such as solidarity measures.

Reasoning that social class assumptions might underlie reactions toward speakers of Spanish-accented English, we conducted an investigation (Ryan & Sebastian, 1980) in which social class information and ethnicity were independently varied to examine the separate and joint effects of these factors on social reactions to accented speakers. Williams (1976) had reported data from a similar study in which teachers rated brief videotaped samples of Anglo- and Mexican-American children described as lower class or middle class. Although the primary dependent variables examined were not directly evaluative, the teachers' expectations regarding the children's performance in academic subjects reflected an interaction between class and ethnicity such that social class affected teacher expectations for Mexican-American children much more than for the majority-group children. Since the Williams research programme was focused upon other issues, this particular finding with both speech and physical appearance cues to ethnicity received little interpretation. Nonetheless, it certainly provides tentative support for the present hypothesis regarding reactions to unseen speakers.

The independent variation of style of speech and social class background information in the Ryan and Sebastian (1980) study allows one to postulate that accentedness acts predominantly as a cue to ethnicity while the social class background information more directly affects assumptions about attitude and belief similarity. The research can therefore be viewed as conceptually similar to investigations of the effects of race (or ethnicity) and belief congruence on attraction and social distance (e.g., Rokeach & Mezei, 1966; Stein, Hardyck, & Smith, 1965; Triandis & Davis, 1965). Thus, the evaluative reactions to the speakers should be affected both by their style of speech and by social class background information. Additionally, in line with previous research on race (or ethnicity) and belief congruence as determinants of social distance judgements (Goldstein & Davis, 1973; Triandis & Davis, 1965), ethnicity was predicted to become an increasingly important determinant of social distance responses as the relationships involved became increasingly intimate. Since speech is a cue to ethnic group membership, this project differs from several earlier studies (i.e., Aboud, Clément, & Taylor, 1974; Bradac, Courtright, Schmidt, & Davies, 1976; Triandis, Loh, & Levin, 1966) in which speech style variations served only as second cues to social class and not as cues to ethnic differences.

In this research, middle class, Anglo-American, undergraduate participants listened to tape-recorded readings of the same formal-style passage by four male speakers and gave a number of social reactions to each speaker immediately after hearing him. In both the experimental and control conditions, the participants listened to readings by two speakers of Spanish-accented English and two speakers of standard American English. In the experimental condition, each speaker was introduced on the tape by a social class background description read by a male standard English speaker. The descriptions contained information about the occupations of the speaker's parents and his place of residence. The 80 participants in the experimental condition were instructed to judge the speakers on the basis of the background information and voice cues, whereas the 40 control subjects were told to respond on the basis of voice cues alone. Listeners rated each speaker on eight personality characteristics and two speech items and also made 11 social distance judgements. The eight personality items included three to represent a status dimension (successful, intelligent, and wealthy), three to represent a solidarity dimension (kind, friendly, and likeable), and two to represent social class and ethnic stereotyping (ambitious and dirty). The speech items asked the participants to indicate how easy it was to understand the speaker and how uncomfortable listening to the speaker made them feel.

An overall multivariate analysis of variance performed on the five major dependent measures (status, solidarity, stereotype, speech, and social distance) for the experimental condition supported the major predictions of the research. The mean status ratings are presented for illustration in Fig. 5.1. The evaluative reactions and social distance judgements of the listeners were significantly influenced by both the speaker's style of speech and social class background. Univariate analyses revealed significant main effects for speech style on all five dependent variables and for social class background information on all dependent measures except solidarity. These main effects indicated that speakers of standard English and middle class persons were generally preferred to the Spanish-accented and lower class speakers. These overall findings, however, were qualified by the presence of an interaction between the two independent variables for all measures. The interactions generally indicated that being *either* a standard speaker *or* a middle class person resulted in favourable evaluations while being *both* a Spanish-accented speaker *and* a lower class person led to especially negative evaluations. In other words, a sharper distinction was drawn between middle and lower class accented speakers than between standard speakers with different social class backgrounds.

To determine the relative importance of ethnicity and social class background information on the social distance judgements involving varying degrees of intimacy, analyses were carried out on the individual items. In accordance with past research, the comparisons between standard and accented middle class speakers revealed that more subjects preferred to enter the most intimate interactions (date my sister, have as a close personal friend) with a standard rather than an accented speaker. Similar comparisons within the lower class produced the same results. Other comparisons between middle and lower class accented speakers indicated preference for the middle class persons, with the most substantial difference occurring for the item concerned with living in the same apartment building.

The analyses performed on the subjects' responses in the control condition revealed no significant effects. On all measures except the speech ratings, the direction of the differences did, however, favour the standard

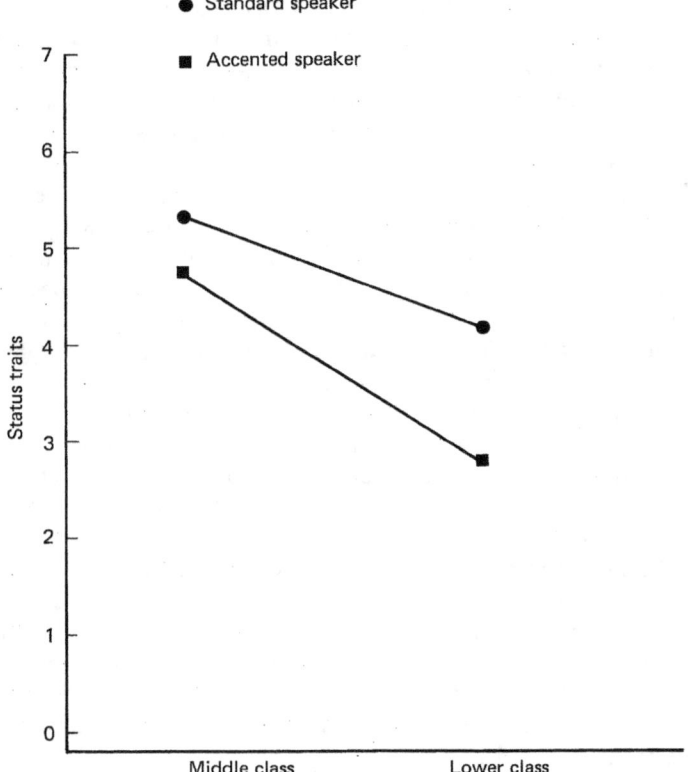

Fig. 5.1 Mean status ratings for standard and accented speakers with middle and lower class backgrounds.

speakers. The substantial variability in the subjects' responses to the speakers with regard to speech ratings, especially the two standard speakers, evidently contributed to the failure to obtain significant results. Nondialect voice differences have been found to affect evaluative reactions in other research (Arthur, Farrar, & Bradford, 1974) and apparently were especially influential in this control condition.

The results offer strong support for the major hypothesis examined in the research—social class background information substantially affects reactions to speakers of Spanish-accented English. Should the assumption that speakers of Spanish-accented English are members of the lower class be disconfirmed, this would markedly attenuate the usually observed negative reactions to these individuals. Confirming the assumption, on the other hand, results in especially negative evaluations. The only exception to this general pattern occurs for the more intimate social distance judgements where the ethnicity of the individual assumes greater importance. It should be noted that recent replications of this design have shown only accent and class main effects for German-accented English (Ryan & Bulik, 1982), Cockney English (Giles & Sassoon, 1983), and American English as contrasted with RP English (Stewart, Ryan, & Giles, 1985). These contrasting findings for other ethnolinguistic groups highlight the particularly strong influence of social class assumptions in the reactions towards Spanish-accented speakers in the American context.

Although the results for the experimental condition are quite straightforward and consistent with expectations, two important issues were not addressed. First, one wonders what assumptions listeners actually do make about the social class of speakers of Spanish-accented English when this information is not provided. Are Spanish-accented speakers perceived as lower in social class than standard speakers? Related to this, do these class judgements consistently vary with the speaker's perceived accentedness? Secondly, an implicit assumption in Ryan and Sebastian (1980) was that social class information was associated with perceived belief and attitude similarity, but the validity of this assumption was not tested. The major purpose of a recent investigation by Sebastian, Ryan, and Corso (in press) was to examine these issues. It was expected that the more accented an individual's speech was judged to be, the lower his or her perceived social class and the greater the individual's assumed attitude dissimilarity from majority group subjects. In general, it was expected that the more accented the individual's speech, the more unfavourable the reactions to him would be.

In this research, middle class, Anglo-American undergraduate participants listened to ten male speakers reading a formal-style text. Four of the stimulus persons were speakers of standard English. The remaining six spoke Spanish-accented English, with two speakers at each of three levels of accentedness (low, medium, and high). After listening to each speaker, the respondents indicated the speaker's social class and evaluated his personality on two items stressing "status" (successful and intelligent) and two stressing "solidarity" (friendly and trustworthy). They then indicated the extent to which they thought the speaker would agree with them on five controversial social issues (legalization of marijuana, value of college education, legislation against environmental pollution, expansion of the welfare system, and rugged individualism). Finally, the participants were asked whether or not they would be willing to enter into five different social relationships with the speaker (date my sister, be a close personal friend, invite home to dinner, live in the same apartment building and attend the same school).

The subjects then listened to the same speech samples in a second random order and made a number of additional responses after listening to each speaker. They, first of all, rated the speaker's accentedness, the discomfort they experienced while listening to the speech and the intelligibility of the speech. The respondents then simply identified the speaker as either an Anglo American or Mexican American. Finally, because the research also explored individual differences in reactions to Spanish-accented speakers, the subjects completed a version of the California F scale of authoritarianism (Adorno, Frenkel-Brunswick, Levinson, & Sanford, 1950).

An analysis of variance performed on the subjects' ratings of the speakers' accentedness resulted in a highly significant main effect for accentedness. Subsequent comparisons among the average accentedness ratings for the standard speakers and low-, medium-, and high-accented speakers revealed that all means differed significantly from one another, with the standard speakers receiving the lowest accentedness ratings and the high-accented speakers receiving the highest ratings. Thus, the respondents did perceive the different levels of accent in the intended way.

To examine the major predictions, both analyses of variance and correlational analyses were conducted. For the analyses of variance, the subjects' scores on the California F scale were trichotomized, and the subject's level of authoritarianism served as a between-subjects variable. Analyses of variance with three levels of authoritarianism and four levels of accentedness were carried out on the social class, belief similarity and social distance judgements. For all three measures, highly reliable main effects for accentedness were obtained. Subsequent comparisons among the means revealed that the standard speakers were more favourably evaluated than all accented speakers and that the high-accented speakers were the least favourably evaluated group of accented individuals. For the belief similarity and social distance measures, the low- and medium-accented speakers were not responded to differentially. However, the medium-accented individuals were responded to more favourably than the low-accented speakers on perceived social class. With the exception of this unexpected reversal, the results from these analyses were very orderly and confirmed the major predictions of the study. Accented speakers were perceived as lower in social class, less similar in beliefs, and less desirable as partners in a range of relationships than standard speakers. In general, the stronger the speaker's accent was perceived to be, the more negative these evaluations were. The only effect obtained for authoritarianism in these analyses was on the social distance measure where it was found that high authoritarian respondents were more likely to reject all speakers as partners in social interactions (see Giles, 1971; Kalin, Rayko, & Love, 1980).

To compare the relative downgrading of Spanish-accented speakers on the status and solidarity dependent measures, the subjects' responses on these two variables were analysed together in a three-factor analysis of variance (3 levels of authoritarianism × 2 types of personality ratings × 4 levels of accentedness). While no significant effects involving authoritarianism were found, main effects for type of personality rating and accent levels were obtained along with a significant interaction between these two variables. The interaction indicated that a stronger distinction between accent levels occurred for status than solidarity scores. An analysis carried out on the status ratings alone yielded a main effect for accent levels, and subsequent comparisons among the means showed that all means differed significantly from one another. The means were ordered as expected, except that medium-accented speakers were viewed more favourably than the low-accented speaker. This is the same kind of reversal which was earlier noted for the similar measure of perceived social class. The analysis performed on the solidarity measure alone resulted in a significant effect for accent. The comparisons among the means showed only that the standard speakers were viewed more positively than any of the accented speakers. These results were basically consistent with the hypotheses. The accented individuals were viewed more negatively than standard speakers, and for the status measure more negative evaluations were generally associated with stronger accents. The sharper downgrading on status measures relative to solidarity ones is furthermore consistent with previous research (Ryan & Carranza, 1975).

Correlational analyses were carried out to examine directly the relationship between speech ratings and the social reactions, and these analyses provided striking support for the hypothesis that the speakers' perceived accentedness would be associated with the unfavourable reactions to them. Significant correlations were obtained between perceived accentedness and each of the social reaction indices. Even stronger results were obtained for the correlations computed between the social reaction measures and the speech ratings of "comfortable" and "understandable." These latter findings may reflect the possibility that these speech ratings contain stronger social evaluative components than the accentedness rating.

To examine further the prediction that assumptions about social class and belief similarity are important mediators of the reactions to Spanish-accented speakers, partial correlations between perceived accent and social judgements were computed. When the effect of social class ratings was partialled out, no correlations between accentedness and social judgements remained significant. On the other hand, when the effect of belief similarity ratings was partialled out, the only correlation was that between accentedness and social class.

Taken together, these two studies indicate that social class assumptions and to a lesser extent attitude/belief similarity assumptions are important mediators of the reactions to speakers of Spanish-accented English. For most of the reactions which have been examined, the results offer strong support for the mediation of ethnic prejudice by social class assumptions (see Taylor & Giles [1979] for a general discussion of the overlap between the speech features which signal ethnicity and social class membership). One notable exception to this general pattern occurs for the more intimate social distance judgements where ethnicity has been found to have a powerful effect. In this context, it also should be mentioned that social class membership seems to be a more potent determinant of evaluative reactions for accented than standard speakers. Depending on the ethnicity of the speaker, it appears that the same class information may have a different meaning (Schneider, Hastorf, & Ellsworth, 1979). In any event, despite the importance which social class membership has been found to have in the research, it appears that the outgroup prejudice which has been observed cannot be simply reduced to class prejudice.

Several features of the results from Sebastian et al. (in press) deserve further comment. First of all, the lack of strong effects for authoritarianism was probably due to the restricted range available in the sample. Further research with extreme groups would seem worthwhile. Second, the unexpected switch in ordering between low- and medium-accent speakers on status and social class responses suggests that degree of accent may not be as salient in that range, thereby allowing other aspects of individual voices to exert greater influence. Furthermore, it was found that the two low-accented speakers were misidentified by 89% and 31% of the listeners, and this misidentification occurred when the listeners perceived the speech as less accented. There was, in fact, a significant difference in the accentedness rating of the two low-accented speakers when they were misidentified as compared to when they were correctly identified. Despite this difference, there was a tendency for the Mexican American misidentified as Anglo American to be evaluated less positively than the Mexican American correctly identified. These findings accord with those reported by Fraser (1973) where black speakers were rated more negatively when misidentified as white than when accurately identified. The implication is that majority members hold a higher criterion for acceptable speech for Anglo Americans than for minority speakers. This hypothesis deserves further investigation and may also partially account for the switch in ordering observed in the research.

Our previous studies suggest several additional directions for future research. Two straightforward extensions would involve, first, manipulations of the speakers' similarity to the listeners in attitudes and beliefs, and, second, variations in the speakers' own social class rather than that of their parents. Examinations of the impact of multiple cues to ethnicity (speech and appearance) on evaluative reactions would enable assessments of the separate and joint effects of these stimuli. Finally, further research should attempt to identify the kinds of information (social class, occupation) or personal attributes (physical attractiveness, sex) which would result in more positive, instead of negative, evaluations for nonstandard relative to standard speakers.

### Negative-Affect Arousal and Evaluative Reactions

The downgrading of speakers of Spanish-accented English and other nonstandard language varieties is a well-documented phenomenon. Although the complex social stereotyping mechanisms just described can account for many of the findings, it is quite plausible that other mechanisms also contribute to the commonly observed devaluation of speakers of nonstandard language varieties by members of the majority group.

One such mechanism is suggested by the Byrne-Clore reinforcement-affect model of evaluative responses (Byrne & Clore, 1970; Clore & Byrne, 1974) which is also basically compatible with related ideas offered by the Lotts (Lott & Lott, 1972, 1974). The Byrne-Clore model makes a number of simple assumptions and straightforward predictions. It, first of all, assumes that most environmental stimuli can be identified as either rewarding or punishing. Secondly, rewarding stimuli arouse positive affect whereas punishing stimuli arouse negative affect. An individual's evaluation of any stimulus is then equal to the net affect aroused by the stimulus. Finally, neutral stimuli associated with rewarding stimuli will come to arouse positive affect and thus be positively evaluated through a classical conditioning process. Similarly, neutral stimuli associated with punishing stimuli will come to arouse negative affect and hence be negatively evaluated.

For our purposes the model applies in the following manner. One needs to assume that listening to speakers of nonstandard language varieties arouses negative affect among speakers of the standard variety. This negative affect may result from the difficulty listeners have in understanding these nonstandard speakers and from consequent difficulties in interpersonal communication and/or task performance based on the nonstandard speaker's message. The speakers themselves are therefore associated with the negative affect and are consequently evaluated negatively. A similar explanation for the differential response to speakers of powerless vs. powerful styles of English has been suggested by Erickson, Lind, Johnson, and O'Barr (1978).

Support for the assumption that understanding speakers of Spanish-accented English is relatively difficult and leads to discomfort in the listeners has been obtained in our earlier studies (Ryan & Sebastian, 1980; Sebastian et al., in press). Furthermore, in the Sebastian et al. research, the correlations between evaluative reactions and ratings of comfortableness and understandability were significant and substantial. The more discomfort the respondents experienced while listening to the speakers and the more difficulty they had in understanding the speakers, the more negative their evaluations of the speakers were found to be. This suggests that the negative affect experienced by the listeners contributed to their evaluative reactions toward the speakers, even though unfavourable stereotypes may affect discomfort and understandability ratings to some extent.

As indicated above, the effects of such a negative affect mechanism should be particularly pronounced in interpersonal communication situations where the individuals are at least minimally motivated to understand one another. The standard speaker's difficulty in understanding the nonstandard speech may be at least mildly frustrating under such circumstances. Even further frustration would be anticipated if the difficulty in understanding the communicated information interfered with the standard speaker's ability to carry on a conversation or attain some other goals. Derogation of the speaker, then, should be readily expected from theories of interpersonal attraction which predict that persons associated with punishing stimuli are disliked.

A fairly direct test of the negative affect mechanism can be made by experimentally varying the affective circumstances under which subjects are exposed to the same speaker. Exposure to white noise, especially intermittent and unpredictable white noise, is known to be subjectively annoying (Glass & Singer, 1972). An individual associated with this kind of noise should be evaluated more negatively than the same person who is not associated with this irritating stimulation, particularly if the people being evaluated are not physically present (Kenrick & Johnson, 1979). For our purposes, using noise has advantages over other procedures used to vary affect in studies of interpersonal attraction, such as showing subjects happy or sad films (Gouaux, 1971) or varying room temperature and spatial density (Griffith & Veitch, 1971). Noise, in addition to its intrinsic effects on affect, may be presented to interfere with a communicated message, thereby also impairing performance of a task based on the communicated information. The resulting frustration should lead to even further devaluation of the speaker associated with it.

To test the validity of this reasoning, we have recently carried out two experiments (Sebastian, Ryan, Keogh, & Schmidt, 1980). Both experiments were presented as colour recognition studies. The subjects listened to tape-recorded descriptions of six difficult-to-describe colours. After listening to each description, the subjects were required to select the colour described from a set of five stimulus colours. Finally, in both experiments the subjects were asked to complete a questionnaire about the speaker and the experiment. The questionnaire included scales for the evaluation of the speaker's personality, assumed attitude/belief similarity, perceived social class, subject's willingness to participate in a future communication experiment with the speaker, effectiveness of the colour communications, and separate items for assessing the responsibility of the speaker and the tape-recording for difficulties experienced with the task. The questionnaire also contained three items for evaluating the communicator's speech: accentedness, discomfort associated with listening to the speech, and ease of understanding the communicator.

The initial study was simple and straightforward in design and included only two experimental conditions. In this between-subjects design, the colour descriptions were given by the same male speaker of standard English over either noise-free tapes (normal condition) or tapes punctuated by bursts of white noise (noisy condition). As an explanation for the noisy tapes, the subjects were told that mechanical difficulty during preparation of some of the tapes had caused some static or noise. It was expected that the speaker in the noisy condition would be evaluated more negatively than the speaker in the normal condition.

The results of this experiment were as straightforward as its design and highly supportive of the basic prediction. The colour recognition performance of the subjects was substantially worse in the noisy, rather than the normal, tape condition. Furthermore, the noisy speech was rated as significantly more difficult to understand and uncomfortable than the speech in the normal condition. The accentedness ratings of the speakers in the two conditions were identical, an expected but important outcome. Thus, the noise variation had the intended effects on performance and perception of the speech. Consistent with these findings and the association of the speaker with the presumed arousal of negative affect, the speaker in the noisy condition was more negatively evaluated than he was in the normal condition. The pattern of results obtained for the noisy speaker closely resembled that typically found for speakers of non-standard English. As can be seen in Fig. 5.2, he was viewed as lower in status, solidarity, and social class, and was perceived as a much less desirable partner for a future experiment (essentially a social distance judgement). The noisy descriptions were seen as less effective but, interestingly enough, the subjects did not directly assign more responsibility to the noisy speaker for their task difficulties and instead blamed the tape. All in all, strong support was obtained for the hypothesis that individuals associated with punishing stimuli and negative affect would be relatively poorly evaluated.

The second study extended the first by examining evaluative reactions to Spanish-accented and standard speakers and by using tapes with continuous white noise, bursts of white noise, or no noise. The potentially

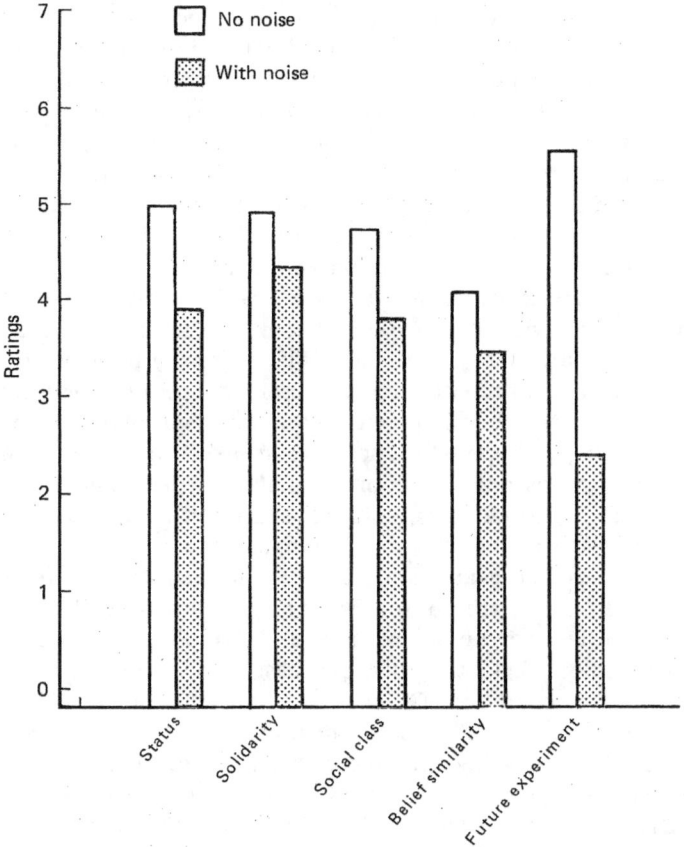

FIG. 5.2 Mean evaluations of a standard English speaker heard with or without noise.

striking influence of affective context on the evaluation of accented speech has been illustrated by Nisbett and Wilson (1977), who found that reactions to the foreign accent of a college instructor depended on the warmth or coldness of the speaker's manner. Tape recordings of the same colour descriptions used in the first study were prepared for each of the three noise conditions by three male speakers of standard English and three male speakers of Spanish-accented English. Fifteen subjects were randomly assigned to each of the six experimental conditions in this between-subjects design (two levels of accent, three levels of noise), so that five subjects listened to each of the three speakers in each condition.

Several additional changes were made in the second study. To conduct a purer test of the effects of noise on evaluative reactions without the added effects of frustration from poor task performance, two modifications were introduced. For the bursts condition, the noise was placed on the tapes so that it would not mask critical colour information. Secondly, two of the stimulus colour sets were changed to improve the average level of recognition accuracy. Finally, the respondents were asked to complete a short mood scale after completion of the colour recognition task and before evaluation of the speaker. The mood scale was added to check more directly on the subjects' affect. In this second study, it was expected that speakers of Spanish-accented English and speakers in the noise conditions would be evaluated more negatively than the other speakers.

A number of significant results were obtained for noise, accent, and the interaction of these variables. Colour recognition accuracy was affected by both variables and their interaction. The especially poor performance of subjects in the continuous noise, accented speaker condition was largely responsible for the main effects for noise and accent. Consistent with one of the major hypotheses, accented speakers were reacted to more negatively than standard speakers on a number of personality and social dimensions—status, social class, and attitude/belief similarity. While the noise variations failed to affect the participants' responses on the major personality and social evaluations, main and interaction effects were found for noise on other responses. For example, a marginally significant ($p<.10$) main effect for noise on the speaker responsibility measure indicated that subjects held the speakers least responsible for their difficulties in the bursts condition. Other results indicated this was mainly true for the standard speaker. The speech measures were also affected by the independent variables. Accent significantly influenced all speech measures in the expected manner. The accented speakers were rated as more accented, difficult to understand, and uncomfortable to listen to. A main effect for noise on the difficulty in understanding measure indicated that the subjects had particular trouble in the continuous noise condition. The analysis of the mood scale revealed that subjects in the continuous noise condition reported the most negative affect, while subjects who heard accented speakers tended to experience more unpleasant feelings than those who heard standard speakers.

In this second study, the speakers associated with noise were not in general more negatively evaluated on the major personality and social dimensions. The noise manipulations used may not have been sufficiently unpleasant (i.e., unpredictable, loud) since variations in noise per se without additional frustration have been shown to influence attraction toward stimulus persons (Kenrick & Johnson, 1979). Nonetheless, if the noise has the added effect of impairing task performance, as it did in the first study, then the resulting frustration should be very likely to lead to devaluation of the individual associated with these experiences. The frustrating effects of nonstandard speech styles in naturalistic situations may be especially important determinants of reactions to the speakers.

The negative affect mechanism, as it has been conceptualized for this research on evaluation and speech style, seems capable of partially accounting for the results. The devaluation of the standard speaker in the first study simply cannot be explained in terms of ethnic stereotyping processes. Moreover, to the extent that frustration and discomfort do stem from interactions with nonstandard speakers, the resulting speaker devaluation predicted from the negative affect mechanism would have a more realistic basis than would negative evaluations derived from learned stereotypes, a process which may involve no contact whatsoever with the outgroup. If conceptualized more broadly, the negative affect mechanism may prove even more useful. At least as far as social groups are concerned, it seems to be the case, sadly, that different is bad (LeVine & Campbell, 1972; Tajfel, 1970). In other words, a sufficient basis for the occurrence of negative affect, devaluation, and discrimination at times seems to be nothing more than the mere classification of people into groups. In summary, for both empirical and theoretical reasons the negative affect mechanism deserves consideration in understanding reactions to speakers of nonstandard language varieties.

### Behavioural Effects of Ethnicity: Avoidance, Discrimination and Aggression

A number of studies have now clearly shown that listeners have negative attitudes toward and beliefs about speakers of Spanish-accented English. Relative to speakers of standard English, speakers of Spanish-accented English are viewed as lower in status and social class, less similar in attitudes and beliefs, less desirable as "partners" in a range of social situations, and sometimes less friendly. To the extent these reactions are categorical, one may describe speakers of Spanish-accented English as the victims of prejudice and negative stereotyping.

A question which arises is whether these negative verbal evaluations find expression in more intense forms of rejection. That is, in comparison to speakers of standard English, are speakers of Spanish-accented English more likely to be avoided, discriminated against, and even physically attacked? A natural outgrowth of the previous work is to examine what overt behavioural consequences, if any, these negative attitudes and beliefs have.

In his discussion of the behavioural expressions of prejudice, Allport (1954) identified five increasingly intense and negative manifestations of prejudice: (1) anti-locution or verbal rejection; (2) avoidance; (3) discrimination; (4) physical attack; and (5) genocide or systematic extermination. Clear evidence for anti-locution has been obtained in our previous research. Viewed somewhat generously our social distance results can be taken as indicators of avoidance and perhaps even discrimination (live in the same apartment building), at least at the level of behavioural intentions. Examining our previous findings much more rigorously, however, one finds no data regarding actual behaviour toward speakers of Spanish-accented English.

To fill this void, Buttino and Sebastian (1978) carried out a simple study. In this research, the aggressive behaviour of Anglo-American males towards individuals of either Spanish ethnicity or other Anglos was examined. In addition to varying the ethnicity of the target, the research also independently varied anger arousal. Thus, the subjects in this study were initially either angered by their supposed partner (actually an experimental accomplice) or they were treated more positively. The anger-arousal manipulation was similar to one which is commonly used in aggression research and involved a shock evaluation of the subject's performance on a problem as well as a verbal evaluation. In the angered condition, the subjects received nine out of a possible ten electric shocks and a series of negative verbal comments as an evaluation of their performance on a problem. The nonangered subjects received only a single electric shock and more positive verbal comments. The shocks used in the research had been pretested and were judged, on average, to be moderately painful.

The subject's partner was either easily identifiable as an individual of Spanish ethnicity or as another Anglo American. Several cues to ethnicity were involved in the research, including style of speech. The individuals of Spanish ethnicity spoke with quite pronounced Spanish accents, had Spanish surnames, and were also readily identifiable as individuals of Spanish ethnicity on the basis of visual cues (hair and skin colour). Two individuals from each ethnic category participated in the research.

After the manipulation of anger, the subjects were ostensibly provided with the opportunity to retaliate in a modification of the procedure developed by Buss (1961). In this procedure, subjects are instructed to administer a shock to their partner after each mistake he or she makes on a learning task. The subjects are free to administer shocks from any of ten buttons which supposedly correspond to increasingly intense levels of shock. The subjects can also control the duration of shocks they administer. The average intensity and duration of shocks the subjects think they have delivered constitute the major dependent measures of aggression. By means of this procedure, the subjects were provided with 20 aggression opportunities. After this phase of the experiment was completed, the subjects were asked to fill out a short questionnaire which assessed the effectiveness of the manipulations and also asked the subjects to report their perceptions of, and feelings about, other aspects of the experiment.

The analyses of the subjects' responses to the questionnaire indicated that the manipulations were perceived in the manner intended. The subjects in the angered condition reported a significantly higher level of anger than the nonangered subjects. The speech of the confederates of Spanish ethnicity was rated as significantly more accented than the speech of the Anglo Americans. Finally, all subjects correctly identified their partners as either Anglo Americans or individuals of Spanish ethnicity.

The overall analyses of the aggression data yielded a main effect for anger with the angered subjects delivering more intense shocks than the nonangered individuals. Although the targets of Spanish ethnicity were given shocks of higher average intensity than the Anglo-American targets, the difference did not reach conventional levels of statistical significance. The interaction between ethnicity of the target and anger was not significant.

An internal analysis of the data did yield some interesting effects. On the final questionnaire, the subjects were asked to indicate how concerned they were about the experimenter's evaluation of their performance. Angered subjects who reported minimal concern on this item were found to be significantly more aggressive towards the target of Spanish ethnicity than toward the Anglo-American target. The opposite pattern of results was obtained for the angered subjects who were very concerned about the experimenter's evaluation of them. Although these findings must be interpreted cautiously, they suggest that more aggression is directed toward individuals of Spanish ethnicity by angered subjects whose inhibitions are weak.

Despite the interesting results obtained in the internal analysis, the findings from this study were somewhat surprising. In view of the frequently observed devaluation of speakers of Spanish-accented English, it was expected that they would be the targets of more intense aggression especially after they had angered an Anglo American. However, after further examination of relevant theory and research, the outcomes of the study appear more sensible. Research on inter-racial aggression and the relationship between attraction and aggression has shown that attitudinal variables (such as prejudice and liking) influence aggression only when anger arousal is *not* manipulated (e.g., Donnerstein & Donnerstein, 1976; Kelley & Byrne, 1977; Shuntich, 1976). On the other hand, when anger arousal is varied in these studies, as it was in our examination of inter-ethnic aggression, the anger manipulation is the major determinant of aggressive behaviour (e.g., Genthner & Taylor, 1973). Current research is therefore in progress to investigate further the impact of ethnicity on avoidance, discrimination and aggression under circumstances where anger either has or has not been manipulated. Regardless of outcome, the research will provide information about the nature and intensity of Anglos' attitudes towards individuals of Spanish ethnicity. It is fully recognized that the target variations rest on more than speech cues alone, but strong manipulations are preferred in early stages of research. Later research can examine the influence of the various cues to ethnicity alone and in combination in order to understand further their influence on overt behaviours.

## AGE ESTIMATES AND AGE-RELATED INFERENCES

A person's style of speech affects inferences about ethnicity, social class and a variety of other personal attributes. One could surmise that speech cues would also permit inferences about an individual's age. Helfrich (1979) has, in fact, recently written at length about age markers or ". . . speech cues which potentially differentiate between members of different age groups . . .[p. 63]." If an individual's age can be fairly reliably estimated from speech cues, attitudes towards the elderly could be unobtrusively examined by exposing listeners to speakers who varied in age, and examining evaluative reactions to these individuals.

This kind of research is important for a number of reasons. First of all, attitudes towards the elderly have long occupied the interest of social gerontologists. Knowledge about attitudes towards the elderly is important because the attitudes towards this group, like those directed towards any social category, may well affect the treatment they receive and even the group members' self-conceptions (Ward, 1979). Secondly, although a vast literature on attitudes toward the elderly has accumulated, relatively little is known about the reasons for the frequently observed negative attitudes towards old people in the United States (see Bennett & Ekman, 1973; McTavish, 1971). Research aimed at understanding these reactions is clearly needed. Finally, an indirect measurement procedure has advantages over more direct approaches. Problems associated with social desirability response sets or evaluation apprehension can be circumvented with indirect methods.

The initial question which needs to be addressed is, therefore, whether untrained listeners can reliably and accurately estimate the age of individuals on the basis of voice cues alone (see Chapter 6). Answering this question was the major purpose of the research by Ryan and Capadano (1978), while a second purpose was to examine evaluative reactions to speakers varying in age by means of an indirect procedure. Two experiments employing the same procedure were conducted. The first experiment investigated reactions to female speakers who ranged in age from 12 to 71 years, whereas the second experiment involved male speakers between the ages of 17 and 68 years. In each case, the undergraduate participants listened initially to tape-recorded readings of the same passage by 16 speakers. After listening to each speaker, the participants were asked to rate the speaker on six age-related stereotype scales (e.g., active-passive; with-it—out-of-it). The subjects then listened to a second tape which consisted of 32 readings of only the first two sentences from the original passage. The first 16 speakers were the same as those used in the first tape but were presented in a different random order. The remaining 16 speakers were additional stimulus persons of the same sex and age range as the initial 16. After listening to each speaker on the second tape, the subjects were asked to guess the age of each speaker.

Pearson correlation coefficients between the real and mean guessed age of the speakers for each sex were computed. For both the male and female speakers, positive and highly significant correlations were obtained. Further analyses indicated that the listeners showed substantial agreement among themselves in estimating the speakers' ages. The results clearly indicated that an individual's age can be reliably and accurately estimated from voice cues alone.

For the female speakers, their real and guessed ages correlated significantly with a number of the evaluative reactions. The older women were viewed as significantly more reserved, passive, out-of-it, and inflexible than their younger counterparts. The only evaluative reaction which correlated significantly with the real and guessed age of the male speakers was the rating of flexibility. Older men were viewed as less flexible than younger ones.

The demonstration that age can be estimated reliably from voice cues alone is the most important feature of the study. This information allows one to use the procedure as an unobstrusive means of examining attitudes towards, and stereotypes of, the elderly and to explore possible reasons for these responses. Different inferences regarding speaker age may play a significant role in judgements of voices whose rates and pitches have been artificially modified. Thus, slowed speech and altered pitch/intonation for male voices (Apple, Streeter, & Krauss, 1979; Brown, Strong, & Rencher, 1974) have led to negative evaluations on characteristics related to age stereotyping (e.g., slow, passive, weak, less competent, less benevolent). If age estimates for such modified voices should be reliable, then the extent to which the differential reaction to these voices depends on age stereotyping could be profitably examined.

Additional research by the authors aimed to explicate some of the reasons for the commonly observed negative attitudes towards, and stereotypes of, the elderly and old age in the United States. As mentioned earlier, there is a remarkable paucity of research concerned with understanding negative reactions to the elderly. Nonetheless, a number of hypotheses have been offered by various writers. One major possible explanation holds that negative attitudes towards old age and the elderly reflect other negative attitudes towards characteristics or experiences commonly associated with old age, such as low socioeconomic status, poor health, and loneliness (e.g., Bennett & Eckman, 1973). A second hypothesis states that the elderly are devalued because they fail to exhibit behaviours highly valued by Americans, such as independence, achievement and personal productivity (Cowgill & Holmes, 1972). A third commonly proposed explanation for the negative attitudes and stereotypes individuals hold towards the elderly contends that age stratification occurs in the United States. These structural conditions result in ignorance and/or misinformation about the elderly, and these factors, in turn, lead to negative attitudes and stereotypes (McTavish, 1971).

An investigation by Colette-Pratt (1976) offers some evidence pertinent to these several hypotheses. From the set of predictor variables included in her study, Colette-Pratt found that negative attitudes towards poor health were the most consistent and powerful predictors of negative attitudes towards old age across all age groups (young, middle-aged, older) included in her work. Negative attitudes toward death were also related to the devaluation of old age among the young and middle-aged subjects. Finally, some evidence was obtained that attitudes towards achievement, independence and personal productivity influenced the attitudes of the young, middle-aged and older subjects, respectively, towards old age.

One of our recent projects, which employs the indirect methodology of obtaining evaluative reactions to speakers, also explored several hypotheses for the downgrading of old age and the elderly (Sebastian, Ryan, & Abbott, 1981). First, the relationships among a variety of characteristics associated with old age (e.g., health, intelligence, ambition, activity) and perceived age were examined. The importance of assumed attitude/belief similarity in determining evaluative reactions to others has been noted earlier. Assumed attitude/belief dissimilarity may be especially relevant in examinations of reactions to the elderly, since it seems closely related to the notion of the "generation gap." The relationship between perceived age and assumed attitude similarity was also investigated.

Thirty-two undergraduates listened to two different random orders of the tape-recorded readings of the same passage by 12 male speakers. On the basis of age estimates from an independent group of subjects, two speakers were selected to represent each of six age categories (21-30, 31-40, 41-50, 51-60, 61-70, 71+). After listening to each speaker the first time, the subjects gave their impressions of the speaker by rating him along a number of dimensions: independence; ambition; intelligence; physical activity; physical health; extent of attitude/belief similarity; financial status and educational level. After listening to each speaker the second time, the respondents simply estimated the person's age.

The findings were highly significant and rather remarkable. The correlations between the average perceived age of each of the 12 speakers and the mean rating for each of the attributes listed above were highly significant and negative in *every* case ($p < .001$). Thus, older speakers were judged to be less physically healthy ($r = -0.92$), lower in financial status ($r = -0.81$), less intelligent ($r = -0.83$), ambitious ($r = -0.81$), physically active ($r = -0.91$), independent ($r = -0.80$), similar in attitudes and beliefs ($r = -0.82$), and lower in educational level ($r = -0.85$). Virtually identical results were obtained for the correlations between the speakers' actual ages and their assumed qualities. These results point to the usefulness of the procedure and indicate that increasing age is associated with a number of negative attributes.

In our most recent research project, Stewart and Ryan (1982) examined the joint effects of speaker age and rate of speech on the first impressions of young adult listeners. In response to Kogan's (1979) interpretation of our earlier findings as dependent upon the repeated measures design, this experiment presented young adult speakers (20–22 years) to one group of listeners and older speakers (60–65 years) to another group. Even with this design, the older speakers (all male) were perceived as significantly lower in competence and social class, as having attitudes and beliefs less similar to the judges', and as being more socially distant from the judges than younger speakers. Also consistent with earlier studies, the older adults were viewed to be less flexible and more old-fashioned. Furthermore, the fact that the older speakers were considered more benevolent than younger adults appears to fit the stereotype as well (Crockett, Press, & Osterkamp, 1979). Analyses of causal attributions for successes and failures essentially supported the findings for the personality and social ratings

Within the design, speech rate was employed as an indirect manipulation of perceived competence (see Apple et al., 1979; Brown, Strong, & Rencher, 1974). It was hypothesized that disconfirmation of the positive stereotype of the younger speaker (i.e., slow speech rate) and of the negative stereotype of the older speaker (i.e., fast rate) would yield an important rate × age interaction. Even though the especially negative evaluations of the slow young speaker were observed, evidence for the especially favourable evaluation of the fast older speaker was obtained in only one aspect of the causal attribution data (i.e., stability of causes for success in a competence situation).

We would argue that the Stewart and Ryan (1982) study offers a good illustration of the type of age attitude research which should be conducted. Now that the effectiveness of speaker age as an indirect manipulation has been demonstrated, it is important to move on to more complex designs. For the immediate future, it would be of special interest to examine the interactions between age and speech rate for female speakers.

## FUTURE RESEARCH DIRECTIONS

### Old Age and Racial-Ethnic Minority Group Membership: Double Jeopardy

Old people are devalued in the United States and most other modern societies (Palmore & Manton, 1974). They are furthermore often discriminated against because of their age, and some research indicates that discrimination based on age is at least as pronounced as that due to sex and race (Palmore & Manton, 1973). Belonging to various racial-ethnic minority groups in the United States also frequently results in prejudice, negative stereotyping and discrimination. Being a member of two outgroups, the aged and a racial-ethnic minority, has consequently been seen as a situation involving double jeopardy, That is, while blacks and Mexican Americans, for example, are relatively disadvantaged at all ages compared to whites, their disadvantage is presumed to be even greater in old age than it was in earlier years. An alternative point of view is that ageing "levels" the differences which earlier existed between racial-ethnic groups (Kent, 1971). The effects of age, in other words, cut across racial-ethnic boundaries and reduce the differentials between groups in such areas as health, income and life satisfactions. Regardless of racial-ethnic group, older people have less money, poorer health and lower life satisfaction relative to their more youthful counterparts.

Dowd and Bengtson (1978) examined the competing hypotheses of double jeopardy and age-as-leveller. The survey responses of a large sample of middle-aged and older black, white and Mexican Americans were used for this purpose. The respondents were questioned about their health, income, life satisfaction and social participation (contact with friends, relatives, etc.). While some support for the levelling hypothesis was found for life satisfaction and social participation measures, strong support for the double jeopardy hypothesis was found for income and subjective health. Minority elderly were worse off than middle-aged minority persons and older whites, suggesting they suffered more because they belonged to two minority groups.

Discrimination need not result from prejudice, but prejudice is a common cause of discrimination (Simpson & Yinger, 1972). The techniques used in other research reported in this chapter again provide an indirect means of examining negative attitudes and stereotypes towards the minority aged. The double jeopardy hypothesis can, in other words, be examined at the level of individual attitudes and beliefs. If the results showed that the minority aged were more negatively evaluated than both older whites and younger minority group members, the research would suggest an explanation for the differential treatment afforded older minority people. Interestingly enough, especially pronounced devaluation of the minority aged would be conceptually similar to another kind of double jeopardy already described—lower class, minority group membership. Extensions of these ideas to cases of triple and perhaps even quadruple jeopardy are possible (Manuel, 1977). Cues about a person's sex, race or ethnicity, and age may all be conveyed by speech. At the level of discrimination, triple jeopardy has already been found for black, elderly women (Palmore & Manton, 1973). To the extent that social class may also be readily inferred from speech cues, examinations of quadruple jeopardy on the basis of voice cues alone are possible.

### Adapting Speech for Aged or Minority Individuals

Among possible behavioural measures of interpersonal evaluation, variations in speech addressed to minority or elderly target persons seem especially worthy of future investigation. In dyadic situations, individuals may communicate some of their evaluative reactions towards an interlocutor by adapting their own speech (see Chapter 10). In particular, inferences about limited linguistic and/or intellectual capabilities based on voice cues (e.g., ethnic or lower class speech style, youth or advanced age) may lead to simplifications in the form and content of speech. The psycholinguistic literature (Helfrich, 1979; Snow & Ferguson, 1977) has documented the manner in which adults simplify their speech to young children in terms of pronunciation, grammar and vocabulary, as well as exaggerated intonations (see Chapter 4). Although systematic research has not yet been conducted with respect to adaptions toward members of other social categories, similar simplifications have been observed for "foreigner talk" by Ferguson (1972) and for messages to the elderly by Rubin and Brown (1975). This type of adaptation is similar to the accommodation discussed by Giles and his colleagues (see Giles & Powesland, 1975). However, the principles governing simplification will undoubtedly be somewhat different from those affecting convergence toward or divergence from the accent or language of an interlocutor.

An important contribution to the analysis of behaviour toward minority group members would definitely be made by research examining the extent and manner in which interlocutors simplify the form and content of messages to accented and aged individuals. The critical methodological difficulty to be faced in such an investigation is the identification of appropriate speech characteristics which could be reliably and easily assessed. Candidates for initial consideration include: loudness, pitch, and rate of speech; pause patterns and exaggerated pronunciations; alterations of standard pronunciations and simplification of consonant clusters; mean length of utterance, proportion of multiclause sentences and ungrammatical or nonstandard forms; type-token ratio and abstractness of vocabulary.

Analyses of such variables would yield important psycholinguistic information concerning linguistic simplification, but more importantly would also provide for behavioural measures indicating how representatives of minority groups (including the elderly) are evaluated. Furthermore, once such adaptation to individuals from minority groups has been documented, the responses of minority group members to the changes can be examined. It would be important to know under what circumstances these modifications are viewed as, for example, offensive and insulting or courteous and obliging.

## SUMMARY AND CONCLUSIONS

Information gleaned from nothing more than a sample of a person's speech has been shown to be a powerful and reliable determinant of social reactions. With regard to social evaluations and inferences, strong support for this proposition has been obtained in our research on speakers of Spanish-accented English and in the related work of others who have studied responses to speakers of other nonstandard language varieties. The basic methodology used in this research is also beginning to prove useful in advancing knowledge and understanding of attitudes towards and beliefs about the elderly and old age. Whether speech cues *alone*, or in combination with other cues to group membership, will influence negative interpersonal behaviours is a question which will be answered by the findings of current and future research. Regardless of the outcomes in these ongoing investigations, the impact of voice cues on some forms of social behaviour is unequivocally established.

Accounting for the influence of speech cues on evaluations remains a major concern. Two distinct mechanisms for explaining the evaluative responses of individuals to speech cues have been presented in this chapter. The negative affect mechanism, which was developed quite explicitly, essentially postulates that negative affect stems directly from the unusual speech cues themselves and/or from problems related to the listener's difficulty in understanding the communication. The speaker is associated with the negative affect and is consequently evaluated unfavourably.

The second major mechanism which has guided our work and served as an explanation states that listeners use voice cues to make inferences about the speaker's membership in one or more social categories. In the case of speakers of Spanish-accented English, accentedness apears to serve as a cue to ethnicity which, in the absence of additional information, then leads to inferences about social class membership. Categorization into this multiple criterion group then results in evaluative reactions. Context-related standards also influence these evaluations, and the speaker's degree of accent affects the extent to which the speaker assumes the affective and ideational content of the category. Providing information about the social class of the accented speaker evidently prevents listeners from making their usual inferences about social class on the basis of ethnicity.

From the perspective of this second mechanism, the responses to speakers of nonstandard speech styles appear to be at least minimally determined by their ethnic and social class categorizations. The age and sex of the speakers are also personal attributes which can be inferred from voice cues and lead to other social categorizations which may significantly influence evaluative reactions. In other words, it appears that listeners make multiple classifications of speakers and that their evaluations result from an interaction of these category assignments which are not readily predictable from an average or summation of the evaluations based on individual categories. It instead appears that the interpretation and evaluation of stimulus persons, as presented in our research, changes as a function of the specific combination of the information possessed or inferred by the judge. The complexity of this interpretation is commensurate with that of the data it addresses.

We have discussed evidence that downgrading of accented speakers is directly related to two sources of negative affect: discomfort associated with the effort required to understand different speech; and negative inferences (in particular, lower social class) based on the social category of ethnicity. Future research will focus upon clarifying which factors influence the direct and the socially-mediated arousal of negative affect towards accented speakers as well as older speakers. The potential generality of these two mechanisms to varied settings as well as their specific adaptations in particular intergroup contexts argues strongly for examination of their effects in diverse contexts (e.g., Ryan, 1983).

## REFERENCES

Aboud, F. E., Clément, R., & Taylor, D. M. Evaluational reactions to discrepancies between social class and language. *Sociometry,* 1974, *37,* 239–250.

Adorno, T. W., Frenkel-Brunswik, E., Levinson, D. J., & Sanford, R. N. *The authoritarian personality.* New York: Harper, 1950.

Allport, G. W. *The nature of prejudice.* Reading, Mass.: Addison-Wesley, 1954.

Apple, W., Streeter, L. A., & Krauss, R. M. Effects of pitch and speech rate on personal attributions. *Journal of Personality and Social Psychology,* 1979, *37,* 715–727.

Arthur, B., Farrar, D., & Bradford, G. Evaluation reactions of college students to dialect differences in the English of Mexican-Americans. *Language and Speech,* 1974, *17,* 255–270.

Bennett, R., & Eckman, J. Attitudes toward ageing: a critical examination of recent literature and implications of future research. In C. Eisdorfer & M. P. Powell (Eds.), *The psychology of adult development and ageing*. Washington, DC.: American Psychological Association, 1973.

Bradac, J. J., Courtright, J. A., Schmidt, G., & Davies, R. A. The effects of perceived status and linguistic diversity upon judgements of speaker attributes and message effectiveness. *Journal of Psychology*, 1976, *93*, 213-220.

Brennan, E. M., & Brennan, J. S. Accent scaling and language attitudes: reactions to Mexican-American English speech. *Language and Speech*, 1981, *24*, 207-221. (a)

Brennan, E. M., & Brennan, J. S. Measurements of accent and attitude toward Mexican-American speech. *Journal of Psycholinguistic Research*, 1981, *10*, 487-501. (b)

Brennan, E. M., Ryan, E. B., & Dawson, W. E. Scaling of apparent accentedness by magnitude estimation and sensory modality matching. *Journal of Psycholinguistic Research*, 1975, *4*, 27-36.

Brown, B. L., Strong, W. J., & Rencher, A. C. Fifty-four voices from two: the effects of simultaneous manipulations of rate, mean fundamental frequency, and variance of fundamental frequency on ratings of personality from speech. *Journal of Acoustic Society of America*, 1974, *55*, 313-318.

Buss, A. H. *The psychology of aggression*. New York: Wiley, 1961.

Buttino, A. J., & Sebastian, R. J. *Effects of target's ethnicity and anger arousal on aggression*. Unpublished manuscript, University of Notre Dame, 1978.

Bryne, D. *The attraction paradigm*. New York: Academic Press, 1971.

Byrne, D., & Clore, G. L. A reinforcement model of evaluative responses. *Personality*, 1970, *1*, 103-128.

Cantor, N., & Mischel, W. Prototypes in person perception. In L. Berkowitz (Ed.), *Advances in experimental social psychology* (Vol. 12). New York: Academic Press, 1979.

Carranza, M. A. Attitudinal research on Hispanic language varieties. In E. B. Ryan., & H. Giles (Eds.), *Attitudes towards language variation: social and applied contexts*. London: Edward Arnold, 1982.

Clore, G. L., & Byrne, D. A reinforcement-affect model of attraction. In T. L. Huston (Ed.), *Foundations of interpersonal attraction*. New York: Academic Press, 1974.

Colette-Pratt, C. Attitudinal predictors of devaluation of old age in a multigenerational sample. *Journal of Gerontology*, 1976, *31*, 193-197.

Cowgill, O., & Holmes, L. C. *Ageing and modernisation*. New York: Appleton-Century-Crofts, 1972.

Crockett, W. H., Press, A. N., & Osterkamp, M. The effect of deviations from stereotyped expectations upon attitudes towards older persons. *Journal of Gerontology*, 1979, *34*, 368-374.

De la Zerda, N., & Hopper, R. Employment interviewers' reactions to Mexican-American speech. *Communication Monographs*, 1979, *46*, 126-134.

Dienstbier, R. A. A modified theory of prejudice emphasizing the mutual causality of racial prejudice and anticipated belief differences. *Psychological Review*, 1972, *79*, 146-160.

Dion, K. K., Berscheid, E., & Walster, E. E. What is beautiful is good. *Journal of Personality and Social Psychology*, 1972, *24*, 285-290.

Donnerstein, E., & Donnerstein, M. Research in the control of inter-racial aggression. In R. G. Geen & E. C. O'Neal (Eds.), *Perspectives on aggression*. New York: Academic Press, 1976.

Dowd, J. J., & Bengtson, V. L. Ageing in minority populations: an examination of the double jeopardy hypothesis. *Journal of Gerontology*, 1978, *33*, 427-436.

Ehrlich, H. J. *The social psychology of prejudice*. New York: Wiley, 1973.

Erickson, B., Lind, E. A., Johnson, B. C., & O'Barr, W. M. Speech style and impression formation in a court setting: the effects of "powerful" and "powerless" speech. *Journal of Experimental Social Psychology,* 1978, *14,* 266-279.

Ferguson, C. A. *Towards a characterization of English foreigner talk.* Paper presented at the International Congress of Applied Linguistics, Copenhagen, Denmark, 1972.

Fraser, B. Some "unexpected" reactions to various American-English dialects. In R. Shuy & R. Fasold (Eds.), *Language attitudes: current trends and prospects.* Washington, D.C.: Georgetown University Press, 1973.

Genthner, R. W. & Taylor, S. P. Physical aggression as a function of racial prejudice and the race of the target. *Journal of Personality and Social Psychology,* 1973, *27,* 207-210.

Giles, H. Ethnocentrism and the evaluation of accented speech. *British Journal of Social and Clinical Psychology,* 1971, *10,* 187-188.

Giles, H., & Powesland, P. F. *Speech style and social evaluation.* New York: Academic Press, 1975.

Giles, H., Scherer, K. R., & Taylor, D. M. Speech markers in social interaction. In K. R. Scherer & H. Giles (Eds.), *Social markers in speech.* Cambridge: Cambridge University Press, 1979.

Giles, H., & St. Clair, R. M. (Eds.) *Language and social psychology.* Baltimore: University Park Press, 1979.

Giles, H., & Sassoon, C. The effects of speakers' accent, social class background and message style on British listeners' social judgements. *Language and communication,* 1983, *3,* 305-313.

Glass, D. C., & Singer, J. E. *Urban stress: experiments on noise and social stresses.* New York: Academic Press, 1972.

Goldstein, M., & Davies, E. E. Race and belief: a further analysis of the social determinants of behavioural intentions. *Journal of Personality and Social Psychology,* 1978, *22,* 346-355.

Gouaux, C. Induced affective states and interpersonal attraction. *Journal of Personality and Social Psychology,* 1971, *20,* 37-43.

Griffith, W., & Veitch, R. Hot and crowded: influences of population density and temperature on interpersonal affective behaviour. *Journal of Personality and Social Psychology,* 1971, *17,* 92-98.

Helfrich, H. Age markers in speech. In K. R. Scherer & H. Giles (Eds), *Social markers in speech.* Cambridge: Cambridge University Press, 1979.

Kalin, R., Rayko, D. S., & Love, N. The perception and evaluation of job candidates with four different ethnic accents. In H. Giles, W. P. Robinson, & P. M. Smith (Eds.) *Language: Social psychological perspectives.* Oxford: Pergamon Press, 1980.

Karlins, M., Coffman, T. L., & Walters, G. On the fading of social stereotypes: studies in three generations of college students. *Journal of Personality and Social Psychology,* 1969, *13,* 1-16.

Katz, D., & Braly, K. W. Racial stereotypes of 100 college students. *Journal of Abnormal and Social Psychology,* 1933, *28,* 280-290.

Kelley, K., & Byrne, D. Strength of instigation as a determinant of the aggression-attraction relationship. *Motivation and Emotion,* 1977, *1,* 29-38.

Kenrick, D. T., & Johnson, G. A. Interpersonal attraction in aversive environments: a problem for the classical conditioning paradigm? *Journal of Personality and Social Psychology,* 1979, *37,* 572-579.

Kent, D. P. The Negro aged. *Gerontologist,* 1971, *11,* 26-29.

Kogan, N. Beliefs, attitudes and stereotypes about old people. *Research on Ageing,* 1979, *1,* 11-36.

Lambert, W. E. A social psychology of bilingualism. *Journal of Social Issues*, 1967, *23*, 91-109.

LeVine, R. A., & Campbell, D. T. *Ethnocentrism: theories of conflict, ethnic attitudes, and group behaviour.* New York: Wiley, 1972.

Lott, A. J., & Lott, B. E. The power of liking: consequences of interpersonal attitudes derived from a liberalized view of secondary reinforcement. In L. Berkowtiz (Ed.), *Advances in experimental social psychology* (Vol. 6). New York: Academic Press, 1972.

Lott, A. J., & Lott, B. E. The role of reward in the formation of positive interpersonal attitudes. In T. L. Huston (Ed.), *Foundations of interpersonal attraction.* New York: Academic Press, 1974.

Manuel, R. *Double, triple, and quadruple jeopardy: the black aged.* Paper presented to the Annual Meeting of the Gerontological Society, San Francisco, 1977.

McTavish, D. G. Perceptions of old people: a review of research methodologies and findings. *Gerontologist*, 1971, *11*, 90-101.

Nisbett, R. E., & Wilson, T. D. The halo effect: evidence for unconscious alteration of judgements. *Journal of Personality and Social Psychology*, 1977, *35*, 250-256.

Palmore, E. B., & Manton, K. Ageism compared to racism and sexism. *Journal of Gerontology*, 1973, *28*, 363-369.

Palmore, E. B., & Manton, K. Modernisation and status of the aged: international correlations. *Journal of Gerontology*, 1974, *29*, 205-210.

Rey, A. Accent and employability: language attitudes. *Language Sciences*, 1977, *47*, 7-12.

Rokeach, M. Some unresolved issues in theories of beliefs, attitudes, and values. In *Nebraska Symposium on Motivation* (Volume 27). Lincoln: University of Nebraska Press, 1980.

Rokeach, M., & Mezei, L. Race and shared belief as factors in social choice. *Science*, 1966, *151*, 167-172.

Rubin, K. H., & Brown, I. D. R. A life-span look at person perception and its relationship to communicative interaction. *Journal of Gerontology*, 1975, *30*, 461-468.

Ryan, E. B. Social-psychological mechanisms underlying native speaker evaluations of non-native speech. *Studies in Second Language Acquisition*, 1983, *5*, 148-159.

Ryan, E. B., & Bulik, C. M. Evaluations of middle class and lower class speakers of standard American- and German-accented English. *Journal of Language and Social Psychology*, 1982, *1*, 51-61.

Ryan, E. B., & Capadano, H. L. Age perceptions and evaluative reactions towards adult speakers. *Journal of Gerontology*, 1978, *33*, 98-102.

Ryan, E. B., & Carranza, M. A. Evaluative reactions towards speakers of standard English and Mexican-American accented English. *Journal of Personality and Social Psychology*, 1975, *31*, 855-863.

Ryan, E. B., Carranza, M. A., & Moffie, R. W. Reactions towards varying degrees of accentedness in the speech of Spanish-English bilinguals. *Language and Speech*, 1977, *20*, 24-26.

Ryan, E. B., & Giles, H. (Eds). *Attitudes towards language variation: social and applied contexts.* London: Edward Arnold, 1982.

Ryan, E. B., & Sebastian, R. J. The effects of speech style and social class background on social judgements of speakers. *British Journal of Social and Clinical Psychology*, 1980, *19*, 229-233.

Schneider, D. J., Hastorf, A. H., & Ellsworth, P. C. *Person perception* (2nd ed.). Reading, Mass.: Addison-Wesley, 1979.

Sebastian, R. J., Ryan, E. B., & Abbott, A. R. *Social judgements of speakers of different ages.* Paper presented at the Annual Meeting of Midwestern Psychological Association, Detroit, 1981.

Sebastian, R. J., Ryan, E. B., & Corso, L. Social judgements of speakers with differing degrees of accent. *Social Behaviour and Personality,* in press.

Sebastian, R. J., Ryan, E. B., Keogh, T., & Schmidt, A. The effects of negative affect arousal on reactions to speakers. In H. Giles., W. P. Robinson., & P. Smith (Eds.), *Language: social psychological perspectives.* Oxford: Pergamon Press, 1980.

Shuntich, R. J. Some effects of attitudinal similarity and exposure on attraction and aggression. *Journal of Research in Personality,* 1976, *10,* 155-165.

Shuy, R. W. Subjective judgements in sociolinguistic analysis. In J. E. Alatis (Ed.), *Linguistics and the teaching of standard English to speakers of other languages or dialects.* Washington, D.C.: Georgetown University Press, 1969.

Simpson, G. E., & Yinger, J. M. *Racial and cultural minorities: An analysis of prejudice and discrimination* (4th ed.). New York: Harper & Row, 1972.

Smedley, J. W., & Bayton, J. A. Evaluative race-class stereotypes by race and perceived class of subjects. *Journal of Personality and Social Psychology,* 1978, *36,* 530-535.

Snow, C. E., & Ferguson, C. A. (Eds.). *Talking to children: language input and acquisition.* Cambridge: Cambridge University Press, 1977.

Stein, D. D., Hardyck, J. A., & Smith, M. Race and belief: an open and shut case. *Journal of Personality and Social Psychology,* 1965, *1,* 281-290.

Stewart, M. A., & Ryan, E. B. Attitudes towards younger and older adult speakers: effects of varying speech rates. *Journal of Language and Social Psychology,* 1982, *1,* 91-109.

Stewart, M. A., Ryan, E. B., & Giles, H. Accent and social class effects on status and solidarity evaluations. *Personality and Social Psychology Bulletin,* 1985, *11,* 98-105,

Tajfel, H. Experiments in intergroup discrimination. *Scientific American,* 1970, *223,* 96-102.

Taylor, D. M., & Giles, H. At the crossroads of research into language and ethnic relations. In H. Giles & B. Saint-Jacques (Eds.), *Language and ethnic relations.* New York: Pergamon Press, 1979.

Triandis, H. C., & Davis, E. E. Race and belief as determinants of behavioural intentions. *Journal of Personality and Social Psychology,* 1965, *2,* 715-725.

Triandis, H. C., Loh, W. D., & Levin, L. A. Race, status, quality of spoken English, and opinions about civil rights as determinants of interpersonal attitudes. *Journal of Personality and Social Psychology,* 1966, *3,* 468-472.

Triandis, H. C., & Triandis, L. M. Race, social class, religion, and nationality as determinants of social distance. *Journal of Abnormal and Social Psychology,* 1960, *61,* 110-118.

Tucker, G. R., & Lambert, W. E. White and Negro listeners' reactions to various American-English dialects. *Social Forces,* 1969, *47,* 463-468.

Ward, R. A. *The ageing experience: an introduction to social gerontology.* New York: H. B. Lippincott, 1979.

West, S. G., & Brown, T. J. Physical attractiveness, the severity of the emergency and helping: a field experiment and interpersonal simulation. *Journal of Experimental Social Psychology,* 1975, *11,* 531-538.

Williams, F. *Explorations of the linguistic attitudes of teachers.* Rowley, Mass.: Newbury House, 1976.

# 6 Towards a Social Psychology of Voice Variations

Bruce L. Brown and Jeffrey M. Bradshaw
*Brigham Young University*

## INTRODUCTION

A number of reviews of the personality-speech and emotion-speech literature appeared in the early 1960s (Diehl, 1960; Kramer, 1963; Mahl & Schultze, 1964). Scherer has brought us up to date with valuable recent overviews of the functions of vocal signs in conversation (1979a) emotion and speech (1979b) and personality and speech (1979c). Siegman (1978) has also contributed an important review of the speech research that bears upon clinical concerns such as anxiety, pathology, personality and emotional state. Rather than duplicate what has already been treated very competently, our purpose in this chapter will be to re-examine (and sometimes re-analyze) a select few of the older studies in order to propose remedies for the apparent artificialities of much of current paralinguistic research. In other words, we aim to demonstrate how social-psychological studies of voice variations can uncover verifiable information about personality dynamics and social processes.

Two fundamental features of vocal qualities are distinctive: they are totally quantifiable (Brown, Strong & Rencher 1975, pp. 11-12) and are central mediators of social processes and interpersonal dynamics. In this chapter, we focus primarily upon the reflections of *personality* and *emotion* in vocal characteristics. We refer to and attempt a critique of some of the major contributions and established findings from the three Scherer reviews and tie them in with additional studies not reviewed there.

As Laver and Trudgill (1979)[1] convincingly argue, there is a wealth of information within the voice concerning the intentions, dispositions and dynamics of individuals: their physical selves as well as their inner worlds are reflected in their speech. Laver and Trudgill identify seven muscle systems which it is possible to isolate (respiratory, phonatory, pharyngeal, verlopharyngeal, lingual, labial and mandibular) and propose that:

> Speaking thus requires the most complex and skillful collaboration between the different muscle systems, whose cooperative actions all have to be precisely and intricately coordinated in time. It is not at all surprising, therefore, that in learning to control such a complex apparatus sufficiently to be able to produce auditorily acceptable imitations of speech patterns heard in one's social environment, speakers would nevertheless develop idiosyncracies of pronunciation that serve to individuate them within their own social group [p. 5].

Undoubtedly this individuation is intricately tied to the development of people's unique personalities, both through (1) the reflections of their intentions and preferences in their selection of *vocal patterns* and (2) the view they get of themselves through their biologically-fixed *vocal features* and the reactions others have to them. The problem is in unravelling the tremendous complexity of the vocal information. Substantial progress is being made in working out the ways in which anatomical variations and the functioning of the seven muscular systems of speech are realized acoustically (see, for example, the work of Laver, 1968, 1975 and 1978; and of Titze, 1973 and 1974). The major difficulties have been, and will be, in dealing with the psychological dimensions: personality and emotion.

## PERSONALITY AND VOCAL PATTERNS

The widespread public interest in radio during the 1930s and 1940s was reflected in part by the vast amount of research at that time which looked at the voice as a mirror of the personality. By the next decade, however, such research effort had been almost entirely abandoned because of repeated failures to find any noteworthy correspondence between subjective judgements of personality from voice and the results of standardized measures of personality.

Since that time, most research has ignored the accuracy question and has split into two divergent directions (See Fig. 6.1).[2] These have been identified by Scherer (1979c):

---

[1]The Laver and Trudgill chapter is a very good summary of the phonological and linguistic work that has been done in categorizing, taxonomizing and defining various kinds of linguistic markers.

[2]See Scherer's (1979c) chapter where he uses an adaptation of the Brunswik "lens model" to set this distinction out in more detail.

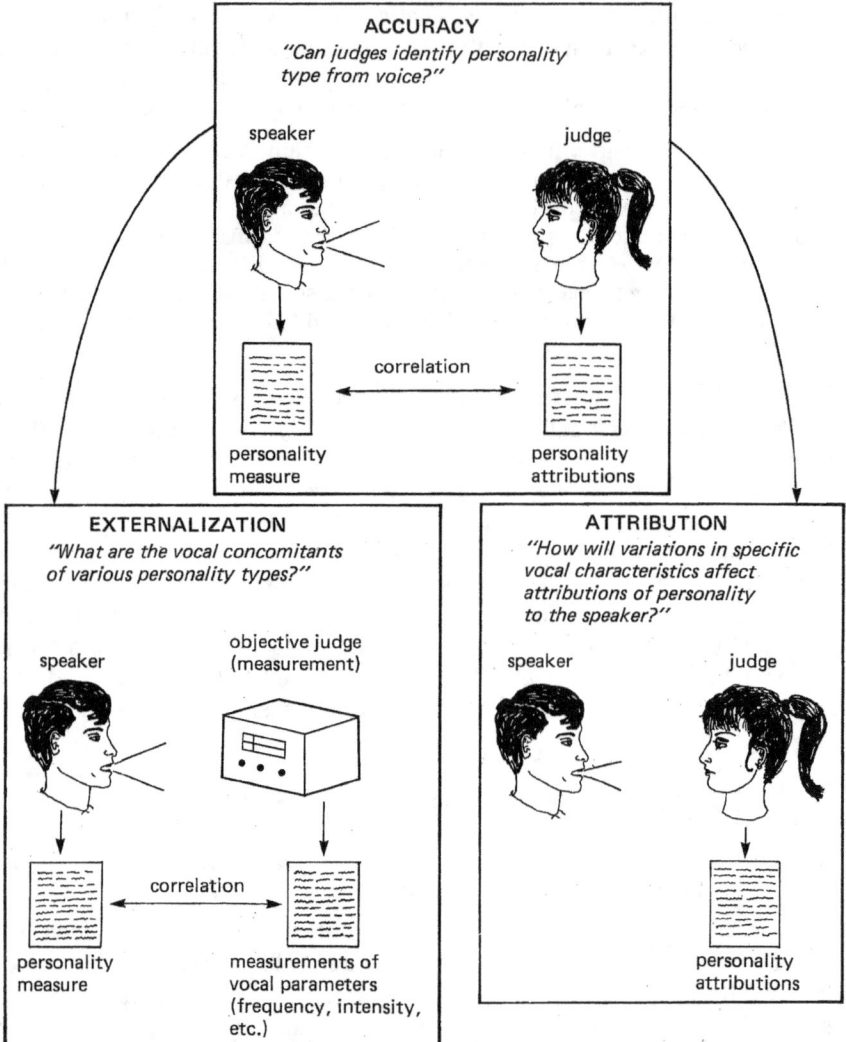

FIG. 6.1 A comparison of the standard accuracy, externalization and attribution research paradigms for studying the relationship between personality and voice.

1. *Externalization* studies, which have more or less kept the older research paradigm but have replaced naive subjective judgements with "expert ratings, systematic coding, or electro-acoustic analyses [p. 151]." These analyses are then compared with standardized personality measures.

TABLE 6.1
Potential Sources of Problems for Studies of Speech and Personality

|  | Inadequate Speech Measurement? | Nonexperimental (Correlative)? | Inadequate Personality Measurement? |
|---|---|---|---|
| Accuracy Studies | no | yes | yes |
| Externalization Studies | yes | yes | yes |
| Attribution Studies | no | no | no |

2. *Attribution* studies, which continue to rely on subjective judgements of personality but which make no attempt to relate them to a criterion of accuracy.

Table 6.1 shows a list of potential trouble spots for studies of speech and personality. As can be seen, the accuracy and externalization studies hold the monopoly on these problems, while attribution studies are relatively problem free. Why this is so becomes clear in examining Fig. 6.2.

Figure 6.2 shows the dilemma of externalization studies — the independent variable is one based on social judgement, but the dependent variable is objective. Also, it is hard to conceive of how the independent variable could be manipulated, so externalization studies are hopelessly correlational. Attribution studies reverse this, giving the right combination for good experimental studies: An objective, manipulable independent variable and a dependent variable that is, although subjective, measureable without argument. Attributions of personality are straightforwardly social judgements, conceptually simple and quite easily measureable, compared to the conceptual difficulties of measuring personality. Accuracy studies also share the problem of the clouded conceptual status of personality measurement.

The first problem of Table 6.1, *inadequate speech measurement,* is soluble. It is possible now with Fast Fourier transforms and related acoustic analysis methods almost totally to capture numerically the information in speech (see Chapter 7). Speech that is synthesized from the numerical representation is, in the best examples, very similar to real speech (Brown et al., 1973).[3] The very important work left to be done in speech analysis is that of finding the most useful ways of summarizing the tremendous

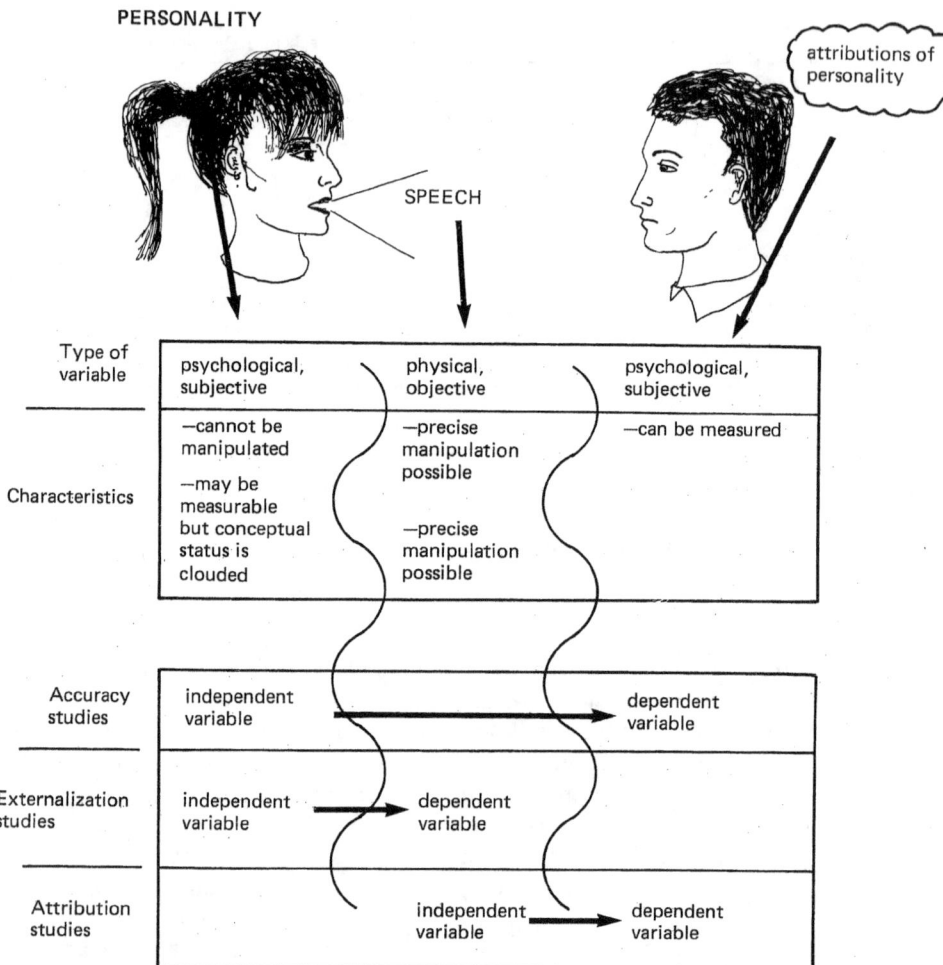

FIG. 6.2  The relative strength of attribution studies and the weaknesses of externalization and accuracy studies.

amount of data that comes from the numerical representation of pitch-tempo patterns and power spectrum, and pulling it together in a theory that relates the acoustic realization to physiological/anatomical causes.[4]

The *correlative* nature of the accuracy and the externalization studies has prevented researchers from obtaining the kind of clean results needed for the formulation of testable hypotheses and cogent theory. Even in the best studies, correlations are small and the relationships are tenuous and unstable from one study to another. Little emerges in the way of a coherent, convincing pattern.

One way to stabilize and give some coherence to the results is to use factor analysis of the correlation matrices. There is usually considerable redundancy in both speech and personality variables, and factor score plottings show the relationships in terms of "bundles" of variables, which are more stable than single variables. (See Figs. 6.3 and 6.4 on pp. 159 and 160, for example.)

Another way to improve studies of personality reflections in speech so that they show "cleaner" results is to examine unique or extreme exemplars of various traits. In this way the chances are better of getting clear "ideal" patterns of vocal properties that differentiate one trait from another, rather than just correlating a bunch of vocal measures with a bunch of trait measures on a more randomly varying sample. Looking at the whole *gestalt* of vocal patterns characteristic of extreme exemplars of various traits will give much clearer results than endless correlational tables.

*Inadequate personality measurement* has also plagued accuracy and externalization studies from the very beginning. What is most surprising in examining this literature is that the quality of the paper and pencil tests used in this research has only rarely been questioned. When, for example, correlations between personality measures and personality attributions have been slight, fault has typically been assigned to the inaccurate "vocal stereotypes" which presumably bias subjective ratings. But, as we shall argue below, it is just as likely (perhaps more so) that inadequate personality measures have been largely responsible for the paucity of useful findings.

---

[3]Scherer's presentation (1979c, footnote 5, p. 184) of the results of "realism" tests is misleading. Whereas his account suggests that rate changed synthetic speech only sounds normal 50% to 58% of the time, what we in fact found was that when judges are told that some voices are synthetic and some are natural, they *mistake* synthetic for natural 50% to 58% of the time. It is important to add that even natural voices are judged to be synthetic about 5% of the time. Also, the quality of synthesized voices has improved since that time. Scherer's reference for the data is from a summary paper (Brown et al., 1975). Perhaps he did not have access to the original study (Brown et al., 1973).

[4]Titze (1973) in his doctoral dissertation used classical mechanics to mathematically model the relation between vocal anatomical functioning and its acoustic realization. Scherer in his 1979 review of emotion in speech (Scherer, 1979b) proposed a similar integration of anatomical correlates with the acoustic and psychological data, and even though he does so on the basis of the rather limited data available, the value of such an approach in producing testable hypotheses is obvious. Theoretical integration of externalization studies, giving a coherent account of why particular vocal qualities are associated with particular personal characteristics, will be heavily dependent upon the findings of such acoustical-anatomical work, exemplified in the work of Laver (1968; 1975; and 1978) and that of Titze (1973; 1974; and Titze & Talkin, 1979).

We propose, as an alternative to standard tests, to use the more direct method of nomination by social consensus to select exemplars of various traits.[5] In interpreting results, we would then say, "This vocal pattern is characteristic of those who are nominated by a number of other persons as being the most dominant person they know," rather than ". . .characteristic of those who judge themselves to be high in dominance," or ". . .characteristic of those who answer questions on a standardized scale in a way that is scored (for whatever reason, logical or empirical) as being dominant."

We would not wish, of course, to make the mistake of assuming that a social consensus can be the criterion in an accuracy study. If there is one lesson from the flurry of interpersonal-perception accuracy studies of the 1950s and 1960s, it is that we have no basis for talking about accuracy unless we have an objectively assessable reality. If we were to ask judges, for example, to identify the voice of a dominant person, we would have little basis for saying they were wrong or right according to whether their choice agreed with our social consensus nomination. If we give them all the information (e.g., that some person was nominated more than anyone else in his dormitory as being dominant) and then ask them to identify which voice it is, accuracy can be assessed because we are asking them to identify a social decision, which is real, did happen, etc., rather than appealing to some "ideal" of dominance separate from social judgement.

### Accuracy Studies

The first, and largest in scale, of the accuracy studies is T. H. Pear's (1931) collection of judgements of personality from the radio voice. With the assistance of the British Broadcasting Company, he secured the judgements of 4,000 listeners concerning birthplace, occupations, age, and place of residence of each of nine speakers. Although these judgements were difficult to quantify, given their basis in the auditors' free descriptions, his results enabled him to make some tentative conclusions about their accuracy. Not surprisingly, sex (see Chapter 4) was always judged

---

[5]In one study (Dicks, Brown & Wells, 1977) our research group found that extreme high and low scorers on the POI, a test based upon "self-actualization" theory, did not differ in their ability to recognize portrayed emotions or their ability to portray them, but when we switched to a "nomination" strategy, comparing those who had been nominated as being unusually well adjusted with two control groups, the nominated group was substantially better at judging emotion portrayals. Scherer (1972, 1978) has also had good results with nomination strategies. He has shown that "both self and peer ratings of extroversion can be accurately inferred from voice quality for American speakers. For German speakers, peer ratings of dominance and assertiveness correlate significantly with respective attributions made on the basis of voice quality samples." (Scherer, 1979c, p. 190.)

correctly (except in the case of one eleven year-old child). Vocation and physical descriptions were sometimes judged with astonishing success. Age was estimated quite well by the listeners, although there was a strong tendency for estimates to centre in the thirty age group (see Chapter 5).

Allport and Cantril (1934), inspired by Pear's (1931) and Herzog's (1933) auspicious beginnings, set out to design a more careful study of personality judgements from voice in eight separate experiments with a total of 587 judges and 18 different speakers. Information pertaining to eight "objective" criteria (age, height, complexion, appearance in photographs, appearance in person, handwriting, vocation, and political preference) was gathered. Information was also obtained for three other criteria: extroversion/introversion was measured by the Heidbreder scale; ascendance/submission by the Allport "A-S Reaction Study"; and dominant values by the Allport and Vernon "Study of Values." In each experiment, standard passages from Charles Dickens, Lewis Carroll, and similar sources were used. Judges in each of these experiments were given descriptions of personality characteristics of speakers and asked to match them with the voices.

Age was identified quite accurately but, as in Pear's study, there was a tendency for estimates to centre in the thirty age group. Contrary to Herzog's (1933) findings, height was identified successfully in only one of four experiments. The one experiment involving complexion yielded somewhat significant results, as did the ones on appearance in photographs and in person. Vocation and political preferences were identified with moderate success, but handwriting yielded no results of significance.[6]

One of the personality measures (dominant values) gave positive and significant results in half of the studies. With the other two personality measures (extroversion and ascendance) an interesting thing happened, which Allport and Cantril (1934) state is "quite typical of our findings" — namely, that both "significantly positive" and "significantly negative" results are reported,[7] leading them to conclude that "the uniformity of opinion regarding the personality of radio speakers is somewhat in excess of the accuracy of such opinion (p.50)."

Also in 1934, Taylor published the results of his study. Recordings were

---

[6]It is unfortunate that most of these old studies do not give enough data from their results to construct a "contingency table" which shows the distribution of judged values for each measured speaker type. (This particular type of contingency table is often called a "confusion matrix" in that it displays the patterns of confusion in the judgements of actual categories.) When enough data is given, we can use Information Theory statistics to judge accuracy in a way that allows across-study comparisons (see footnote 9).

[7]The index of accuracy in this study is particularly obscure and is incomparable with other studies.

made of 20 subjects, including two groups measured high and low on neuroticism (Thurstone Personality Schedule) and a group that was randomly selected, and each recording was played to at least 20 judges. Subjects had previously filled out a self-descriptive questionnaire by putting a plus, minus or question mark next to 136 items concerning various personality traits (32 items from Freyd's list of introvert characteristics, 25 from the Thurstone Personality Schedule, and the remainder from "words commonly used to describe people"). Judges filled out the same questionnaire for each voice they heard but despite a high degree of agreement between judges, the correlations between their ratings and the subjects' self ratings indicated no relationship whatsoever. In fact, Taylor (1934) concluded that there "is a slight but statistically significant tendency for the auditors to be most consistent in their judgements when they agree least with the subjects themselves [p. 24-7]."[8]

Eisenberg and Zalowitz (1938) selected eight extremely dominant and eight extremely non-dominant women using the Maslow "Social Personality Inventory" and a personal interview. Phonograph records of their voice were played for 43 judges who were only able to judge dominance a little better than chance. This is in contrast to Allport and Cantril's positive findings with their personality measure of dominance. As in previous studies, social agreement was high despite the "inaccuracy" of the judgements.

From 1939 to 1943, a series of studies was carried out by Fay and Middleton including, among other things, judgements of Spranger personality types from voice (1939, from the Allport and Vernon "Study of Values"), Kretschmerian body types (1940b, no actual morphological measurements were made), intelligence (1940a, Terman Group Test of Mental Ability), sociability (1941, Flanagan sociability scale of the Bernreuter "Personality Inventory"), introversion (1942, also from the Bernreuter), and leadership (1943, ratings by fraternity brothers). Although the Spranger personality-type and Kretschmer body-type studies showed a better-than-chance accuracy,[9] judgements of intelligence from voice were "only fairly reliable" and sociability and leadership ratings revealed no more than chance accuracy. In each study, however, the phenomenon of significant inter-judge reliability was reported.

If one takes these studies at face value the inaccuracy of judgements of

---

[8]It is unfortunate that Taylor did not use an "accuracy of response prediction" paradigm in which the judges estimate what speakers would put on the questionnaire for themselves rather than putting what they think the speakers "are." In this case, there would be an "assessible reality," which would probably give much higher accuracy scores, and even if not, we would know that it was due to the judge's inability rather than the conceptual confusion of what the speaker "really is.")

personality from voice seems apparent. In every review of accuracy research only one conclusive finding emerges: *There is nearly always astonishingly high inter-judge agreement despite the poor accuracy (in the sense of personality ratings agreeing with the standardized tests of the trait in question).*

The standard way of interpreting this has been to assume that the judges are rating on the basis of inaccurate "vocal stereotypes." To quote Allport and Cantril (1934), "the various features of personality are associated in the minds of the judges (with) some preconception of the type of voice to which these features correspond [p.50]." Although judges share these preconceptions about what the voice of a certain personality type sounds like, researchers have assumed that these stereotypes have little or no basis in reality because of their disparity from assessments of personality made by paper and pencil measures.

We propose an alternative view: *That the inaccuracy of personality judgements from voice has far more to do with the inadequacy of the personality measures used than the incompetency of judges to assess traits from vocal properties.* This view is especially admissible in the light of the fact that, as Kjeldergaard (1968) points out, there is considerable accuracy whenever certain *objectively measurable* characteristics such as age, sex, social class, etc. are measured. (Social class judgements typically correlate .80+ with actual numerical social class indices, see Brown & Lambert, 1976.) Other more recent studies and reviews of the vocal realization of objective characteristics such as sex (Smith, 1979), age (Helfrich, 1979; Ryan, 1979; Ptacek & Sander, 1966), social class (Robinson, 1979; Brown & Lambert, 1976), and ethnicity (Giles, 1979) also show surprising accuracy.

In retrospect, especially with the well-established unreliability of most of the personality tests used in these studies,[10] it seems strange that it would have been assumed that the "stereotyped" judgements were in error rather than the tests. It seems particularly strange since the concept of personality is itself rooted in the perception one person has of another. The question of whether person $A$ is "dominant" is ultimately a social

---

[9]Fay and Middleton's 1939 "Spranger personality types" study, and their 1940b "Kretschmer body types" study *did* give us enough information to make confusion matrices and to compute Information Theory statistics as suggested in footnote 6. For most of the sub-studies within the "Spranger" study, the percentage of personality information being communicated to judges by the vocal qualities was between 20% and 25% (taken from the "coefficients of constraint" in the Information Theory statistics). For the "Kretschmer" study the amount of "body type" information communicated was 5% to 8% for male judges and 14% to 17% for female judges.

[10]See for example, Tyler's (1953) critique of the Bernreuter "Personality Inventory," which formed the criterion for many of the personality and voice studies.

perception question.[11] We cannot be satisfied in any final way by agreeing that he or she is dominant if scoring high on a particular dominance test, since it is ultimately only a secondary derivative from social judgement (some particular personality theory, explicit or implied); if his or her test is "construct validated," or if consensual validation is used, we are correlatively referred to some social perception criterion. A number of personality theorists (e.g., Mischel, 1973) have articulated the dilemma: *Although personal identity seems to be a very stable thing, personality tests are notably unreliable, with little agreement among alternate measures of the supposed same trait.*[12]

Other researchers (Meehl & Hathway, 1946) have come to the conclusion that self-report scales are "notoriously susceptible to 'faking' or 'lying' in one way or another, as well as . . .even greater susceptibility to unconscious self-deception and role playing on the part of individuals who may be consciously quite honest and sincere[13] in their responses [p. 525]." More recently Sackeim and Gur (1979) concluded from their study that self-deception contributes significantly to the invalidity of self-report inventories and more substantially than does intentional lying.

We propose that if adequate alternatives to standard personality measures (such as the nomination technique described above, or selecting speakers on the basis of objective categories that are related to personality, e.g., occupation, college major or age) are utilized we will find judges to have high accuracy in identifying these from voice.

### Externalization Studies

Scherer (1979c) describes the present state of research on externalization as "bleak" and "the amount of hard data negligible," and he hastens to add that this is not because of a lack of effort (there are more than 1500 references in Görlitz's 1972 review). A coherent pattern does not emerge from these "gargantuan proceedings."

---

[11]One may argue that the action pattern, the behaviour of a person, is public data, assessable by a third person observer. One way to be freed from this delusion is to carefully read Taylor's influential account (1964) of how identifying actions requires introspective attribution. There is no meaning to the action "pattern" until imposed by a human judge (either the actor himself or an observer).

[12]Could this be, for example, why Allport and Cantril (1934) in reporting judgements of dominance from voice using Allport's "A–S Reaction Study," reported findings not in accord with Eisenberg and Zalowitz's (1938), who used Maslow's "Social Personality Inventory"?

[13]Note this strange implicit hypothesis of a conscious honesty and an unconscious dishonesty that is so common in psychological literature. Compare to footnote 32 and the accompanying text and references.

The crude speech variables used in almost all of the externalization studies reviewed by Scherer are not the primary defect, since such studies could be used for preliminary hypotheses to be tested with more precise methods, and the parallel comparisions of the subjective speech judgements with the quantitative ones would be valuable. The really serious problems are (1) the correlative nature of the studies and (2) the monumental problem of personality measurement, particularly in the accuracy studies. One of the best externalization studies, Scherer's "juror study," which uses precise measurements of speech, still gives very tenuous conclusions. (The complete study is not yet in print but a partial report is given in Scherer, 1979c.) The primary data are correlations among self- and peer-ratings for extroversion and emotional stability and a set of precise measures of fluency-related variables as well as pitch and "effort". The largest correlation reported between personality ratings and speech is −.65 (42% common variance). Even tenuous results are better than none, and a summary of the major findings of the best of the externalization studies on specific dimensions of voice may provide some groundwork for future work. We shall concentrate on three specific dimensions of voice: fundamental frequency, vocal intensity, and articulation/timbre.

*Fundamental Frequency:* Scherer, in his juror study, reports that higher fundamental frequency (F$\emptyset$) seems to be associated with self-ratings of competence and dominance in male Americans (and to a lesser degree in male German speakers), as well as self-ratings of discipline and dependability in male German and female American speakers.[14] He hypothesizes that a high degree of arousal may be associated with competence and dominance in males, which is in turn reflected in a heightened degree of muscle tone leading to characteristically higher F$\emptyset$. However, as Scherer (1979c) points out, this hypothesis is at present highly speculative since the only evidence results from studies of an increase in transitory states of arousal under stress.

---

[14]These variables, the self-ratings on specific trait dimensions, must undoubtedly have considerable redundancy with one another, and a much clearer and coherent pattern could probably be given by summarizing them with factor analytic plots like the one in Fig. 6.4 and other figures in this chapter.

Scherer finds in his (admittedly limited) sample that the mean F$\emptyset$ for American speakers (128Hz) is significantly lower that that of German speakers (161Hz, $p < .001$) which supports Laver's (1975, p. 268) impression of a very low pitch range in American males. As Scherer (1979) points out, "it would be a challenging task for social psychologists to determine whether the difference is due to physiological factors—possibly related to national character or modal personality—or to differential expectations or evaluations concerning desirable pitch levels—strongly influenced by historical tradition or mass media portrayals—or the interaction of both of these factors [pp. 157-158]."

*Vocal Intensity.* The personality trait most consistently associated with vocal intenstity is extroversion (Allport & Cantril, 1934; Trimboli, 1973). Consistent with these findings, Mallory and Miller (1958) report a very small (.14) correlation between "inadequate loudness" as rated by members of the speech department faculty and introversion as measured by the Bernreuter Personality Inventory. Mallory and Miller (1958) also report a negative correlation ($-.32$) between "inadequate loudness" and "dominance," but no such correlations were found in Scherer's juror study.

*Articulation and Timbre.* Moses' classic work *The voice of neurosis* (1954), which discussed a number of hypotheses concerning voice changes in patients experiencing affective disturbances, inspired Rousey and Moriarty (1965, and later, Rousey, 1974) to extend and substantiate some of these ideas. These authors propose that, as well as Freud's popular ideas on the meanings of slips of the tongue as applied to words, we consider his indirect suggestion of the psychological significance of an individual's misuse of specific sounds.

Rousey's (1974) analyses of detailed case studies have led him to form inferences concerning the relationship of personality patterns to the inability to master proper speech sounds. An example of one of these inferences is the following: "The misarticulation of the vowel *r* reflects lack of impulse control and minimal neurological disfunction [p.12]." Although the strength of the evidence for his specific hypotheses and his adoption of a psychoanalytic framework may not be convincing, his work certainly represents a pioneering effort to apply our knowledge of personality and speech to the practical diagnostic setting, and the possibility of linking specific vocal characteristics to their concomitants in the development of a child's personality is an exciting one. Undoubtedly anomalies of speech are reflective of personality, and a careful working out of that relationship will be a major contribution.

Lomax (1974) has speculated that phonatory and articulatory patterns are influenced by sociological as well as psychological factors, claiming that "back, loosely enunciated and lax sounds decrease, and front, narrow, sharply enunciated sounds generally increase as culture grows more complex and laden with rules [pp. 204-205]."

Ostwald (1963, 1965) was one of the first to use spectrographic methods of voice analysis to investigate the relationship between acoustical parameters of speech and types of personality. There are now very precise methods available for looking at power spectrum of voice, such as the "fast Fourier transform" method and the "predictor coefficient" method used in Scherer's "juror study" (see Scherer, 1979c), the Brown, Strong and Rencher speech synthesis studies (1973, 1974), Smith, Brown, Strong and Rencher (1975) and Apple, Streeter and Krauss (1979) and Stewart, Brown and Stewart (in preparation). Before these methods were well developed and became generally known, Ostwald (1965) devised a procedure that uses filters to obtain amplitude values for octave and half octave bands to provide a crude approximation to the power spectrum.

He identified certain qualitative categories of voice, such as "flat voice," associated with monotonous speech indicating depression, with sound energy spread evenly across the spectrum; "hollow voice," with only the fundamental frequency having much sound energy, the harmonics dropping off markedly in energy; "robust voice," associated with oratorical or theatrical speech. In later work, he used sound spectrograms which show the changes in power spectrum energy patterns over time, but his qualitative analysis of crude power spectrum data is much more interesting and illuminating. Even though in today's world the acoustic descriptions appear simplistic and naive, they suggest exciting possibilities for attribution studies in which experimental designs using speech synthesis methods could be used to test his hypotheses. For example, Ostwald (1965) suggests that:

> It is a fundamental fact of auditory perception that the human ear is most sensitive to tonal stimuli above 500 cycles per second. Almost all sounds calculated to arouse human beings — whistles, cries, sirens, screams — contain a large amount of sound energy above 500 cycles per second. On the other hand, the fundamental tone of the human voice, which is located at lower frequency levels, is so dispensable in ordinary conversation that telephone companies do not even bother to transmit it. We advance the hypothesis that speakers increase the amount of sound they emit at higher frequencies when they want to be listened to and reduce their high-frequency output when they prefer to be ignored. [pp. 85-86].[15]

## Attribution Studies

As Scherer points out in his review (1979c), the results of attribution studies are much clearer and much more stable than externalization studies, and it is possible to approach the attribution problem experimentally.[16]

---

[15]It is interesting to note Ostwald's "medical model" approach to voice as a symptom of "emotional disturbance" (he is an M.D.), such as his statement (1965) that "one man we studied in this way entered the hospital in a state of severe depression *resulting from* manic-depressive psychosis; his voices were uniformly flat [p. 84, our italics]." He views vocal qualities as rather involuntary indices of disturbance. In contrast, Warner (1982), and Beier (1966) see both the vocal properties and the "disturbance" as primarily intentional and communicative, even insistent. (See discussion of these authors on pp. 175-176.)

[16]There is an interesting example of a very recent study in which the much weaker correlation methodology is used even in an attribution setting (Aronovitch, 1976) where an experimental method could have been used.

Stagner (1936) was the first to study the ways in which specific vocal cues are used in the process of making judgements about personality, countering Allport and Cantril's (1934) view that such an undertaking would be "absurdly atomistic." The reliability of Stagner's (1936) findings, however, are questionable, given the small number of speakers and the lack of adequate instrumentation.

One of the best of the more recent attempts at an experimental paradigm is a study by Addington (1968) in which two male and two female trained speakers simulated a number of different voice qualities, pitch patterns and speaking rates (generating 252 "voices" from four), which were then rated by a large number of judges on semantic differential type adjectives.[17] We re-analyzed his data to simplify and clarify the effects of these subjective manipulations for the two male voices and obtained some interesting hypotheses to test with computer manipulation methods. Fig. 6.4 gives the results, but Figure 6.3 helps one to understand how to read Fig. 6.4

Suppose that we were to plot 14 of Addington's 252 voices (the two male speakers doing each of seven manipulations: breathy, thin, flat, nasal, tense, throaty and orotund) on only two of his 24 paired opposite adjectives, "feminine vs masculine" and "intelligent vs. stupid." Suppose also, that we knew enough about the geometry of correlation so that, instead of putting the two axes (feminine-masculine and intelligent-stupid) perpendicular to one another, which would only be proper if they were independent ($r = .00$), we put them with their positive poles 95.5° away from one another (as shown in Fig.6.3) because they are found to correlate with one another $r = .096$, the cosine of which is 95.5°. The position of one of the voice manipulations for one of the speakers in this two-dimensional space, then, is found at the intersection of a perpendicular from his score on the masculine-feminine axis and a perpendicular from his score on the intelligent-stupid axis. Speaker 1's "breathy" voice, for example, has a score of $1.2\sigma$ on the masculine-feminine axis (this is a $z$ score, and since the positive end of this axis is feminine, a positive score means toward the feminine end of the axis) and a score of $1.43\sigma$ on the

---

[17]Even though this study could in a sense be called experimental, because the same two male voices and the same two female voices are used with a number of voice dimensions manipulated in systematic combinations, it is not a precise experimental paradigm since it is doubtful that one can subjectively hold all other speech dimensions constant while altering a particular one. There is some evidence, however, that at least for the dimension of speech rate, subjective alterations give very similar patterns of judge ratings to those of computer altered voices (Stewart et al., in preparation). If such is also true of other vocal and speech dimensions, the findings of Addington may be essentially corroborated when the same speech dimensions are more carefully evaluated with the speech synthesis experimental methodology.

6. Towards a Social Psychology of Voice Variations    159

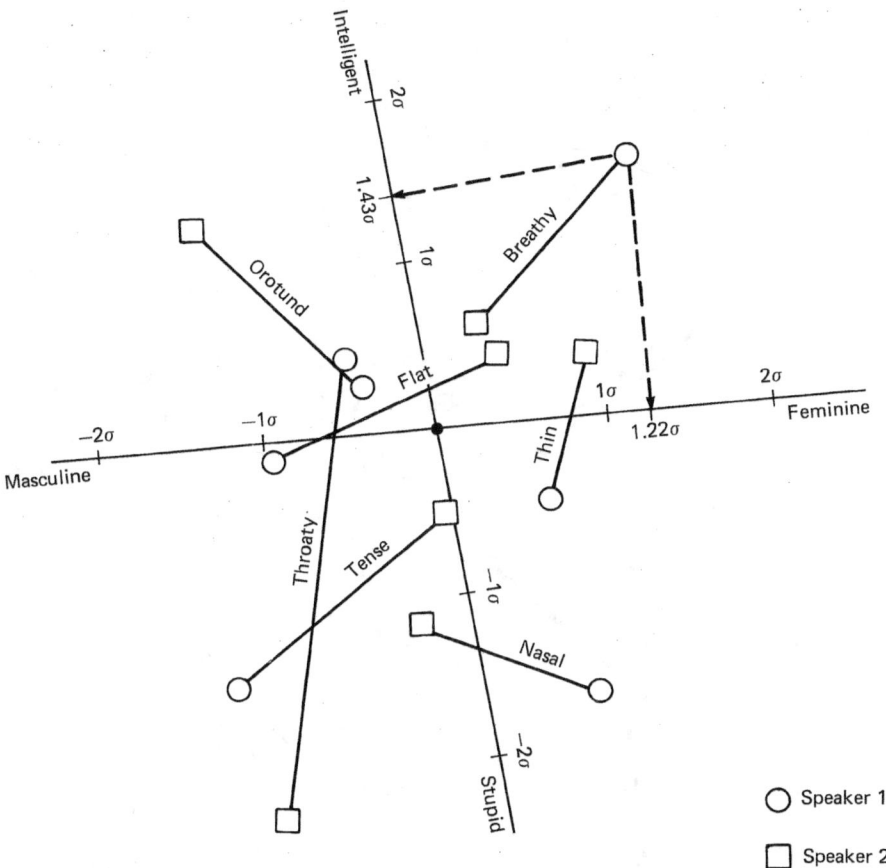

FIG. 6.3  Two male speakers in seven voice manipulations, plotted on only two of the 24 adjectives (Figure constructed from our reanalysis of the data from Addington, 1963, 1968). *Note:* The line connecting Speaker 1 with Speaker 2 for each manipulation is simply to make the two voices for each manipulation easier to find.

intelligent-stupid axis, so his point for the "breathy" voice in the two-dimensional space is located at the intersection of the two perpendiculars as shown in Fig. 6.3.

Suppose now that we wanted to see the positions of these seven manipulations for the two speakers for the other adjectives as well. If all gave independent information (all were uncorrelated with one another), this would require a 24-dimensional space representation for the 24 adjective pairs, or, more realistically, 276 graphs like Fig. 6.3 to show the plotting of all pair combinations of the 24 adjective pairs. Fortunately, there is considerable redundancy in the adjectives and they can all be

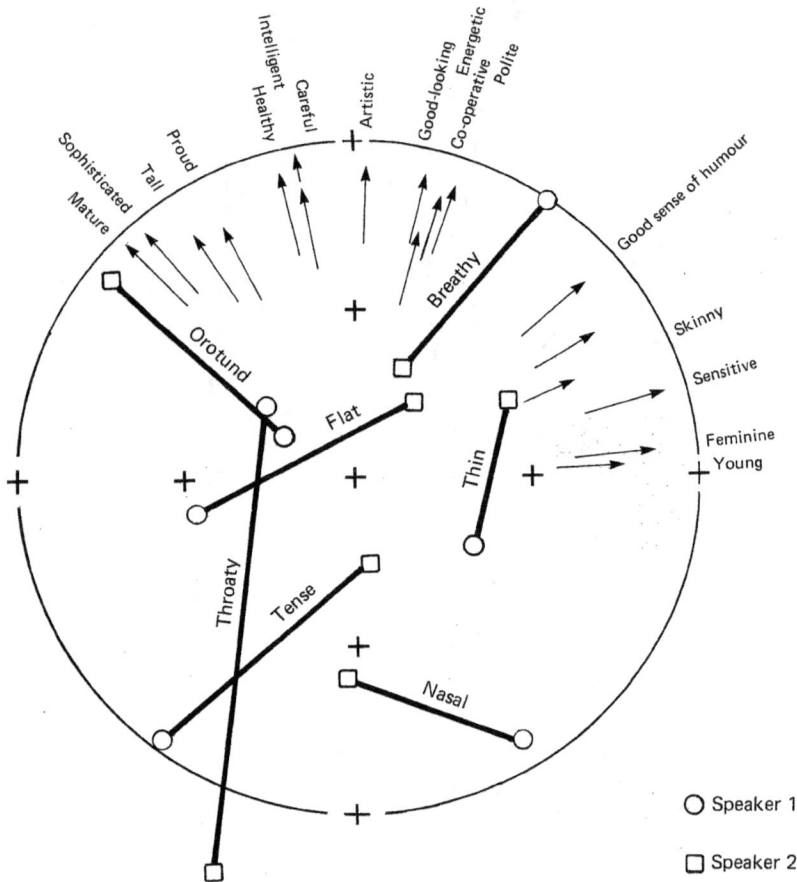

FIG. 6.4 Two male speakers in seven voice manipulations, plotted on all 24 adjectives. (Figure constructed from our reanalysis of the data from Addington, 1963, 1968: 17 of the 24 adjectives shown.)

located mostly in the same two-dimensional space of Fig. 6.3. Fig. 6.4 shows the same plotting with the other adjectives added. To know the standard score of any voice on any adjective, one simply drops a perpendicular from the plot of that voice to the adjective vector or axis in question.[18] Of course, not just any two-dimensional plane within the 24-

---

[18]If our factor analysis accounted for all the variance in the 24 adjectives with two factors, these projected scores on any adjective from the two-dimensional plotting would be exact. The length of the adjective vectors in Fig. 6.4 indicates the amount of variance in that adjective pair accounted for by the two factors. For those vectors that are shorter, then, the scores estimated from projections would be the least accurate.

dimensional space will do. This one was located by means of the principal factors method of factor analysis.

Although Addington also used a factor analysis to summarize his rating data, his factor structure is virtually uninterpretable, presumably because he computed correlations over both speakers and judges (thus causing a conflation of two sources of variance) and making an unnecessarily complex factorial structure. It is not clear from the paper whether this is the case, but this is a common error in analyzing data of this kind. Professor Addington graciously helped us obtain the original data from this study, his dissertation. From our factor analysis of ratings averaged over judges (found in Appendix II beginning on page 172 of Addington, 1963) we obtained the clear pattern shown in Fig.6.4. This figure gives a very terse summary of the findings of Addington's study. In examining the factor score positions of Speaker 1 and Speaker 2 (the two male speakers on the "orotund" manipulation) both voices can be seen to be relatively high on the vectors for such variables as "sophisticated," "mature," "tall," and "proud", Speaker 2 being considerably higher than Speaker 1 on these dimensions for that manipulation. Similarly, the "thin" manipulation gives rise to ratings high on "sensitive," "feminine," and "young". This is the case for both speakers. By contrast, there is considerable variance in the effect the "throaty" manipulation has on the two speakers' ratings, Speaker 2 being very low on vectors like "good looking," "cooperative," "polite," etc. for this manipulation, but Speaker 1 being about in the middle of the plotting on this manipulation. It is very difficult to pull this much information out of the original study because of the method in which the data are presented there. When one understands how to read them, factorial plots of this kind are very efficient summaries of multivariate data. Addington's study is by far the richest in information of any of the attribution studies up to the present time, and it would be very worthwhile to continue the kind of simplifying re-analysis begun in Fig. 6.4 to the remainder of the 252 speaker-manipulation combinations. The results will then have to be confirmed either by trying to do the same things using speech-synthesis technology (as employed in the studies described in the following paragraphs) to generate manipulations precisely, or by doing a careful acoustic analysis of Addington's original voice tape to determine just what the speakers were manipulating for each type of "voice."

At about the same time that Addington was doing his work, Kjeldergaard (1968), working with John Carroll at Harvard, did a similar experimental attribution study with five original voices, but with only four manipulations of each: "normal," "fast," "shouting," and "soft." Kjeldergaard's manipulations were incomplete (he had all of the manipulations for three of the speakers but only normal voices on two), not completely crossed, and the polarity on his adjective pairs was not sufficiently clear in the version of the paper we have to enable us to put it in the form of Fig. 6.4 for comparison. Therefore, we replicated his study with the rate manipulation ("fast" vs "normal") completely crossed (all possible combinations) with the "shout" vs. "soft" vs. "normal" manipulation, using a Latin-square presentation of six speakers each doing each of the six manipulation combinations and using natural speech (answers to three questions, to give three replications of the experiment), rather than a standard passage as Addington and Kjeldergaard had done. The detailed results of both this and the other Addington manipulations are being compiled, but would require much more space than the whole of this chapter, but Fig. 6.5 displays just the means for "normal" rate and "fast" placed in opposition, and the means for "shout" and "soft" placed in opposition. A "soft" voice is seen as more humble, unemotional, submissive, etc. and a "shout" voice is seen as more outgoing, energetic,

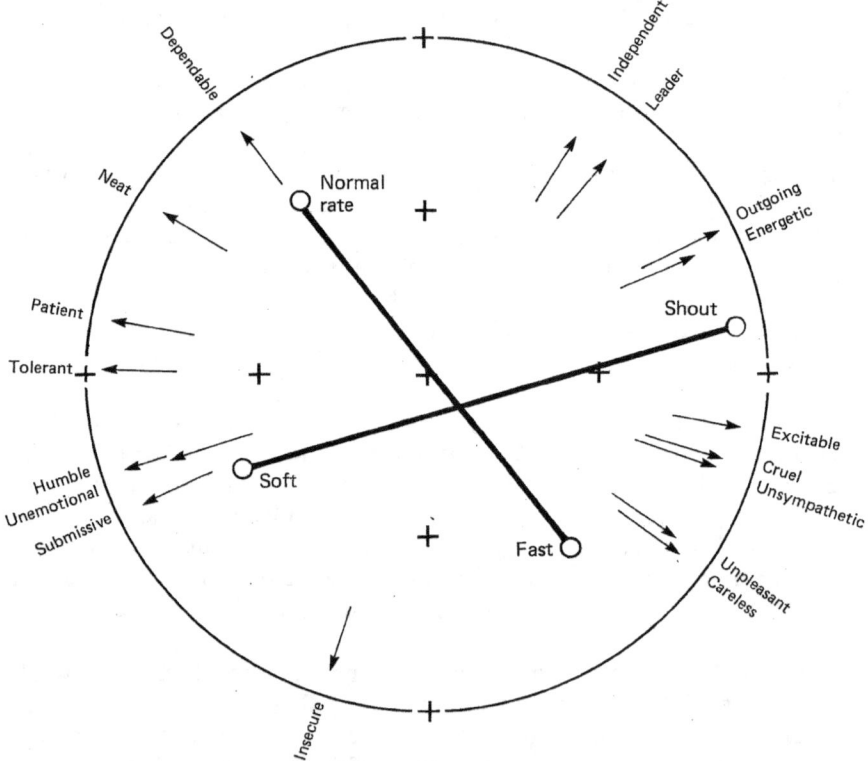

FIG. 6.5 A plotting of the mean factor scores for the "normal" rate vs. "fast" manipulation and for the "soft" vs. "shout" manipulation (Data from our replication of Kjeldergaard, 1968).

excitable, etc.[19] A "fast" voice is seen as more unpleasant, careless, unsympathetic, cruel, etc., whereas a "normal" rate voice is seen as more dependable, neat, patient, etc.

The first truly experimental studies, using a fast Fourier transforms speech synthesis method to manipulate precisely one parameter of voice at a time, were conducted in the early 1970s (Brown et al., 1973, 1974; and Smith et al., 1975) and tested the effects of rate, pitch (average F∅.) and intonation (variance of F∅.) on personality adjective judgements. The findings with respect to rate are clear cut and stable and most accurately demonstrated in the study by Smith et al. (1975).[20] Here it is shown that judgements on adjectives related to competence are a monotonically increasing function of phonemes per second. Moreover judgements on adjectives related to benevolence are an "inverted U" function of phonemes per second, with the most positive rating being given to the normal rate voice for each speaker (see Fig. 6 of Smith, et al., 1975; and the triple replication of these results under different circumstances in Brown, 1980b). The effects of intonation and pitch were much less clear cut and accounted for much less variance than rate in a three-way factorial comparison of them (Brown et al., 1974).[21]

MacLachlan (1979) prepared persuasive messages where the speaker subjectively varied his rate in three conditions: slow (111 words per minute), normal (140 wpm), and fast (191 wpm). Subjects who heard the tapes rated the speakers on the degree of their agreement with the

---

[19]To make the two-dimensional plottings more easy to read, we have only placed one pole of the bi-polar adjective pairs on the plottings, but we could just as well say that "shout", for example, is "proud", "emotional" and "dominating," since these are the opposite poles that were used for the adjective pairs "humble," "unemotional" and "submissive," which are located directly across the centre of the graph from the "shout" voice average.

[20]Scherer (1979c) questions the generalizability of these results on the basis that the manipulations may have been too extreme to sound like natural speech, but claims that one cannot determine this since the speech rates for the voices are not given. Again, this may be a problem of getting his information from a summary paper (Brown et al., 1975) rather than from the primary source (Smith et al., 1975). Fig. 6 of the primary source clearly gives the average rate of each of the nine manipulations in phonemes per second. A replication of this rate study (see Brown, 1980b) which used natural answers to questions rather than standard passages and kept the rates of manipulated speech well within bounds of believeability, gave results which are remarkably similar to the results of the Smith et al. study. It is a very reliable effect.

[21]One finding conflicts with Scherer's from correlational studies. While he finds increased competence with higher pitch (average F∅), Brown et al. (1974) found that an experimentally increased F∅, with all other vocal features controlled, resulted in a slight decrease in competence as well as benevolence ratings. However, only two "seed" voices were used in this study and the speakers were reciting a standard passage. The question will need to be settled with improved experimental methods like those discussed below (Stewart, et al. in preparation).

speaker, his intelligence and his objectivity. Although full statistics for adequate comparision with our studies are not reported, MacLachlan states that in each case the faster speaker was rated more highly. These results conflict with the findings of the Kjeldergaard replication given in Fig. 6.5 which show the fast manipulation to make a voice sound more careless, unpleasant, unsympathetic, etc. They also conflict with the many times replicated findings of the precise experimental studies (summarized in Brown, 1980b) that when a voice is increased in rate with everything else held constant, it is perceived as lower on benevolence-related adjectives generally. MacLachlan in the same paper reports an experiment in which a "time compression technique" was used to speed speech by 25%. The faster speakers were rated as "more knowledgable, intelligent and sincere than those who spoke slowly [p. 114]." These results are very consistent with those of an almost identical study reported in Brown et al. (1973) in which an Eltro-Automation Rate Changer (an electronic time compression device that holds pitch constant while altering rate) was used to both speed and slow voices. The results were presented in a similar plotting to Figs. 6.4 and 6.5 of this chapter from a factor analyisis of 22 adjective pairs, and slowed voices were found to be rated lower in all competence-related adjectives and all benevolence-related adjectives. However, speeded voices were found to be rated higher on competence-related adjectives, but lower on benevolence-related adjectives.

A recent study (Brown, Giles & Thakerar, 1985) shows clearly that making generalizations from such results should be taken with a pinch of salt, unless judges' attributions of the speaker's intent are also taken into account, i.e., the judges' perceptions of *why* the speaker is speaking that way. This was a factorial study of the interactive effects of rate ("slow," "normal," and "fast"), dialect ("standard" vs. "non-standard" in a British setting) and context (context given or not given). In the non-context or "monologue" condition, judges were unaware of the situation that led to the utterance, but in the "context" condition they were told that a psychologist was explaining some principles to a group of dentists. Fig. 6.6 gives the results for a part of the study with male judges only. For this factor analysis a three-factor solution was needed to account for over 60% of the variance. In order to plot the information for the three factors, two plottings must be given, a "front" view and a "side" view. In order to see what effect any manipulation had on all of the adjectives we must look at both plottings, Factor I by Factor II ("benevolence" by "competence") and Factor I by Factor III ("benevolence" by "social attractiveness"). The "standard, monologue" condition corresponds to all of the old studies of the effects or rate, since in those we did not have dialect or context introduced. The results for that condition are consistent with those of the older studies: Increased rate gives rise to increased

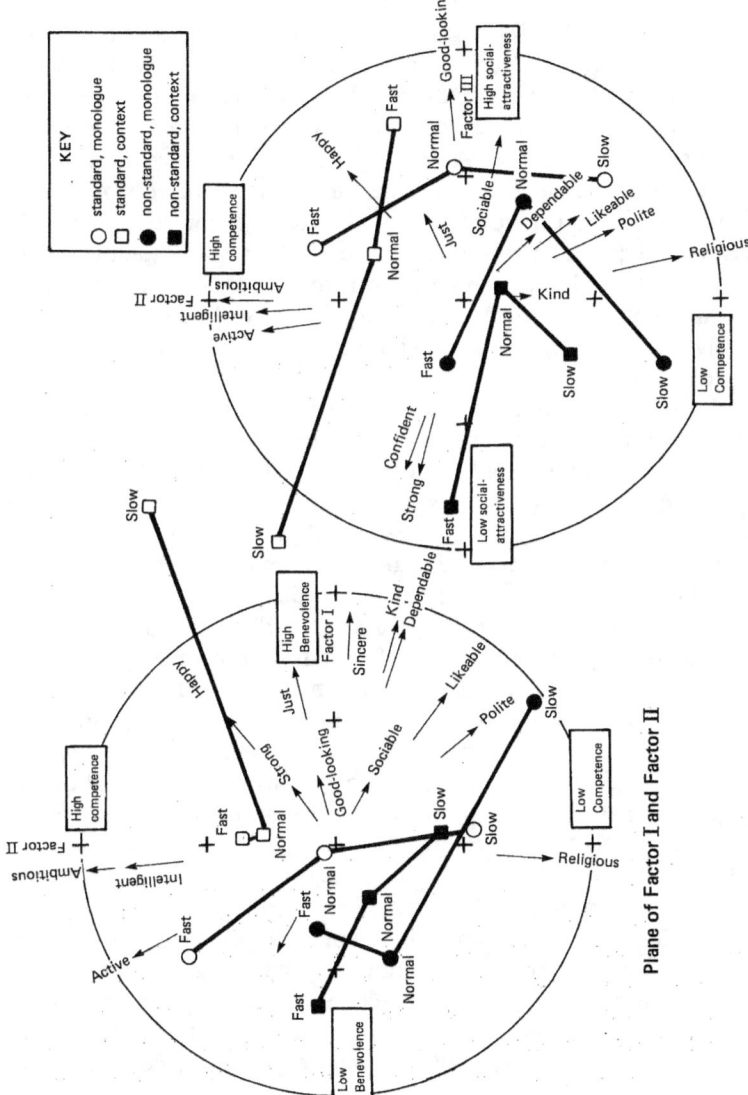

FIG. 6.6 A plotting of the factor scores for the twelve manipulations superimposed upon the factor pattern of the fifteen adjectives—male judges.

competence ratings and decreased benevolence ratings, and decreased rate gives rise to a decrease in both competence and benevolence ratings. Additionally we find in this study that both increasing and decreasing rate give rise to dereased social-attractiveness (Factor III).

The really interesting finding is the way in which context affects these old results. When judges are given context, i.e., a reason for slow speech (to make oneself intelligible to dentists), the slow rate is no longer perceived as a decreased competence but an increased benevolence, with even a slight increase in competence. A nonstandard dialect voice sounds less competent and less benevolent to judges than the standard version, but if one slows the nonstandard voice it sounds more benevolent and only slightly less competent. The study shows clearly that many factors affect judgements of voice with strong interactions among them, and, therefore that we can not know the effect of a vocal change without knowing also what meaning the judge gives to the change and, to what speaker intention it is attributed.

Perhaps the most serious defect of the early experimental studies was the artificiality of the speech samples used: recitation of standard sentences. Apple et al. (1979) tested the effects of rate and pitch manipulations using speech synthesis methods in an improved design in which the stimuli were actual spontaneous answers of subjects to one of two questions. However, there were methodological problems (see Brown, 1980b) with this study which made it difficult to evaluate whether the results agreed with those of the earlier, less natural studies. Stewart et al. (in preparation; see Brown, 1980b for a brief description of their method and results) tested the rate question with a design that also used natural speech in the form of spontanteous answers to questions, but improved upon the Apple et al. (1979) study by using a Graeco-Latin square design that uses each speaker as his or her own control. In this way they controlled for pre-manipulation characteristics of speakers, the problem that makes the Apple et al. data difficult to interpret.

The findings of the Stewart et al. study corroborated the fundamental findings of the old studies, with only slight variation across different speech content. The effects of subjective manipulations were found to be essentially the same as those of computer synthesis manipulations, suggesting that the studies that use subjective manipulation to investigate rate probably give results very close to those that would be obtained with the more precise but much more difficult and expensive speech synthesis methods.

The Graeco-Latin square paradigm worked out in the Stewart et al. study is a very sensitive and powerul one for examining the effects of even subtle vocal manipulations. In future work, it may be valuable to combine an "externalizing" methodology with this experimental method for examining attributions. That is, after getting extreme exemplars of various traits by social consensus nomination (as described in the proceeding section), it could be valuable to test the hypotheses that come from acoustic analysis of their voices by synthesizing a voice, both in its normal form and with the hypothesized vocal index of that trait, to see if it does in fact cause an attribution of the trait.[22]

### Attribution and Temporal Patterns

A serendipitous finding with respect to actual and perceived speech rate has led to some important questions related to pauses and temporal patterning. In the Stewart et al study, each voice was increased and decreased in rate both synthetically by the computer method and subjectively by the speaker. Although the two methods of manipulating rate gave almost the same results in the relative personality trait ratings, when ratings were obtained of how fast the voice sounds to judges and plotted as a function of actual rate (Fig. 6.7) it became clear that the rate of the normal spontaneous voice and the fast, medium and slow synthesized voices (which are merely mathematical transformations of the spontaneous voice) were relatively overestimated in rate. However those "acted back" (the person speaking the same thing again, as much as possible like the first time) at fast, medium and slow rates were relatively underestimated. We think this was because it is not by phonemes per second that a person subjectively judges rate, but by the rhythm of the speech (the distance between stress or accent points) independent of pauses.[23] That is, in spontaneous speech a person pauses to think, but a listener does not include the pause in a subjective assessment of rate, only reckoning it on the basis of rhythm. When one is acting back the same words, "thought pauses" are not so necessary. Although the rhythm may not be any faster, the elapsed time will be shorter and so the actual phonemes per second will be underestimated. We are now developing a method of automatically categorizing every ten millisecond slice of speech time as either "voice speech," "unvoiced speech," or "background noise." This scheme will allow a detailed micro-analysis of the temporal pattern of speech that will provide a test of these hypotheses. We expect the microanalysis of the temporal pattern of speech in natural emotion situations to be particularly revealing.

---

[22]Scherer (1979c) suggests a similar strategy of using "complementary externalization and attribution studies, to derive at least some hypotheses about the existence of further personality markers in speech [p. 191]."

[23]These, and related findings, underscore the importance of differentiating between aspects of speech and voice as they are objectively measured (distal cues) and as they are subjectively experienced (proximal percepts). (See Scherer, 1979c.) Failure to distinguish between these apsects is a serious problem in many studies.

168  Brown and Bradshaw

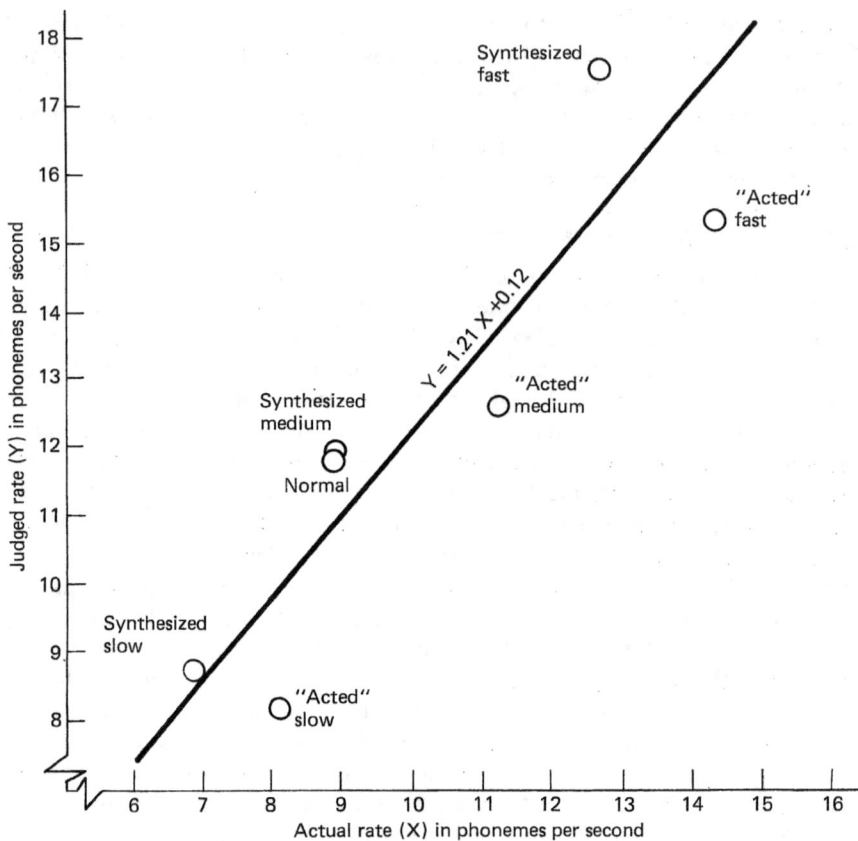

FIG. 6.7 Bi-variate scatter plot and regression line for the relationship between actual and perceived speaking rates for the average of the normal voices and for the averages of six manipulations. (from Brown, 1980b, Fig. 2, p. 296).

When Howard Giles was collaborating with our research group, he mentioned that he found it very hard to believe that slower speech is always perceived as less competent, since he knows a number of very competent slow talkers. We carefully listened to the tapes from the Stewart et al. study and made an interesting discovery: In order to subjectively slow one's speech without sounding less intelligent, one must do it with pauses. Rate decrease studies utilizing speech synthesis have slowed all aspects of the utterance uniformly. An important direction for future studies will be to test the effects of slowing through pauses. It may be possible to predict in advance the effect a pause will have from the position in which it appears. At major syntactic breaks it may be more an "emphasis pause", but in the midst of syntactic units it may be a disruption or a "thought pause." A number of important findings have emerged from the many studies of pauses and temporal patterns in vocal interaction (see Rochester & Gill, 1973; Siegman, 1978; and Feldstein & Welkowitz, 1978, for reviews), but the development of the micro-analysis temporal patterning method mentioned above will allow more precise specification of temporal pattern. Some important advances should come from the careful analysis of the temporal patterns of voices under natural emotion conditions (which we describe in the next section) as compared with the same voices when not under emotive stress.

## EMOTION AND VOCAL PATTERNS

Scherer (1979b) has also conducted a superb review of the current state of knowledge in the area of the vocal and speech reflections of emotion. Again, we do not attempt a duplication of his effort here, but instead discuss a few of the classic studies of emotion and speech in terms of their major findings and problems. Studies in this area tend to fall into one of two categories:

1. *Externalization studies:* acoustic analysis of vocal and speech cues accompanying discrete emotions (usually only portrayed rather than real) or non-specific arousal.
2. *Accuracy studies:* i.e., subjective judgements of which of several emotions is being evoked or portrayed (usually portrayed).

In principle, there is no reason why there should not also be attribution studies of emotion in speech, but these have seldom been done. For example, it would be possible to use the Graeco-Latin square design, developed for the Stewart et al. study, to make manipulations in speech to fit specific hypotheses about the vocal properties that mediate given emotive states, and to test the effects of such manipulations upon attributions of emotion from a group of judges.

### Externalization Studies

Fairbanks (Fairbanks & Provonost, 1939; Fairbanks, 1940; Fairbanks & Hoaglin, 1941) was one of the first to study specific vocal indicators of discrete emotions by acoustic measurement. Since his technique was limited to the use of a modified oscillograph, the major object of his studies was to examine the relationship between $F\emptyset$ (fundamental frequency) and emotion.

In one study (Fairbanks & Provonost, 1939), six male actors read a standard passage while simulating emotions of contempt, anger, fear, grief, and indifference. These portrayals were played to a group of 64 "auditors" who were instructed to identify the emotions being portrayed. Their high degree of accuracy verified the correspondence between speech patterns and their intended emotions. As far as variation in pitch over time is concerned, Fairbanks noted the "few extremely wide variations in the simulation of contempt, the generally wide, rapid inflections of anger, the irregularity of the pitch changes in fear, the consistent vibrato in grief and the lack of distinguishing features in indifference [p. 458]." The mean pitch levels of the emotions in order of ascendency were, indifference (108 Hz), contempt (124 Hz), grief (136 Hz), anger (229 Hz) and fear (254 Hz)

In one of the most sophisticated approaches to the emotion-speech question, Williams and Stevens (1972) recorded the voices of professional actors reading short scenarios written to portray anger, fear, sorrow and a neutral situation. The study is carefully done and a good source for hypotheses, but much of the data are qualitative descriptions and even the quantitative results are presented in graph form or are described rather than tested for statistical significance. With such a small sample, the observed consistencies may not be applicable to a larger sample of actors, let alone the general populace. There is sufficient inter-actor inconsistency to leave the reader with a considerable burden of interpretation. The contour of fundamental frequency vs. time was found to be the strongest indicator of the emotions of the speaker. Lower fundamental frequency, with decreased range and reduced rate of articulation, were indicative of sorrow. Anger was characterized by both raised pitch and increased pitch variance. The analysis did not reveal any consistent acoustical correlates for portrayals of fear.

### Accuracy Studies

One major problem in accuracy studies of emotion and speech is that of obtaining content-free speech. If we do not do this, content (*what* is being said) may be the cue for recognition of an emotion rather than vocal properties (*how* the thing is said). Davitz and Davitz (1959) dealt with this problem in a novel way by having subjects express each of ten emotions by reciting the alphabet "using letters as if they were words," after reading a brief description of a situation which might generate the feeling in question. Judges were then faced with the task of deciding which feeling situation was being expressed. They found the highest percentage of correct identification for anger (65%),[24] followed by nervousness (54.2%), sadness (49.2%), happiness (43.3%), sympathy (38.8%), satisfaction (30.8%), fear and also love (25%), jealousy (24.6%), and pride (20.8%).

The Kramer (1964) study only used five emotions but their acted portrayals used actual speech rather than letters of the alphabet and the results were displayed more completely in confusion matrix form (thus allowing more careful comparison, using Information Theory statistics, to the other studies cited in this chapter which use an accuracy paradigm). In order to hold verbal content constant so that it would not be a cue in identifying the emotion portrayed, they arranged to have three sentences that were equivalent for each of the scenarios for the five emotions. Only those three sentences were presented to judges for the identification task. The three sentences of recorded portrayals were presented to judges in three ways: untouched English portrayals, the same English portrayals filtered to pass only frequencies below 400 Hz., and untouched portrayals in Japanese. These conditions were used to test the consistency of the pattern of confusions under each method of disguising content (filtering and using a language unknown to the judges). Table 6.2 displays the results of the Kramer study presented in a format that allows maximum comparison with the other studies of this chapter. Two of the emotion names, anger and love, are the same for the Kramer study and the Davitz and Davitz study. Other emotions which are fairly comparable are grief, which was used by the Kramer study, and sadness, which was an emotion Davitz and Davitz wanted to identify. Let us see what the comparable results were for these three emotions: anger, grief/sadness, and love. In both studies, anger is most often correctly indentified (between 67% and 77% in the three Kramer conditions and 65% correct in Davitz and Davitz). Sadness/grief is next (58% to 90% in Kramer and 49.2% for Davitz and Davitz), and love is least correctly identified in both studies (38% to 56% in Kramer, and 25% in Davitz and Davitz).

One of the greatest gaps in the emotion/speech literature is the absence of studies of real, naturally occurring emotion.[25] If one wishes to be

---

[24]Davitz and Davitz (1959) do not report percent-correct statistics but they do give, in their Table 1, the number of correct identifications for each emotion portrayed. These percentage figures were obtained by dividing the number correct for each emotion by the total number of portrayals, which was 240 in each case.

[25]One notable exception is an externalization study included in Williams and Stevens (1972) which they carried out collateral to the main one. They analysed acoustically the recorded commentary of the radio announcer who witnessed and described the Hindenberg disaster as it happened. It is difficult to imagine a speech sample more realistic and natural or a situation more extreme. Comparisons between the actual recording and a portrayal by an actor who had not heard the recording, but only read the transcript, showed similar emotion/non-emotion differences, suggesting that, at least for this one kind of very extreme emotion, portrayals can be fairly accurate. What is missing in this data is replications to determine whether such emotion cues are consistent across persons and across time. An experimental study with a number of emotion-producing situations and a number of speakers would allow statistical inference and tests of consistency as to the relationships between emotive states and vocal properties.

### TABLE 6.2

Confusion Matrices, Information Theory Statistics and Percent-correct Statistics for English Unfiltered, English Filtered and Japanese Voices Portraying Five Emotions. (The Information Used to Construct this Table is from Kramer, 1964, p. 392, Table 1, with Information Theory Statistics and Corrected Percent-correct Statistics Added.)

| English Unfiltered Voices | | | | | | Percentage of Correct Judgements | Corrected Percentage of Judgements | Percentage of Information Transmitted (Coefficient of Constraint) |
|---|---|---|---|---|---|---|---|---|
| Intended Emotion | Judged Emotion | | | | | | | |
| | a | c | g | i | l | | | |
| anger | 74 | 26 | 0 | 0 | 0 | 74%[a] | 67.5% | 46.4% of the |
| contempt | 3 | 85 | 3 | 9 | 0 | 85% | 81.25% | information |
| grief | 2 | 5 | 58 | 4 | 31 | 58% | 47.5% | for the five |
| indifference | 1 | 16 | 4 | 76 | 3 | 76% | 70% | emotions was |
| love | 2 | 14 | 17 | 11 | 56 | 56% | 45% | transmitted |

| English Filtered Voices | | | | | | | | |
|---|---|---|---|---|---|---|---|---|
| Intended Emotion | Judged Emotion | | | | | | | |
| | a | c | g | i | l | | | |
| anger | 77 | 23 | 0 | 0 | 0 | 77% | 71.25% | 38.0% of the |
| contempt | 6 | 48 | 4 | 36 | 6 | 48% | 35% | information |
| grief | 0 | 3 | 71 | 5 | 21 | 71% | 63.75% | for the five |
| indifference | 6 | 11 | 7 | 63 | 13 | 63%[a] | 53.75% | emotions was |
| love | 0 | 12 | 20 | 19 | 48 | 48% | 35% | transmitted |

| Japanese Voices | | | | | | | | |
|---|---|---|---|---|---|---|---|---|
| Intended Emotion | Judged Emotion | | | | | | | |
| | a | c | g | i | l | | | |
| anger | 67 | 29 | 0 | 3 | 1 | 67%[a] | 58.75% | 42.5% of the |
| contempt | 0 | 20 | 17 | 52 | 11 | 20% | 0% | information |
| grief | 0 | 0 | 90 | 1 | 10 | 90% | 87.5% | for the five |
| indifference | 2 | 21 | 2 | 73 | 2 | 73% | 66.25% | emotions was |
| love | 1 | 7 | 3 | 52 | 38 | 38% | 22.5% | transmitted |

[a] = median

precise, neither the Kramer study nor the Davitz and Davitz study really measures judgement accuracy. In both cases the experimenters have defined the emotion that they wish the judges to portray more in the actual scenarios used to exemplify the emotion rather than just an emotion name or label, and yet judges are only given the emotion labels to choose from. It would be much more defensible to allow the judges to read the scenarios as well so that they would have the same opportunity as the speakers to interpret the emotion labels. The investigators have not established a logically tight *assessable reality* against which to measure judge accuracy.[26]

In order to move one step closer to natural emotion in spontaneous speech, we designed an experiment (Brown, Bowen, and Hamblin, 1977, see also the partial report of it in Brown, 1980b) to obtain speech samples of five male undergraduates in reaction to six films quite diverse in emotional impact. It is not easy to define the emotion generated by each film, but having the judges also view the film provides a situational definition. That is, judges are faced with the question "which film led to this utterance?" to which there is one indisputably correct answer and five indisputably incorrect ones. The emotion involved is probably somewhere between real emotion and portrayed. It is the vicarious emotion of the spectator. We found that judges could, on the basis of only the vocal qualities (for content was obscured by having speakers in a foreign tongue) identify the film with an accuracy almost as great as portrayed emotion in the earlier Davitz and Davitz and Kramer studies.

Even though it could be argued that this is one step further removed from real emotion than portrayals, in that it is an observation of a portrayal, one crucial element makes it more comparable to real emotion: the emotion is *subsidiary* to the task the viewer is carrying out rather than being the *focus* of his attention as in portrayals.[27] A great weakness of accuracy studies which use portrayed emotion lies in the fact that it is one thing to ask whether the feelings and emotions a person experiences in natural situations are detectable in vocal qualities, and quite a different thing to ask whether a person can produce portrayals of emotion or feelings vocally that are recognizable. The former are likely to be subtle. The latter run the risk of being nothing more than stylized caricatures.

We have been carrying out additional studies (see Brown, 1980a for some of the initial data) to gather recordings of vocal emotion in natural

---

[26]Polanyi (1962, p. 139) and Taylor (1964, pp. 76–80) both argue this kind of point effectively. The Polyani reference clearly shows the motivation behind "operationism" or "operational definitions" and the Taylor reference is a demonstration of the fallacy in operationism logic.

[27]"Subsidiary" and "focal" are being used here in the same sense that Polanyi (1962, chapter 4) uses them.

situations such as: the birth of the first child;[28] patients before and after a serious operation; college athletes before and after a major event; etc. All of these voices are being judged by a small group of listeners (with the voices played backwards or low pass filtered to occlude intelligibility) to evaluate the accuracy with which they can identify which voice sample came from which situation.

The next step will be a careful acoustic analysis of the temporal patterns, pitch/amplitude patterns and long-term power spectrum associated with the voice in various situations in order to test the hypotheses of the vocal marker links with specific emotions. From these results and the ones summarized by Scherer (1979a), hypotheses will be constructed and tested with an experimental design using speech synthesis methods.

An example of a major issue in the vocal realization of emotion that could be tested effectively using this research paradigm is whether the important markers are found in the temporal patterning of FØ) and amplitude or in the characteristic timbre (long term power spectrum).[29] The bulk of the research so far has dealt with the former. Scherer, both in the emotion/speech review chapter (1979b) and the personality/speech chapter (1979c) expresses the view that power spectrum data will be a rich source of information about an individual's psychological state, proposing as an example that the relative increase of energy above 500 Hz is an indicator or marker of stress and tension in the voice.[30] However, more research is needed.

---

[28]We realize that some of these studies deal with matters of great import and personal concern, and require interpersonal respect and sensitivity. The value of even very good data (which we hope some of this will be) is very small compared to the other values involved in such an event. We have sought to act in accord with the feelings of each couple and to give them adequate knowledge of how the voices will be used, in order to allow them to decline if they wish. (Participation is voluntary in the first place, but after the tape is made they are given a chance to indicate if they prefer the tape not to be used further.) We have also been aware of the need for selectivity in the kind and size of listener groups involved in accuracy tests—it would not do to have large unselected groups of undergraduates as listener subjects.

[29]A "long term power spectrum" is simply the summation of the power spectrum over a number of time slices. It is a stabilized indicator of timbre of the voice over the utterance as contrasted with the temporary timbre characteristics of any one time slice.

[30]Scherer quotes Laver (1975) in connection with this hypothesis. Laver's clarification of it (personal communication) is that the voice of stress and tension is increased in amplitude both above and below 500 Hz, but that the relative increase is greater above 500 Hz than below. However, it can be argued that driving any resonant sound box at higher amplitudes will result in disproportionately higher amplitudes above 500 Hz, and this particular power spectrum configuration may be only an artifact of the increased amplitude, rather than a separate vocal marker for tension. (See Strong and Plitnik, 1977 for a clear demonstration of this principle in connection with the clarinet, p. 244, the oboe, p. 247, and the flute, p. 256.)

In connection with the studies of emotion, there is also a need for work on the conceptual clarification of emotion theory as it can be applied to vocal reflections. Particularly of interest is the taxonomy and very clever conceptual analysis of emotions by Solomon (1977) from within the tradition of existentialism and self-deception theory (such as Nietzsche, Sartre and Camus). Especially relevant is his emphasis on a differentiation between those emotions that are more reactive (in which a vocal accompaniment could be considered an index of an inner state) and those that can be seen as a communicative message. For example, anger can be used as a way of accusing others as Lewis Carroll expressed in *Alice in Wonderland:* " 'I'll be judge, I'll be jury,' said cunning old fury."

The shortcomings of Skinner's *Verbal behaviour* (1957) have received at least as much criticism as they deserve, but there may be some important insights to be gained from dichotomizing language functionally into "mands," verbal operants intended to bring about a certain state of affairs, and "tacts," the conveyors of information (see also Chapter 9.) Beier (1966) in his theory of "evoking messages" clearly points out the habitual ways in which vocal operants can be an important part of personality structure:

> As an illustration of the evoking message we can consider an individual who thinks of himself as lonely and without any friends. In a careful analysis of his messages, we discover the coding of very subtle cues that are likely to create an emotional climate in the people he addresses, resulting in negative and angry feelings. The sender evokes this negative response but is nevertheless able to see himself as the victim of circumstances. As he was not aware that he coded this information, he does not have a feeling of responsibility for the response he obtained. Indeed, the evoking message seems to be the type of communication which maintains the patient's present state of adjustment. With this message he helps to create those responses in his environment which confirm his view of the world. Through the responses he elicits, he constantly obtains proof that the world is exactly the place he thinks it is!. . .The evoking message is probably one of the basic tools used by individuals to maintain their consistency of personality. . .The person with emotional conflict. . .creates a world in which he typically feels victimized by others, in which he experiences great unhappiness, though he has little awareness that he is often the creator of this world [pp. 12–13].

It seems reasonable to assume that a manner of speech that evokes rejection is often because of a lack of social skill, that it constitutes a failure, but Beier's position turns the tables by viewing it as a manifestation of skill. He suggests three observations that will demonstrate that it is skillful and purposive: (1) it is frequent; (2) it is integrated with the person's total personality; and, most importantly, (3) there seems to be no learning, no improvement associated with it.[31] We have, then, purposive messages, the intent of which are directly contradictory to the person's avowed intent— a perfect fit to the classic description of self deception (*mauvaise foi*) given by Sartre (1943/1969, pp. 96-98)[32] and others (Fingarette, 1969; Warner, 1982) i.e., purposive messages which are directly contradictory to the subject's intentions.

Although the illustrations in Beier's 1966 book of the phenomenon are mostly anecdotal accounts from clinical experience, he has, with a rotating group of students, done considerable empirical work in this area.[33] A common paradigm in these studies is to have subjects (some of them with severe adjustment problems) portray various "moods" and then to have groups of judges categorize the voice according to mood. High inter-judge reliability in an assessment that is contradictory to the person's insistence of what he or she is portraying is taken as an index of the person's problem. The logic is that it is not so much a question of who is right about the mood, but that it is a blatant demonstration of social reality— that the person is not communicating to others what he or she acknowledges as his or her intention. It is argued further that this mistake is not accidental. There is a resistance to learning. There is no increment of improvement. Therefore, it must be the social impact intended by the person.

As the concept of emotion becomes less elusive, we can begin to focus on understanding processes underlying the judge's perception of emotion. Just as the Beierian theory leads us to expect that vocal paralinguistic cues are more accurate indicators of a person's intentions than his or her own avowals, we would also expect on the basis of some recent studies (e.g. Dicks, Brown & Wells, 1977; Sackeim & Gur, 1978) that judges' involuntary "tacit" reactions (perhaps eventually measurable by EEG, EMG of facial muscles, etc.) would be more accurate than explicit judgements to the extent that the judges are themselves self-deceived we theorize that those who are more well adjusted personalities will have explicit verbal judgements more in accord with their primary tacit apprehensions and will, therefore, be more accurate in their perceptions of emotions and personality traits in others. It may be time to re-open the accuracy-of-the interpersonal-perception research tradition. One of the most important directions for future work may be a return to the accuracy issue, using a

---

[31] This is our own summary drawn from discussions with Beier.

[32] This is the example of the woman who colludes in her own seduction, though the realization of the intent that is betrayed by the total purposive pattern of her actions would horrify her.

[33] Most of that work is only in the form of dissertations and theses available at the University of Utah libary. A summary of the findings has not yet been written.

6. Towards a Social Psychology of Voice Variations 177

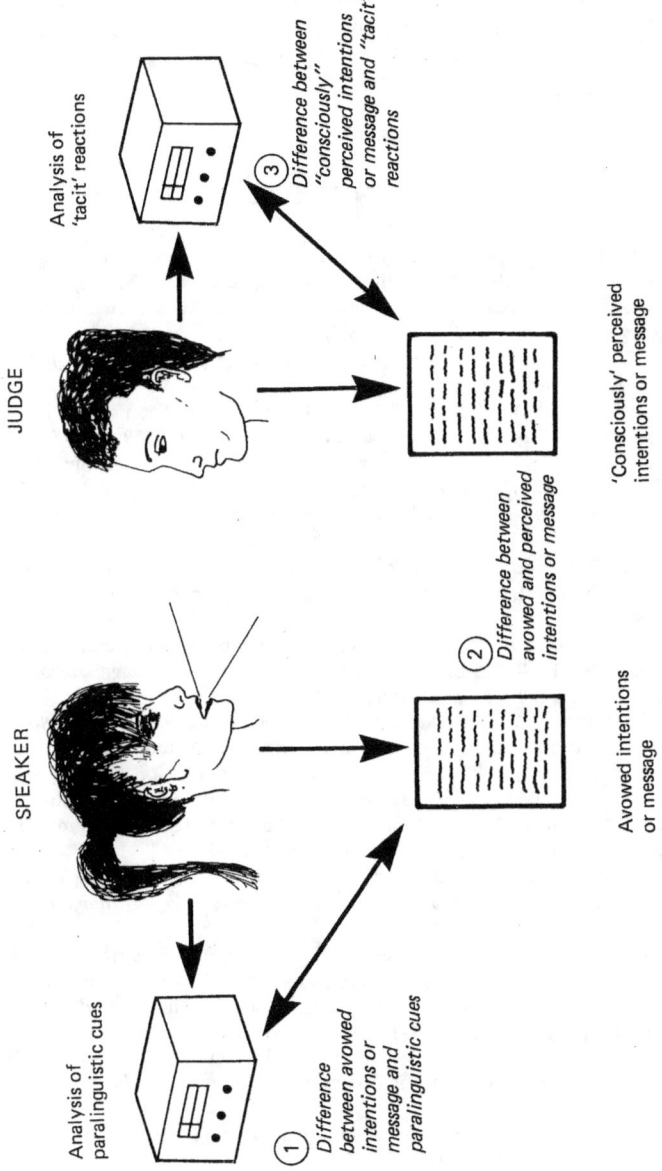

FIG. 6.8 Three possible research paradigms for a more adequate conception of emotion and speech.

logically tight accuracy paradigm to select accurate and inaccurate judges and then using the very precise attribution paradigms now in existence to uncover and analyze the attributional basis of inaccuracy and its relation to so-called "emotional disturbance" and what Szasz (1974) calls "the myth of mental illness," perhaps with research paradigms like those outlined in Figure 6.8.

## REFERENCES

Addington, D. W. *The relationship of certain vocal characteristics with perceived speaker characteristics.* Unpublished dissertation, University of Iowa, 1963.

Addington, D. W. The relationship of selected vocal characteristics to personality perception. *Speech Monographs,* 1968, *35,* 492-503

Allport, G. W., & Cantril, H. Judging personality from voice. *Journal of Social Psychology,* 1934, *5,* 37-54.

Apple, W., Streeter, L. A., & Krauss, R. M. Effects of pitch and speech rate on personal attributions. *Journal of Personality and Social Psychology,* 1979, *5,* 715-727.

Aronovitch, C. D. The voice of personality: stereotyped judgements and their relation to voice quality and sex of speaker. *Journal of Social Psychology,* 1976, *99,* 207-220.

Beier, E. G. *The silent language of psychotherapy.* Chicago: Aldine Publishing Company, 1966.

Brown, B. L. The detection of emotion in vocal qualities. In H. Giles., W. P. Robinson., & P. M. Smith (Eds.), *Language: social psychological perspectives.* Oxford: Pergamon Press, 1980. (a)

Brown B. L. Effects of speech rate on personality attribution and competency evaluations. In H. Giles., W. P. Robinson., & P. M. Smith (Eds.), *Language: social psychological perspectives.* Oxford: Pergamon Press, 1980. (b)

Brown, B. L., Bowen, D. E., & Hamblin, D. L. *The recognition of film-induced emotion from vocal qualities.* Unpublished manuscript, Brigham Young University, 1977.

Brown, B. L., Giles, H., & Thakerar, J. N. Speaker evaluation as a function of speech rate, accent and context. *Language and Communication,* 1985, *5,* in press.

Brown, B. L., & Lambert, W. E. A cross-cultural study of social status markers in speech. *Canadian Journal of Behavioural Science,* 1976 *8,* 39-55.

Brown, B. L. Strong, W. J., & Rencher, A. C. Acoustic determinants of perceptions of personality from speech. *International Journal of the sociology of language,* 1975, *6,* 11-32.

Brown, B. L., Strong, W. J., & Rencher, A. C. Fifty-four voices from two: the effects of simulations manipulations of rate, mean fundamental frequency and variance of fundamental frequency on ratings of personality from speech. *Journal of the Acoustical Society of America,* 1974, *55,* 313-318.

Brown, B. L., Strong, W. J., & Rencher, A. C. Perceptions of personality from speech: effects of manipulations of acoustical parameters. *Journal of the Acoustical Society of America,* 1973, *54,* 29-35.

Davitz, J. R., & Davitz, L. J. The communication of feelings by content-free speech. *Journal of Communication,* 1959, *9,* 6-13

Dicks, R. H. Brown, B. L., & Wells, M. G. *A comparision of groups differing in mental health in their ability to judge and portray emotions.* Unpublished manuscript, Brigham Young University, 1977.

Diehl, C. F. Voice and personality: an evaluation. In D. A. Barbara (Ed.), *Psychological and psychiatric aspects of speech and hearing.* Springfield, Illinois: C. Thomas, 1960.

Eisenberg, P., & Zalowitz, E. Judgements of dominance-feeling from phonograph records of voice. *Journal of Applied Psychology,* 1938, *22,* 620–631.

Fairbanks, G. Recent experimental investigations of vocal pitch in speech. *Journal of the Acoustical Society of America,* 1940, *11,* 457–466.

Fairbanks, G., & Hoaglin, L. W. An experimental study of the durational characteristics of the voice during the expression of emotion. *Speech Monographs,* 1941, *8,* 85–90.

Fairbanks, G., & Pronovost, W. An experimental study of the pitch characteristics of the voice during the expression of emotion. *Speech Monographs,* 1939, *6,* 87–104.

Fay, P. J., & Middleton, W. C. The ability to judge sociability from the voice as transmitted over a public address system. *Journal of Social Psychology,* 1941, *13,* 303–309.

Fay, P. J., & Middleton, W. C. Judgement of intelligence from the voice as transmitted over a public address system. *Sociometry,* 1940, *3,* 186–191. (a)

Fay, P. J., & Middleton, W. C. Judgement of introversion from the transcribed voice. *Quarterly Journal of Speech,* 1942, *28,* 226–228.

Fay, P. J., & Middleton, W. C. Judgement of Kretschmerian body types from the voice as transmitted over a public address system. *Journal of Social Psychology,* 1940, *12,* 151–162. (b)

Fay, P. J., & Middleton, W. C. Judgement of leadership from transmitted voice. *Journal of Social Psychology,* 1943, *17,* 99–102.

Fay, P. J., & Middleton, W. C. Judgement of Spranger personality types from the voice as transmitted over a public address system. *Character and Personality,* 1939, *8,* 144–155.

Feldstein, S., & Welkowitz, J. A chronography of conversation: in defence of an objective approach. In A. W. Siegman & S. Feldstein (Eds.), *Nonverbal behaviour and communication.* Hillsdale, New Jersey: Erlbaum, 1978.

Fingarette, H. *Self-deception.* New York: Humanities Press, 1969.

Giles, H. Ethnicity markers in speech. In K. R. Scherer & H. Giles (Eds.), *Social markers in speech.* Cambridge: Cambridge University Press, 1979.

Gorlitz, D. D. *Ergebnisse und probleme der ausdruckspsychologischen sprechstimm-forschung.* Königstein, FRG: Meisenheim, 1972

Helfrich, H Age markers in speech. In K. R. Scherer and H. Giles (Eds.), *Social markers in speech.* Cambridge: Cambridge University Press, 1979.

Herzog, H. Stimme und Personlichkeit. *Zeitschrift für Psychologie,* 1933, *130,* 300–379.

Kjeldergaard, P. M. *Changes in perceived personality traits as a function of manipulation of vocal characteristics.* Unpublished manuscript. Harvard University, 1968.

Kramer, E. Elimination of verbal cues in judgements of emotion of voice. *Journal of Abnormal and Social Psychology,* 1964, *68,* 390–396.

Kramer, E. Judgement of personal characteristics and emotions from non-verbal properties of speech. *Psychological Bulletin,* 1963, *60,* 408–420.

Laver, J. Voice quality and indexical information. *British Journal of Disorders of Communication,* 1968, *3,* 43–54.

Laver, J. *Individual features in voice quality.* PhD dissertation, University of Edinburgh, 1975.

Laver, J. The concept of articulatory settings: an historical survey. *Historiographia Linguistica,* 1978, *5,* 1–14

Laver, J., & Trudgill, P. Phonetic and linguistic markers in speech. In K. R. Scherer and H. Giles (Eds.), *Social markers in speech.* Cambridge: Cambridge Univeristy Press, 1979.

Lomax, R. Social structure and sound change. In R. W. Wescott (Ed.), *Language origins,* Silver Springs, Md:, Linstock Press 1974.

MacLachlan, J. What people really think of fast talkers. *Psychology Today,* November 1979, 113–117.

Mahl, G. F., & Schulze, G. Psychological research in the extralinguistic area. In T. A. Sebeok, A. S. Hayes, & M. C. Bateson (Eds), *Approaches to Semiotics.* The Hague: 1964.

Mallory, P., & Miller, V. A. A possible basis for the association of voice characteristics and personality traits. *Speech Monographs,* 1958, *25,* 255–260.

Meehl, P. E., & Hathway, S. R. The *K* factor as a suppressor variable in the Minnesota Multiphasic Personality Inventory. *Journal of Applied Psychology,* 1946, *30,* 525–564.

Mischel, W. Towards a cognitive social learning reconceptualization of personality. *Psychological Review,* 1973, *80,* 252–283.

Moses. P. *The voice of neurosis,* New York: Grune & Stratton, 1954

Ostwald, P. F. Acoustic methods in psychiatry. *Scientific American,* 1965, *212,* 82–91.

Ostwald, P. F. *Soundmaking: the acoustic communication of emotion.* Springfield, Illinois: Charles C. Thomas, 1963.

Pear, T. H. *Voice and Personality.* London: Chapman & Hall, 1931.

Polanyi, M *Personal knowledge: towards a post-critical philosophy.* New York: Harper & Row, 1962.

Ptacek, P. H., & Sander, E. K. Age recognition from voice. *Journal of Speech and Hearing Research,* 1966, *9,* 266–272.

Robinson, W. P. Speech markers and social class. In K. R. Scherer and H. Giles (eds.), *Social markers in speech.* Cambridge: Cambridge University Press, 1979.

Rochester, S. R., & Gill, J. Production of complex sentences in monologues and dialogues. *Journal of Verbal Learning and Verbal Behavior,* 1973, *12,* 203–210.

Rousey, C. L. (Ed.) *Psychiatric Assessment by speech and hearing behavior.* Springfield, Illinois: Charles C. Thomas, 1974.

Rousey, C. L., & Moriarty. A. E. *Diagnostic implications of speech sounds.* Springfield, Illinois: Charles C. Thomas, 1965.

Ryan, E. B. Why do low-prestige language varieties persist? In H. Giles & R. N. St Clair (Eds.), *Language and social psychology.* Oxford: Blackwell, 1979.

Sackeim, H. A., & Gur, R. C. Self-deception, other-deception, and self-reported psychopathology. *Journal of Consulting and Clinical Psychology,* 1979, *47,* 213–215.

Sackeim, H. A., & Gur, R. C. Self-deception, self-confrontation and consciousness. In G. E. Schwartz and D. Shapiro (Eds.), *Consciousness and self-regulation: advances in research and theory* (Vol. 2). New York: Plenum Press, 1978.

Sartre, J. P. *Being and nothingness.* H. E. Barnes (trans.). New York: Washington Square Press, 1969. Originally published as *L'etre et le neant* in 1943.

Scherer, K. R. The functions of nonverbal signs in conversation. In R. N. St Clair & H. Giles (Eds.), *The social and psychological contexts of language.* Hillsdale, N.J. Lawrence Erlbaum Associates, 1979. (a)

Scherer, K. R. Inference rules in personality attribution from voice quality: the loud voice of extroversion. *European Journal of Social Psychology,* 1978, *8,* 467–487.

Scherer, K. R. Judging personality from voice: a cross-cultural approach to an old issue in interpersonal perception. *Journal of Personality,* 1972, *40,* 191–210.

Scherer, K. R. Nonlinguistic vocal indicators of emotion and psychopathology. In C. E. Izard (Ed.), *Emotions in personality and psychopathology.* New York: Plenum Press, 1979. (b)

Scherer, K. R. Personality markers in speech. In K. R. Scherer and H. Giles (Eds.), *Social markers in speech.* Cambridge: Cambridge University Press, 1979. (c)

Siegman, A. W. The tell-tale voice: nonverbal messages of verbal communication. In A. W. Siegman & S. Feldstein (Eds.), *Nonverbal behaviour and communication.* Hillsdale, N. J.: Lawrence Erlbaum Associates, 1978.

Skinner, B. F. *Verbal behaviour.* New York: Appleton-Century-Crofts, 1957.
Smith, B. L., Brown, B. L., Strong, W. J., & Rencher, A. C. Effects of speech rate on personality perception. *Language and Speech,* 1975, 18, 145-152.
Smith, P. M. Sex markers in speech. In K. R. Scherer and H. Giles (Eds.), *Social markers in speech.* Cambridge: Cambridge University Press, 1979.
Solomon, R. C. *The passions: the myth and nature of human emotion.* Garden City, New York: Anchor Books, 1977.
Stagner, R. Judgements of voice and personality. *Journal of Educational Psychology,* 1936, 27, 272-277.
Stewart, M., Brown, B. L., & Stewart, S. *A comparison of computer manipulated speech rate with subjectively manipulated speech rate in effects upon personality attributions.* Manuscript in preparation, Brigham Young University.
Strong, W. J. & Plitnik, G. R. *Music, speech, and high fidelity.* Provo, Utah: Brigham Young University Press, 1979.
Szasz, T. S. *The myth of mental illness: foundations of a theory of personal conduct.* Revised edition. New York: Harper and Row, 1974.
Taylor, C. *The Explanation of behaviour.* New York: The Humanities Press, 1964
Taylor, H. C. Social agreements on personality traits as judged from speech. *Journal of Social Psychology,* 1934, 5, 244-248.
Titze, I. R. The human vocal cords: a mathematical model, part I. *Phonetica,* 1973, 28, 129-170.
Titze, I. R. The human vocal cords: a mathematical model, part II. *Phonetica,* 1974, 29, 1-21.
Titze, I. R., & Talkin, D. T. A theoretical study of the effects of various laryngeal configurations on the acoustics of phonation. *Journal of the Acoustical Society of America,* 1979, 66, 60-74.
Trimboli, F. Changes in voice characteristics as a function of trait and state personality variables. *Dissertation Abstracts International,* 1973, 33, 3965.
Tyler, L. E. Test review No. 77. In O.K. Buros (Ed.), *The Fourth Mental Measurements Yearbook.* Highland Park, N.J: The Gryphon Press, 1953, 135-140.
Warner, C. T. *Bondage and emancipation: a conceptual introduction to the study of motivation.* Unpublished 19-chapter manuscript, Brigham Young University, 1982.
Williams, C. E., & Stevens, K. N. Emotions and speech: some acoustical correlates. *Journal of the Acoustical Society of America,* 1972, 52, 1238-1250.

# 7
# Temporal Patterns of Speech and Gaze in Social and Intellectual Conversation

**James M. Dabbs, Jr.**
*Georgia State University*

The simplest conversations are very complex. There is always more than one person involved, each with unique ideas, aims, skills and conceptions of what is going on. The persons may be acquaintances, enemies, lovers, children or strangers. The occasion may be frivolous or serious, friendly or hostile. The speech may be fast or slow, formal or informal, expressionless or full of feeling. About all conversations have in common is that the speakers use words and alternate in taking turns.

This chapter considers whether two global functions might underlie and account for the surface qualities of conversation. It is the thesis here that two functions, social and intellectual, deal respectively with interpersonal relationships and with ideas about the world. Which function is more or less salient at a given moment may be revealed in the patterns of relatively simple, content-free parameters of sound and silence. Unlike most research on conversation, this ignores words and tones of voice. Such an approach will seem sterile to many, but the research tradition that is identified with Jaffe and Feldstein (1970) and their colleagues, indicates that on-off patterns of speech and silence carry a great deal of information.

## SOCIAL AND INTELLECTUAL FUNCTIONS

To consider the function of a conversation is to ask why conversation takes place, with subordinate questions ranging from why two partners talk to why they use particular words. There is little agreement in classifying functions of conversation or of language in general (see

Halliday, 1973; Robinson, 1972), and considering the functions of language is not a popular pastime among linguists. Functions of language are probably as varied as the functions of any other aspect of behaviour. People want to learn, teach, influence, gain friends, deflect attacks and sometimes simply be with others. Language helps to accomplish these ends.

One approach to classifying the functions of conversation would emphasize the essentially social nature of human beings. While people do spend time alone, thinking, making plans and solving problems, their attention is repeatedly drawn to one another. They live in groups, learn about the world from others and join with others in coping with the world. They develop alliances and networks of social relationships while working and sharing information.

Every conversation takes place between partners in a world that includes and extends beyond the conversation itself. The partners are concerned with each other and with happenings in the larger world. The conversation serves these respective concerns, which we label here "social" and "intellectual." "Social" conversation deals with establishing and maintaining a relationship with an immediate social partner. "Intellectual" conversation deals with information that goes beyond this relationship. We would expect social conversation to be oriented more toward the partner and intellectual conversation oriented more toward practical issues or abstract ideas. How this difference in orientation might be detected from the audible and visible features of a conversation is the topic of this chapter.

Purely social conversation is generally lightly loaded with significant ideas and what we normally call "thinking." Langer has emphasized the mindlessness of much social behaviour (Langer, Blank, & Chanowitz, 1978). The ethnomethodologists note that conversations are often made up of strings of *non sequiturs* that hang together because each party presumes, rightly or wrongly, knowledge of what the other is talking about (Gamson, 1974; see Chapters 2 & 3). The philosopher Hannah Arendt (1978) notes that thinking is "out of order" when action is called for, because thinking cannot move fast enough to guide contemporaneous action. Social interaction is tied only loosely to the thoughts a person had before entering into a social encounter. The ideas in social conversation are often of little consequence, and conversations can be easily entered or left at any point without loss.

In purely intellectual conversation, ideas are more central than social relationships. The partners talk to learn or teach or explore. They process information and communicate matters of fact. They solve problems, formulate ideas, stimulate each other's thoughts, and use each other as sounding boards. The purpose of their conversation is to pursue the consequences of theoretical or practical matters; how they feel about one another is not at issue.

Most conversation mixes social and intellectual elements, because both are needed for the partners to continue talking. The social orientation keeps them interested in each other, and the intellectual content keeps the words from degenerating into sighs, grunts, growls or murmurs. The social relationship need not be friendly and the intellectual activity need not be productive. But the subjects must have some interest in one another—either positive or negative—and they must use words, with the intellectual meanings inherent in words. Any conversation will have both social and intellectual elements, even though at any given moment the social or the intellectual aspects may predominate.

The contrast between social and intellectual is an old one in social psychology. In studies of impression formation, "social" traits in others have been reported to affect initial liking, while "intellectual" traits affect respect (Hamilton & Fallot, 1974). A similar distinction exists in Fiedler's (1964) description of differences between social and task leaders. The distinction is closely related to Bales' system for scoring social interaction (Bales & Strodtbeck, 1951). The Bales system analyses group interaction, including communication, using categories that might be called social (dealing with tension, agreement and solidarity) and intellectual (dealing with suggestions, options, and information). But the Bales system, as it has been employed historically, examines the content of what is said. It is used to analyze groups performing tasks and the data generally come from typscripts of verbal interaction taken at face value, though it purports to deal with the meaning behind the words. The present scheme of dividing conversation into social and intellectual arises from a similar desire to treat the meaning behind the words (the "music," not the words), but it pays less attention to the actual words than does the Bales system. The present schema presumes that a social or intellectual orientation will emerge in enough different ways in the behaviour of a conversing pair to be detected by an observer who does not even hear the individual words.

### An Evolutionary Basis

Mattingly (1972), a linguist who studies physical qualities of speech, presents an appealing evolutionary model of how social and intellectual functions might have come together out of two originally independent systems. He suggests that speech began as a set of species-specific "sign stimuli," stereotyped displays that automatically trigger stereotyped responses in another member of the same species. Many animals have such displays, mostly related to sexual or agonistic behaviour. Peacocks posture with brilliant feathers; the dominant rhesus monkey walks with tail and head erect; and people emit cries, tones, gestures and facial expressions that arouse others and move them to action.

People presumably had vocal sounds before thay had language. Vocal sounds can support some of the universal activities of social life—courting, mothering, fighting. An archaic link between vocal sounds and social feelings is still with us. We recognize the voices of acquaintances immediately, even after a long absence. We know immediately from the tone of a voice what kind of message will follow. We use words as other animals use sounds, in the service of social interaction. The words are complex but the message in the voice is simple. We elaborate upon the same themes over and over again.

But while people have some of the simple social concerns that other animals have, they differ from other animals in their intellect. The most average person can deal with abstract problems to a degree unmatched by any other animal. Human intellect, evolving along with other human abilities, has been shaped by nature and adapted to deal with nature. Intellect carries with it a practical understanding of the world of the here and now and of likely variations in this world that might be encountered in the future. The intellect, emerging from dealings with the world, encompasses a system for abstracting and categorizing the properties of the world, providing in effect a *grammar* of the world.

The intellectual grammar manipulates abstract symbols, but it does so in a social context. Other persons are part of the natural environment and the intellectual grammar must encompass these other people. Other persons are needed to help one cope with the world and the originally primitive vocal display system provides a flexible medium for communicating the activities of intellect. Anthropological evidence (Lieberman & Crelin, 1971) suggests that the adaptive value of speech was so great that the throat evolved toward improved speaking ability at the expense of efficient swallowing, introducing a lethal component and giving a new meaning to the admonition, "Don't talk with your mouth full!"

Language today, in Mattingly's (1972) view, has emerged from a marriage of two systems, one evolving primitive vocal stimuli that convey information about recurring social themes, and the other involving a grammar based upon strategies the intellect has found useful in dealing with the world. A complex intellect has been combined with a simple social display system. Both systems benefit from the marriage because physical qualities of the voice are complex enough to articulate complex ideas, and the intellect provides new ways of expressing the same old social themes.

This state of affairs is useful to the social actors but confusing to eavesdroppers listening to the words. It is difficult to know when the words are important and when they are only being used as vehicles for tones that convey simple social effects. The words will evoke ideas in the listener, whether or not the ideas were important to the speaker. The situation is especially confusing when social and intellectual aspects of a message are intermixed. One partner may try to instruct the other or gather information, while the other wants a purely social exchange. One partner may flirt while the other is serious. One partner may try to please, in order to make a sale or win a vote, using social tactics to persuade the other about a new idea. A speaker may alternate between social and intellectual concerns, even within a single utterance.

The present chapter is concerned with monitoring and scoring the functions that underlie conversation. Complex conversations must eventually be dealt with, but as a starting point it seems advisable to focus upon the simple situation in which both parties are oriented either towards social or towards intellectual issues. Further, if the words are not to be trusted, as has been suggested here, it might be preferable to begin with ignoring the words and searching for the meaning of a conversation in content-free parameters. The parameters to be considered here come from the stuff behind the words, the patterning of sound and silence and tone of voice and the flow of smiles and gestures and eye contact that accompanies conversation. The first study reported below was done to see whether social and intellectual segments of conversation might somehow "look" different from one another.

## THE "LOOK" OF A CONVERSATION

In unpublished exploratory work, Gloria Choo and I found that observers can agree in their moment-by-moment scoring of a conversation as social or intellectual, based solely upon watching the speakers' faces, without hearing their voices. Subjects were 13 male and 13 female university students who had not previously met and who conversed in opposite-sex pairs for half an hour each. They were asked to get to know each other, talking about their backgrounds, likes and dislikes, school activities and so forth, and also to spend time discussing more serious issues, such as presidential politics, Mexican-U.S. relations and problems in the Middle East. The subjects' faces were recorded using two television cameras with zoom lenses, and images of the two faces were merged side by side onto a single videotape.

Two judges watched the videotapes with the sound turned off and a partition between the judges so that they would not influence each other. Each judge used a three-way switch to indicate continuously whether the conversation at each moment was:

1. Social, with subjects attending to each other and displaying responsive nods, smiles or facial expressions:
2. Intellectual, with subjects appearing to be caught up in their own ideas, displaying thoughtful expressions and markedly less attention toward each other.
3. Not clearly either social or intellectual.

TABLE 7.1
Percentage of Time Judges Agreed and Disagreed in Scoring Moments of Conversation

|  |  | Social | Judge B<br>Neither | Intellectual |
|---|---|---|---|---|
|  | Social | .12 | .04 | .00 |
| Judge A | Neither | .03 | .59 | .03 |
|  | Intellectual | .00 | .03 | .16 |

Table 7.1 shows mean proportions of agreement and disagreement between the judges on the three coding categories. As can be seen in the cells along the diagonal of the table, the judges agreed a total of 87% of the time, and they agreed that the conversation was social 12%, intellectual 16%, and neither 59% of the time. It never happened that one judge scored "social" while the other scored "intellectual." The mean weighted Kappa index was .72, where Kappa reflects the degree to which agreement exceeds chance (.00) and approaches perfection (1.00) (Cohen, 1968). We take this high level of agreement as evidence that judges can score the social-intellectual distinction reliably, even though the occurrence of purely social or intellectual episodes was relatively infrequent.

This demonstration leaves a number of questions unanswered. It is based upon data from only two judges, and it treated social and intellectual as pure types of conversation. It did not attempt to analyse combinations of social and intellectual elements. A basic issue concerns the question of whether responsiveness of *facial expression* has any bearing upon social versus intellectual *oral conversation*. We do not know how judges would have scored the sound track, nor do we know what the subjects really had in mind while they were talking. But the point of this chapter is that conversation to a large extent reflects the use of a primitive display system to convey simple social effects. Facial expressiveness is only one aspect of this display system (voice being another), but we did find that judges using a nonverbal classification system could agree in scoring a dimension that we thought would distinguish between social and intellectual conversation.

## Temporal Patterning and the Form of a Conversation

The judges agreed that different segments of conversation "looked" social or intellectual. The next step would seem to be to find out whether these segments also "sounded" different from one another. Unfortunately, in the conversations described above, technical problems made it impossible to separate the voices of the two subjects, and we decided to collect additional conversations for study. Before describing these conversations, let us consider what aspects of a vocal exchange should be studied.

We wish to avoid dealing with the actual words spoken, because of the difficulty in scoring the meaning of words and because focusing upon the words can obscure the issue of what a conversation is about. Even when the aim of a conversation has little to do with words, the words will be there, because conversation without words is impossible. Sometimes the words will serve only as "filler," providing a vehicle to convey simple social affects, and the elaborate symbolic meaning of the words will be superfluous. This notion was supported by fragments we heard in the Choo and Dabbs' conversations. In one episode of apparent great good humour and laughter, upon turning up the sound we could hear that the subjects were talking about suicide. Their casual and happy manner belied the seriousness of their words.

If the words themselves are not useful, what is left is how the words are said. This includes style, or form, the structure into which words and ideas are fitted. Form has diverse meanings as can be seen throughout this volume; it can refer to stock phrases, dialect used with a particular audience or setting, the fitting together of sounds with rhyme and metre, or even the connotations of words chosen to express an idea. It includes rhythm in English and melody in a tonal language. It includes the auctioneer's fast speech and the preacher's "stained glass voice" Of all the possible varied meanings of form, this chapter will consider only one; temporal patterning. Specifically, we will deal with the patterning of sound and silence and eye contact that provides a continuous background for the lexical content of a conversation.

There are a number of reasons for focusing upon temporal patterning. Measures of timing provide a link to a currently popular tradition in cognitive psychology (Posner, 1978). Timing can vary independently of the words being used and, as a result, can convey information independent of the words. In common parlance, we refer to a person's ability to say the right thing at the right time and to the skillful timing of a comedian or public speaker. Timing can be related to the ideas being discussed, to a speaker's internal state, or to stimuli from the audience or elsewhere in the environment. Timing of speech and gaze will vary as the speaker searches for words, considers ideas, waits for a response, watches the partner's reaction, or sets up a pattern of leading or following the partner in a series of utterances. Timing could be keyed to more global factors, such as the emotional tone of an exchange, or the speaker's skill, or even personality differences associated with childhood experiences with rhythm (Ayres, 1973). Even changes in body temperature can affect a speaker's subjective sense of time (O'Hanlon, McGrath, & McCauley, 1974), perhaps in turn affecting the overall pace of any time-based processes.

Finally, temporal patterning can be studied objectively and automatically. The tradition of studying the temporal patterning of speech is most closely associated with the work of Jaffe & Feldstein (1970). Jaffe and Feldstein worked with an Automated Vocal Transaction Analyzer, which allowed them to ignore the content of speech and focus upon regularities in the detailed patterning of speaking and pausing. Feldstein and Welkowitz (1978) review a number of studies that have used this approach and present a schema that treats conversation as a stream of alternating *turns* between partners. A turn begins when one partner speaks alone and lasts until the other partner speaks alone. Each turn is made up of *vocalizations* and *pauses:* a pause that ends a turn is a *switching pause.* An utterance by one partner when the other is talking is called *simultaneous speech;* simultaneous speech is *interruptive* if it leads to a change of turn and *noninterruptive* if it does not. *(Noninterruptive simultaneous speech* will result either when the listner interjects a word or when the listener tries, and fails, to gain the floor.)

This schema, with vocal parameters that can be scored electronically and analyzed by computer, will be emphasized in the rest of this chapter. In addition to speech, the pattern of each partner's gazing toward the face of the other will be considered. Gaze is generally regarded as important in conversation (Ellsworth & Ludwig, 1972; Exline, 1972; Vine, 1973). Speech and gaze change rapidly, and information in the patterning of speech and gaze in a conversation lasting several minutes is enormous.

There are many ways in which the parameters of speech and gaze describing a conversation can be summarized. *Simple parameters* can be examined. One could describe the percentage of time, number of occurrences and mean length of occurrence of each vocal and visual parameter. For example, a subject might pause 85 times in 10 minutes, have an average turn length of 5.8 seconds, or look at his or her partner 60% of the time. Such simple parameters might characterize a conversation as erratic and halting or fast-paced and smooth. *Pairs of parameters* can be examined. The co-occurrence of behaviours often has special meaning. For example, a high level of looking at the partner may be quite normal when one is listening but less so when one is talking. *Sequential patterns of parameters* can be examined, using time series techniques to show how a subject's speech or gaze is affected by what happened in preceding moments. Such patterns can show us the extent to which the partners are responsive to one another or behave independently of one another. Finally, *spectral techniques* can detect repetitive or cyclical variation in speech or gaze over the course of a conversation. Such cyclical variation would appear if a conversation alternates between being fast and slow, halting and smooth, or even social and intellectual.

## PROBABLE DIFFERENCES BETWEEN SOCIAL AND INTELLECTUAL FORM

Given that there are ways of scoring and summarizing the form that might reside in the patterning of speech and gaze, let us return to the question of how this form might differ between social and intellectual conversations. Real conversations must be examined, but it might be useful first to speculate upon the kinds of differences that would be expected to follow from our conception of these two kinds of conversation. The patterning of speech and gaze should be affected by the subject's focus of attention and by the complexity of the ideas being communicated.

Social conversations focus upon the partner and relationships with the partner. Partners should look at one another more, because looking is needed for them to coordinate their behaviour and respond to one another. Looking will tend to ensure continued thoughts about the partner, which in turn should lead to continued looking. In most conversation, the listener's looking is high, but in social conversations the speaker's looking should also be high. If the speaker is already thinking about the partner, he or she will not be distracted from other thoughts by the sight of the partner.

The pace should be faster in social rather than intellectual conversation, with shorter vocalizations. Social communication, because it deals with simple and stylized information, should itself tend to be simple and stylized. We deal with social relationships that have existed since time immemorial, variations on themes of playing, working, protecting, loving and fighting. We communicate these themes easily because our listeners are largely replications of ourselves and quick to understand what we mean (see, however, Chapter 2). The messages are stereotyped and can be delivered in a few words. Sometimes a message is carried completely by tone of voice or hesitancy of speech.

Speech in social conversation should also be affected by social arousal. The presence of fellow creatures of the same species increases arousal in both people and animals (Zajonc, 1965). Arousal can occur in intellectual conversation, of course, as one becomes excited about ideas. But arousal should be more likely in social conversation because attention will be directed toward the partner, making this potential source of arousal especially and continuously salient. Arousal has an energizing effect. Words should be spoken more rapidly, allowing turns to be completed more quickly. Pauses should become shorter and fewer. Switching pauses should become shorter, and there should be more occasions on which turns change with no switching pause at all. Arousal should also speed up the pace of conversation by reducing the likelihood of complicated and involved thoughts; thoughts that are already relatively unlikely in social conversation. An exception to this tendency for arousal to facilitate speech would occur in situations when subjects do not know what to say, in which case the arousal would facilitate the dominant responses of hesitating, stammering or waiting for the other to speak.

Intellectual conversations focus more upon ideas. One effect of this should be to reduce the amount of gaze toward a partner. The sight of the partner is both distracting and arousing. It interferes with the ability to think and leads the speaker towards simple and stereotyped utterances. The need to think should cause the speaker's gaze to be reduced. Gaze is ordinarily low during a speaker's vocalizations and pauses, and during vocalizations and pauses in intellectual conversation it should be even lower.

The pace should be slower in intellectual than in social conversation. The speaker is considering notions that go beyond social feelings; notions that may not be readily understood by the listener. The speaker has to explain more of what he or she is talking about and words become important. Complex messages cannot be conveyed by facial expression and tone of voice, and more dependence upon words should lead to longer vocalizations and turns. There should be longer pauses between the vocalizations within a turn, as the speaker searches for words, and longer switching pauses between turns, as the partner thinks more before responding. Speech parameters might be more variable in intellectual conversation, as ideas alternate between flowing smoothly and becoming elusive. Long pauses are accepted by the participants in intellectual conversation as a normal result of trying to "figure things out," while long pauses in social conversation indicate things are not going well and will tend to be avoided.

A focus upon the partner in social conversation could lead to a tendency for the partners to copy or mimic one another (see Chapters 4 & 10). In the literature on nonverbal communication there is a discussion of synchrony, the tendency for persons to mimic one another's physical posture and gestures (Scheflen, 1964). Even newborn infants mimic the facial expressions of their caretakers (Meltzoff & Moore, 1977). It has frequently been reported that partners in conversation emit pauses of similar length (Feldstein & Welkowitz, 1978), though this could be because both partners are affected by the same conversational topic or by other shared stimuli. Time series analysis might provide an appropriate technique for revealing a greater responsiveness to the partner in social rather than in intellectual conversations.

Rhythmical components in the exchange between conversational partners could be examined using spectral techniques. We would expect the overall cadence of a conversation to be slower when the conversation is more intellectual. Different kinds of rhythm are possible. One partner, for example, might hold forth and dominate the conversation with a series of long turns, while the other partner emits short utterances. Then, with a shift in the conversation, the other partner would have a series of long turns while the first partner emits short utterances. Here the partners would be completely out of phase with one another in the lengths of their turns. In other conversations, the partners could be in phase with one another, following the same cycle. For example, there could be episodes in which both partners speak in short turns, or look at each other a great deal, or pause for long periods. Finally, the partners could follow cycles slightly out of phase with one another, with one partner leading the other in changes of behaviour. For example, one partner's rising enthusiasm, reflected in interruptions, could in subsequent moments induce similar enthusiasm—and interruptions—in the other party.

It is possible that social and intellectual conversations will differ in their moment-to-moment predictability. Social conversations deal with archaic social relationships, and simple and stereotyped themes are repeated with slight variations in the words used. Often the important thing is that conversation takes place, with the content being secondary. Because there is little essential content, there is little to disrupt the underlying pattern of turns, vocalizations, pauses, glances and other content-free parameters into which content is fitted.

In intellectual conversation, participants discuss the complex possibilities of a world that involves more than the here and now of social relationships. Communicating this novelty requires a more careful arrangement of words than does communicating social feelings. Words and ideas follow their own rules of grammar and logic, independent of the relationship between speaker and listener, and unpredictably long or short turns, vocalizations and pauses would be expected to occur more frequently.

Some Social Conversations

Two studies provide some beginnings for the examination of temporal patterning in different kinds of conversation. These studies show that we can generate conversations in the laboratory that differ on a social-intellectual dimension. They also show that temporal patterning of speech and gaze varies along some of the lines suggested here.

The first study, by Dabbs, Evans, Hooper, and Purvis (1980), examined pairs of subjects getting acquainted. Subjects were selected to be high or low in social skill, as measured by Snyder's (1974) self-monitoring scale. High self-monitors are responsive to their social environments, monitoring their actions and what happens around them, changing their behaviour to do what is appropriate and performing continuously as if acting out a part in a play. Low self-monitors, on the other hand, attend less to social demands and behave more similarly from situation to situation. The behaviour of the high self-monitor is flexible, perhaps even superficial; the low self-monitor lacks either the motivation or the ability to be flexible. High self-monitors have been found to be more popular in undergraduate campus organizations, and it seemed reasonable to us to treat self-monitoring as an index of social skill. In getting acquainted with one another, high self-monitors were expected to converse in a more "social" manner than lows, directing more attention toward their partners and showing less indication of abstract thought.

Twelve high and 12 low self-monitoring pairs were selected from the extremes of a sample of 164 college students who completed the self-monitoring scale. Subjects in each pair were of the same sex, and low and high groups were equally divided among male and female pairs. Subjects were not previously acquainted. They reported in pairs to a social psychology laboratory where they were seated on opposite sides of a table. They spent 10 minutes getting to know one another, talking about their backgrounds, activities in school or things outside of school. On the table between them was a wooden box with a window through the centre, through which they could see each other's faces (Dabbs, 1979). Transparent mirrors in the window gave subjects unobstructed views of each other but at the same time diverted images of their faces into a television camera and thence into a videotape recorder. Subjects wore lapel microphones and their voices were recorded on two audio channels of the same videotape. Subjects appeared to become accustomed to this set-up and converse normally fairly quickly.

The videotape recordings were later scored by sending the voice channels through an electronic interface into a microcomputer (Dabbs & Evans, 1982) and by having judges view the tape on a monitor and press a switch whenever each subject appeared to look toward his or her partner. Gaze was easy to score, and reliability between judges was high. The microcomputer monitored the voice channels and the judges monitored the gaze switches, and this information was transmitted to a larger computer. The larger computer maintained a continuous record of the state of each subject's gaze and speech, including turns, vocalizations, pauses, switching pauses, interruptive simultaneous speech and noninterruptive simultaneous speech.

Analysis of summary scores for each subject on each speech and gaze parameter suggested that high self-monitors talked in a more "social" manner than lows. The experimenters had observed informally that high self-monitors in the experiment were more enthusiastic than lows and more interested in one another. The analyses supported these impressions, showing that high self-monitors had significantly shorter turns than lows and emitted significantly more interruptive simultaneous speech, being more likely to initiate their turns before their partners stopped talking. Shorter turns would seem to indicate ideas that are less complex or less completely worked out than longer turns, and the interruptive changes of turn suggest that high self-monitors were not pausing to think about their ideas in any great detail before responding. Thus, it appeared that high self-monitors, more than lows, were oriented toward facile and superficial responding to their partners.

While the high self-monitor's pattern of speech appeared to reflect a more social orientation, initial analysis of their gaze parameters showed no such effect. High self-monitors looked at their partners no more than lows did. Perhaps this should not be surprising, because others have found gaze patterns to be similar even among people as different as infants and adults (Peery & Stern, 1974). Females gazed more than males, however, and under other conditions a more or less social orientation might produce differences in gaze. A different pattern of gaze did appear in a study of more intellectual conversations, which is to be described next.

## Some Intellectual Conversations

The second study examined conversations that were more purely intellectual. Subjects were 12 male and 12 female pairs of undergraduate students, not selected on the basis of self-monitoring scores. Each pair was told that the investigator had been studying conversations among people getting acquainted and now wished to study more serious conversations. Each subject was given a sheet of information about the 1979 U.S. fuel crisis, containing questions of how serious it was, whose fault it was and what should be done about it. Subjects sat alone in separate rooms for 10 minutes to gather their thoughts, then went to the experimental room to converse for 10 minutes. Procedures for recording and analyzing the speech and gaze patterns were the same as in the earlier study.

There were differences in temporal patterning between these intellectual conversations and the earlier social conversations among high and low self-monitors. Patterns of speech and gaze seemed to show more cognitive activity and less social involvement in the intellectual conversations. Intellectual conversations had fewer and longer turns than social conversations. Noninterruptive simultaneous speech was higher, perhaps because longer turns always elicit more interjections from a listener. Gazes were shorter, although overall amount of gaze was about the same as before. Gaze also differed from the earlier social conversations in being especially low during the pauses within a subject's turn and during the switching pause just before a subject's turn. Cognitive processing is presumed to occur during pauses (Allen & Guy, 1977), and the particularly low gaze here could have reflected the speaker's need to think about the issue and avoid being distracted by the sight of the partner.

Time series and spectral techniques were used to contrast the sequential patterning of speech between the intellectual conversations and the earlier social ones. In the time series approach, each conversation was treated as a string of alternating turns between partners. Each turn may have a degree of predictability arising from a history going back a number of turns into the past. For each turn the values of each parameter were computed, such as turn length, amount of pausing, amount of gaze and so forth. Auto-correlations were used to see whether a parameter during a subject's turn could be predicted from parameters in prior turns of the subject or the partner. Contrary to expectations, the time series analysis generally did not reveal differences between high and low self-monitors or between social and intellectual conversations. This approach revealed little continuity in subjects from turn to turn and little responsiveness, or back and forth flow of mutual influence between subjects, in these content-free parameters. This is not to say that there is no continuity and influence, but none showed up in the content-free parameters. The findings here are in contrast to the generally reported findings that the average value of parameters across the course of a conversation shows congruence or synchrony between subjects (Feldstein & Welkowitz, 1978). When the data was analysed as described by Feldstein & Welkowitz, based upon each subject's average scores, high correlations were found between subjects within a pair (among the social conversations, $r = .72$ for pause length and $r = .69$ for switching pause length), but this relationship disappeared when we examined the moment-by-moment patterning. It could be that both subjects in a pair tend to be similar because they are influenced by the same factors, even though their mutual moment-by-moment influence upon one another is small.

Much more success was encountered using spectral techniques to contrast social and intellectual conversations (Dabbs, 1983a). A curve was first generated to display the flow of turns and pauses across each 10-minute conversation. The curves showed the state of each conversation at each quarter second, with $A$'s vocalizations plotted as $+1$, $B$'s vocalizations plotted as $-1$, pauses plotted as zero and simultaneous speech ignored. Visual examination of the resulting curves suggested that subjects alternated in such a fashion that $A$ would tend to have a string of long turns, followed by $B$ having a string of long turns, and so forth. A Fourier analysis was performed to break each overall curve down into its sine wave components, or cyclical alterations, and analysis of variance was used to test the significance of the difference in the Fourier results between the 24 social and 24 intellectual conversations.

The findings indicated that long cycles were more characteristic of intellectual than of social conversation. The dominant cycle length was in the range of 32–124 seconds for intellectual conversations and 2-8 seconds in social conversations. It appears likely that long cycles in intellectual conversations, which might be called "megaturns", result from the ideas being discussed, ideas that take longer to complete than the simple affects and pleasantries of social conversation. A more detailed contrast between the social conversations in the self-monitoring study and the intellectual discussions on the fuel crisis is provided by Dabbs (1983b).

## CONCLUSIONS

These analyses of speech and gaze indicated differences in the patterning of speech and gaze between social and intellectual conversation. The differences fit with expectations about conversations geared toward serving the disparate functions of promoting social bonds and promoting an exchange of ideas. It would be incorrect to regard the conversations studied as pure manifestations of social or intellectual activity. The conversations were complex and determined by many factors, but it seems that the social-intellectual dimension was a salient one. For this reason, the present findings can be taken as support for the notion that the social-intellectual difference with be reflected in temporal patterns of speech and gaze.

The next step might be to use the techniques described here to explore how social and intellectual functions account for the activity of everyday conversation, examining segments of conversation that are not clearly social or intellectual, but contain elements of both. One application would be to examine the patterns of speech and gaze in persuasive speakers, persons who can talk about intellectual matters in a manner that makes whatever they say acceptable (cf. Chapter 8). Such people may be salesmen, teachers, political leaders, psychotherapists, psychopaths or ordinary citizens to whom people like to listen. An analysis of temporal patterning may show some of these persons skilled in blending social and intellectual styles, building social bonds that help get their ideas accepted.

Such speakers may present intellectual ideas while disarming their listeners with an attentive or responsive social manner. Successful social actors may be flexible enough to produce various combinations of social or intellectual content with an underlying social or intellectual form.

It is likely that some of the findings will bear upon the nature of social skill. Social skill is often presumed to involve being responsive to the other; this is how the high self-monitor is usually described. But there is also skill in providing a model for the other to follow, especially if the other is socially less competent than oneself. This may be what some therapists do with shy and retiring clients. We need to learn more about the outcome, both in terms of current satisfaction and future social competence, of interacting with others who are especially skilled in conversation. We also need to know more about the antecedents of conversation skill, of how one person learns the characteristic patterns of social conversation, while another learns a more intellectual style. And, finally, is there any intrinsic tie between the content of a conversation and the underlying style used to express this content?

The approaches described in this chapter are statistical ones, and their strength will be greatest in analyzing long conversations or large numbers of conversations. Short utterances may always have to be understood in the light of the content of what is said, because the underlying temporal patterning is too fragmentary to be informative. But over longer periods of time the way that words are strung together, with sound and silence and changing facial expression, may tell us more than the words themselves about what is going on.

## REFERENCES

Allen, D. E., & Guy R. F. Ocular breaks and verbal output. *Sociometry,* 1977, *40,* 90–96.

Arendt, H. *The life of the mind: vol. 1. Thinking.* New York: Harcourt Brace Jovanovich, 1978.

Ayres, B. Effects of infant carrying practices on rhythm in music. *Ethos,* 1973, *1,* 387–404.

Bales, R. F., & Strodtbeck, F. L. Phases in group problem solving. *Journal of Abnormal and Social Psychology,* 1951, *46,* 485–495.

Cohen, J. Weighted Kappa: nominal scale agreement with provision for scaled disagreement or partial credit. *Psychological Bulletin,* 1968, *70,* 213–220.

Dabbs, J. M., Jr. Portable apparatus for recording direct frontal views of conversing subjects' faces. *Behaviour Research Methods and Instrumentation,* 1979, *11,* 531–532.

Dabbs, J. M., Jr. Fourier analysis and the rhythm of conversation. Atlanta, Ga.: Georgia State University (ERIC Document Reproduction Service No. ED 222 959) 1983.(a)

Dabbs, J. M., Jr. Measuring the cognitive load of conversation: speech rhythm and speech-gaze patterns. *Psychological Documents,* 1983b, *13,*3.

Dabbs, J. M., Jr., & Evans, M. S. Electronic AVTA: signal processing for automatic vocal transaction analysis. *Behaviour Research Methods and Instrumentation,* 1982, *14,* 461–462.

Dabbs, J. M., Jr., Evans, M. S., Hooper, C. H., & Purvis, J. A. Self-monitors in conversation: what do they monitor? *Journal of Personality and Social Psychology,* 1980, *39,* 278–284.

Ellsworth, P. C., & Ludwig, L. M. Visual behaviour in social interaction. *Journal of Communication,* 1972, *22,* 375–403

Exline, R. V. Visual interaction: the glances of power and preference. In J. Cole (Ed.), *Nebraska Symposium on Motivation* (Vol. 19). Lincoln: University of Nebraska, 1972.

Feldstein, S., & Welkowitz, J. A chronography of conversation: in defense of an objective approach. In A. W. Siegman & S. Feldstein (Eds.), *Nonverbal behavior and communication.* Hillsdale, NJ: Erlbaum, 1978.

Fiedler, F. E. A contingency model of leadership effectiveness. In L. Berkowitz (Ed.), *Advances in experimental social psychology* (Vol. 1). New York: Academic, 1964.

Gamson, W. A. Ethnomethodology. In W. A. Gamson & A. Modigliani (Eds.), *Conceptions of social life.* Boston: Little, Brown, 1974.

Halliday, M. A. K. *Explorations in the functions of language.* London: Edward Arnold, 1973.

Hamilton, D. L., & Fallot, R. D. Information salience as a weighting factor in impression formation. *Journal of Personality and Social Psychology,* 1974, *30,* 444–448.

Jaffe, J., & Feldstein, S. *Rhythms of dialogue.* New York: Academic, 1970.

Langer, E., Blank, A. & Chanowitz, B. The mindlessness of ostensibly thoughtful action: the role of "placebic" information in interpersonal interaction. *Journal of Personality and Social Psychology,* 1978, *36,* 635–642.

Lieberman, A. M., & Crelin, S. On the speech of Neanderthal Man, *Linguistic Inquiry,* 1971, *2,* 203–222.

Mattingly, I. G. Speech cues as sign stimuli. *American Scientist,* 1972, *60,* 327–337.

Meltzoff, A. N., & Moore, M. K. Imitation of facial and manual gestures by human neonates. *Science,* 1977, *198,* 75–78.

O'Hanlon, J. F., McGrath, J. J., & McCauley, M. E. Body temperature and temporal acuity. *Journal of Experimental Psychology,* 1974, *102,* 788–794.

Peery, J. C. & Stern, D. N. Gaze duration frequency distributions during mother-infant interaction. *Journal of Genetic Psychology,* 1974, *129,* 45–55.

Posner, M. I. *Chronometric explorations of mind.* Hillsdale, N.J.: Lawrence Erlbaum Associates, 1978.

Robinson, W. P. *Language and social behaviour.* Baltimore: Penguin, 1972.

Scheflen, A. E. The significance of posture in communication systems. *Psychiatry,* 1964, *27,* 316–331.

Snyder, M. The self-monitoring of expressive behaviour. *Journal of Personality and Social Psychology,* 1974, *30,* 526–537.

Vine, I. The role of facial-visual signalling in early social development. In M. Cranach & I. Vine (Eds.), *Social communication and movement.* New York: Academic Press, 1973.

Zajonc, R. B. Social facilitation. *Science,* 1965, *149,* 269–274.

# 8 An Expectancy Interpretation of Language and Persuasion

Michael Burgoon
*University of Arizona*

Gerald R. Miller
*Michigan State University*

## INTRODUCTION

Our language affects our lives powerfully. By evaluating our language choices, others make attributions about social and professional status, background and education and even the intent of communication (see Chapters 5 & 6). Those intrigued with social influence, whether classical scholars or media image-makers, have long pondered the influence of such language choices on the success or failure of persuasive attempts. The decision to appeal to people's logical or emotional side is manifest in the language used in persuasive messages: Persuaders try to mollify, justify, terrify, or crucify by altering the language of their appeals.

Though few would deny the suasive power of language, relatively little research has examined the effects of differing language strategies on attitudinal and behavioural change. Granted, some studies have examined the relationships between specific language and message variables (e.g., fear appeals, emotional appeals, intense language) and persuasive effectiveness, but fewer attempts have been made to provide a theoretical perspective that explains more adequately the role of specific message variables in facilitating or inhibiting changes in attitudes and behaviours. This chapter develops a line of reasoning which holds that since language is a rule-governed system, people develop norms and expectations concerning appropriate usage in given situations. In many transactions, the language used confirms these norms and expectations—indeed, frequent confirmation helps to explain the maintenance of the norms and expectations. In some persuasive situations, however, communicators, intentionally or accidentally, violate norms governing appropriate language usage, thus violating the expectations of message receivers; and, in turn, affecting their receptivity.[1]

Obviously, many cultural and sociological forces shape our patterns of ordinary language and determine normative and non-normative usage. As communicators mature, they not only learn the mechanics of language but also *what* to say and *when* to say it—or at least they think they do. Besides cultural and sociological forces that shape the appropriateness and effectiveness of language choices, several communicator, situational, and context variables also influence the persuasive effectiveness of different message strategies.

Turning to the persuasion literature, Brooks (1970) demonstrated that receivers have shared expectations about the behaviours a communicator should exhibit. When these expectations are violated, receivers overreact to the behaviours actually exhibited. If the communicator initially is perceived negatively, but he or she demonstrates more positive behaviours than anticipated, receivers overestimate the positiveness of the unanticipated behaviours. The reverse also holds: If an initially positive communicator exhibits unexpectedly negative actions, recievers exaggerate their negative evaluation of the communicator and/or the message. Research by McPeek and Edwards (1975) further supports the proposition that positive violations of expectations increase persuasibility only for initially negatively evaluated sources.

Though much of this research involved situations where communicators took unexpected positions or advanced unexpected arguments, some evidence also suggests that people develop general expectations about the linguistic properties of messages. Burgoon and Chase (1973) found that when inoculation messages differed in linguistic structure from attack messages, the amount of persuasion prompted by those messages differed. Based on this finding, Burgoon and Stewart (1975) posited that when communicators positively violate linguistic expectations, attitude change toward the advocated position increases; when communicators negatively violate linguistic expectations, a boomerang effect occurs, with receivers changing to the position opposite to the one advocated by the communicator. Both of these studies are discussed later in this chapter, but the important point is that people develop expectations about the appropriateness of the content and the language of persuasive messages. Violations of these expectations can either facilitate or inhibit persuasion.

---

[1]We grant that our position could be couched in an attribution theory perspective. Since much of the research described adopted an expectancy framework and since "attribution theories" refer to such a wide variety of theoretical perspectives, we opted for a more restricted perspective as reflected in our expectation interpretation.

Thus, our first major proposition can be stated as follows:

*Proposition 1.* People develop expectations about language behaviours which subsequently affect their acceptance or rejection of persuasive messages.

Moreover, two corollary propositions constitute the beginning point for developing a more complete theoretical synthesis of the relationship between specific language variables and persuasion:

*Proposition 1A.* Use of language that negatively violates normative expectations about appropriate communication behaviour inhibits persuasive effectiveness
*Proposition 1B.* Use of language that positively violates expectations by conforming more closely than anticipated to normative expectations of appropriate communication behaviour facilitates persuasive effectiveness.

Obviously, these propositions provide but a modest beginning toward developing an understanding of the relationship between language use and persuasion. Nevertheless, they have stimulated our research questions, propositions and hypotheses for more than a decade. The rest of this chapter discusses studies that have addressed questions and hypotheses derived from the previous three propositions.

To date, our research has focused on three different persuasive paradigms. Several studies examined the traditional *passive message reception paradigm* (Miller & Burgoon, 1973), where communicators create messages designed to change the attitudes and/or behaviours of message receivers. A second series of studies investigated a radically different persuasive situation labelled the *active participation paradigm*. Most of these studies required the intended persuadees to engage in counterattitudinal advocacy; thus, the research sought to determine the effects of specific language variables on persons actively engaged in advocating positions they themselves did not privately believe. In both the active and passive paradigms, primary interest centred on discovering the relationship between language choices and persuading either the self or some target audience. A final communication situation examined was the *resistance to persuasion paradigm*. Obviously, this third paradigm differs substantially from the first two since the relationship between differences in language usage and subsequent inhibition of persuasive attempts was of paramount concern. The three persuasive paradigms provide the major divisions for this chapter.

Although our research can be grouped under these three broad contextual headings, numerous other questions were also addressed. Perhaps it would be useful to list some of the major issues dealt with at various stages:

1. The research examined selected language variables commonly used in persuasive appeals.[2] Attention was directed at three broad classes of appeals: Those meant to arouse fear and threat; those reflected in opinionated rejection and acceptance statements; and those varying in the linguistic intensity with which they argued a position. These three types of appeals permitted us to identify normative expectations about appropriate communication so as to determine the effects of violations of expectations on persuasive impact.

2. Considerable attention was devoted to determining the relationship between specific communicator attributes and language choices as determinants of persuasive success or failure. Since communicator credibility has a strong impact on persuasive efficacy, a major thrust of our research was to determine more precisely the effectiveness of different language strategies when used by people with varying levels of credibility. A related line of research examined the sex of communicator as a factor in persuasive success, given the use of differing language strategies.

3. Some attention was given to investigating selected receiver attributes as predictors of receptivity to varying persuasive strategies. Though these receiver variables have not yet received the lion's share of our attention, some knowledge has been gained about the effects of sex of the receiver and relative open- and closed-mindedness on receptivity to specific message appeals.

4. In almost every study, interest was focused on the effects of cognitive stress, whether chronic or induced, on communicator language choices and/or receiver responses to various message strategies. In some studies, stress was induced in the communicators by forcing them to use specific kinds of language. In others, stress was induced in the receivers by using language strategies designed to threaten or frighten them. Yet other studies examined the receptivity of receivers placed under induced stress to various language strategies.

Although these general concerns guided our research, one study built upon others and often suggested new methods for discovering knowledge

---

[2]We have dealt with different forms of language intensity. Others, such as Moscovici (1976) Sandell (1977), and Scherer (1979) have examined a wider range of linguistic variables in their syntheses.

about the role of expected language behaviour in determining people's responses to persuasive messages. This continuity will be further revealed as we examine the three broad areas of research concern.

## PASSIVE MESSAGE RECEPTION PARADIGM

Unquestionably, most published research on persuasion has focused on situations where a communicator prepares and delivers a message designed to produce some kind of behavioural change in the people who receive the message. Three kinds of message appeals interested us in this kind of persuasive situation.

The first message strategy examined was *fear-arousing appeals*. The questions of how communicators use language to arouse fear and how such arousal affects persuasive receptivity can be approached from a cognitive consistency perspective (Festinger, 1957; Heider, 1946; Newcomb, 1953; Osgood & Tannenbaum, 1955). These theories assume that individuals strive to maintain consistency between various cognitive elements, e.g., their covert attitudes and their overt behaviours. Since cognitive consistency is assumed to be the preferred psychological state, any perception of inconsistency will stimulate activities aimed at restoring consistency. Thus, any persuasive message can be conceived as having two functions: (1) arousing cognitive inconsistency in message recipients; and (2) providing specific recommendations for restoring cognitive consistency.

Several early studies assumed that messages containing strong fear-arousing appeals would result in more cognitive inconsistency than messages using milder language. The explicit language of the strong fear-arousing appeal emphasizes the harmful consequences of failure to comply with the advocated message position, while the language of the mild appeal does not. Since strong language should produce more stress in receivers, greater motivation to comply with requested changes so as to restore cognitive consistency should occur.

Using a different theoretical perspective, Janis and Feshbach (1953) stimulated considerable controversy with their findings that mild fear messages were more persuasive, both in terms of immediate compliance and resistance to subsequent persuasive attacks, than their strong fear counterparts. Because of several procedural problems in research supporting a negative relationship between fear arousal and attitude change (De Wolfe & Governale, 1964; Janis & Terwilliger, 1962), only limited support can be claimed for this position. Additional studies have reported a positive relationship between level of fear arousal and attitude change (Leventhal & Niles, 1964, 1965; Niles, 1964; Singer, 1965). To add to the theoretical confusion, others have found no relationship between level of fear arousal and subsequent attitude change (Beach, 1966; Powell, 1965). These inconsistent findings suggest that other variables are important determinants of the effects of fear-arousing appeals on subsequent persuasive impact.

To investigate some of these specific mediating variables, Miller and Hewgill 1966) examined: (1) the relationship between source credibility, fear arousal, and attitude change; (2) the effects of the referent of the fear-arousing language on persuasive impact; and (3) various types of fear-arousing appeals that can be employed. These investigators hypothesized that if a source has high initial credibility, appeals eliciting strong fear will be more persuasive than messages using mild appeals. They also posited the converse for low credibile sources: Mild fear-arousing appeals will result in greater attitude change than strong appeals, though change will generally be less for low credible communicators.

In two studies by these authors, the highly credible source was identified as a professor of nuclear research recognized as a national authority on the biological effects of radioactivity. The low credibile source was identified as a high school student whose information was based upon a social studies term paper and whose father was a contractor who built underground schools. Since the message advocated construction of such schools to protect students in case of nuclear attack or natural disaster, this manipulation was expected to produce differences in both perceived competence and trustworthiness, an expectation confirmed by subsequent manipulation checks.

The strong fear-arousing message made 14 references to death or serious injury which might result from war or natural disaster if children were housed in conventional school buildings. These references were eliminated from the mild fear messages, and language of a nonemotive, low threat nature was substituted. In both studies, the strong fear appeals proved more effective than mild appeals when presented by the highly credible source. Listeners exposed to the low credible source were no more influenced by a strong than a mild fear message. Moreover, listeners in the low-credibility conditions demonstrated no more attitude change than a no-message control group. In their second study, Miller and Hewgill (1966) hypothesized that a low credible source using strong language would reduce his credibility further by his language choices while an initially high credible source would enhance his credibility by using strong fear-arousing language. The results generally support these hypotheses.

In yet a third study, Miller and Hewgill (1966) hypothesized that when presented by a highly credible source, strong fear-arousing appeals having as their referent the message recipient's valued other—i.e., the recipient's "family" and "wife and children"—will produce greater attitude change than strong fear-arousing appeals having as their referent the recipient himself. Although they found no support for the hypothesized differences between self- and valued-other referents when the messages were attributed to a highly credible source, both messages were persuasive when compared to a no-message control condition. This study represents yet a third case in which communicators with high credibility were successful using strong fear-arousing language in their persuasive appeals.

Much early fear appeal research focused on appeals stressing the harmful *physical* consequences of failure to comply with advocated positions (Berkowitz & Cottingham, 1960: Janis & Feshbach, 1953; Leventhal & Niles, 1965). A second type of fear-arousing appeal stresses the harmful *social* consequences of failure to adopt message recommendations. Messages containing social approval or disapproval cues are frequently used in everyday conversations and in advertisements promoting everything from peanut butter to feminine hygiene products, but little research had dealt with the persuasive impact of such cues prior to a study by Powell and Miller (1967). They found that messages advocating voluntary blood donations to the Red Cross were most effective when they contained social approval cues (i.e., cues stressing that donors would be perceived as unselfish and socially concerned), intermediately effective when they contained social disapproval cues (i.e., cues indicating that non-donors would be seen as selfish and socially unconcerned) and least effective when neither approval or disapproval cues were present.

The second message strategy involves the use of *opinionated language*. Rokeach's (1960, pp. 80-87) discussion of opinionated and non-opinionated language identifies a specific type of appeal emphasizing undesirable social consequences. Non-opinionated statements only indicate the communicator's attitude towards a particular idea or concept—e.g., "I support abortion on demand." By contrast, opinionated statements not only indicate the communicator's attitude toward an idea or concept, they also indicate the communicator's attitude toward those who agree or disagree with him or her—e.g., "Any intelligent person supports abortion on demand" (opinionated acceptance), or "Only a stupid fool opposes abortion on demand" (opinionated rejection). In terms of a social reinforcement model, non-opinionated statements can be considered mild fear-arousing messages; while opinionated statements can be viewed as strong fear-arousing messages, since they explicitly indicate that the communicator's approval or disapproval of the receiver is contingent upon the latter's compliance with the position advocated in the message.

Miller and Lobe (1967) investigated the relative persuasiveness of non-opinionated and opinionated language. These researchers reasoned that a receiver's open- or closed-mindedness should mediate responses to a highly credible source using opinionated language. Closed-minded persons rely more heavily on authority as a basis for beliefs; hence, social approval and disapproval attributed to a positive message source should induce high levels of cognitive inconsistency in closed-minded receivers. Moreover, Powell (1962) demonstrated that closed-minded people have great difficulty separating message sources from message content. For these reasons, it was hypothesized that opinionated language attributed to a highly credible source would be especially persuasive in instances involving closed-minded receivers. By contrast, open-minded people should be more capable of evaluating the message content on its own merits, because they should be less influenced by the external sanctions of the authoritative communicator. In fact, the *ad hominem* attacks contained in the opinionated statements could reduce persuasive impact, for such attacks are antithetical to the consensually developed norms for appropriate, rational discourse. Consequently, such language could result in negative violation of expectations for open-minded receivers, leading to the hypothesis that nonopinionated language will be more persuasive than opinionated language for open-minded receivers. Finally, Miller and Lobe predicted that open-minded receivers would also derogate the credibility of the communicator when he violated their expectations negatively by using opinionated language. Such derogation was not expected for closed-minded receivers.

A written message which advocated making the scale of cigarettes illegal was attributed to a popular astronaut whom all receivers perceived to be highly credible. The content of the opinionated and nonopinionated messages was identical save that in the opinionated message, two opinionated acceptance statements—e.g., "Anyone of any intelligence can plainly see that smoking is related to certain physical ailments"—and two opinionated rejection statements—e.g., "Some irresponsible citizens seem to feel that tobacco products should be kept on the market"—were included. To equalize message length, phrases containing nonopinionated language were inserted in the nonopinionated language message.

The results only partially supported Miller and Lobe's reasoning. Highly credible sources were more effective using opinionated language regardless of the relative open- or closed-mindedness of the receiver. Obviously, highly credible communicators who give added information about their attitude toward those who agree or disagree with them facilitate rather than inhibit attitude change. Though the findings for closed-minded receivers are consistent with Miller and Lobe's original expectations, the results for the open-minded receivers ran counter to prediction since they were also more influenced by opinionated than non-opinionated language.

In a later study, Miller and Baseheart (1969) investigated the relationship between a communicator's trustworthiness and his persuasive impact when using opinionated or nonopinionated language. They reasoned that language cues denoting social disapproval should be differentially effective, depending on the receiver's perception of the source's trustworthiness. If a source is initially perceived as trustworthy, such language cues should result in greater acceptance of the message; conversely, linking social disapproval cues to an unliked, distrusted communicator should reduce persuasiveness. Specifically, it was predicted that low trustworthy sources would be more persuasive using nonopinionated language while highly trusted communicators would be more effective using opinionated language.

The results supported the reasoning of Miller and Baseheart. When the communicator was initially perceived as trustworthy, opinionated language was more effective than nonopinionated; however, when the source was initially perceived as relatively untrustworthy, an opinionated message produced less attitude change than a nonopinionated one. Once again, these results held for both open- and closed-minded receivers.

The studies by Miller and Lobe and by Miller and Baseheart yield results consistent with those obtained in the previously discussed study by Miller and Hewgill (1966): Highly credible sources have more freedom in their language choices. Taken together the studies suggest that if a source has high crediblity, stronger language specifying harmful consequences of failure to comply will be more effective than messages employing milder language, regardless of whether the message cues allude to undesirable social *or* physical consequences. The evidence is clear that low credible sources do not have the freedom to select language strategies which attempt to frighten people into complying. The consistent lack of differences between open- and closed-minded receivers suggests that this variable does not mediate attitudinal shifts.

Other personality constructs have received little or no attention in this area. Baseheart (1971) did find that *approval-dependence* produced different effects on recipient attitude change. As predicted, receivers with a high need for social approval were more vulnerable to persuasive appeals containing opinionated language than people with low social approval needs. This finding indicates that other personality variables may enter into the relationships between various language alternatives and subsequent persuasive effectiveness.

The third general language strategy to be discussed in this section involves *the language intensity of the persuasive appeal*. Actually, the previously discussed studies of fear appeals and opinionated language can be conceived as representing special operationalizations of language intensity. Most investigators have adopted Bowers' (1963, p.345) definition of language intensity as "the quality of language which indicates the degree to which the speaker's attitude deviates from neutrality." Such a conceptual definition leads to the conclusion that a strong fear appeal would indicate a marked deviation from neutrality on a concept and would be classified as an instance of high intensity encoding. Similarly, both opinionated acceptance and opinionated rejection statements enhance the perception that a communicator is intensely committed to the position he or she is advocating.

Though Miller and Lobe (1967) briefly commented on the relationship between their opinionated language study and the early research of Bowers (1963), most work on language intensity has existed as a parallel but distinctly separate area from the related fear appeal and opinionatedness research. No attempt has been made to synthesize the conceptual and research similarities of these related areas.

In the conceptualizations developed about fear-arousing messages, opinionated language, and language intensity, there appears to have been an intuitive bias for predictions that stronger, highly graphic language would be more persuasively effective. When Janis and Feshbach (1953) found that mild fear-arousing language was more persuasive than strong fear appeals, a flurry of research addressed this apparently counter-intuitive finding. An analogous situation ensued when Bowers (1963) failed to confirm the hypothesis that speeches using highly intense language would produce greater attitude change than speeches using language of low intensity. In fact, Bowers found that low intensity speeches arguing against concepts were significantly more persuasive than high intensity speeches opposing issues or concepts. In no case was high intensity persuasively superior to low intensity encoding, a finding Bowers could not explain. When viewed apart from the research on fear-arousing messages and opinionated language, this superiority of low intensity language appeared to be counter-intuitive and stimulated a great deal of later research.

More than a decade later, Burgoon (1975) sought to explain the superiority of the low intensity language in Bower's (1963) persuasive messages from an expectancy theory perspective. Bowers (1963), Brooks (1970) and Burgoon and Chase (1973) all provide evidence that receivers develop expectations about the syntax, language and content of persuasive messages. When sources positively violated receiver expectations (e.g., a militant speaking moderately), attitudes toward the topic changed significantly in the direction of the advocated position. These studies suggest that when receivers expect communication behaviour to affect them negatively and this expectation is disconfirmed by the sources, the resultant messages are persuasively effective. The findings suggest that even extremely low credible sources can produce dramatic shifts of attitude when they positively violate receiver expectations.

Burgoon (1975) extended the language intensity research by examining interactive effects of communicator credibility and language intensity on persuasive effectiveness. Employing a rationale similar to the earlier fear appeal (Miller & Hewgill, 1966) and opinionated language (Miller & Lobe, 1967) studies, Burgoon predicted a highly credible source would be expected to use more intense persuasive language and thus be more effective when emphatically advocating acceptance of a position. The conventional portrait of an effective male speaker portrays an aggressive, dynamic and outspoken advocate. Despite this, low credible communicators are often seen as "pushy" or "obnoxious" if they use highly intense language in their attempts to persuade. Burgoon therefore predicted that low intensity language would result in more attitude change than highly intense language when the communicator is initially low in credibility.

Findings conformed with expectations. The high credible source was more persuasive when using highly intense language, while the low credible source (a salesman) was more persuasive using low intensity language. Apparently it was a positive violation of expectations for the salesman to use relatively low intensity language in a persuasive message. Cultural stereotypes portraying salesman as extroverted and aggressive, along with the efforts of the experimenter to create such expectations in the experiment's induction period, created a situation where the source could positively violate receivers' perceptions of his character and competence. When the highly credible source used highly intense language, he was more persuasive but was seen as less competent than when he used low intensity language. Obviously, person perception and persuasiveness are relatively independent factors in some persuasive situations.

Continued use of masculine pronouns to refer to communicators in these experiments is not a sexist slip of the pen but a descriptive statement about the gender of sources used in the research reviewed thus far. Exclusion of female speakers is of concern given the expectancy violation rationale we have advanced. Generalizations concerning the use of fear-arousing appeals and opinionated language are largely limited to male speakers, as are most of the conclusions that can be drawn from the language intensity literature, and must be based upon the expectations receivers have about appropriate communication behaviour *for males.*

Despite the recent emphasis on equality for men and women in American society, most people still accord the two sexes very different roles in the social structure (Bem, 1975; Bem & Lenney, 1976). With these relatively fixed perceptions of proper sex roles, develop some prescriptive generalizations about appropriate and inappropriate behaviours for females. Bem and Bem (1970) suggest that whether intentional or not, the socialization process has programmed females to be complementary to rather than independent of males, submissive rather than dominant, domestic rather than business- or scientific-minded, and to consider themselves less knowledgeable than men. These submissive, dependent stereotypes imply that men and women would be expected to differ on certain communicative behaviours.

Burgoon and Stewart (1975) posited that most people would expect women to advocate positions less intensely than men. Specifically, they hypothesized a direct, positive relationship between level of language intensity and subsequent attitude change for male communicators and a negative, linear relationship between level of language intensity and attitude change for females. Their prediction was based both on notions of expectancy theory and earlier research (e.g., Miller & McReynolds, 1973) suggesting that, in general, male speakers are seen as more credible than females.

A second concern of Burgoon and Stewart involved the receptivity of male and female receivers to messages of varying intensity delivered by female and male sources. Research (e.g., Scheidel, 1963) has suggested that females are generally more persuasible than men. Unfortunately, critics have contended that these studies suffer from consistent selection of "male topics," i.e., issues about which males have more information and higher involvement. Burgoon and Stewart included sex of the receiver to try to replicate earlier sex differences in persuasibility while avoiding alleged procedural biases. Moreover, the manipulation of receiver sex allowed them to probe interactions between communicator sex, intensity of the message and sex of the receiver; permitting more precise statements about expectations concerning male and female communicators for receivers of both sexes.

As predicted, males were more persuasive when they used highly intense language while females fared better when they used language of low intensity. There were no significant interactions between sex of receiver and the language intensity or communicator sex variables, although a trend suggested that females were especially receptive to highly intense messages by male communicators. In addition, females proved to be more persuasible than males. Since the topic—admitting students to the university only if they had a 3.25 grade average—was salient to both males and females, topic bias cannot be advanced to explain the sex differences.

The findings of Miller and Hewgill (1966), Miller and Lobe (1967), and Miller and Baseheart (1969) conform to those of Burgoon (1975) and Burgoon and Stewart (1975). High credible sources apparently do not violate people's expectations negatively when they use fear-arousing appeals, opinionated language or highly intense language. These studies suggest that Janis and Feshbach's (1963) and Bower's (1963) finding that milder language facilitates attitude change should at best be treated as a main effect finding that is often overridden by interactions with other mediating variables. The findings of Burgoon and Stewart indicate that most females have less freedom than males in selecting language strategies if they wish to be effective persuaders. Differing expectations concerning appropriate communication behaviour for men and women appear to prevail in U.S. society; the effects of violations of these expectations are gender specific.

While the studies discussed thus far have examined messages which intentionally arouse anxiety, threat, or fear in receivers; another line of research has investigated a type of appeal labelled *irrelevant fear*. Irrelevant fear reflects anxiety caused by anticipating future negative events unrelated to the persuasive message content or to any potential harmful consequences of failure to comply with the communicator's recommendations. If people are fearful about specific future events like the possibility of war or economic ruin, they are more susceptible to influence. This assertion is consistent with the results of investigations of the effects of general anxiety on social influence (Lundy, Simonson, & Landers, 1967; McNulty & Walters, 1962; Simonson & Lundy, 1966; Staples & Walters, 1961; Walters & Ray, 1960). Irrelevant fear presumably makes people more attentive and supposedly increases their vulnerability to persuasive attacks; however, several studies (Burgoon, 1970a; Carmichael & Cronkhite, 1965) demonstrate that various kinds of cognitive stress have different effects on message reception and acceptance. Based on their results, Carmichael and Cronkhite argue that already highly aroused persons reject stimuli that lead to further arousal. Consistent with this position, Jones and Burgoon (1975) reasoned that people in highly anxious states would react negatively to intensely worded, persuasive appeals. Specifically, they hypothesized that individuals in irrelevant fear conditions would be aroused enough to be more susceptible to social infuence than individuals in no-irrelevant fear conditions, but that such arousal would produce the most attitude change with low language intensity messages since the high arousal state induced by irrelevant fear would cause receivers to respond negatively to the additional arousal produced by highly intense, persuasive messages.

Jones and Burgoon first administered the 34-item Emery and Krumboltz (1967) Test Anxiety Inventory to all participants. At a later session conducted during regularly scheduled class meetings, participants in the irrelevant fear conditions were told that the only fair way to grade the class was to give them a test on all material covered in class, and that this examination would occur later in the class period. Participants in the no-irrelevant fear conditions were told nothing about an examination.

Participants then read a message containing either high or low intensity language and advocating a position on a controversial issue unrelated to the university. To control for general test anxiety, so that the attitude measures would be influenced only by situationally specific irrelevant fears, the Test Anxiety Inventory scores were used as a covariate.

Only irrelevant fear/low intensity message receivers reported significantly more favourable attitudes toward the position advocated in the message. The least attitude change occurred in the irrelevant fear/high intensity condition, confirming Carmichael and Cronkhite's (1965) prediction that highly aroused individuals will avoid further arousing stimuli. In terms of our expectancy rationale, it can be argued that highly aroused receivers will pay more attention to any persuasive message. Since they might well expect relatively intense messages, more moderate presentations should positively violate their expectations, thus lowering their arousal by permitting them to consider calmly worded, rational arguments and maximizing the likelihood of successful persuasion. While admittedly *post hoc*, such an interpretation is warranted by the findings of Jones and Burgoon (1975).

Other special forms of intensity, such as obscene language, have also received some research attention. Bostrom, Baseheart, and Rossiter (1973) and Mulac (1976) demonstrated the negative consequences of using obscene language in persuasive appeals. Pawlovich (1969) found that the credibility of female communicators who used obscene language dropped sharply, while males using the same language did not suffer marked loss of credibility, In general, these findings fit our expectancy perspective: In situations where obscenity is clearly inappropriate, as has typically been true for women, use of profane language would negatively violate receiver expectations and inhibit persuasive impact.

In summary, it seems reasonable to interpret the research discussed thus far using the general expectancy position articulated in our initial propositions. The following propositions relate to persuasive attempts occurring within the passive message reception paradigm. Each is consistent with our expectancy rationale:

*Proposition 2.* Receivers have normative expectations about the level of fear arousing appeals, opinionated language, and magnitude of language intensity appropriate to persuasive discourse.

*Proposition 3.* Highly credible communicators have the freedom to select varied language strategies in developing persuasive messages, while low credible communicators must conform to more limited language options if they wish to be effective.

*Proposition 3A.* Because of differences in perceived credibility, highly credible sources can use low intensity appeals and be more persuasive than low credible communicators using either strong or mild language.

*Proposition 3B.* Highly credible communicators can often enhance the persuasive impact of messages by using intense language.

*Proposition 3C.* Communicators perceived as low in crediblity or those unsure of their perceived credibility with a given audience will usually be more persuasive if they employ appeals of low intensity.

*Proposition 4.* Receivers have normative expectations about appropriate communication behaviours which are gender specific.

*Proposition 4A.* Because of these expectations, males are usually more persuasive when using highly intense persuasive appeals.

*Proposition 4B.* Because of these expectations, females are usually more persuasive when using persuasive appeals of low intensity.

*Proposition 5.* Fear arousal that is irrelevant to the content of the message or the harmful consequences of failure to comply with the advocated position often mediates receptivity to different levels of language intensity.

*Proposition 5A.* Receivers aroused by induction of irrelevant fear or suffering from specific anxiety are most receptive to persuasive messages containing low intensity appeals.

*Proposition 5B.* People aroused by induction of irrelevant fear or suffering from specific anxiety are relatively unreceptive to highly intense persuasive appeals.

## THE ACTIVE PARTICIPATION PARADIGM

The active and passive participation paradigms differ importantly. In the passive message reception paradigm, the persuader *acts,* by transmitting a message, while the persuadee is *acted upon.* In the active participation paradigm, usually characterized by persuadee/communicators who have been induced to present belief-discrepant messages publicly, *a change occurs in the roles* taken by the persuader and the persuadee(s). The persuader is no longer the active agent; rather, once the persuadee has been induced to prepare and deliver a counterattitudinal message, the persuader assumes a relatively passive role. By contrast, the persuadee engaged in counterattitudinal communication is highly involved throughout the persuasive attempt: rather than being acted upon, persuasion occurs only if the persuadee acts upon himself or herself (Miller & Burgoon, 1973).

Limited attention has been focused on the effects of specific language choices made by persuadee/communicators in the active participation paradigm. Burgoon (1970b), in a review of the counterattitudinal advocacy literature, claims that while research evidence suggests that communicators shift their attitudes to conform more closely with their advocated positions, most research has specified conditions leading to attitude change without studying overall persuasiveness or quality of counterattitudinal messages. Published studies have usually evaluated only belief-discrepant messages without comparing them to belief-congruent communications and have neglected to analyze the content or style of messages at a level of abstraction less than overall judgements of message quality.

In other areas of research, evidence suggests a relationship between psychological stress and verbal behaviour. Greenberg and Tannenbaum (1962) found that communicators experiencing high cognitive stress produced less readable messages than did their counterparts who were placed under low stress. Osgood and Walker (1959) compared suicide notes to other kinds of writing and concluded that communicators under stress use less intense language: writers of suicide notes used a higher percentage of ambivalent constructions, e.g., "maybe" and "possibly," and a greater number of ambivalent assertions.

Burgoon (1970b) reasoned that since communicators were advocating something they did not privately believe, counterattitudinal advocacy should create considerable cognitive stress. His initial interest in counterattitudinal message analysis was prompted by the often contradictory and confusing results obtained in studies dealing with the effects of variables, such as justification, on attitude change following counterattitudinal advocacy. Burgoon suggested that the kinds of messages produced might differ in studies reporting conflicting results. In one study (Burgoon, 1970b), only 49% of a sample of supposed belief-discrepant messages were judged as advocating the position the communicators had been asked to support, with 31% of the messages being deemed neutral. By contrast, 96% of the belief-congruent messages were accurately judged as to the position being advocated by the communicator. The results indicate that communicators were manipulating the language of messages to avoid taking public stances that conflicted with their private beliefs.

In the first of three studies, Burgoon and Miller (1971) examined differences in language intensity manifested by persons in free encoding situations where either a counterattitudinal or belief-congruent message was produced. As predicted, communicators placed in the stressful situation of counterattitudinal advocacy created less intense messages supporting mandatory on-campus residency than communicators allowed to create belief-congruent messages opposing such a university policy.

Apparently, people are more ambivalent and less intense when they create messages advocating positions they do not privately support.

Although Festinger (1957) posited that "believing $X$" and "advocating not-$X$" fosters cognitive inconsistency which prompts the communicator to change attitudes to conform more closely with the advocated position, no prior research had demonstrated that "believing $X$" and "strongly advocating not-$X$" leads to more attitude change than "moderately advocating not-$X$." Nevertheless, cognitive consistency theories suggest several reasons for positing a direct relationship between counterattitudinal message intensity and attitude change. First, intense language commits communicators to the position advocated in the counterattitudinal messages and prevents them from avoiding the task by constructing ambivalent, neutral messages. Moreover, intense advocacy makes it difficult for advocates to reverse their public positions by claiming that a counterattitudinal statement was not really made. Less intense, more moderate messages allow communicators to concede that their belief-congruent positions may be correct; intense messages reduce the possibility of such concessions. In short, the irrevocable, unambiguous nature of high intensity messages should produce considerable cognitive inconsistency which, in turn, should increase the magnitude of post-counterattitudinal advocacy attitude change.

Burgoon and Miller (1971) describe two studies in which a direct linear relationship between level of language intensity in counterattitudinal messages and subsequent attitude change toward the belief-discrepant position was hypothesized. In the first study, male and female participants were asked to partially create counterattitudinal messages advocating mandatory on-campus residency during all four years of college attendance. Some of the word choices for the message were controlled so that each communicator was required to create a low, moderate or highly intense counterattitudinal message. In the second study, draft-eligible college students were induced to create counterattitudinal messages advocating the abolition of student draft deferments, again with language choices partially controlled. In both studies, the hypothesized direct relationship between language intensity and attitude change following counterattitudinal advocacy was confirmed.

These studies yield information about certain language norms which influence counterattitudinal encoding. When creating counterattitudinal messages in free-encoding situations, communicators generate more ambivalent, less intense messages than when advocating a position congruent with their private attitudes. When unexpectedly placed in situations that force them to create highly intense counterattitudinal messages, communicators are required to violate *their own* norms about acceptable communication behaviour. Such self-violations heighten cognitive stress, which subsequently increases the amount of attitude change following counterattitudinal advocacy. Apparently, in the active participation paradigm, stress affects language choices and language choices affect stress. When combined with the previously discussed research of Jones and Burgoon (1975), these findings indicate that cognitive stress affects receptivity to various language strategies, influences production of persuasive appeals and is a potent predictor of attitude change in both the active and passive paradigms.

We are unaware of any research dealing with the impact of cognitive stress on message production and attitude change that has examined language variables other than intensity. Stress probably produces measurable effects on a variety of language variables and future research aimed at determining these effects should prove useful. The following propositions summarize our present knowledge about the active participation paradigm:

*Proposition 6.* Communicators experiencing cognitive stress produce less intense, more ambivalent messages.

*Proposition 7.* When forced to violate their own norms about appropriate communication behaviour by encoding highly intense messages, communicators experience increased cognitive stress.

*Proposition 8.* There is a direct linear relationship between level of language intensity and attitude change following counterattitudinal advocacy.

## RESISTANCE TO PERSUASION PARADIGM

The first two paradigms discussed in this chapter are primarily concerned with attitude *change*. The paradigm discussed in this section focuses on processes for making people more *resistant to change*. Though attempts to bring about change and efforts to induce resistance to change differ in certain ways, the resistance to persuasion paradigm is best viewed conceptually as an extension of the persuasion process. In order to induce resistance to change, communicators typically transmit messages which seek to change the way persons process later messages. In simple terms, an initial message seeks to reduce the vulnerability of receivers to later persuasive appeals.

Much of the research on resistance to persuasion has centred on various tests of McGuire's inoculation viewpoint. Based on a biological analogy, this approach argues that just as people are immunized by pre-exposure to weakened forms of a disease, a persuader can immunize people against future persuasive appeals by exposing them to weakened forms of these appeals. The inoculation model requires that pretreatment messages stimulate but do not destroy defences, so that receivers become resistant to later persuasive messages.

A large body of research (McGuire, 1964, 1966; Tannenbaum, 1966 Tannenbaum & Norris, 1965) has demonstrated that resistance to persuasion can be conferred with a variety of pretreatment strategies. Controversy has surrounded the best explanation of reasons for the effectiveness of these techniques. Congruity theorists (Tannenbaum, 1966) have relied on such explanations as *concept boosting* (supporting existing beliefs and attitudes) and *assertion weakening* (refuting opposing arguments). The inoculation model assumes a refutational pretreatment strategy is superior to belief-supportive strategies since the former provides the two necessary conditions for inducing resistance to persuasion; threats to existing beliefs and defences against future attacks. There are findings to support both interpretations: In some cases, supportive pretreatment strategies are more effective; in others, refutational strategies have resulted in more resistance to persuasion.

Some studies have examined the structural properties and the content of pretreatment messages, but few have manipulated language variables in either pretreatment or persuasive attack messages to determine their effects in inducing resistance to persuasion. Moreover, research matching the linguistic properties of pretreatment and attack messages so as to induce resistance or provide a means of overcoming resistance to persuasion is limited.

Operating from an expectancy perspective, Burgoon and Chase (1973) sought to extend prior findings concerning language intensity to the resistance to persuasion paradigm. Based on the assumption that relatively credible communictors can use high levels of language intensity persuasively and on the (1966) Tannenbaum, Macaulay, and Norris finding that the more one bolsters an existing attitude, the more resistant it becomes to subsequent attacks; they predicted that when supportive pretreatment messages are used, attitude change following a moderately intense persuasive attack will vary inversely with the intensity of the pretreatment message. In effect, communicators using a supportive pretreatment strategy must argue intensely to confer resistance to persuasion.

Use of the refutational pretreatment strategy leads to different expectations. As previously noted, Bowers (1963) found a boomerang effect resulting from adverse reactions to the credibility of speakers taking unconventional and unexpectedly strong positions. Burgoon (1970a) and Brooks (1970) obtained unexpected persuasive effects when audience expectations and the subsequent language intensity of speakers were incongruent. McEwen and Greenberg (1970) stress the importance of matching the intensity of message with the intensity of feelings about the source. If receivers expect a certain level of language intensity and the message violates their expectations, the persuasive impact of the message varies depending upon other factors in the situation.

Burgoon and Chase argued that when refutational pretreatments are used, receivers are forewarned of, and develop expectations about, arguments that may be used in future attack messages. If a receiver expects a highly intense persuasive message and the communicator delivers a moderate one, the communicator may seem "reasonable" and succeed with the persuasive appeal. Furthermore, a communicator expected to argue with low intensity may be persuasive by arguing somewhat more intensely than expected, since receivers exposed to low intensity refutational pretreatments may not feel threatened enough to prepare themselves for subsequent persuasive attacks. In other words, a moderate attack can overcome the inoculation effects of a pretreatment message of low intensity. Indeed, Burgoon and Chase posit that any refutational pretreatment, by design, creates expectations about the nature of the forthcoming persuasive attack. Though some of these expectations concern content, receivers also develop linguistic expectations by virtue of the language used in the pretreatment message. Consequently, the most effective means for conferring resistance to persuasion when using a refutational strategy is to match the intensity of the pretreatment message with the intensity of the subsequent persuasive attack message. Stated differently, when the expectations of receivers are not violated in any way, maximum resistance to persuasion is conferred. When the expectations of receivers are negatively violated (e.g., expecting a highly intense attack and receiving a moderate one) or positively (e.g., the intensity of the attack message exceeds a low intensity pretreatment) attitude change in the direction advocated by the second communicator will occur.

The attack message used in the study argued for admitting only juniors and seniors to the university; participants were uniformly opposed to this policy. Supportive pretreatment message recipients read statements prepared by other students opposing such a policy. Key words and phrases were changed to create supportive pretreatments of three levels of language intensity. The high intensity messages used qualifiers, such as, "very bad," the moderate used "bad," and the low used "poor." The messages were identical save for the selection of 11 words or phrases of varying intensity.

Before constructing the refutational pretreatment, it was necessary to create the persuasive attack message. This message contained 11 arguments which used only moderately intense words or phrases. These arguments differed from the supportive arguments generated by the student communicators. Since the refutational pretreatment needed to be an implicit rebuttal of the persuasive attack, 11 rebuttal statements were written. The same blanking procedure was used to create high, moderate and low intensity refutational pretreatments.

There were no significant main effect differences between refutational and supportive pretreatments. As predicted, the highly intense supportive pretreatment conferred more resistance to persuasion than the moderate intensity pretreatment which, in turn, conferred more resistance than the low intensity pretreatment. Moreover, there was a negative linear relationship between the level of intensity in the pretreatment message and the attitude change following the attack message. These results supported a congruity theory interpretation by indicating that highly intense supportive pretreatments were more effective in bolstering existing attitudes.

In the refutational pretreatment conditions, a curvilinear relationship between level of language intensity in the pretreatment message and attitude change following the attack message was observed. The moderate pretreatment message, which was of identical intensity to the attack message, conferred the most resistance to persuasion. Both the high and low intensity refutational pretreatments were less successful in conferring resistance to the moderate attack message. Evidently, the refutational pretreatment created expectations about the forthcoming persuasive attack. When receiver expectations coincided with the intensity of the attack, minimal attitude change occurred. Given differences between pretreatment and attack intensity, receivers changed their attitudes as much as a group of receivers not previously inoculated. Obviously, the success of both supportive and refutational pretreatment strategies is partially determined by the language intensity of both the pretreatment and attack messages.

Burgoon and King (1974) examined strategies for overcoming resistance to persuasion previously conferred by inoculation techniques. In so doing, they attempted to integrate prior language intensity research conducted in both the passive message reception and active participation paradigms.

Burgoon and King reasoned that given the effectiveness of highly intense encoding in the active participation paradigm, this level of intensity should also be effective in persuading persons who had previously been inoculated with pretreatment messages. Specifically, they predicted that the level of language intensity used in the active participation paradigm would have to be relatively high to overcome the effects of pretreatment messages. They also predicted that language of low intensity would be more effective for the passive message reception paradigm, since such language would violate expectations positively, given a relatively high intensity pretreatment inoculation.

The same issue and message construction procedures were used as in the earlier Burgoon and Chase (1973) study. The results generally conformed to Burgoon and King's predictions. In the active participation conditions, there was a direct relationship between language intensity and attitude change following creation of the messages. Moreover, persons in the high intensity, active participation conditions changed their attitudes as much as an uninoculated control group. Thus, highly intense, active participation completely overcame the inoculation effects of pretreatment messages. Actively created, low and moderate intensity messages were less successful in overcoming induced resistance to persuasion; in fact, persons in the low intensity, active participation condition reported no more attitude change than persons in a pretest/post-test only control condition, indicating that the active creation of low intensity messages was unsuccessful in overcoming inoculation.

In the passive message reception conditions, the level of language intensity in the attack message was inversely related to subsequent attitude change. The low intensity message produced as much attitude change as did the same message given to an uninoculated control group, demonstrating that the low intensity message completely overcame the effects of inoculation. Since persons receiving a highly intense message did not change significantly from the pretest/post-test only control group, it appears that intense messages presented to passive audiences are ineffective in overcoming previously induced resistance to persuasion. Care was taken to ensure that the attack message was persuasive and that the inoculation message did produce the expected resistance.

There were no effects for kind of pretreatment message and no interpretable effect demonstrating the superiority of active participation or passive reception. The findings for the active participation conditions extend Burgoon and Miller's (1971) results by using previously inoculated individuals. Moreover, they indicate that a relatively high threshold of language intensity must be reached before inoculated persons will overcome the effects of induced resistance. That low intensity attacks were more persuasive in the passive message reception conditions is again consistent with the view that moderate language sometimes violates expectations positively and functions as an effective strategy for overcoming resistance to persuasion.

Taken as a whole, this research underscores the fact that questions dealing with strategies for inducing resistance to persuasion are considerably more complex than whether supportive or refutational pretreatments are superior. The type of language used in both pretreatment and attack messages clearly interacts with other variables to mediate resistance to persuasion.

Burgoon, Cohen, Miller, and Montgomery (1978) contended that the rather singular interest in testing the inoculation model, with its emphasis on pretreatment message variables, restricts theoretical development in the area of resistance to persuasion. Like Miller and Burgoon (1973), they argue that conferring resistance to persuasion should be conceptualized as an extension of the persuasion process. This approach permits integration of the persuasion findings with knowledge about the process of inducing resistance to persuasion.

While Burgoon et al. (1978) emphasize the limitations of the inoculation model, they do not discard all of its propositions. They develop a communication-oriented perspective positioning three primary factors that mediate people's ability to resist persuasive appeals:

1. The amount of motivation to counterargue the position advocated in the persuasive message.
2. The extent to which the communication fulfils or violates receiver expectations of appropriate communication behaviour.
3. The context in which the communication occurs.

Burgoon et al. also argue for expanding the traditional view of what constitutes a pretreatment message. They hold that any communication which prompts counterarguing to defend present beliefs can be viewed as a pretreatment message. For instance, any message advocating a position counter to current attitudes that motivates people to counterargue can be viewed as a pretreatment inhibiting acceptance of a second message arguing the same side of an issue. Since persuasion is seldom a one-shot attempt, any message could affect acceptance of a subsequent message, regardless of its content or the position it advocates.

The first proposition of Burgoon et al. states that resistance to persuasion is a function of practice in defending one's beliefs, with practice being a function of motivation. Considerable research supports the notion that threatening an attitude motivates its holder to defend it; which, in turn, increases resistance to persuasion. Of major theoretical importance, then, are the defence mechanisms through which increased motivation is manifested.

Several writers (Festinger & Maccoby, 1964; Osterhouse & Brock, 1970) emphasize that persons exposed to persuasive attacks actively subvocalize counterarguments. Such subvocalization is presumed to create resistance to the persuasive message. If so, the effectiveness of the threat component of pretreatment messages results from increased counterarguing stimulated by the awareness that one's attitudes are vulnerable to attack.

The interest in counterarguing as a mediator of attitude change has stimulated research focusing on the effects of inhibiting counterarguing, primarily by introducing some form of distraction concurrent with the persuasive attack. Festinger and Maccoby (1964) found that distraction inhibits counterarguing and leads to increased acceptance of the persuasive message. Some researchers have reported a direct relationship between distraction and attitude change; others have found an inverse relationship; while others have been unable to detect a relationship. Kiesler and Mathog (1968) observed a direct relationship between distraction and attitude change, but only when the source was relatively high in credibility. This finding supports the "distraction leads to increased acceptance" hypothesis, for if the communicator has low credibility, counterarguing is unnecessary because resistance can be obtained by derogating the communicator. Zimbardo, Snyder, Thomas, Gold, and Gurwitz (1970) observed an interaction between distraction and the perceptual set of message recipients: Distraction increased attitude change when receivers were primarily set to attend to the persuasive message, but distraction decreased attitude change when receivers were primarily set to attend to the distracting task. In short, the evidence indicates that subvocal counterarguing does occur and that this phenomenon mediates the attitude change process.

Burgoon et al. (1978) also incorporated the expectancy notions discussed in this chapter as a second proposition in their resistance model. It is not necessary to again review the contention that people develop expectations, and the violations of these expectations mediate both attitude change and inducing resistance to persuasion.

A third proposition advanced by Burgoon et al. attempts to integrate knowledge about the impact of distraction and audience expectations with McGuire's (1964) notions about the importance of threat in creating different persuasive contexts. The authors suggest that receiver expectations and attitudinal threats can be affected by directing the attention of receivers to different types of distracting tasks during presentation of a persuasive message. Varying tasks are assumed to induce differing critical response sets, or receiver expectations; which, in turn, are related to the amount of counterarguing produced both during and *subsequent* to presentation of an initial persuasive message. These differences in counterarguing are assumed to facilitate or to inhibit attitude change resulting from subsequent persuasive messages.

More specifically, Burgoon et al. posit that when receivers are asked to evaluate critically the attributes of a communicator, i.e., to look for negative source and/or delivery characteristics, they are vulnerable to subsequent persuasive appeals. This vulnerability stems from the interaction of several variables, including type of critical task, presence of distractors and amount of situational threat. Emphasis on the task of identifying negative characteristics should minimize the persuasiveness of the initial message and the amount of perceived threat to the receiver. Furthermore, attention to negative source characteristics should distract receivers from counterarguing crucial arguments in the message. Thus, they will be unprepared to defend their attitudes and relatively unmotivated to counterargue in the future. Conversely, attention to positive communicator attributes should enhance the effectiveness of an initial persuasive message and increase its threat, since receiver attitudes are shown to be vulnerable to attack by a relatively effective communicator. This vulnerability should increase motivation to counterargue following the receipt of the initial message, thereby conferring increased resistance to later messages advocating the same position. Results of the study supported these predictions.

While incorporating notions of receiver expectancy in their model, Burgoon et al. did not deal explicitly with the importance of confirmation or disconfirmation of these expectations. This omission is a logical shortcoming of their model. They assume that the expectations per se affect the amount of threat to a receiver. Although their research appears to support this view, it can be argued that an equally important factor is whether these expectations are confirmed or, if disconfirmed, what form the disconfirmation takes: Specifically, when expectations are positively violated, the persuasiveness of an initial message is enhanced; when they are negatively violated, the persuasiveness of the initial message is inhibited.

In a later study, Miller and Burgoon (1979) incorporated type of violation, as well as including language intensity as a key variable. They posited that when persons are asked to evaluate the highly intense characteristics of a counterattitudinal message and the message consists entirely of low intense language, expectations are positively violated. This positive violation should produce a contrast effect that enhances attitude change after the first message, a prediction consistent with all of the research reviewed in this chapter.

In addition, Miller and Burgoon make a crucial prediction of great import to their model. They reason that the realization that opposing arguments can be advanced in a reasonable, moderate manner should threaten receivers and motivate counterarguing following receipt of the initial message but prior to presentation of a second message. Thus, upon exposure to the second message, *attitudes should revert to the original negative position.*

Similarly, when receivers are asked to evaluate the low intense appeals of a counterattitudinal message and the message consists entirely of highly intense language, a negative violation of expectations occurs. This negative violation should prove distracting and inhibit counterarguing. Reasoning analogous to that of Kiesler and Mathog (1968) suggests persuasive appeals can be resisted by derogating the source or message style and thus rendering counterargument unnecessary. This ability to resist without counterarguing should decrease the threat to receivers and reduce their motivation to counterargue prior to receiving a second message. Consequently, they should be vulnerable to subsequent messages arguing the same position as the first message.

Results generally conformed with theoretical expectations. As predicted, receivers whose expectations were violated positively were initially more favourable toward legislation of heroin (the position advocated in the message), but reverted to their original attitudes after hearing a second message advocating the same policy. Receivers whose expectations were violated negatively were relatively unpersuaded after receiving the first message, but demonstrated significant attitude change after exposure to a second message.

The findings of Burgoon et al. (1978) and Miller and Burgoon (1979) fall outside the domain of both inoculation theory and congruity theory. These approaches deal strictly with pretreatment message strategies, ignoring the possibility of one persuasive message affecting resistance to subsequent persuasive appeals. The expectancy position developed in this chapter does, however, provide a framework for interpreting the results. Indeed, the finding that receivers whose expectations were positively violated by an initial message were persuaded by it, but then reverted to their initial attitudes after exposure to a second message *advocating the same position*, is counterintuitive without reference to our expectancy rationale and conflicts with inoculation and cognitive consistency viewpoints. Although Zajonc (1960, 1969) speculates about the effects of disconfirmed expectancies on attitude structure, his speculation does not explain the attitude changes and reversals observed in the different message reception conditions employed by Burgoon and his associates.

The importance of these reversals and changes is apparent when considered in the light of the research reviewed in this chapter. Most previous persuasion research has been conducted in one-shot message situations not dissimilar to the initial message conditions used by Burgoon and his colleagues. Relatively few studies have looked at persuasion in situations involving sequential message reception. Perhaps, as Burgoon and his associates demonstrate, some appeals are persuasive for a single message but result in boomerang effects when receivers are exposed to later messages advocating the same position. Conversely, some strategies that produce little attitude change following a single message may actually make receivers more vulnerable to future messages advocating the same position. Obviously, this possibility applies to the research on fear appeals, opinionated language and language intensity discussed earlier.

The following propositions summarize the major results of research investigating the role of expectations and language variables in the process of inducing resistance to persuasion:

*Proposition 9.* When supportive pretreatment strategies are used, attitude change following a subsequent persuasive attack varies inversely with the linguistic intensity of the supportive pretreatment message.

*Proposition 10.* Refutational pretreatments create expectations by forewarning receivers about the nature of forthcoming attacks.

*Proposition 10A.* When persuasive attack messages do not violate the linguistic expectations created by a refutational pretreatment, maximum resistance to persuasion is conferred.

*Proposition 10B.* If the linguistic properties of attack messages violate the expectations created by refutational pretreatments, either positively or negatively, receivers are less resistant to persuasion.

*Proposition 11.* Given passive message reception, low intensity attack messages are more effective in overcoming resistance to persuasion conferred by supportive, refutational, or combination pretreatments.

*Proposition 12.* When the persuasive attack relies on an active participation strategy, a direct relationship exists between language intensity in the actively created attack and overcoming resistance conferred by supportive, refutational, or combination pretreatments.

*Proposition 13.* When receivers are exposed to more than one message arguing the same position, the confirmation or disconfirmation of linguistic expectancies in the first message systematically affects the acceptance of the second message.

*Proposition 13A.* When linguistic expectations are positively violated in an initial message, the initial message is persuasive, *but* a reversal of attitudes to the original position occurs after exposure to a subsequent message advocating the same counterattitudinal position.

*Proposition 13B.* When linguistic expectations are negatively violated in an initial message, the initial message is not persuasive, *but* receivers are more vulnerable to the arguments of a subsequent message advocating the same counterattitudinal position.

## SOME CONCLUDING COMMENTS

Although we have not attempted an exhaustive review of all research demonstrating relationships between language choices and attitude change—or even a report of all the research we ourselves have carried out—the studies summarized in this chapter underscore the fact that specific language variables are potent predictors of persuasive success. The conceptual framework provided by or expectancy perspective allows us to reinterpret a number of findings that have been grouped under various theoretical umbrellas. As we have noted, some findings appear counterintuitive unless they are interpreted from an expectancy framework. Although certain findings "fit" various theoretical explanations, we are unaware of another conceptual scheme that consistently accounts for the findings of numerous studies concerning the effects of intense language on both persuasion and inducing resistance to persuasion.

During the conduct of this research, we have frequently been struck by a reaction of at least mild surprise. Our surprise stemmed not so much from the fact that most of our hypotheses were confirmed, for social scientists usually become so egotistically involved in their own predictions that they have difficulty entertaining the possibility that they are wrong. Rather, our surprise resulted primarily from the dramatic effects of these language variables on persuasive outcomes. The size of the differences and strength of the relationships for many of the dependent variables have demonstrated how even relatively minor variations in the linguistic and syntactic properties of messages can influence persuasive success. Such positive violations of our expectations, as expected, persuaded us to continue our quest for additional relationships between language choices and attitude and behaviour change.

Our modest propositional framework is almost entirely limited to a single language variable, *language intensity,* conceptualized and operationalized in various ways. Bradac, Bowers and Courtwight (1979) have reviewed the variables of lexical diversity and immediacy, along with language intensity, and have offered some generalizations about the impact of these variables in differing communicative contexts. These are but two additional language variables that could benefit from additional studies to examine their relationship with success at social influence. Though many of our claims remain tentative, we are convinced that scientific understanding of the persuasion process can be markedly increased by continuing research on the ways that language strategies facilitate or inhibit persuasive success.

## REFERENCES

Baseheart, J. R. Message opinionation and approval-dependence as determinants of receiver attitude change and recall. *Speech Monographs,* 1971, *38,* 302–310.

Beach, R. I. The effect of a "fear-arousing" safety film on physiological, attitudinal and behavioural measures: A pilot study. *Traffic Safety Research Review,* 1966, *10,* 53–57.

Bem, S. L. Sex role adaptability: One consequence of psychological androgyny. *Journal of Personality and Social Psychology,* 1975, *31,* 634–643.

Bem, S. L., & Bem, D. J. Case study of a nonconscious ideology: Training the woman to know her place. In D. J. Bem, *Beliefs, attitudes, and human affairs.* Belmont, California: Wadsworth, 1970.

Bem, S. L., & Lenney, E. Sex typing and the avoidance of cross-sex behaviour. *Journal of Personality and Social Psychology,* 1976, *33,* 48–54.

Berkowitz, L., & Cottingham, D. R. The interest value and relevance of fear-arousing communications. *Journal of Abnormal and Social Psychology,* 1960, *60,* 37–43.

Bostrom, R. N., Baseheart, J. R., & Rossiter, C. M. The effects of three types of profane language in persuasive messages. *Journal of Communication*, 1973, *23*, 461–475.

Bowers, J. W. Language intensity, social introversion and attitude change. *Speech Monographs*, 1963, *30*, 345–352.

Bradac, J. J., Bowers J. W., and Courtright, J. A. Three language variables in communication research: Intensity, immediacy, and diversity. *Human Communication Research*, 1979, *5*, 257–269.

Brooks, R. D. The generalizability of early reversals of attitudes toward communication sources. *Speech Monographs*, 1970, *37*, 152–155.

Burgoon, M. The effects of response set and race on message interpretation. *Speech Monographs*, 1970, *37*, 264–268.(a)

Burgoon, M. Empirical investigations of language intensity: III. The effects of source credibility and language intensity on attitude change and person perception. *Human Communication Research*, 1975, *1*, 251–256.

Burgoon, M. *Prior attitude and language intensity as predictors of message style and attitude change following counterattitudinal communication behaviour.* Unpublished doctoral dissertation, Michigan State University, 1970.(b)

Burgoon, M., & Chase, L. J. The effects of differential linguistic patterns in messages attempting to induce resistance to persuasion. *Speech Monographs*, 1973, *40*, 1–7.

Burgoon, M., Cohen, M., Miller M. D., & Montgomery, C. L. An empirical test of a model of resistance to persuasion. *Human Communication Research*, 1978, *5*, 27–39.

Burgoon, M., & King, L. B. The mediation of resistance to persuasion strategies by language variables and active-passive participation. *Human Communication Research*, 1974, *1*, 30–41.

Burgoon, M., & Miller, G. R. Prior attitude and language intensity as predictors of message style and attitude change following counterattitudinal advocacy. *Journal of Personality and Social Psychology*, 1971, *20*, 240–253.

Burgoon, M., & Stewart, D. Empirical investigations of language intensity: I. The effects of sex of source, receiver, and language intensity on attitude change. *Human Communication Research*, 1975, *1*, 244–248.

Carmichael, C. W., & Cronkhite, G. Frustration and language intensity. *Speech Monographs*, 1965, *32*, 107–111.

De Wolfe, A. S., & Governale, C. N. Fear and attitude change. *Journal of Abnormal and Social Psychology*, 1964, *69*, 119–123.

Emery, J., & Krumboltz, J. Standard versus individualized hierarchies in desensitization to reduce test anxiety. *Journal of Counselling Psychology*, 1967, *14*, 204–209.

Festinger, L. *A theory of cognitive dissonance.* Stanford: Stanford University Press, 1957.

Festinger, L., & Maccoby, N. On resistance to persuasive communications. *Journal of Abnormal and Social Psychology*, 1964, *68*, 359–366.

Greenberg, B. S. & Tannenbaum, P. H. Communicator performance under cognitive stress. *Journalism Quarterly*, 1962, *39*, 169–175.

Heider, F. Attitudes and cognitive organization. *Journal of Psychology*, 1946, *21*, 107–112.

Janis, I. L., & Feshbach, S. Effects of fear-arousing communications. *Journal of Abnormal and Social Psychology.* 1953, *48*, 79–92.

Janis, I. L., & Terwilliger, R. An experimental study of psychological resistance to fear-arousing communication. *Journal of Abnormal and Social Psychology*, 1962, *65*, 403–410.

Jones, S. B. & Burgoon, M. Empirical investigations of language intensity: II. The effects of irrelevant fear and language intensity on attitude change. *Human Communication Research*, 1975, *1*, 248–251.

Kiesler, S. B., & Mathog, R. B. Distraction hypothesis in attitude change: Effects of effectiveness. *Psychological Reports*, 1968, *23*, 1123-1133.

Leventhal, H., & Niles, P. A field experiment on fear arousal with data on the validity of questionnaire measures. *Journal of Personality*, 1964, *32*, 459-479.

Leventhal, H., & Niles, P. Persistance of influence for varying durations of exposure to threat stimuli. *Psychological Reports*, 1965, *16*, 223-233.

Lundy, R. M., Simonson, N. R., & Landers, A. D. Conformity, persuasibility and irrelevant fear. *Journal of Communication*, 1967, *17*, 39-54.

McEwen, W. J., & Greenberg, B. S. Effects of communication assertion intensity. *Journal of Communication*, 1970, *20*, 340-350.

McGuire, W. J. Attitudes and opinions. *Annual Review of Psychology*, 1966, *17*, 475-514.

McGuire, W. J. Inducing resistance to persuasion: Some contemporary approaches. In L. Berkowitz (Ed.), *Advances in experimental social psychology* (Vol. 1). New York: Academic Press, 1964, pp. 191-229.

McNulty, J., & Walters, R. H. Emotional arousal, conflict and susceptibility to social influence. *Canadian Journal of Psychology*, 1962, *16*, 211-220.

McPeek, R. W., & Edwards, J. D. Expectancy disconfirmation and attitude change. *Journal of Social Psychology*, 1975, *96*, 193-208.

Miller, G. R., & Baseheart, J. Source trustworthiness, opinionated statements, and response to persuasive communication. *Speech Monographs*, 1969, *36*, 1-7.

Miller, G. R., & Burgoon, M. *New techniques of persuasion*. New York: Harper & Row, 1973.

Miller, M. D., & Burgoon, M. The relationship between violations of expectations and the induction of resistance to persuasion. *Human Communication Research*, 1979, *5*, 301-313.

Miller, G. R., & Hewgill, M. A. Some recent research on fear-arousing message appeals. *Speech Monographs*, 1966, *33*, 377-391.

Miller, G. R. & Lobe, J. Opinionated language, open- and closed-mindedness and response to persuasive communications. *Journal of Communication*, 1967, *17*, 333-341.

Miller, G. R., & McReynolds, M. Male chauvinism and source competence: A research note. *Speech Monographs*, 1973, *40*, 154-155.

Moscovici, S. *Social influence and social change:* New York: Academic Press, 1976.

Mulac, A. Effects of obscene language upon three dimensions of listener attitude. *Communication Monographs*, 1976, *43*, 300-307.

Newcomb, T. M. An approach to the study of communicative acts. *Psychological Review*, 1953, *60*, 393-404.

Niles, P. The relationship of susceptibility and anxiety to acceptance of fear-arousing communications. Unpublished doctoral dissertation, Yale University, 1964.

Osgood, C. E., & Tannenbaum, P. H. The principle of congruity in the prediction of attitude change. *Psychological Review*, 1955, *62*, 42-55.

Osgood, C. E., & Walker, E. G. Motivation and language behaviour: A content analysis of suicide notes. *Journal of Abnormal and Social Psychology*, 1959, *59*, 58-67.

Osterhouse, R. A., & Brock, T. C. Distraction increases yielding to propaganda by counterarguing. *Journal of Personality and Social Psychology*, 1970, *15*, 344-359.

Pawlovich, K. J. The effects of offensive language on initial impressions of unknown communication sources. Unpublished master's thesis, Michigan State University, 1969.

Powell, F. A. The effects of anxiety-arousing messages when related to personal, familial, and interpersonal referents. *Speech Monographs*, 1965, *32*, 102-106.

Powell, F. A. Open- and closed-mindedness and the ability to differentiate source and message. *Journal of Abnormal and Social Psychology*, 1962, *65*, 61-64.

Powell, F. A., & Miller, G. R. Social approval and disapproval cues in anxiety-arousing communications. *Speech Monographs*, 1967, *34*, 152-159.

Rokeach, M. *The open and closed mind.* New York: Basic Books, 1960
Sandell, R. *Linguistic style and persuasion.* New York: Academic Press, 1977.
Scheidel, T. M. Sex and persuasibility. *Speech Monographs,* 1963, *30,* 353-358.
Scherer, K. R. Voice and speech correlates of perceived social influence in simulated juries. In H. Giles and R. St. Clair (Eds.), *Language and social psychology.* Baltimore: University Park Press, 1979.
Simonson, N. R., & Lundy, R. M. The effectiveness of persuasive communication presented under conditions of irrelevant fear. *Journal of Communication,* 1966, *16,* 32-38.
Singer, R. P. *The effects of fear-arousing communication on attitude change and behaviour.* Unpublished doctoral dissertation. University of Connecticut, 1965.
Staples, F., & Walters, R. H. Anxiety, birth order, and susceptibility to social influence. *Journal of Abnormal and Social Psychology,* 1961, *62,* 716-719.
Tannenbaum, P. H. Mediated generalization of attitude change via the principle of congruity. *Journal of Personality and Social Psychology,* 1966, *3,* 493-499.
Tannenbaum, P. H., Macaulay, J. R., & Norris, E. L. Principle of congruity and reduction of persuasion. *Journal of Personality and Social Psychology,* 1966, *3,* 233-238.
Tannenbaum, P. H., & Norris, E. L. Effects of combining congruity principle strategies for the reduction of persuasion. *Sociometry,* 1965. *28,* 145-157.
Walters, R. H., & Ray, E. Anxiety, social isolation, and reinforcer effectiveness. *Journal of Personality,* 1960, *28,* 358-367.
Zajonc, R. B. The concepts of balance, congruity, and dissonance. *Public Opinion Quarterly,* 1960, *32,* 445-452.
Zajonc, R. B. Cognitive theories in social psychology. In G. Lindzey and E. Aronson (Eds.), *Handbook of social psychology* (Vol. 1, 2nd ed.). Reading Mass.: Addison-Wesley, 1969, pp. 320-411.
Zimbardo, P., Snyder, M., Thomas, J., Gold, A., & Gurwitz, S. Modifying the impact of persuasive communications with external distraction. *Journal of Personality and Social Psychology,* 1970, *16,* 669-680.

# 9 Pragmatics Versus Reinforcers: An Experimental Analysis of Verbal Accommodation

Howard M. Rosenfeld
*University of Kansas*

Pamela K. Gunnell
*University of Hartford*

## INTRODUCTION

A favourite question in comprehensive examinations of doctoral candidates in social psychology is "What is social psychology?" It may appear that the purpose of this question is to assess the student's familiarity with consensually accepted answers. But an additional motive of the faculty who make up the tests is their hope that they may evoke from the creative student a more satisfactory conception of the discipline. Thus, when students ask faculty what to read in preparation for their comprehensives in social psychology, it is not pure sadism that prompts the common reply, "Read everything." The audacious search for a comprehensive theory that has been the hallmark of social psychology accounts for both its appeal and its frustration.

The formidable task of developing a workable social psychological explanation of human behaviour in the real world deserves to be approached with considerable humility and open-mindedness. Unfortunately, that is not always the case. Social psychologists are no less susceptible to battles over conceptual dominance than other mortals. Of course, vigorous competition among alternative viewpoints can have very productive consequences. On the other hand, premature exclusion of certain viewpoints on prejudical grounds can have a deleterious effect on the development of a field.

The preceding introductory comments are offered to encourage the reader of this chapter to persist through it even though it argues for incorporating into social psychology a theoretical perspective that is widely believed to be incompatible with currently more acceptable viewpoints. We refer to the well-known antagonism between behavioural learning explanations and contemporary cognitive explanations of social behaviour. One outcome of that controversy has been a relative neglect of the learning process in contemporary social psychological theory. The field has made greater advances in our knowledge of how persons process social information than about how behaviour is altered by, or adapts to, changes in the social context. Much of the current antagonism between cognitive and learning explanations is due to the residue of historical events that lack current validity. A primary purpose of this chapter will be to demonstrate that, with some qualifications, reinforcement and cognitive explanations are, in fact, complementary, interdependent and mutually enhancing.

This chapter will briefly review and evaluate some of the major historical events that have led up to the existing controversies. But the principal contribution will be the presentation of new evidence that empirically demonstrates the value of a *rapprochement* between cognitive and behavioural perspectives. Although the evidence is compelling, it is admittedly limited in scope. It is based upon a serendipitous discovery by the present authors during their exploration of initially puzzling results from a unique, laboratory study of human social influence processes. None of these limiting circumstances require apology; but it is important to note that considerably more work is needed to explore further the generality of application of the discovery.

The focus of attention will be on human communicative behaviour methodology was initially developed by Rosenfeld and Baer (1969, 1970) to determine if social speech would be susceptible to interpersonal behaviour modification when the artificial awareness-inducing features of earlier procedures were eliminated. Evidence of such modification was obtained with the new procedure, but it was not consistently replicable. In puzzling over the variability in results, the present authors happened upon the discovery of a hitherto unnoticed cognitive variable in the social interaction process that permitted much more precise prediction of when utterances were, versus when they were not, susceptible to subtle efforts at social control via reinforcement and punishment. To validate objectively the effects of the process variable, a new experimental control was added to the double agent procedure.

The improved predictions obtained by the re-analyses of old data, and their verification with new methods and data, indicate that the social modifiability of speech content depends upon the interaction of social reinforcement contingencies and the cognitive or pragmatic properties of specific utterances. It is not a matter of one or the other being the correct explanatory variable. Thus, we conclude that advocates of cognitive explanations and advocates of behavioural learning explanations of human influence can benefit from the incorporation of each other's conceptions. At this time, it appears that both sociolinguistic and learning theories are capable of incorporating the broader perspective that is necessary to account for the present data. Each discipline deals with problem areas that could benefit from the interactive perspective. If social psychology is to attain its aspiration of comprehensive explanation, it too needs to recognize and incorporate the interactive contributions of pragmatic and reinforcement variables.

## PERSPECTIVES ON VERBAL BEHAVIOUR

Students of human behaviour are not immune to disputes over conceptual territory, but few controversies have generated as much antagonism as those that deal with spoken language. Traditionally, human speech was considered the territory of linguistics, a field in which the structure of each human utterance could be studied in its own right. But increasing attention has been given by linguistics to the pragmatic and sociolinguistic functions of speech—its connections to the persons who utter and hear it and to the larger social context within which it is embedded (Ervin-Tripp, 1969). Other disciplines also have attended to the relationship between speech and the contextual variables (see also Chapter 10). To the personality psychologist, speech provides a channel to the speaker's state of mind (see Chapter 6). To the social psychologist, speech is, in addition, a major instrument of communication and persuasion and an object of such efforts (see Chapter 8). Each discipline interprets speech within its own conceptual domain and tends to extend its conception to explain events of primary interest to the other disciplines. Such "encroachments" tend to give rise to paradigmatic conflicts. The conflicts, in turn, can result in non-productive attacks and defences or in productive intradisciplinary development and interdisciplinary integration.

Probably the most controversial publication of a particular perspective regarding the interpretation of spoken language was B. F. Skinner's (1957) book, *Verbal behaviour,* in which the noted behavioural psychologist formally organized a conception that he had been developing for over two decades. The thrust of Skinner's argument was that verbal behaviour should, at least initially, be studied in terms of the same principles that are applicable to other forms of behaviour, rather than as a special variety subject to its own rules. From his behaviourally-oriented operant conditioning perspective, this conclusion required that verbal behaviour be interpreted primarily in terms of its controlling variables rather than its content. Furthermore, from his viewpoint, the controlling variables of primary interest were located in the reinforcing or punishing consequences of behaviour, those that increased or decreased the probability of repetition of the behaviour. In support of Skinner's position, a substantial number of empirical studies were published in the late 50s and early 1960s purporting to demonstrate that the content of verbal utterances was indeed susceptible to conditioning (Kanfer, 1968).

In the typical verbal conditioning experiment (e.g., Greenspoon, 1955), the subject was prompted to speak a discrete sequence of words or other simple utterances. If the contents of the utterance fell within a particular class (e.g., animate objects or plurality) then the experimenter would follow it with a brief verbal reply (e.g., "mm-hmm" or "good") which was presumed to have a general, socially reinforcing function. If the designated class of utterances increased in relative frequency of occurrence as a result of the selective consequences, conditioning was assumed to have been demonstrated.

This assault upon the traditional territory of the linguist and cognitive psychologist unleashed an equally famous critical retort (Chomsky, 1959). The attacks on verbal conditioning by Chomsky and others were broad based, with arguments ranging from the reasonable to the dubious. Among the credible arguments was the one that similarities in the ontogeny and structure of language across cultures implied that language is indeed a unique variety of behaviour affected by the evolution of specialized capacities of the human brain, and thus that conditioning could not constitute a complete explanation of its acquisition and performance. It was true also that the verbal conditioning studies had dealt with relatively simple forms of utterance, usually a single word, thus leaving unanswered the question of whether or not they could work as well with the more complex forms of natural speech. Furthermore, not all verbal conditioning studies were successful.

However, it was not clear how many of the failures could be attributed to inadequacies of conditioning theory or how many to a variety of procedural flaws in much of the existing research (Holz & Azrin, 1966). The argument that verbal conditioning could not affect the acquisition of language because infant utterances were rarely followed by reinforcing replies from parents was considered by behavioural psychologists (e.g., MacCorquodale, 1970) to reflect both an inadequate comprehension of the nature of reinforcers (they are actually functionally defined by their demonstrated effectiveness and not substantively defined by their contents) and schedules of reinforcement (reinforcement actually is most often and most effectively provided only occasionally rather than regularly).

Perhaps the most influential criticism was based upon empirical evidence that the research paradigms for demonstrating verbal conditioning had confounded reinforcement effects with the occurrence of an awareness by the subjects of the experimenter's intentions (Brewer, 1974; Spielberger & DeNike, 1966). The typical awareness study was similar to the typical verbal conditioning study described above, except that the subject was also encouraged to try to work out what was going on in the experiment. If an increase in the rate of the reinforceable utterance of the subject followed the occurrence of other comments elicited from the subject which indicated awareness of the experimenter's reinforcement paradigm, then the change in verbal behaviour was attributed to this awareness rather than to the effect of the reinforcing consequences per se. However, the awareness argument was answerable on the logical grounds that awareness is not incompatible with reinforcement, on the epistemological grounds that the role of awareness is empirically untestable, and on the related methodological grounds that the experimental paradigms for demonstrating awareness were unnecessarily biased towards actually eliciting the awareness (Rosenfeld and Baer, 1969, 1970).

As a result of the paradigmatic conflicts, students of human verbal communication became polarized to a degree from which they have not fully recovered. Some integration of behavioural and cognitive-linguistic positions has gradually occurred over the years. Clearly, operant conditioning researchers have been paying more attention to linguistically relevant considerations, such as the generative properties of speech (Sherman, 1971), and it is becoming more common for cognitive-linguistic theorists to give at least limited recognition to the role of reinforcement processes in the explanation of language usage and development (e.g., Bowerman, 1978). Yet, the battle scars that remain are reflected in the persistence of inter-disciplinary misunderstandings and antagonisms and, relatedly, in the neglect of potentially integrative theory and research that may prove productive for the analysis of verbal interchanges.

## MANDS AND ILLOCUTIONARY ACTS

By the mid-1960s, basic research on the Skinnerian explanation of verbal behaviour had diminished substantially as operant conditioning researchers shifted their efforts to more applied problems. Unfortunately, most of the published research on Skinner's theory had been limited to demonstrations that verbal behaviour has operant properties, i.e., that it is reinforceable. Virtually no attention had been paid to Skinner's most relevant concept for social psychology—the "mand" (Skinner, 1957). The essential property of the verbal "mand" is that it is functionally defined in terms of its relationship to both the person who speaks it and the audience who hears it. In colloquial terms, a mand is an utterance whose content refers to both the motivational state of the speaker and the corresponding incentive properties of the environment. In the terminology of behavioural psychology, the mand specifies both the nature of the state of deprivation of the speaker and the correspondingly relevant reinforcers in the environment. Most often the reinforcers are provided by other persons in the environment (social reinforcers). Thus the mand is a very *social*-psychological concept.

A unique advantage of the functional definition of the mand is that it specifies the contextual conditions (state of deprivation, reinforcers) that are necessary for the acquisition and performance of the mand, and it is not bound by utterance content. Thus, the utterance "I need a drink" would be a mand if it could be demonstrated that it followed from a state of thirst and that it occurred in an environment that tended to provide thirst-quenching beverages. Under similar circumstances, the substantively less direct utterance "It's hot in here" would be functionally equivalent. However, as a purely descriptive comment unrelated to an actual deprivational state of the speaker, it would not qualify as a mand. Furthermore, if uttered in reaction to a state of deprivation of attention, and not of liquid, it would be a mand of different variety.

Not long after Skinner's book was published, a concept very similar to the mand became popularized in linguistics—the "illocutionary act" (Austin, 1962)—an utterance which specifies the motivation of the speaker and thus also indicates what social responses constitute a satisfactory reply (called a "perlocutionary act"). The above example of a request for a drink also could fall within Austin's subcategory of "exercitive" illocutionary acts, which refer to advocacy of a certain course of action on the part of the recipient. As such, an appropriate perlocutionary reply might consist of an offer of a drink.

The conceptions of both the mand and the illocutionary act recognize the imbeddedness of their respective utterance classes within the sequential contexts of social interaction. Both recognize that one conversant's utterance (mand, illocution) can serve as an antecedent (discriminative stimulus, condition for speech act) and as a consequence (reinforcer, perlocutionary effect) to the utterances of other conversants. Thus it is surprising that to this day, in publications on illocutionary acts, it is difficult to find any comparison with the mand, nor even any acknowledgement of the existence of the latter concept. One would suspect that the insulation of the two conceptions might be attributable to the paradigmatic conflict referred to earlier.

However, the major importance of comparing the mand and the illocution is not for determining which came first; such chicken-and-egg issues are rarely productive and, besides, even more remote antecedents probably can be claimed. Rather, the comparison is important because the two conceptions offer *complementary* perspectives on a class of utterance that is relevant to the social psychology of language. A general difference is that the illocutionary act is primarily a theoretical concept which specifies in detail the psychological assumptions of the speaker that are necessary for attributing a particular illocutionary force to an utterance. In contrast, the mand is basically a methodologically-grounded concept which emphasizes the social interactional sequences that must be observed to account for the emergence and repetition of the act. The conception of the illocutionary act specifies mental preconditions that are logically required for a satisfactory theoretical explanation of certain classes of utterances. The conception of the mand specifies the sequential contingencies between overt events that are required for the prediction and control of the performance and the acquisition of such classes of utterances. Thus it would appear that if the linguist and the operant conditioner could get their respective acts together, so to speak, they could combine their perspectives into one that had greater theoretical elegance, methodological soundness and practical applicability.

The present chapter is an effort to promote a more productive integration between the complementary social-behavioural conception of the mand and the cognitive-linguistic conception of the illocutionary act, because these are relevant to a fuller understanding of verbal communication and influence. In particular, we will describe and validate an objective basis for identifying illocutionary acts within a controllable social-experimental setting, and we will demonstrate how repertoires of illocutionary acts are, as mands, affected by verbal reinforcement contingencies.

## A SERENDIPITOUS OPPORTUNITY: THE DOUBLE AGENT REVISITED

The involvement of the present authors in the paradigmatic controversy reviewed above was due to our attempts to account for the inconsistent results we obtained in efforts to replicate the evidence of verbal conditioning without awareness that was reported by Rosenfeld and Baer (1970). Our solution to this problem, which led to the present perspective on the paradigmatic conflict, was intimately related to our reconceptualization of the "double agent" research methods of Rosenfeld and Baer. Thus a brief review of their conception and procedures is necessary for our presentation of supporting arguments and data.

The double agent researchers argued that although awareness could not be conclusively proved or disproved in verbal conditioning studies and although an awareness interpretation was not inherently incompatible with a reinforcement explanation, it would still be prudent to design a procedure in which the probability of awareness was minimized. As noted earlier, in the prototypical, verbal conditioning laboratory experiment the subject's only task was to say words or short utterances one at a time, and the experimenter's only task was to reply to a subclass of the utterances with a purported verbal reinforcer. Under such circumstances, the subject is likely to be curious about the experimenter's purposes and to pay special attention to trying to figure it out. In contrast, the double agent procedure was an effort to distract the subject from suspicions about the intentions of the experimenter.

Overall, the procedure was an attempt to include both the experimental control of the verbal conditioning experiment and to approach the active social involvement of participants in real life verbal interaction. This involvement was promoted by treating subjects as if they were experimenters whose task was to reinforce selectively the verbal behaviour of another person. But, in actuality, the other person was a confederate whose verbal behaviour was subtly used to reinforce the verbal behaviour of the subject.

As in real life conditions of espionage, it can get difficult to keep track of the identities of characters who play double agent roles. Thus, for the sake of simplicity, the conventions will be used of referring to the real subject in the conventional way as $S$, the double agent confederate as $C$, and the experimenters as $E$s. Also, inasmuch as $C$ and most $S$s were female, they will be referred to by feminine pronouns.

The procedure was as follows. An $S$ was hired by the $E$s to serve as an experimenter whose task was to devise an effective reinforcement schedule for improving the speech of a supposed subject *(C)*. $S$ would communicate with $C$ via an intercom, and would operate an add-subtract point counter visible to $C$. $S$ was informed that $C$ was instructed by the $E$s to say nouns one at a time, on request by $S$. Actually, $C$ was a confederate robot; a multi-track tape recording, one track of which contained fluently spoken nouns while the other track contained the same nouns preceded by an "uh"-type disfluency. In an initial baseline period, $C$ emitted the disfluent forms on a random 50% schedule, while an assessment was made of the forms of request spoken by the $S$. A stable lexical characteristic of the $S$'s requests was selected by the $E$s as a target for subsequent reinforcement or punishment. In the conditioning period that followed the baseline assessment, $S$ was instructed to continue requesting nouns and to reinforce fluent nouns with points to be delivered by an electro-mechanical device. $S$ could give from zero to three positive or negative points.

If $S$'s request was a designated form (e.g., contained the word "please"), a word from $C$'s fluent track was played as a reinforcement; requests in any other form produced the word from the disfluent track.

The conditioning period persisted until $S$ either increased the relative frequency of the reinforceable request form to a criterion level (two consecutive 25-response blocks different from baseline at the .05 level by the binomial distribution) or until an arbitrary number of unsuccessful blocks occurred. If evidence of conditioning occurred, at least one more experimental period was added in which either a reversal of the conditioning effect was attempted or in which a different form of request was selected for reinforcement. Periodically, a break was called during which the $E$s interviewed $S$ to probe for awareness. Inasmuch as the awareness data have no clear implications for present purposes, they will not be referred to further. The other procedural details described above are reviewed in Table 9.1, except that the probe phase in Table 9.1 was added later for the present study and will be discussed in a subsequent section of the chapter.

TABLE 9.1
Subject and Experimenter Roles in Confederate Double Agent Robot Procedure

| Experimental Period | Subject Role | Experimenter Role |
|---|---|---|
| Baseline | Give points randomly. Select $CR$* from $E$'s words. | Give disfluencies randomly. Select $CR$ from $S$'s requests. |
| Probe | Give points contingently. Decrease $E$'s disfluencies. | Give disfluencies randomly. Assess $S$'s request functions. |
| Conditioning | Give points contingently. Decrease $E$'s disfluencies. | Give disfluencies contingently. Change $S$'s rate of $CR$s. |
| Reversal | Give points contingently. Decrease $E$'s disfluencies. | Reverse preceding contingency. Reverse $S$'s rate of prior $CR$s. |

*Critical response (to be increased or decreased).

Rosenfeld and Baer (1970) successfully applied the procedure to two $S$s. The present authors applied this procedure to twelve additional $S$s, and found that the outcomes were about equally divided into the following subsets: $S$s who were repeatedly conditioned across experimental phases, $S$s who were initially conditioned but who could not be further modified, and $S$s who did not condition at all. Also, as in the cases studied by Rosenfeld and Baer, among the $S$s who were successfully conditioned there was a wide variation in the number of trials required for the effect.

We were curious about the reasons for the variability in effectiveness of the conditioning procedures between and within subjects. So we instigated a detailed analysis of the fully-recorded sequential data from all of the above Ss to determine if any previously undetected overt variable might have contributed to the variability in success. Ultimately, one such variable was revealed by the search. This variable, which was crucial to the prediction of success and failure of attempts at verbal conditioning, was the emergence of differential pragmatic functions among request forms.

## Functional Differentiation of Requests

The Es in the double agent studies had treated the various forms of request of Ss as if they were equivalent in their susceptibility to reinforcement. But evidence was later uncovered that Ss often made a pragmatic differentiation in the forms of their requests. Their requests tended to differentiate into two categories—those directed at maintaining fluent responses and those directed at discontinuing disfluent responses from the confederate. As will be shown, everyday language meanings of the verbal contents of two types of request often, but not always, reflected their functional use. Although there was no evidence that the subjects were doing so intentionally, in a sense they were acting as if they were "triple agents." While formally following the experimenters' instruction to speak to the confederate only for the purpose of soliciting additional responses, the subjects were also subtly varying the forms of their requests in ways that could be expected to promote only desired forms of response by the confederate.

Our identification of pragmatic usage of requests to facilitate positive outcomes was done on the objective basis of computing the relative probability that a given form of request followed fluent versus disfluent utterances, under the condition that the subject has been motivated to increase fluent utterances. In the illustrative cases to be described in this chapter, most of the evidence of functional differentiation of request forms was sufficiently clear for it to be unproductive to perform and report the results of formal statistical analyses at each of the many relevant data points. However, for purposes of future applications of the method, it is useful to spell out the statistical procedures to be followed.

For the inference of positive function, the most relevant summary statistic is the transitional probability that a given category of utterance $(U_i)$ follows fluent responses $(F)$, i.e., $P(U_i/F)$. For the inference of negative function, the corresponding statistic is $P(U_i/D)$, where $D$ stands for disfluent response. The dominant function is the one with the higher transitional probability. The statistical sampling reliability of the dominant function can be computed by tests of the significance of the difference between the two transitional probabilities. (For more detailed discussions of relevant computational procedures see Allison and Liker,

1982). To determine if the function of a response category changes significantly across conditions, the differences between the two transitional probabilities can be compared across the periods. Examples of such conditions are the experimental periods described in Table 9.1 and illustrated in Figs. 9.1, 9.2 and 9.3 of this chapter. The result of one such statistical test is given in Footnote 1.

By "forms" of request, we refer to simple categorical distinctions between the lexical contents of requests, although if would be possible to consider more elaborate criteria, including paralinguistic features. Using our lexical criterion, it turned out that the request forms that typically followed fluent responses tended to be composed of conventional terms implying a request for repetition of a prior event (e.g., "Okay, again please."), whereas those that followed disfluent responses semantically implied a request for change (e.g., "Another word.") Several actual examples are given in Figs. 9.2 and 9.3.

From a linguistic standpoint, the requests appeared to have met the requirements of illocutionary acts (Austin, 1962). Although classification of the varieties of illocutionary acts has been undergoing substantial transformation, the performative verb "request" commonly appears within one of the subcategories. In Austin's classification scheme, they would fall within the more general category of "exercitives" which generally refers to advocacy of a certain course of action on the part of the recipient and which contains such performative verbs as entreat, urge, direct, beg and recommend (Austin, 1962, pp. 154–155).

Searle (1977, p. 35) explicitly considers requests to fall within a category of "directives." in which the speaker attempts to fit the "world to words" by means of causing the listener to do something in particular. Elsewhere, Searle (1969, p. 66) specifies how requests must fit four basic rules of illocutionary acts: Propositional content (they specify a future act for the listener to perform); preparation (speaker can be presumed to believe that the hearer is capable of doing the act); sincerity (speaker can be presumed to be gratified by performance of the listener's act); and essence (the utterance is an effort to get the listener to perform the act). Although we did not assess explicit evidence for these assumptions, the structure of the experiment made it highly likely that they were operating.

The requests also apparently met the definitional criteria of mands (Skinner, 1957, pp. 34–35) including both evocation by a state of deprivation (here, deprivation of fluent utterances from the confederate as defined by the experimental procedures) and the specification of rewarding outcomes (here, repetition of fluent utterances or change from disfluent utterances to fluent ones). Among his own extensive listing of subclasses of mands, Skinner explicitly included the "request", which is "an occasion for successful giving" in which the utterance specifies the reinforcer and indicates the speaker's readiness to accept it (p. 38). However, a complete functional definition of mands must include objective evidence of a supportive reinforcement history.

Thus, major variables in the present analysis will be the functional differentiation of forms of request by subjects with respect to their motivated usage as mands or illocutions, their implications for the perlocutionary and reinforcing properties of the confederate's replies, and also the degree to which the actual replies support the requests. We will now offer a more thorough theoretical analysis of the interaction of reinforcement and pragmatic principles in the double agent research paradigm and then illustrate the value of these principles in the interpretation and prediction of data.

### A Reconception of the Double Agent Situation

According to the official rules of the double agent experiment, the $S$ should vary the functional usage only of her point-giving responses. Officially, $S$ is to use her verbal capacities only to notify $C$ of the occasions on which to utter nouns, although $S$ is asked by the $E$s to do so in an interesting way so as to keep $C$ involved. But, inasmuch as $S$'s differentiated point-giving per se is rendered ineffective by the experimental structure, the only remaining mode of the influence by $S$ is her verbal prompt. The $E$s in the double agent experiment, like experimenters in traditional verbal conditioning studies, expected that $S$ would differentiate her verbal prompts into rewardable and punishable subclasses as the responses were subjected to the reinforcement contingencies imposed by $E$, via $C$.

But, unlike subjects in traditional verbal conditioning experiments and like persons in normal social encounters, the $S$ in the double agent experiment has no reason to doubt that she can potentially influence $C$ via the normal language usage of her utterances, nor that $C$ is motivated to be normally accommodative to $S$'s requests. Thus, within the rules of permissible behaviour in the experiment, $S$ should be expected to select from her behavioural repertoire those verbal response forms which, from direct or vicarious prior experience in analogous situations, are most likely to evoke desirable responses from $C$. However, as in many natural social encounters, to effectively influence $C$ without violating the rules of the encounter $S$ must differentiate her utterances in very subtle ways. The $S$ cannot blatantly utter, "Please speak your nouns without an antecedent filled pause."

In natural conversational encounters, it may be difficult to determine the different pragmatic uses of utterances of participants. In verbal conditioning studies, however, such a determination is made less problematic because the $E$ or $C$ can provide clearly distinguishable verbal reactions that are highly likely to serve positive or negative reinforcing functions to the $S$. Thus, the $S$ should be expected to utter those request forms that she has found to be, or expects to be, most successful in maintaining positive or reinforcing social reactions and those likely to inhibit negative or punishing social reactions. We refer to the former usage as "positive requests" on the assumption that their intent is to encourage repetition of rewarding outcomes, and the latter as "negative requests", assuming that their goal is to replace negative outcomes with positive ones. The relative frequency with which $S$ utters a particular request form after the rewarding versus punishing utterances of $C$ is an objective measure of the degree to which $S$'s form of utterance is functionally differentiated.

The $E$ in traditional verbal conditioning studies operates from a different perspective than was described above for the $S$. The $E$ tends to ignore differentiated sociolinguistic usage of utterances by $S$. Rather, $E$ differentiates them on such criteria as their reliability of measurement and stability of baseline rate. If $E$ falsely considers the $S$'s repertoire to consist only of a diverse but functionally equivalent set of prompts, rather than of subsets of differential social responses (mands or illocutionary forces), then $E$'s programme for reinforcement may be incompatible with $S$'s sociolinguistic habits and expectations. This is, $C$ may fail to provide perlocutions that are appropriate to $S$'s illocutions (or reinforcers that are appropriate to $S$'s mands).

For example, $C$ may use disfluent nouns to punish forms of request that say in effect, "Stop speaking disfluently." From an illocutionary standpoint, if $S$ thinks that $C$ is capable of controlling disfluency then $S$ is likely to repeat the request form. After the request repeatedly fails to obtain the perlocutionary outcome sought by $S$, $S$ may attempt to subtly vary her verbal performance so as to find a more persuasive form. But if none of $S$'s available alternative positive request forms meet $E$'s criteria for a reinforceable response, then $S$ can succeed only by modifying the existing pragmatic usage of her speech. (An additional alternative, is that $S$ confronts $C$ about $C$'s apparent obstinacy. This never occurred in the study, perhaps due to its perceived illegitimacy, or to politeness or lack of awareness. However, several unsuccessful $S$s did complain to $E$ during rest periods about the $C$'s apparent stupidity in failing to recognize $S$'s contingent application of points.)

Thus, knowledge of the relationship between $E$'s reinforcement contingencies and $S$'s illocutionary acts should permit more precise predictions and more accurate interpretations of the processes and outcomes of verbal conditioning studies. Consider the simple case (such as in Case 1, presented later in the chapter) in which $S$ has two functionally differentiated forms of request; one positive (e.g., "Okay") and the other negative (e.g., "Next"). Due to *E*'s arbitrary selection of *S*'s critical response form (the one to be selectively reinforced by fluent nouns or punished by disfluent ones), without consideration of its illocutionary or manding usage by *S*, four combinations of *S* and *E* responses could result. The *E* could: (1) reward *S*'s positive request; (2) punish *S*'s positive request; (3) reward *S*'s negative request; or (4) punish *S*'s negative request. The implications of the different combinations for the success of the experiment are shown in the cells of Table 9.2

TABLE 9.2
Theoretical Effects of *E*'s Verbal Contingencies on Simply-Differentiated Functional Requests by *S*

| | *E's Contingent Response* | |
|---|---|---|
| *S's Functional Request* | *Reward* (By Fluency) | *Punish* (By Disfluency) |
| Positive (to repeat fluency) | (1) Repeat pos. request | (2) Alternate requests |
| Negative (to stop disfluency) | (3) Alternate requests | (4) Repeat neg. request |

*Note* The model in Table 9.1 can be applied to the analysis of Subject 1 (see p. 245) by substituting the utterance class "okay" for the positive request and "next" for the negative request. Cells 2 and 3 represent Subject 1's conditioning period.

*Cell 1.* The most successful combination should occur when the *E* selects *S*'s positive request ("Okay") as the response to be reinforced. In this case, *S*'s first such request, which is likely to be initiated in reaction to a fluent response by *C*, will be reinforced by *C*'s subsequent fluent reply. Thus, *S*'s subsequent response should again be a request to repeat reward. In this manner, *S* should emit a continuing sequence of the positive requests, thereby providing apparent evidence of immediate and consistent verbal conditioning.

*Cell 2.* If, on the other hand, *E* decided to punish *S*'s positive request, then *E* would be unlikely to supress it more than 50% of the time for the following reasons. Each punishment of the positive request would be followed by the negative request by *S* (a request for *E* to terminate the punishing disfluency and substitute a rewarding fluent request for it). The

$E$ would then attempt to reinforce the negative request (to change to fluent responding) by speaking fluently. Thus, the sequential pattern of $S$'s responses would consist of an alternation of positive and negative requests, with the target request consequently occurring half of the time. The degree to which evidence of effective experimental suppresion of the critical response could be claimed would depend upon the degree to which the prior baseline rate of that response had been greater than 50%.

*Cell 3.* A similar alternation pattern would result if $E$ had opted to reinforce $S$'s negative request. (For the $S$ with only one positive and one negative request form, this option would be a necessary concomitant of the preceding combination. As in the preceding combination, the $S$ would shift back and forth between the conditions described in the second and third cells of Table 2).

*Cell 4.* Finally, if $E$ had selected $S$'s negative request as the response to punish, he would be totally and perhaps embarrassingly unsuccessful. Each punishment would elicit a repetition of the negative request, rather than substitution of the positive request desired by $E$. (Note that, again, given a repertoire of one positive and one negative request, this fourth condition would be a necessary accompaniment of the first condition. Consequently, if $S$ happened to emit a positive request as her first response, she should never expose her negative request to the punishment contingency—an outcome that should prove at least puzzling to $E$.)

In summary, the four combinations should generate the following respective patterns of responses by $S$: (1) repetition of reinforceable critical responses; (2 and 3) alternation of critical and noncritical responses; and (4) repetition of punishable critical requests. Thus, Combination 1 should lead to early success and Combination 4 to early failure. Combinations 2 and 3 should lead to an intermediate success rate, the interpretation of which should depend upon $S$'s base rate of critical responses, at least in those experiments in which base rates are assessed. To the degree that $S$'s negative requests had a baseline level above 50%, or that her positive requests had a baseline rate below 50%, the shift to the alternation pattern in the conditioning period would appear to be successful.

## EMPIRICAL EVIDENCE

We will illustrate the interaction between $S$'s request functions and $E$'s reinforcement contingencies in three single-subject cases, each employing a reversal design. Overall, they provide repeated demonstration of the processes of response alternation, repetition, substitution, and change in function that result in varying successfulness of reinforcement contingencies. The cases differed sufficiently in the lexical-grammatical content of functional request repertoires to demonstrate that a diversity of contents may perform similar functions. The first two subjects were selected because they provided the clearest and most consistent evidence of functional differentiation of requests in data obtained by the double agent procedure. Comparison of the two also illustrates the effects of differences in complexity of functional response repertoire on the results of experimental contingencies. The third subject provides the first demonstration of an additional experimental procedure for unconfounded analysis of response functions, which permitted planned experimental testing of predictable interactions between response functions and various reinforcement contingencies.

## Case 1: Simple Repertoire

Subject 1 *(S1)* was the first of two subjects described by Rosenfeld and Baer (1970) as illustrations of successful verbal conditioning without awareness under the double agent robot procedure. Requests containing the word "next" constituted 46% of all requests during the two 25-trial blocks of the baseline period. In the subsequent conditioning period, in which only requests containing "next" were followed by fluent replies by *C*, the percentage of "next" requests increased to 100%. The only deviation of the obtained results from the classical demonstration of reinforcement and multiple reversal of the relative rate of occurrence of the critical response category was that over 125 trials occurred before the rate of response began its increase to criterion level. The present reconception offers an explanation for the lengthy period required for conditioning.

*S1*'s responses in baseline were limited almost exclusively to the terms "Okay" and "Next" at about equal frequencies, with an occasional "Go ahead" or "Next word". The *E* subsequently divided the responses into two arbitrary subcategories to serve as targets for differential reinforcement. One category consisted of utterances containing the word "Next" and other of the remaining responses "Okay" and "Go Ahead." We will refer to these two categories simply as "next" and "okay" "Next" was arbitrarily selected as *S1*'s critical response, the one to be reinforced by *C* in the conditioning period. It should be noted that *E*'s classification of *S1*'s responses into the two forms was based upon their stability of distribution during baseline, with no consideration of the possibility of their differential functional usage by *S*.

For the present report, *S1*'s two response categories were assessed for possible differential request functions by comparing their probabilities of occurrence after *C*'s fluencies versus after *C*'s disfluencies. In the two blocks of baseline (i.e. the first 50 trials) there was no reliable differentiation; the two categories accounted for approximately equal proportions of responses occurring after fluencies and after disfluencies. However, differentiation rapidly appeared with the onset of the conditioning period; that is, the appearance of functional differentiation of $S1$'s responses followed $E$'s identification to $S1$ of $C$'s fluent responses as desirable and disfluent responses as undesirable and $E$'s corresponding instructions to $S1$ to increase the proportion of $C$'s fluent responses by means of giving positive and negative points to $C$.

Inasmuch as $E$ was ineffective in the task of increasing "next" responses until the sixth 25-response block of the conditioning period, it was possible to assess the differential usage of $S1$'s requests through the first five blocks of that period. As shown in Fig. 9.1a, "next" functioned as a negative request, accounting for over 80% of post-disfluent responses throughout the conditioning period and only for 0% to 30% of post-fluent responses.[1] Thus, apparently, "Next", was employed by $S1$ in a way similar to its traditional usage in a crowded barber shop—as a request for change. "Okay" served a complementary function as a positive request, connoting its common meaning that the present state of affairs is satisfactory.

Early in the conditioning period, then, "next" and "okay" became probabilistically differentiated into negative and positive requests. As illocutions or mands the appropriate reaction to each, from $S1$'s point of view, should be a fluent response from $C$. Specifically, appropriate or desirable interactional sequences ($C$-$S$-$C$) from $S$'s perspective should be the following: (1) fluency—"okay"—fluency; (2) disfluency—"next"—fluency. But as a consequence of $E$'s selection of $S1$'s request "Next" as the response to be reinforced, and "Okay" (etc.) as the category to be punished, the following interactional sequences resulted: (1) fluency—

---

[1]The result of one such statistical test is given here. To demonstrate one of the available computational procedures for determining significant changes in functions across conditions, we compare the negative function of "next" in the baseline and conditioning periods (see the top line of Figure 9.1a on page 247.) During the two blocks of baseline, of the 26 disfluencies by $C$, 13 were followed by $S$'s "next," for a probability of .5. During the first five blocks of conditioning, of the 65 disfluencies by $C$, 54 were followed by $S$'s "next," for a probability of .83. Following the formula presented by Allison & Liker (1982, p. 395). the $Z$ statistic for the difference between the two probabilities is 2.64 which is significant at the .01 level of confidence for a two-tailed test. The computations were as follows: $Z$ = Probability of "next" following disfluency in conditioning period, minus the probability of "next" following disfluency in the baseline period, divided by the square root of the product: (combined probability of "next" following disfluency) × (1-probability of "next" following disfluency) × (1/frequency of "next" following disfluency in conditioning + 1/frequency of "next" following disfluency in baseline). Thus,

$$Z = \frac{.83 - .50}{\sqrt{.74\,(.26)\,(.08)}} = 2.64$$

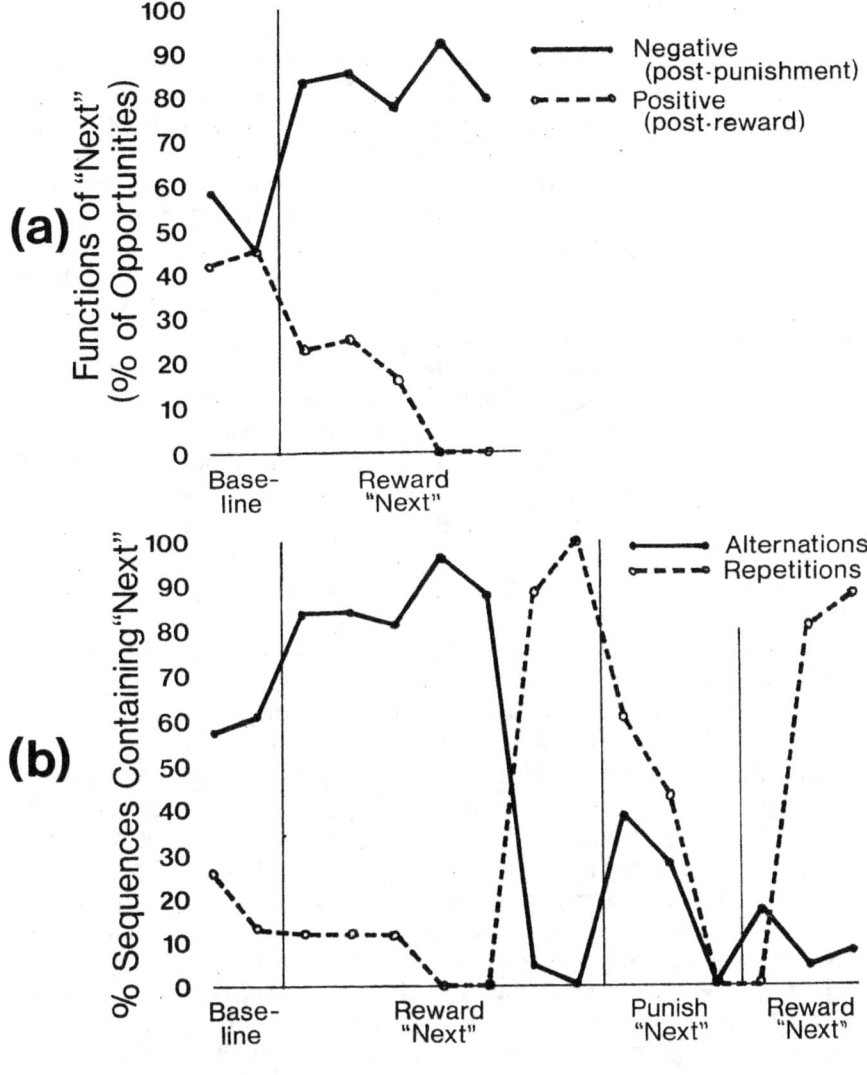

Fig. 9.1. Functions and sequences of $S1$'s responses containing "next." Note: In Fig. 9.1a, negative function refers to the percentage of disfluent utterances of the confederate followed by utterances of the subject containing "next"; positive function similarly refers to post-fluent "next" responses. In Fig. 9.1b, sequences refer to pairs of consecutive utterances by subject, either alternations of "next" and "okay," or repetitions of "next." Baseline period has random disfluencies; punish means follow with disfluency; reward means follow with fluency.

"okay"—disfluency; (2) disfluency—"next"—fluency. Thus, only "next" resulted in the appropriate perlocution or reinforcer.

Given the above information, what should be the predicted outcome of this experiment? *S1* has two socially acceptable possibilities for succeeding. *S1* could substitute a new response form for the ineffective positive request "okay" or break the function of the negative request "next" by using it also as a positive request.

*S1*'s initial reaction should be to respond in function, at least up to the point that she has accumulated sufficient evidence that the positive request is ineffective. Inasmuch as *S1*'s functional request usages were probabilistically rather than absolutely consistent, it should take a while to accumulate sufficient evidence. Furthermore, sticking with the two functional usages would lead *S1* to be successful half of the time, and partial reinforcement schedules are known to maintain behaviour. Specifically, the following social alternation pattern should predominate, as shown on Table 9.2, (p. 243). Cells 2 and 3: disfluency—"next"—fluency—"okay"—disfluency (etc.). But this alternation pattern would result in *S1* evoking a 50% rate of disfluencies from *C*, and the baseline rate of disfluencies was already at 50%. Therefore, by maintaining functional usage of requests, *S1* would not be successful in the task of lowering *C*'s disfluency rate.

To be successful, *S1* must substitute an alternative form of positive request which is not punishable. At a lexical level, no non-"next" lexical substitution would be effective for *S1* because only "next" was reinforceable, but she could vary the contents of longer lexical strings containing "next" (e.g., "Next word.") Another possibility would be for *S* to functionally differentiate "next" at a paralinguistic level, such as by initiating a more pleasant sounding intonational pattern as a positive request, i.e., fluency—pleasant "next"—fluency; in contrast to disfluency—unpleasant "next"—fluency. However, paralinguistic variations were not assessed in this study. Without such a change in the way "next" is uttered, *S1* could succeed only by the drastic action of actually modifying the pragmatic function of "next", by using it as a positive request in addition to a negative one.

Thus, our predicted order of problem-solving efforts by *S1* is: functional usage, substitute functional usage, and modification of function. In agreement with the first prediction (maintain function and alternate request forms), *S1* did in fact say "next" in approximately 50% of the requests throughout the first five blocks of the conditioning period. However, this percentage in itself could be attributed simply to continuation of the baseline rate—the most parsimonious interpretation available in a typical conditioning study in which the functional social usage of *S1*'s responses is not considered. The present interpretation in terms of an interaction between *E*'s contingencies and *S1*'s request functions requires evidence that an *alternation* pattern was instituted in the conditioning period.

The percentage of alternation and repetition of "next" responses over the baseline and conditioning periods are plotted in Fig. 9.1b. (A response by *S* was considered an alternation if it represented a different subcategory from *S*'s prior response, and a repetition if it was from the same response subcategory as the preceding response). Alternation was at a stable rate of approximately 60% per block in baseline. It increased to 80% in the first block of conditioning, when both *E*'s contingencies and *S1*'s instructions regarding the administration of points were changed. Over the next four blocks of conditioning, alternation ranged from 70% to 100%.

There was also some evidence that *S1* attempted to substitute an alternative lexical form of positive request. Recall that during baseline, *S1* had used the response "go ahead" occasionally (specifically, in four of 50 opportunities, or 8% of the time). During the first block of conditioning "go ahead" appeared in 8 of the 25 requests, an increase to 32%. All of these occurrences followed fluent responses of *C*, thus indicating the functional usage of "go ahead" as a positive request. But *E*'s programme required that all such usages result in disfluent outcomes, and "go ahead" dropped out completely early in the third block of conditioning after a total of 13 occurrences. The higher probability response "okay" persisted.

Finally, *S1*'s alternation pattern was broken in the sixth block of conditioning, which was when her rate of "next" first reached the criterion of successful increase over baseline. Thus, *S1* finally broke function, now using "next" as a positive as well as a negative request, and thereby producing the recurring sequence: fluency—"next"—fluency. We do not know whether or not "next" had become differentiated at a paralinguistic level, but there was no functional differentiation of utterances containing "next" at the lexical level. In any case, once *S1*'s request functions were modified, E was able to control *S1*'s utterance forms successfully. In two subsequent periods, successful reversal in the relative rates of uttering "next" were quickly produced.

### Case 2: Complex Repertoire

Subject 2 *(S2)*, a previously unpublished case studied by the present authors, was of interest for several reasons. As with *S1*, her initial conditioning effect was slow, but in this case a different combination of request functions of *S* and contingencies by *E* accounted for the result. Additionally, *S2*'s functional response repertoire was more complex, permitting alternative outcomes to those predicted for *S1*. The more elaborate analysis required for *S2* illustrated processes that are probably more representative of real life verbal interactions.

The verbal requests of *S2* over her 450-response session consisted of 36 different words or combinations of words, many of which contained common components. Optimal separation of the responses into positive and negative request functions would require comprehensive multivariate discriminant analysis of all request forms. For present purposes, it was considered sufficient to informally subdivide 20 of the most common forms, accounting for 97% of *S2*'s requests, into four mutually exclusive subsets. Two subsets tended to function as positive requests and two as negative requests. The subcategorization of each of the two request functions is important because the request component that had been selected by *E* as *S2*'s critical response happened to occur in one subcategory of *each* function. The four request categories, along with their functions and frequencies are shown in Fig. 9.2.

The response component "another," occurring alone or in combination with other words, was selected as the critical response by *E* because it occurred in a stable 46% of baseline responses. Requests containing the word "another" were included in one subset of *S2*'s positive requests, here labelled "'okay' and 'another'." This subset consisted of all requests that contained both terms; for example, "Okay, another word please." The other subset of positive requests, "'okay' and/or 'again'", included either the terms alone or both terms together. The critical response component also was included in one of *S2*'s negative request categories, "'another' without 'okay'"; these requests consisted of all instances of "another" in the absence of "okay." The other negative request category, "'different' or 'new'", contained requests with either "different" or "new" as a component; these two components never happened to occur together in the same request.

The functional usage of the four request categories became increasingly clear as the conditioning period progressed. "'Different' or 'new'" was differentiated within the first block, and "another' without 'okay'" by the second block. The other two requests were differentiated by the subsequent two blocks. As successful illocutions or mands, *S2*'s interaction sequences would appear as follows:

1. Fluency—"'okay' and/or 'again'"—fluency.
2. Fluency—"'okay' and 'another'"—fluency.
3. Disfluency—"'another' without 'okay'"—fluency.
4. Disfluency—"'different' or 'new'" fluency.

But *E*'s programme of punishing responses containing "another" resulted in the following four relevant sequences:

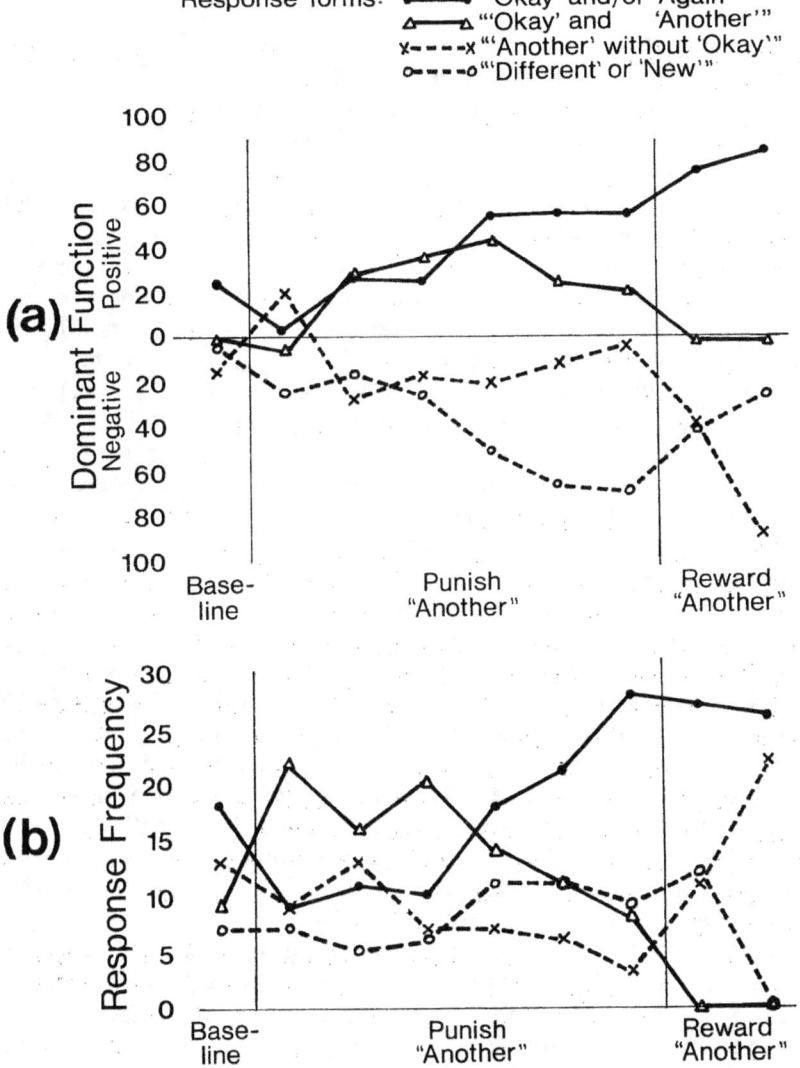

Fig. 9.2 Functions and frequencies of S2's responses. Note: In Figure 2a, dominant function of a response form is the difference in the percentage of disfluent (negative) versus fluent (positive) utterances of the confederate that it follows.

1. Fluency—"'okay' and/or 'again'"—fluency.
2. Fluency—"'okay' and 'another'"—disfluency.
3. Disfluency—"'another' without 'okay'"—disfluency.
4. Disfluency—"'different' or 'new'"—fluency.

Thus *S2* was left with two successful request forms; the other two request forms were rendered ineffective.

What outcomes should we expect in this case? Once *S2* had an opportunity to test the effectiveness of the request usages she should have been expected to decrease performance of the unsuccessful categories. That is, *S2* should have decreased the positive request "'okay' and 'another'" and the negative request "'another' without 'okay.'" Then the expected remaining sequence should have been: disfluency—"'different' or 'new'"—fluency—"'okay' and/or 'again'"—fluency. In contrast to *S1*, there was no need for *S2* to add new forms of functional request or to break functional usage of existing functional requests.

The actual outcome of *S2*'s experiment is shown in Fig. 9.2. *S2* retained her functional usage for ten blocks of 25-trials (five blocks of 50 trials as plotted in Fig. 9.2a.). Fig. 9.2b shows that during the same period the rate of the unsuccessful positive request ("'okay' and 'another'") dropped by about one-half (from about 40% of all requests per block to about 20%), and the unsuccessful negative request ("'another' without 'okay'") dropped from its initial rate of over 20% of requests to 4%. The successful request functions became dominant with the occasional disfluencies of *C* being followed by "'different' or 'new,'" and the subsequent fluency resulting in long chains of "'okay' and/or 'again,'" as predicted. Thus, unlike *S1*, *S2* was able to maintain her request functions while, through a process of elimination of ineffective redundancies within functional categories, succeeding in obtaining a criterion level of reinforcement.

Inasmuch as *S2*'s request functions remained intact at the end of the conditioning period, her behaviour was also predictable in the subsequent reversal period in which responses containing the critical component "another" were reinforced rather than punished. The reversal period resulted in the following four sequences affecting illocutions or mands:

1. Fluency—"'okay' and/or 'again'"—disfluency.
2. Fluency—"'okay' and 'another'"—fluency.
3. Disfluency—"'another" without 'okay'"—fluency.
4. Disfluency—"'different' or 'new'" disfluency.

The expected outcome should be the strengthening of the sequence: disfluency—"'another' without 'okay'"—fluency—"'okay' and 'another'"—fluency. But "okay' and 'another'" never occurred during the reversal period, very likely because it was so strongly suppressed in the prior conditioning period. Thus, it was never exposed to *E*'s positive reinforcement contingency and had no opportunity to become strengthened. In the absence of occurrence of a reinforceable positive request, the prediction for *S2* would be similar to that for *S1*—alternation between the punishable positive request ("'okay' and/or 'again'") and a negative request. In *S2*'s case, the reinforceable negative request "'another' without 'okay'" would be expected to take precedence over the punishable "'different' or 'new.'"

A sequential analysis showed that the dominant characteristic of *S2*'s responses during the reversal period was the predicted alternation between "'okay' and/or 'again'" and "'another' without 'okay.'" These two responses alternated 96% of the time, relative to their respective frequencies of occurrence. The comparable alternation percentage for the prior conditioning period of *S2* was 22%, and for the baseline, 46%. The alternation pattern limited the occurrence of the critical request component "another" to 50% of all requests during reversal. However, for *S2* this percentage represented a sufficient increase over its rate in the prior conditioning period to meet criteria for successful reinforcement.

### Case 3: Improved Experimental Analysis

The new experimental probe for objective detection of response functions was applied to Subject 3 (*S3*). Normally, functional differentiation of *S*'s responses into positive and negative requests would not be detectable until early in the conditioning period. In the baseline period *C* presents fluencies and disfluencies on a random schedule and *S* is not yet informed that the two are differentially desirable. Thus, unless *S* had a natural aversion to disfluency or fluency, she would be expected to say each form of her verbal responses equally often following fluent and disfluent behaviours by *C* during baseline. Differential usage of forms would be expected to begin in the conditioning period after *S* was instructed to decrease *C*'s rate of disfluency. Inasmuch as *S*'s point giving was rendered ineffective, only her verbalizations could influence *C*. Thus, if a category of *S*'s verbal responses differed in relative probability of occurrence after *C*'s fluencies and disfluencies in the conditioning period, functional differentiation would be inferred.

However, verification of the existence of functionally differentiated requests in data previously obtained by the double agent procedures was not always possible because of a methodological limitation. The *S*'s request functions should be assessed after she recieved instructions to modify *C*'s behaviour but *before* *C*'s fluencies were actually made conditional upon the form of *S*'s response. Otherwise, two of the predicted interactions (Cells 1 and 4 in Table 9.2) would result in $C$'s emission of chains of either fluent (rewarding) or disfluent (punishment) responses, depending upon the form of $S$'s initial request. In such cases, there would no longer be available any objective basis by which to test whether or not $S$ performed a request form differentially after reward versus punishment. Even in the case of the other two interactions (Cells 2 and 3 in Table 9.2), in which alternations of $S$'s and $C$'s response forms are predicted, if $C$'s contingencies were able to modify the functional usage of $S$'s responses early in the conditioning period then repetitions of only one request form again would prevail.

To assure an opportunity to assess objectively $S$'s differential use of responses as positive and negative requests, we have devised an additional experimental condition. This probe for response functions is introduced between the baseline and conditioning periods of the double agent procedure, as shown in Table 9.1. In the probe period, $C$ maintains the random schedule of fluent responses from baseline while $S$ receives instructions to increase $C$'s proportion of fluent responses. Thus, $C$ generates a sufficiently large and unconfounded sample of fluent and disfluent responses to permit assessment of $S$'s functional usage of verbalizations. Following the probe period, $C$ initiates contingent application of her fluent responses to categories of $S$'s verbal behaviour. In this way $E$ can *arrange* to test any of the four predictions listed in Table 2.

After two baseline blocks of 25 trials each, the probe for response functions was introduced into $S3$'s session. Four mutually exclusive verbal response categories accounted for virtually all of $S3$'s responses during the probe—"another," "another please," "again," and "again please." Figure 9.3a indicates the functional usages of the responses.

"Another" was predominantly a negative request (75% of its occurrences followed disfluent nouns from $C$), and "another please" was predominantly a positive request (83% followed fluent nouns). Thus, it would appear that "another" by itself served the same kind of negative request function for $S3$ as it had for $S2$. The addition of "please" apparently was sufficient to transform "another" into a positive request, perhaps analogous to $S2$'s use of "okay" prior to "another." Both additions connote ingratiation.

The other two request forms of $S3$ were not reliably differentiated in the probe period, although there were negligible differences in the direction of "again" alone serving a negative function and "again, please" serving a positive function. However, inasmuch as the latter two responses did become clearly functionally differentiated in subsequent experimental periods, it is useful for illustrative purposes to treat them as if they were actually functional by the end of the probe period. If we assume all four forms were functional, appropriate or successful prag-

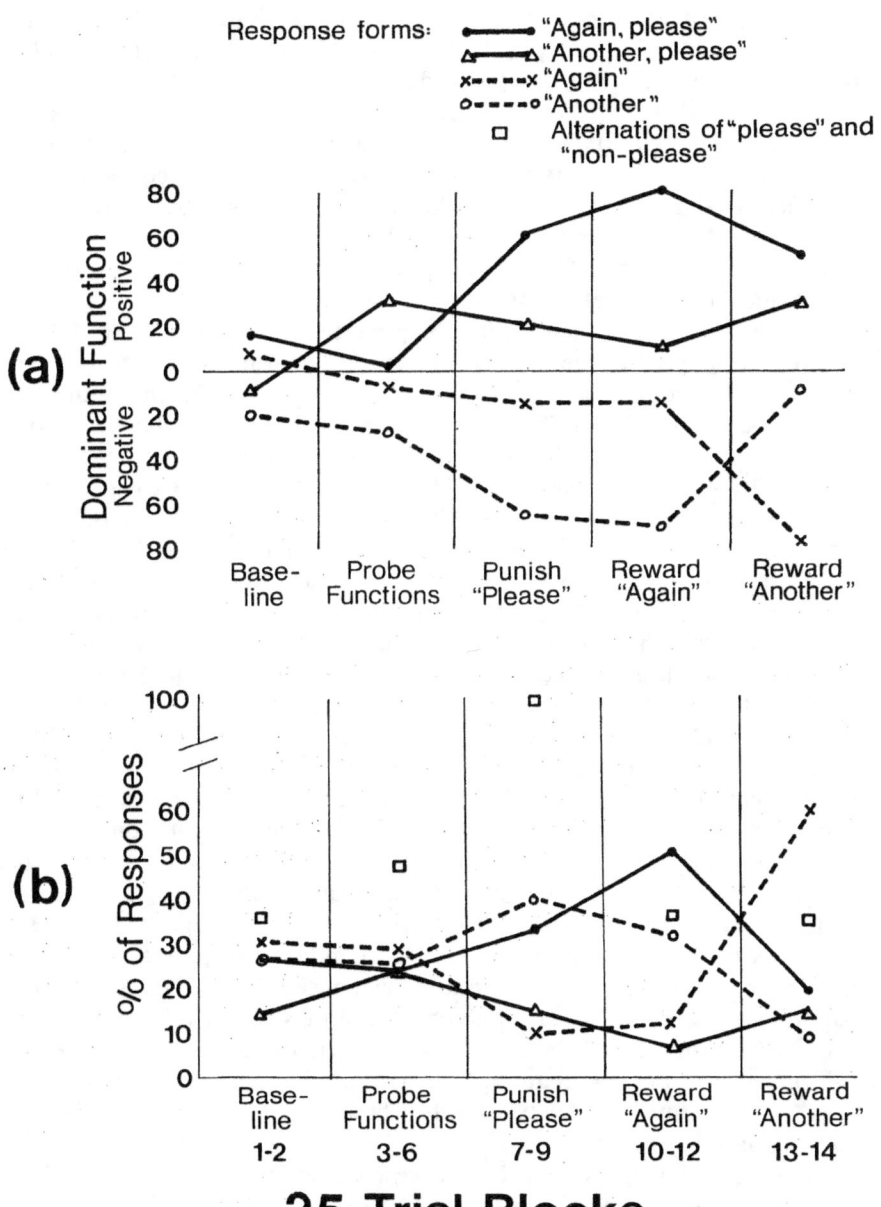

Fig. 9.3 Functions and percentages of *S3*'s responses.

matic usage of *S3*'s request forms would be as follows: (1) fluency—"another please"—fluency; (2) fluency—"again please"—fluency; (3) disfluency—"another"—fluency; (4) disfluency—"again"—fluency.

For the conditioning period, requests containing "please" (46% of all requests) were selected for punishment. Thus *E*'s programme resulted in the following sequences affecting *S3*'s pragmatic uses of request forms; (1) fluency—"another please"—disfluency; (2) fluency—"again please"—disfluency; (3) disfluency—"another"—fluency; (4) disfluency—"again"—fluency. Thus *S3* was left with two potentially effective negative request forms and no effective positive request forms.

Our decision to punish a positive request after the probe period for *S3* allowed us to predict the subsequent pattern of behaviour before it occurred. Our dominant prediction was that *S3* would show an alternation pattern between a "please" and a "non-please" response, based on the same principle that we had applied in the reanalysis of data from *S1* (see Table 9.2). As was the case with *S1*, the only ways for *S3* to succeed in reducing *C*'s disfluency rate below its baseline and probe levels of about 50% would be to introduce a new, non-punishable positive request with lexical content other than "please" (such as "Okay, another"), to paralinguistically differentiate the non-please utterances into positive and negative forms (which we did not assess), or ultimately to break function by using "non-please" utterances as positive, as well as negative requests.

The actual result of the conditioning period was that *S3* contained "please" in 49.3% of all responses, which is about as close to the predicted 50% as one might hope. But as was the case with *S1*, it is critical to the present argument that *S3* show evidence of having instituted an alternation pattern in her sequence of requests during the conditioning period. Again, each sequential pair of responses was considered an alternation if they belonged to different request categories, and a repetition if from the same category. During the probe period, 47% of *S3*'s responses were alternations, while in the conditioning period 93% were alternations (see Figure 9.3). The dominant responses in *S3*'s alternation pattern were "another", which had become more strongly differentiated as a negative request, and "again please", which for the first time clearly functioned as a positive request. The conditioning period was terminated after 75 trials during which *S3* failed to break out of the unsuccessful (to *S3*) alternation pattern.

The request functions detected in the probe period persisted throughout the conditioning period. Thus, it was possible to test a prediction about another interaction between *S3*'s functional request and *E*'s contingencies in a subsequent experimental period. In the second conditioning period, we shifted the contingency from punishment of "please" to the reinforcement of responses containing "again". Note that under this new contingency, reinforcement was applied to both a positive request category ("again please") and a negative request category ("again"). The outcomes of functionally differentiated requests would thus be as follows: (1) fluency—"another please"—disfluency; (2) fluency—"again please"—fluency; (3) disfluency—"another"—disfluency; (4) disfluency—"again"—fluency.

The predicted effects of the second conditioning period upon the four response forms were comparable to those predicted for $S2$'s conditioning period. The unsuccessful requests "another please" and "another" should have decreased in usage, and the successful requests "again please" and "again" should have increased. The dominating interaction sequence should have been: disfluency—"again"—fluency—"again please"—fluency, with "again please" ultimately dominating.

The actual outcome is shown in the fourth column of Figure 9.3b. As expected, the alternation pattern between "please" and "non-please" requests that had dominated the prior period (punish "please") dropped to its baseline level during the second conditioning phase (reward "again"). The predicted change in relative preference for the negative request "again" versus "another" was in the right direction but of negligible magnitude, but the predicted dominance of the positive request "again please" relative to "another please" clearly occurred. "Again please" increased from its 34% of all requests in the first conditioning period to 51% in the second conditioning period, each period lasting three blocks or 75 trials. Over the same two periods, "another please" dropped from 15% to 6%. In fact, nine of the final ten responses in the second conditioning period were "again please", the one exception ("again") occurring in the seventh of the final ten trials, apparently as a result of the $E$'s convention of giving no more than six reinforcers in a row as a distractor from awareness.

Although $S3$ had already been exposed to two different reinforcement contingency periods, one more period was added. In the final period, an attempt was made to weaken $S3$'s newly strengthened reliance on "again please." Reinforcement was switched from responses containing "again" to those containing "another." Thus, predictions similar to the preceding phase were made, except for the utterance content. In particular, "again please" should have decreased and "another, please" increased.

As the data in Figure 9.3b indicate, "again please" did substantially decrease as predicted, from its 50% of all responses in the prior period to 20% in the final period. However, the predicted increase in "another, please" was negligible. Unexpectedly, the dominant response in the final period was the unsuccessful negative request "again."

A likely explanation is that by the end of the prior period, "again" had become strongly entrenched as the successful negative request and "another" had become virtually extinguished in that function. Thus, in the final phase, "another" did not occur often enough to get consistent exposure to the new contingency. Perhaps $S3$ ultimately would have changed, but considering that she had already participated in 350 trials, the experiment was mercifully terminated.

## DISCUSSION

The purpose of this volume is to further our understanding of the relationship between language and social behaviour. We have noted that many disciplines have similar concerns. Yet this commonality of interest is not always reflected in the degree to which writers in one discipline take account of relevant work in other disciplines.

In particular, we compared the concept of the "mand" from operant learning theory and the concept of the "illocutionary act" from linguistic theory. Both represent a social psychological perspective in that they are functionally anchored by their relationship to both antecedent properties of the speaker and subsequent reactions of the listener. Yet neither field has paid sufficient attention to the other's concept, nor has social psychology itself adopted either of them. But recognition of the similarity of the two concepts is less important than is recognition of their complementarity. Linguists (e.g., Searle, 1977) have provided an elaborate conception of the psychological conditions that must exist in a speaker in order to consider an utterance an illocutionary act, although objective methods for assessing such inferences remain to be developed. Operant learning theory (Skinner, 1957) emphasizes how the relationship between a deprivationally instigated speech act and its social reaction affects the probability of the act recurring in the future. Thus linguistic theory is primarily concerned with how to classify an utterance which already has been performed, whereas operant theory is more concerned with demonstrating the environmental conditions under which the utterance will be performed and will change in the likelihood of future performance.

The present study offers an objective method for identifying illocutionary acts or mands that function for the speaker as positive and negative requests. Essentially, the method consists of first establishing social situations in which the speaker is relatively deprived of, or motivated towards, the attainment of a particular class of verbal reply (perlocution, reinforcer). Under conditions in which the motivational state persists, the occurrence of the relevant reply becomes the criterion for identifying the function of the speaker's subsequent utterance. If a particular class (descriptive property) of speaker utterance reliably follows the occurrence of the desired response class of the other participant, then the speaker's utterance is classified as a positive request. If a class of utterance reliably follows nonoccurrence of the desired response, then it is establishing the reliability of positive and negative request uses over repeated conversational exchanges. The method was used to illustrate functional request categories in extensive sequences of utterances obtained in the double agent experimental situation.

The evidence presented illustrated the wide range of surface forms of utterance that can function as positive and negative requests. Particularly noteworthy was the evidence that small variations in form of utterance within a subject can be associated with different functional usages. Both *S2* and *S3* had relatively elaborate variations in the lexical contents of their utterances, each containing multiple uses of the term "*another*". Utterances containing "*another*" functioned as positive requests when other words implying ingratiation either preceded ("*Okay*, another word" by *S2*) or followed "another" ("Another word, *please*" by *S3*). Otherwise, they served as negative requests ("Another word" by either *S*). Although the first subject, *S1*, was limited almost exclusively to the simple utterances "next" and "okay" during the study, it is of interest that "okay" functioned as a positive request as it also did with *S2*.

If a larger sample of subjects were available, it would be possible to apply statistical criteria across subjects to determine the degree to which the surface features of functional requests are normative versus idiosyncratic. As noted earlier, it is also likely that requests are differentiated on paralinguistic grounds and not just the lexical bases analysed in the present study.

The present research also has implications for research on verbal conditioning. Linguists were correct that research on this topic has been limited mostly to simple forms of utterance. But from a social psychological perspective simplicity of utterance is of less concern than is simplicity of the social situation in which it occurs. The double agent research procedure provided a better analog to real life social situations than did most verbal conditioning studies. In particular, it construed the role of subject as an active, influential participant in a social exchange rather than as a more passive object of influence. However, the subject proved to be even more "*social*" than was originally recognized by double agent researchers. Subjects used the ordinary language functions of their speech not only to fulfil the experimenter's instructions to evoke verbal replies, but also to meet their own motives for effectively influencing the substance of the replies.

The current reconceptualization of the double agent studies added consideration of the operation of the mand or illocutionary act as an important variable within the verbal conditioning paradigm. Our experimental analysis of positive and negative requests clearly resulted in a more precise accounting of the sequential performance of utterance classes in two previously puzzling cases. In addition, we elaborated the double agent procedure to test experimentally predictions about the successfulness of verbal reinforcement contingencies in a new case study.

Overall, the studies were very successful in demonstrating how reinforcement contingencies interact with illocutionary functions in determining patterns of verbal response. It is likely, although not provable, that some of the variability in success in past verbal conditioning studies was due to the unnoticed operation of functional responses. More important, future verbal conditioning studies should benefit, both in terms of their success and in their relevance to the field of linguistics, by including objective analyses of response functions. It should be added that the present methods of functional analysis have been applied successfully to nonverbal dimensions of communication behaviour as well (Rosenfeld, Shea & Greenbaum, 1979; Shea & Rosenfeld, 1976). However, the present emphasis has been on verbal behaviour because of the special status it has been given in studies of human relationships.

Other disciplines concerned with the functions of verbal behaviour also could benefit by greater attention to the degree to which utterance forms are affected by the patterns of presence and absence of relevant verbal replies. Linguists concerned with the pragmatics of speech should recognize that perlocutionary acts have the capacity to function as reinforcers of illocutionary acts. By incorporating a more dynamic, social-interactive perspective, linguists could account more effectively for acquisition and performance of illocutionary acts.

Accommodation theory (Giles & Smith, 1979), which is more closely identified with social psychology than are either pragmatic or operant learning theories, is concerned with how interactants change their speech to be more attractive to participants from other groups (see Chapter 10). Prediction of utterance changes in accommodation theory has focused primarily upon the participant's knowledge of speech forms characteristic of members of the other group and the participant's motivation to be accepted by the other group. The present conception might also be applied to an analysis of how response functions and patterns of positive and negative behavioural reactions affect the sequences of utterance forms among the participants who seek to accommodate. For example, it might help to explain and overcome the conflicts that arise from the failure of members of different cultures to interpret correctly each other's proxemic behaviour (Sussman & Rosenfeld, 1982).

In conclusion, we are suggesting that reinforcement processes probably affect verbal performance in a wide range of social encounters. Their identification within the double agent research paradigm lends credence to this assertion. But a general answer can only be obtained by conducting further empirical research, adapted to the specifically relevant social and motivational properties of the particular situation being studied. Clearly the social reinforcement process in conversational exchanges is more complicated than the simple provision of a single form of purported verbal reinforcer (such as "mhm") to an arbitrarily selected response form. Rather, the functions of verbal response categories need to be investigated objectively, including the implications of the response class for the forms of verbal reactions that they are likely to be reinforcing.

It is not really important whether an utterance is labelled a "mand" or an "exercitive," or whatever. The traditional values of a good theory are that it contributes to our sense of understanding, permits prediction, and facilitates control. For social psychology or other social sciences to encompass all of these functions they will need to incorporate further the interactive relationships between cognitive and learning processes.

## ACKNOWLEDGEMENT

The authors wish to thank Susan Kemper for her helpful comments on an earlier draft of this chapter.

## REFERENCES

Allison, P. D. & Liker, J. K. Analysing sequential categorical data on dyadic interaction: A comment on Gottman. *Psychological Bulletin*, 1982, *91*, 393-403.
Austin, J. L. *How to do things with words*. Oxford: Oxford University Press, 1962.
Bowerman, M. Semantic and syntactic development: A review of what, when and how in language acquisition. In R. L. Schiefelbusch (Ed.), *Bases of language intervention*. Baltimore: University Park Press, 1978.
Brewer, W. F. There is no convincing evidence for operant or classical conditioning in adult humans. In Weimer, W. B., and Palermo, D. S. (Eds.), *Cognition and the symbolic processes*. New York: Wiley, 1974.
Chomsky, N. Review of B. F. Skinner's "Verbal behaviour." *Language*, 1959, *35*, 26-58.
Ervin-Tripp, S. M. Sociolinguistics. In L. Berkowitz (Ed.), *Advances in experimental social psychology* (Vol. 4). New York: Academic Press, 1969.
Giles, H., & Smith, P. M. Accommodation theory: Optimal levels of convergence. In H. Giles and R. N. St. Clair (Eds.), *Language and social psychology*. Baltimore: University Park Press, 1979.
Greenspoon, J. The reinforcing effect of two spoken sounds on the frequency of two responses. *American Journal of Psychology*, 1955, *68*, 409-416.
Holz, W. C., & Azrin, N. H. Conditioning human verbal behaviour. In W. K. Honig (Ed.), *Operant behaviour: Areas of research and application*. New York: Appelton-Century-Crofts, 1966.
Kanfer, F. H. Verbal conditioning: A review of its current status. In T. R. Dixon and D. L. Horton (Eds.), *Verbal behaviour and general behaviour theory*. Englewood Cliffs, N. J.: Prentice-Hall, 1968.

MacCorquodale, K. On Chomsky's review of Skinner's "Verbal behaviour." *Journal of the Experimental Analysis of Behaviour,* 1970, *13*, 83-99.

Rosenfeld, H. M. & Baer, D. M. Unbiased and unnoticed verbal conditioning: The double agent robot procedure. *Journal of the Experimental Analysis of Behaviour,* 1970, *13*, 83-99.

Rosenfeld, H. M., & Baer, D. M. Unnoticed verbal conditioning of an aware experimenter by a more aware subject: The double agent effect. *Psychological Review,* 1969, *76,* 425-432.

Rosenfeld, H. M., Shea, M., & Greenbaum, P. Facial emblems of "right" and "wrong": Topographical analysis and derivation of a recognition test. *Semiotica,* 1979, *26,* 15-34.

Searle, J. R. A classification of illocutionary acts. In A. Rogers, B. Wall, and J. P. Murphy (Eds.), *Proceedings of the Texas Conference on Performatives, Presuppositions and Implicatures.* Arlington, Va.: Centre for Applied Linguistics, 1977.

Searle, J. R. *Speech acts.* Cambridge: Cambridge University Press, 1969.

Shea, M., & Rosenfeld, H. M. Functional employment of nonverbal social reinforcers in dyadic learning. *Journal of Personality and Social Psychology,* 1976, *34,* 228-239.

Sherman, J. A. Imitation and language development. In H. W. Reese (Ed.), *Advances in child behaviour and development* (Vol. 6). New York: Academic Press, 1971.

Skinner, B. F. *Verbal behaviour.* New York: Appleton-Century-Crofts, 1957.

Spielberger, C. D., & DeNike, L. D. Descriptive behaviourism versus cognitive theory in verbal operant conditioning. *Psychological Review,* 1966, *72,* 306-326.

Sussman, N. M., & Rosenfeld, H. M. Influence of culture, language and sex on conversational distance. *Journal of Personality and Social Psychology,* 1982, *42,* 66-74.

# 10 Interpersonal Accommodation and Situational Construals: An Integrative Formalisation

Peter Ball
*University of Tasmania*

Howard Giles
*University of Bristol*

Miles Hewstone
*University of Tübingen*

## INTRODUCTION

In this chapter we attempt to extend and systematise some existing contributions to sociolinguistic theory from social psychology. We shall concentrate this extension and systematisation around one particular feature of social situations, namely their location on a dimension of person-versus group-salience, as perceived by the participants. The importance of this dimension for social behaviour in general has been explained in some detail by Tajfel (1978; Tajfel & Turner, 1979) and its specific relevance to language and speech has been pointed out by Giles and Johnson (1981) and Ryan and Giles (1982), though other writers have often been tacitly concerned with it too (e.g., as we shall see, Bernstein, 1958, 1965, 1972, 1981). Nevertheless, its implications for sociolinguistic theory have not yet been very fully explored (see however, Simard, 1983; Gudykunst, in press).

As two of the present authors (Giles & Hewstone, 1982) have argued previously, sociolinguistics has often been simply the study of speech variations, catalogued in relation to different eliciting contexts, a theme which continues to dominate much thinking in the field (see Forgas, 1983). Giles and Hewstone pointed out a limitation of this approach, if pursued slavishly, in restricting speech to the role of a "marker" of situations only, in the sense of reflecting established situational characteristics as a "dependent variable," controlled by situational forces. There is another sense in which speech may be viewed as "marking" situations, namely as a means by which situations themselves become defined for their participants. It was a major purpose of Giles and Hewstone to develop this theme and review already established evidence about how speech operates in this role. This chapter is an attempt to continue the social-psychological contribution to sociolinguistic theory through a process of formulation and formalisation of existing theoretical ideas and their progressive integration with each other. We shall not be concerned mainly with evaluating our suggestions against hard data, but aim to generate more unified and simple theory, which may later be put to empirical test. The "pre-empirical" formulation of theory is an important but neglected part of the scientific enterprise (Shotter & Burton, 1982) and one particularly needed in the sociolinguistic area at the present time.

It is understandable that speech should function actively as well as passively in marking situations, for the two go hand in hand. If we view social phenomena as the handiwork of social individuals, measurable variables do not fall easily into mutually exclusive categories of "cause" and "effect", but function in terms of their significance to social performers. Once a speech variable becomes socially perceived as associated with a given situational characteristic, people put this to use when they wish to create a situation with that characteristic, putting the "mark" upon the situation by means of the speech variable. Again, to prevent a situation developing into one of some given category, speakers are likely to avoid speech markers of that situational category and accentuate those of incompatible categories. Very often, the active and passive roles of speech markers are combined as they are used to maintain situations in their already defined social categories, thus illustrating the close association between the two functions.

## SOCIAL PSYCHOLOGY AND SOCIAL SITUATIONS

Before going into any specific areas of relation between speech and situation, it may be helpful to state briefly our view of how social situations themselves are psychologically organized by participants. In so doing, we draw on a broad evaluation of theoretical and methodological trends in social psychology and sister disciplines.[1] In these we see an emerging

---

[1]We thus boldly summarize the combined drift of some good, old and new thinking which informs social psychology, such as cognitive consistency theories (Festinger, 1957; Heider, 1958; Osgood, Suci, & Tannenbaum, 1957), the motor skill model of social interaction (Argyle, 1978), theories of attribution (Heider, 1958; Jones & Davis, 1965; Kelley, 1967, 1973) and social representations (Moscovici, 1981), as well as so-called "radical" approaches to social psychology, like personal construct theory (Kelly, 1955), ethogenics (Harré & Secord, 1972) and ethnomethodology (Garfinkel, 1967).

scientific paradigm (in the Kuhnian sense) which may be crudely summed up as depicting the Person as Artist and Scientist—i.e. as Creator and Analyser—of the social world. (Oddly enough, social-psychological experiments usually assign subjects to one of two very clear roles: Actor ["Artist"], in which case their own behaviour provides the data, or Observer ["Scientist"], in which case their interpretations of someone else's behaviour are the experimental data.) Both portrayals imply the notions that individuals are active agents, not passive undergoers, of social experience and that they operate according to some parsimony principle. They seek information without waiting for it to impinge upon them, combine and re-combine it in lay theorizing about their world so as to extend the explanatory and predictive power of their theories, while yet minimizing their complexity. They apply their theories to organize their own behaviour and, with others, to create social reality. They test these theories by devising new, better or simpler ways of achieving their social goals, revising them as the outcomes seem to demand. Moreover, individuals do this, not alone, but in concert with others, discussing and refining their theories through social "accounting" (Harré & Secord, 1972), informal reading of newspapers and novels, and sometimes through formal study of social psychology (Gergen, 1973) and other disciplines. They do not even *begin* alone, but have lay social theories bestowed on them through the socialization customs of their cultures. Indeed, their native cultures constitute an extensive body of social theory accumulated over the generations, a paradigm of "normal lay science" within which their personal endeavours are pursued.

What does this perspective on social psychology imply for social situations, the present focus of concern? Within the emerging paradigm, we believe the following type of account can be accommodated. People develop for themselves, mainly within their existing lay theories of social life (but often beyond them and thereby extending them), symbolic working models of the situations in which they are engaged, as those situations unfold (Moscovici & Hewstone, 1983). They use these models to organize their own behaviour, to make guesses about how encounters will proceed, and creatively to change, elaborate and extend the situations themselves, introducing model-derived novelty. An important aspect of this is that the models which participants develop are, as implied earlier, *socially* produced, and in three senses:

1. That the model makers specifically take into account their assessments of their partners' likely reactions and understandings of what goes on;
2. That the models they produce are shaped and constrained to some extent by the culture of which they are a part; and, most importantly,

3. That, at least in fairly successful encounters and when participants are acting in *bona fide* fashion, the models are in fact largely and intentionally *shared* models, joint creations of participants, providing agreed ("negotiated") bases for understanding and situational engineering.

Furthermore, these jointly created situational models have three aspects:

1. Modelling the *actual* (current) state of the encounter;
2. Modelling what the ideal state of the encounter would be (setting goals); and
3. *Evaluating* the current state of the encounter as favourable or not, by comparison of the actual and the ideal states.

To elaborate further, all perception of the progress of a situation takes place, of necessity, *within* the working model actors have so far developed for the current encounter. This means that it normally takes place largely within the *joint* model "negotiated" by them and their partners. Actions are manipulations of the situation's various parameters, designed to modify other variables represented in the shared model. If one actor's model differs significantly from another's, confusion sooner or later ensues, resulting for individual actors in cognitive inconsistency, attributional difficulties, loosened construing, in short, problems which demand revision or re-negotiation of the situational model. This makes all social encounters vulnerable to sabotage by parties who mislead others about their understanding of the model they are collectively building. Moreover, to the extent that actors jointly fail in their mutual model to represent adequately the surrounding material (interpersonal or cultural reality) their purchase upon that reality is thereby limited and their combined endeavours likely to fall short of success.

Language has a role to play in the processes outlined above in two main ways. First, there is the obvious sense in which language can be used by coparticipants in formulating their individual and joint understandings of situations, providing definitional terms and structure for the dialogue in which goals are set, roles apportioned, tactics agreed, and so on. Second, there is the perhaps equally important sense in which speakers' choices of alternative linguistic markers implicitly pre-empt decisions about encounter definition, "manufacturing situational facts," which significantly constrain the situation modelling process. These "facts" are, of course, the active linguistic markers described earlier, and they take the form of different values or (following speech accommodation theory, see Street & Giles, 1982) *changes* in value for linguistic variables at all levels of language from phonetics to discourse. Thus, speech is involved in encounter definition by creating some of the data on which definitional models are built, and also as a medium through which they are negotiated and expressed. Once some degree of situation definition is achieved, the participants' shared definitional model enables them to generate linguistic variants which can function as passive markers of the defined situation.

## SOCIAL PSYCHOLOGY AND LANGUAGE

Social psychology's key theoretical contribution to sociolinguistics has been to elucidate the psychological complexities underlying the distributions of linguistic markers according to setting, participants, goals and other social factors which Hymes (1967) and others have placed on the taxonomic agenda. In so doing, it has begun mapping the most social of social phenomena, language, into the most theoretically fertile concepts of social psychology, such as attitudes, lay explanations and social identity. In this section of the chapter, we note some aspects of this mapping and we suggest further possibilities.

### Intergroup Relations

Recent social-psychological writing on intergroup relations has highlighted the importance of specifically inter*group* processes, emergent from the intergroup context itself, as they affect the experience and actions of individual group members (e.g., Austin & Worchel, 1979; Turner & Giles, 1981). This contrasts starkly with a previously popular presumption that the study of individual and interindividual processes alone would eventually lead to the explanation of intergroup phenomena. However, mere group membership, without either objective intergroup competition for resources or existing group traditions and common characteristics, is now known to generate social identification and intergroup differentiation on value-loaded attributes (Tajfel, 1978). Tajfel has argued (e.g., Tajfel & Turner, 1979) that encounters range along a continuum from those entirely determined by interindividual factors, and unaffected by perceived social categories, to those wholly determined by the perceived group memberships of participants, and in which personal qualities play no part at all. In encounters located towards the intergroup pole, participants show greater uniformity of behaviour towards outgroup members and treat them as members of a homogeneous category, ignoring their individual qualities. It may also be useful to think in terms of intergroup and interindividual contributions towards social behaviour as being orthogonal in *absolute* terms (Giles & Hewstone, 1982; Stephenson, 1981), but the *relativity* between the two is probably of more theoretical and practical interest.² For these reasons, in the discussion which follows we assume a single dimension of relative interindividual-intergroup determination of behaviour.

In a later section of this chapter, we suggest that, even in encounters between fellow members of the *same* group, group membership can have a variable influence upon social interaction, just as when people of different groups meet each other. In anticipation of this, therefore, we drop the "inter-" from Tajfel's dimension and refer henceforth to its two poles as "*person-salient*" and "*group-salient*" (Giles & Ryan, 1982; Ryan, Giles, & Sebastian, 1982).

The person-salient/group-salient continuum is relevant to speech in social encounters because speech variants often function as valued dimensions of intergroup comparison in the formation of social identity (Giles & Johnson, 1981; Taylor, Bassili, & Aboud, 1973). Social identity is defined by Tajfel and Turner (1979) as consisting of "those aspects of an individual's self-image that derive from the social categories to which he perceives himself as belonging" [p. 40], and it may be favourable or unfavourable, according to the individual's evaluation of the ingroup-outgroup differences which he perceives. Speech, unlike some dimensions of social identity (e.g., skin pigmentation), is under considerable voluntary control, making it easy for speakers to accentuate or attentuate group differences in speech at will, in order either to serve the interests of favourable social identity or for other purposes.

### Speech Accommodation Theory

In a number of theoretical publications, Giles and colleagues (e.g., Giles, 1984; Giles & Powesland, 1975; Thakerar, Giles & Cheshire, 1982) have been developing speech accommodation theory. This approach deals with changes in speech style as they relate to interacting individuals of the same or different groups and to their relations, both actual and desired. According to existing speech accommodation theory, style-shifts which increase perceived linguistic similarity between speaker and interlocutor are known as *convergence* and occur when the speaker seeks communicational efficiency or the other's social approval. Style-shifts which linguistically differentiate the speaker from his or her partner are known as *divergence*³ and occur when the speaker either defines the encounter in group-salient terms and seeks positive ingroup identity, or else wishes to

---

²There is no incompatibility between the alternative portrayals, anyway, because, if we think in graphical terms, a 45 degree rotation of orthogonal intergroup and interindividual axes yields a new pair of axes, one of which is intergroup-interindividual relativity and the other an axis representing total degree of determined (i.e., non-random) activity.

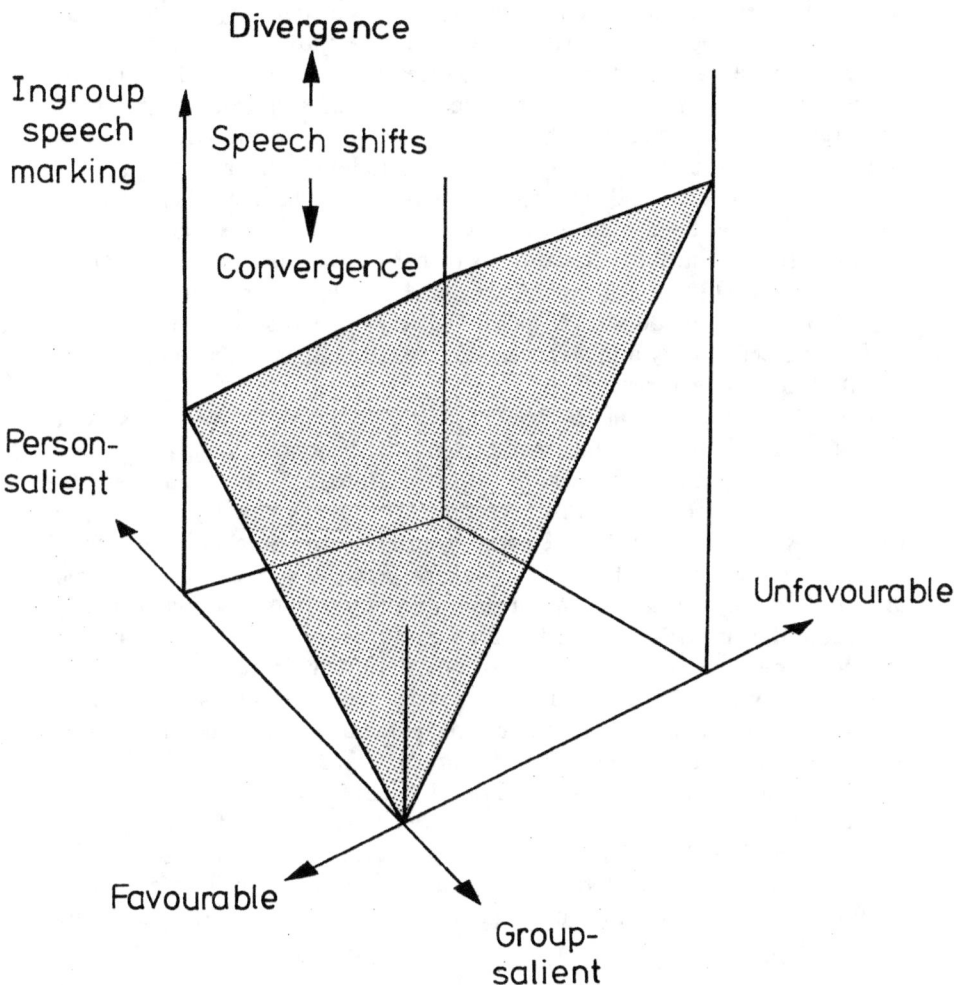

FIG. 10.1 Direction and magnitude of accommodative speech shifts.

---

³Unfortunately, the term "divergence" also features in catastrophe theory (cf. p.273) with a meaning different from its speech accommodation theory sense. To avoid confusion, we use the closely associated term "bifurcation" for catastrophic divergence, retaining "divergence" to mean accentuation of ingroup speech markers.

dissociate personally from the other in an encounter defined as person-salient (Thakerar et al., 1982). However, there is a slight asymmetry about this, since conditions giving rise to convergence and divergence might be expected to be simple theoretical opposites of each other, which is not clearly obvious (e.g., Is person-salience, as such, associated with either convergence or divergence, or both?). One way of restoring symmetry and simplicity could be to portray speech accommodation theory in terms of a simple two-way statistical interaction, in which the person-salient/group-salient dimension determines *magnitude* of convergence or divergence and the speaker's favourablity towards his or her partner determines the *direction* of speech shifts, as shown in Fig. 10.1. Here, the vertical dimension runs from extreme outgroup speech variety upwards towards extreme ingroup speech variety and *shifts* on this axis are either convergent (downward) or divergent (upward).

What this diagram, in its present form, indicates is a basic speech accommodation process when members of different sociolinguistic groups meet, with favourable and cooperative sentiments leading speakers to converge on the other person's speech style, whereas hostile, competitive sentiments lead them to diverge away from it (Doise, Sinclair, & Bourhis, 1976). The extent to which the speakers perceive the encounter to be group-salient is seen as exerting a multiplicative influence upon this process, resulting in greater divergence or convergence, than for encounters viewed as more person-salient. In so far as individuals of the *same* sociolinguistic group differ at all in their speech, their encounters can be seen as like person-salient encounters between members of different groups. However, while this model has some appeal, it lacks plausibility in implying for group-salient encounters wild movement up and down the vertical, convergence-divergence axis as a result of fairly minor fluctuations in favourability-hostility. Clearly, some further modification is needed to restore stability, while at the same time retaining the principle that in group-salient encounters, accommodation processes are somehow accentuated.

## A CATASTROPHE THEORY FORMALIZATION

There is a possible way in which Fig. 10.1 may be extended and at the same time brought into line with some other recent thinking on attitudes and conformity. Flay (1978) and Tesser (1980) have arrived independently at what are, to all intents and purposes, identical models which employ the cusp catastrophe, from the mathematical theory of catastrophes (Thom, 1975; Woodcock & Davis, 1978; Zeeman, 1976), in order to

10. Interpersonal Accommodation and Situational Construals 271

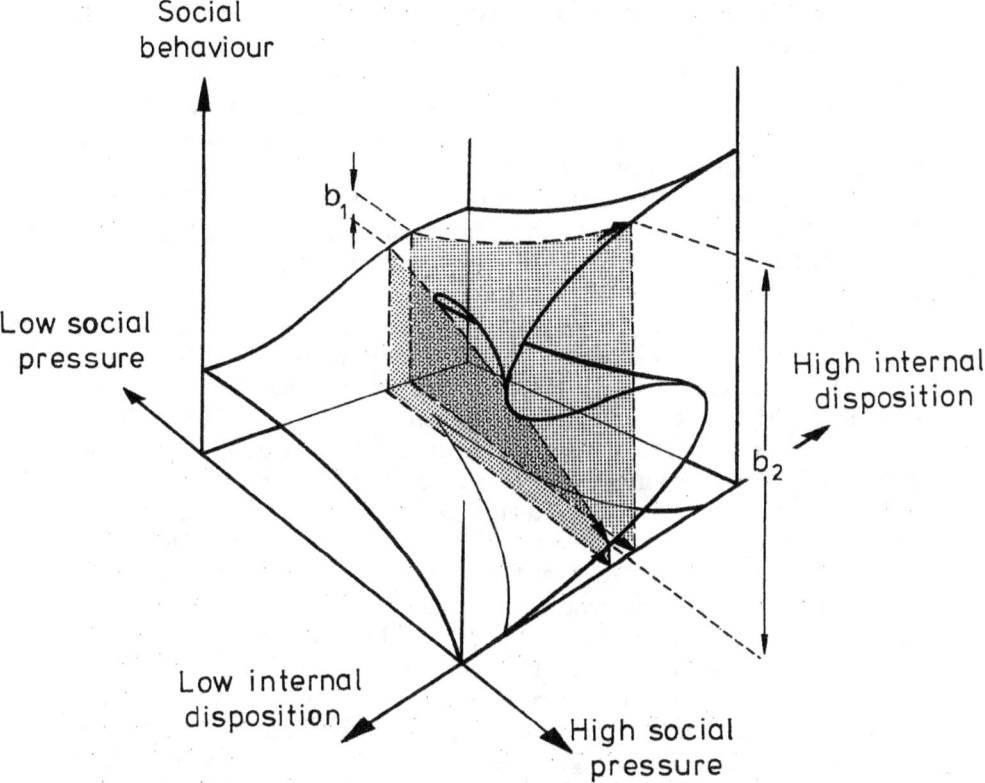

FIG. 10.2 The Flay–Tesser cusp catastrophe model of social pressure, internal disposition, and social behaviour.

describe the joint effects on social behaviour of individual dispositions and social pressures. Tesser's paper focuses mainly on conformity-related behaviour, while Flay deals more with attitudes and attitude change, but both authors are clearly advancing the same principal idea, namely to put a "kink," or fold, into the front edge of a surface like that of Fig. 10.1, thereby producing Fig. 10.2.

At this point, we can use Fig. 10.2 to illustrate a brief background sketch on catastrophe theory, before proceeding to consider its immediate relevance. Catastrophe theory is a recent development in the mathematics of surfaces, which deals with discontinuities (termed catastrophes) which arise from forms such as folds in smooth mappings. Its mathematics is very advanced, but the simpler catastrophes are easily appreciated from pictorial representations. Catastrophe theory offers a cogent understanding of why the behaviour of materials and people is not always the same under the same prevailing conditions, by giving a conceptually powerful rationale for *predicting* unpredictability, and for precisely modelling imprecision. One of the simplest catastrophes is the Cusp Catastrophe, used in Fig. 10.2 to display the hypothesized relation between the dependent variable of socially favourable behaviour under the joint influences of internal disposition and social pressure, as advanced by Flay (1978) and Tesser (1980). In the jargon of catastrophe theory, the vertical axis on a cusp catastrophe diagram is known as a behaviour factor and the two horizontal axes as control factors. The two control factors in this particular application are portrayed as a normal factor and a splitting factor (in Fig. 10.2 internal disposition and social pressure respectively), though this is not the only possible way in which control factors may be arranged. A normal factor shows a consistently positive or negative relation to the behaviour factor, but this varies, with the relation being continuous at one extreme of the splitting factor and behaviour being bimodal at the other extreme. For the splitting factor, the implication of this is that its relation to behaviour is positive at one extreme of the normal factor and negative at the other. We see that the behaviour itself can adopt either of two values in the region where the behaviour surface is folded. This occurs at all points on the behaviour surface above a *cusp*-shaped area on the control surface—hence the name given to this catastrophe. Intermediate levels of behaviour are not possible over the cusp. We also see that changes in the normal factor at the cusp end of the splitting factor, will lead either to very little change in behaviour at all or, if they result in a crossing of the cusp edge and hence a shift from the upper to the lower sheet of the fold (or vice versa), a sudden and fairly massive change, a catastrophic change, in other words. Successive movements to and fro along the normal factor will, in fact, result in successive up-down jumps on the behaviour factor, and the upward and downward jumps will not occur at the same points, but show an overlap. Thirdly, we see that, starting from two points at the back of the diagram, very close together and almost opposite the point of the cusp, representing a very tiny behavioural difference, ($b_1$) and assuming exactly the same movement along the control surface, corresponding to a change in the level of the splitting factor, we can end up with a very large difference ($b_2$) in the resultant behaviour. In other words, the behaviour is seen to diverge, or bifurcate.

The cusp catastrophe can be summed up as a package of five properties:

1. *Bimodality* of behaviour for certain control factor combinations;
2. *Inaccessibility* of intermediate levels of behaviour for these same control factor combinations;

3. *Sudden,* discontinuous changes in behaviour;
4. *Hysteresis,* or overlap between upward- and downward-jumping thresholds;
5. *Bifurcation* (divergence) of originally similar behaviour with changes in the splitting factor.

The Flay and Tesser catastrophe models referred to here as the Flay–Tesser model) depict a relationship between attitudes or individual dispositions (generically denoted here as internal dispositions) and behaviour. They portray this as a smooth monotonic curve when social pressures are weak (at the rear of Fig. 10.2), but as a folded curve (at the front of Fig. 10.2) when social pressures are strong. This generates bimodality of behaviour under strong social pressures, as predicted from psychological reactance theory (Brehm, 1966, 1972), except at extreme values of internal disposition which are either consistent with the social pressure or strong enough to override it. Internal disposition is thus a normal control factor and social pressure is a splitting control factor in the Flay–Tesser cusp.

The Flay–Tesser model, then, suggests that under low social pressure behaviour fairly accurately reflects internal dispositions, but under high social pressure behaviour reflects *neither* internal dispositions *nor* the social pressures themselves in any simple and direct fashion. This echoes the long-running controversy over the relation between attitudes and behaviour (cf. Wicker, 1969) especially given that most research into the issue leaves social pressure uncontrolled and unmonitored. Together with the various other implications Flay and Tesser draw from the cusp model, this is something which we leave readers to follow up themselves while we return to develop speech accommodation theory further along similar lines.

Recall that in Fig. 10.1 (p. 269), we possessed a simple model which showed convergent accommodative speech shifts as controlled by the speaker's favourability towards the listener, and the magnitude of these shifts as a function of the situation's location on the person-salient/group-salient dimension. The favourability factor is an internal disposition just like the Flay–Tesser normal factor, and we now identify the encounter's person-salient/group-salient relativity with the splitting factor of social pressures. Social pressures exist, after all, only in the context of contrasting social groups, physically present or otherwise. When individuals encounter each other strictly and exclusively as individuals, the only possible pressures are those they exert on each other, whereas, if they meet as members of groups, emergent group phenomena immediately affect their behaviour towards each other, as noted earlier. Lastly, in accommodative convergence-divergence, we have a linguistic behaviour factor towards a social target, just as in the Flay–Tesser model. If that

274  Ball, Giles and Hewstone

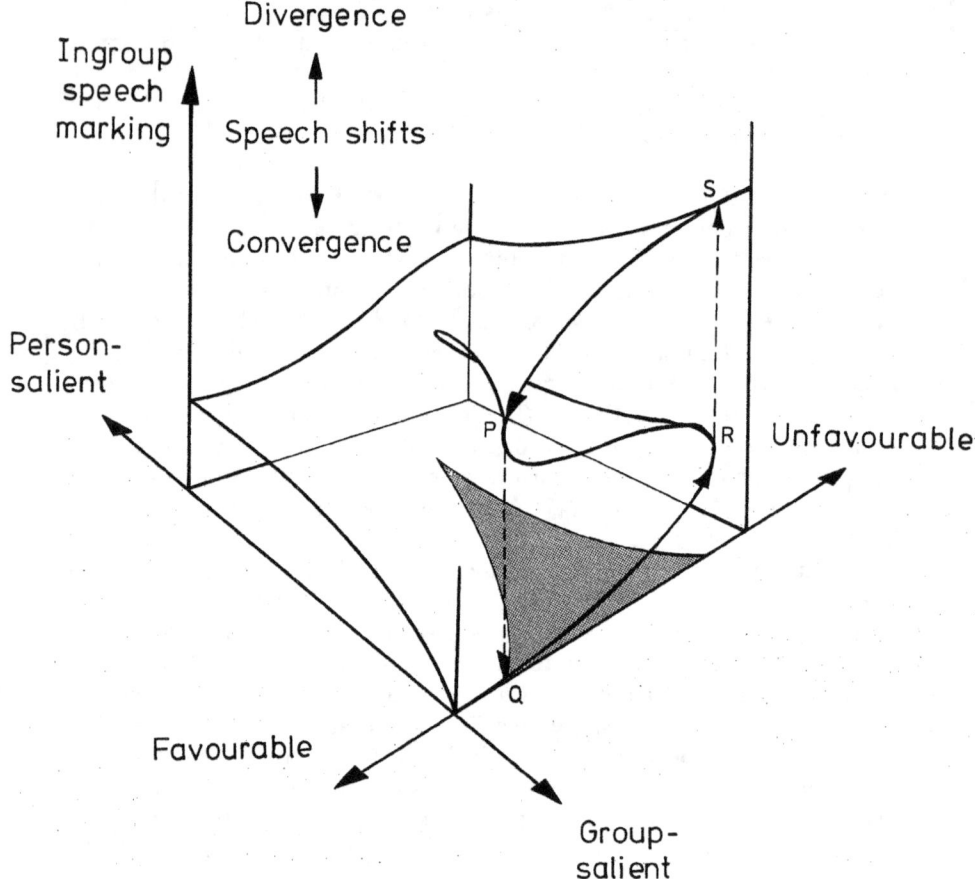

FIG. 10.3  A cusp catastrophe model of speech accommodation.

catastrophe model has any validity, a similar development from Fig. 10.1, along the lines of Fig. 10.3, would make sense. What implications would follow?

Consider the five characteristic properties of the cusp catastrophe, beginning with *bimodality* of behaviour for certain, but not all, control factor combinations. In the present context, we envisage unimodality of behaviour at the person-salient end of the splitting factor. Accommodation will occur as greater or lesser convergence, shading into lesser or greater divergence, as a smooth function of the speaker's friendly or hostile disposition towards the interlocutor, and will typically take the form of finely graded shifts of accent or pronunciation, etc. (see Coupland, 1984). We normally expect interactors who speak widely different languages or dialects to meet as members of different groups, but there are occasions on which group affiliations are tacitly suspended and encounters are therefore person-salient. When this happens, we anticipate that various means will be employed to soften inter-language switching, such as accent-attenuation, lexical and semantic mixings and the use of metalinguistic comments designed to create favourable listener attributions for unavoidable major switches, thereby smoothing an otherwise dichotomy into a continuum (cf. Giles, Taylor & Bourhis, 1973; Scotton, 1976). At the other, group-salient end of the splitting factor we find, except at the most hostile and friendly extremes, *bimodality* of accommodation, observing vigorous convergence and divergence, but no intermediately accommodative speech, thus exemplifying the *inaccessibility* property of the cusp catastrophe. Accommodative changes in speech at this end of the splitting factor are likely to be sudden and gross (the *discontinuity* property), typical of encounters between members of clearly distinct ethno-linguistic groups who discretely switch between languages (Bourhis, Giles, Leyens, & Tajfel, 1979).

From the catastrophe model, it should not surprise us to find two very similar individuals, who share almost identical friendliness-hostility towards a given interlocutor, displaying widely contrasting accommodative speech styles in conversation with the other under equivalent circumstances. This would arise as a result of having arrived at points one vertically above the other on the upper and lower folds over the cusp thereby displaying the *bifurcation* property of the catastrophe (see footnote 3 on p.269). Lastly, we may expect to observe *hysteresis* (the PQRS cycle in Fig.10.3) in successive convergent-divergent speech-switches during group-salient conversations. Divergent changes should occur only after a substantial increase in a speaker's hostility towards his partner above the level at which, as hostility decreases, the corresponding convergent changes occur. Put another way, we should expect that, in group-salient conversations at moderate levels of speaker-favourableness, changes in favourableness would have little or no observable effect on speech accommodation, but that speech would continue as it was until the cusp edge had been crossed and a catastrophic divergent or convergent switch occurred.

So much for the schematic model and its implications, but does all this make psychological sense? In approaching this issue, we need not take each of the five cusp properties separately, because they are really a package and simply different aspects of the cusp as a property in itself. All we need to ask is whether the principal effects of group- vs. individual-focused social interaction correspond to the catastrophe model's implications. Central to Tajfel's approach to intergroup behaviour, as we have seen, is the notion that social behaviour in group-defined contexts is less finely graded than in individually-defined contexts. Members of groups act in a relatively uniform way towards all out-group members and in a contrastingly uniform way towards ingroup members, whereas in person-salient encounters they adjust their behaviour more subtly to the particular other being dealt with. In like vein, our cusp model suggests that as group membership becomes increasingly salient to an encounter the speech options narrow down to approach just two values, maximum accommodative divergence (or ingroup linguistic marking) and maximum accommodative convergence (or total shift to the outgroup's speech style). The bimodality, inaccessibility, discontinuity, bifurcation and hysteresis properties all flow from this.

Whereas Tajfel's own writings on intergroup behaviour focus on negative actions towards outgroup members, existing speech accommodation theory has already gone beyond this to deal with how people speak when they want to be pleasant to outgroup members, with the notion of sociolinguistic convergence. Here, it is made explicit that although, following Tajfel, behaviour towards different outgroup members is indeed uniform, the actor-speaker's individual disposition will influence whether it be favourable or unfavourable. At the same time, our model clearly indicates that change in an individual speaker's favourability towards an outgroup will not immediately, or necessarily ever, manifest itself in any discernible accommodative speech shift. The more the situation is defined by speakers as group-salient, the more likely it is that their actual speech will be trapped by social pressure on either the upper or lower surface of the fold, unable to vary unless the attitude change is sufficient to carry speakers across the edge of the cusp, when the observed speech shifts will be discrete and dramatic. Our present formulation retains this and makes both the uniformity and variability aspects even more central to and comprehensible within the theory.

The Need for a Dynamic

Any application of catastrophe theory should ideally involve specification of some "dynamic" (Zeeman, 1976) or "potential" (Woodcock & Davis, 1978); some resultant force or tension the minimization or maximization of which keeps behaviour on the catastrophe surface and not floating freely around the control-behaviour factor space of the model, although numerous applications omit or defer this. In mechanical catastrophes, the dynamic is typically like tension in a rubber band (Zeeman's pedagogic catastrophe machine) or resistance to buckling in those "clicking" toys which emerge from Christmas crackers. In a previous application of the cusp catastrophe, together with principles from Tajfel's intergroup theory and speech accommodation theory, to second language learning (Ball,

Giles, & Hewstone, 1984), we argued that an appropriate dynamic would be the maximizing of self-esteem (or, after Tajfel, favourableness of social identity), in terms of the kinds of interindividual and intergroup comparisons the person can draw (Festinger, 1954). To employ the same dynamic in our present model would add credibility and further integrate our thinking into what already exists, but such theoretical integration may be too much to hope for yet, at least in any well-elucidated way. However, we may find a plausible dynamic with relevant implications for self-esteem and identity.

The effect of a given behaviour on people's self-esteem is presumably some function of how they see that behaviour presenting them to themselves and, even more, to other individuals. In person-salient encounters, to which participants' and observers' group memberships are irrelevant, an action will be judged good or bad in terms of its individually justified friendliness or unfriendliness toward the recipient. Hence, actors' self-esteem will be equally served as long as their behaviour reflects the friendliness they feel is deserved by the target individual. When groups are salient, though, people themselves have been sorted into contrasting equivalence categories and their behaviour too, as we have noted, tends to be categorical. Cases of extreme hostility or friendliness pose few problems. However, when actors are intermediately disposed towards the target person, they may consider likely intergroup interpretations of their behaviour by witnesses of either group, with the risk of misinterpretation and subsequent misclassifications of themselves if it is at all ambiguous. In group-salient situations, people expect others to maintain clear group identity and they act unfavourably when affiliations are unclear or variable, because that creates uncertainties for them in organizing their own social performance. We may expect that in encounters at the group-salient extreme, self-esteem will be served by avoidance of speech which is not clearly perceptible as convergent or divergent. It may indeed be preferable to converge entirely and "pass" (if non-linguistic factors permit) for one of the outgroup than to be under constant suspicion from both sides of being an interloper (cf. Lambert, 1967). There may be occasions when convergence onto outgroup speech arouses ingroup antagonism (Platt & Weber, 1984), but clear and unambiguous convergence offers the possibility of compensating self-esteem derived from acceptance among the outgroup, and perhaps from migration into it. To complement this, when clear divergence occurs, ingroup identity is emphatically marked and self-esteem thus maintained.

The fold in the behaviour surface of Fig. 10.3 provides the speaker with a means of maintaining consistency of speech-accommodative behaviour, too. It could be uncomfortable in an intergroup relationship continually to shift speech style with momentary fluctuations in positive feelings, because both ingroup and outgroup members (and perhaps oneself) would see one's projected sociolinguistic identity as unstable and unreliable. Hence it is entirely plausible that, after opting for either convergent or divergent speech towards a given other in a given type of situation, one should persevere regardless of moderate changes in internal disposition towards the other, switching only when one's speech has become markedly out of step with one's attitude, and then doing so in a fairly radical fashion, so as to establish an appearance of sociolinguistic stability.

We do not pretend here to have elaborated a thorough account of a dynamic for the present cusp model of speech accommodation, but we suggest that the above indicates something of how it might work and that it bears potential similarity to the self-esteem dynamic in the Ball et al. (1984) version of Giles & Byrne's (1982) intergroup model of second language learning.

## COMMUNICATION WITHIN GROUPS AND CODE-ELABORATION

Up to this point, we have concentrated on conversations between members of *different* groups with constrasting speech varieties, developing the catastrophe model to deal with that context. Consider now the possibility of within-group communication in situations in which group membership is highly salient (in effect, intragroup conversations at the group-salient end of Tajfel's dimension). We ignore the internal disposition dimension of favourability because we are no longer concerned with attitudes towards outgroup members. We thus take leave of the catastrophe model, without necessarily presuming in principle that it may not be brought to bear on intragroup communication. We also have something further to say about communications between speakers when group membership is not salient and it may be pertinent to note here that, by definition, in strictly person-salient conversations there presumably are no differences arising from the interlocutor's membership of an ingroup or an outgroup. In other words, group-salient encounters come in two types, ingroup-ingroup and ingroup-outgroup, but person-salient encounters come in only one type.

Ingroup-ingroup conversations are communication between parties who are conscious that they share certain knowledge, attitudes, skills, and values, certain class, ethnic, physical, religious, or other characteristics which are not shared by others. How should this affect speech? Bernstein (1972) states:

> Sapir, Malinowski, Firth, Vigotsky and Luria have all pointed out from different points of view that the closer the identifications of speakers the greater the range of shared interests and the more probable that speech will

take (a form in which) the range of syntactic alternatives is likely to be reduced and the lexis to be drawn from a narrow range. . . . In these relationships the intent of the other person can be taken for granted as the speech is played out against a back-drop of common assumptions, common history, common interests. As a result, there is less need to raise meanings to the level of explicitness or elaboration. There is a reduced need to make explicit through syntactic choices the logical structure of the communication. . . . Under these conditions, the speech is likely to have a strong metaphoric element. . . . Often in these encounters, the speech cannot be read by those who do not share the history of the relationships. Thus the form of the social relationship acts selectively in the meanings to be verbalized, which in turn affect the syntactic and lexical choices. The unspoken assumptions underlying the relationship are not available to those who are outside the relationship. For these are limited, and restricted to the speakers. The symbolic form of the communication is condensed yet the specific cultural history of the relationship is alive in its form. We can say that the roles of the speakers are communalized roles . . . restricted social relationships based upon communalized roles evoke particularistic, that is, context-tied meanings, realized through a restricted speech variant [pp. 165-166].

In this quotation, Bernstein is outlining what he means by and the conditions which elicit his *restricted code* (R-code), which he contrasts with the *elaborated code* (E-code), a semantically more explicit and less context-bound use of language, generated by the contrasting type of social relationship (i.e., lower interspeaker identification, fewer shared assumptions and more individualized roles): "Thus individualized roles are realized through elaborated speech variants which involve complex editing at the grammatical and lexical levels . . . [p. 167]."

Quite manifestly, Bernstein is formulating here a way of distinguishing between the speech forms most typical of group-salient, ingroup-ingroup conversations, on the one hand, and person-salient (ingroup-ingroup *or* ingroup-outgroup), on the other. Before proceeding, some words of caution, to avoid misunderstanding our position with regard to Bernstein, whose theory of sociolinguistic codes, social class and education (1958, 1965, 1972, 1981) has aroused a controversy (Coulthard, 1969; Labov, 1969; Robinson, 1978) which has created more heat and less light than the issues deserve. In deriving some of our thinking from Bernstein's code formulations, we take up no position here either for or against his substantive assertions about within-class role relations, class differences in code usage, or class comparisons in education attainment. In fact, we suggest that a better understanding of the whole class-code-education issue will be attained only when scholars attempt to separate those elements in Bernstein's writing which formulate and formalise his key concepts and their inter-relationships (cf. Shotter & Burton, 1982) from those elements which go on to make possibly testable empirical statements about their implications for social classes' language and education. Such an exercise will also require clarification and simplification of Bernstein's formulations, parts of which are inconsistent, meandering and obscure. It goes without saying that we believe the formulatory parts of Bernstein include at least some valuable contributions to our understanding of language use.

### One Theory or Two?

As we view it, Bernstein advanced not one theory of sociolinguistic codes, as is popularly believed and as he himself may believe, but two, which, after Einstein, might be termed the general theory and the special theory. The general theory is expressed in statements similar to the quotations previously presented and it makes some useful assertions about the implications of social relationships and structure for the use of language. It points to the consequences of different degrees of knowledge-sharing between interlocutors, as they would make demands upon the various levels of speech production and as those would exert pressures upon each other. Thus, relative lack of shared knowledge requires precise semantic specification of meaning, which in turn makes demands upon syntax, and so on, with the result that it makes sense to seek traces of a sociocultural milieu and its characteristic types of interlocutor relationships in the nuts and bolts of sentence structures. This general theory, which we see as a valiant attempt to delineate a general theoretical connection between social organization and the linguistic nature of the speech product, appears never to have been tested in all the research purporting to concern itself with Bernstein's views. The special theory is the one by which Bernstein's adulators and foes alike have been mesmerized, a theory about social class, language and educability. The special theory has been tested and the prevalent view is that it has been found wanting, but this theory does not necessarily follow from the general theory. The special theory is derivable from the general theory by making certain assumptions about, *inter alia,* class differences in social relations and a nexus between the elaborated code and education. On the present state of the evidence, these assumptions appear more questionable than the general theory with which they combine to yield the special theory.

Bernstein himself can be faulted on numerous grounds. His writings do not make clear that a general and special theory can be distinguished, perhaps because he has been mainly concerned with explaining class differences in educational attainment. He embarked on unnecessary and premature theoretical elaboration, making his writing ever more complex and incomprehensible, an obstacle to any dispassionate examination of the issues over which he and his critics differed, and when outflanked on the political Left he retreated behind an ideological smokescreen. Nevertheless, in the more lucid parts of his writing, the general theory can be discerned; a theory of some inherent plausibility, with perhaps no present competitors, and which has remained twenty years untested. That theory is essentially about the connection between speaker-hearer social relations and the nature of the verbal product, mediated by the central construct of code-elaboration.

In this context, our present concern is to flesh the general theory out with a little social psychology. Like Applegate and Delia (1980), we agree that one of Bernstein's failures was not to recognize fully the psychological character of his theory. It is not social relations between speaker and interlocutor, as such, which make linguistic demands and lead to code-elaboration or code-restriction, but their cognitive representation by the speaker. By invoking the Tajfelian intergroup notion of a person- vs. group-oriented dimension on which an encounter may be cognitively represented, we are attempting to restore a missing link in the chain which leads from culture and society to speech. When ingroup-ingroup encounters are cognitively represented as near the group-salient pole of the dimension, code-restriction is likely to result; when they are represented as near the person-salient pole, code-elaboration is expected. It then remains to be seen which situations and social encounters are represented where on the individual-group dimension, by which language-using participants, and we neither presume nor deny that social class could be relevant here.

We choose, then to identify the R-code as prototypical ingroup-ingroup speech and the E-code as prototypical interindividual speech, in a sense which is conceptually quite independent of any group associations possessed by accents or dialects. We thus take it for granted that Bernsteinian coding is distinguishable from and runs orthogonal to other distinctions between language varieties. Moreover, the E-code can be seen here as a way of using language which is "group-neutral" and a marker of situations as person-salient, rather than group-salient, in character. This could be especially useful when members of different groups wish to deal with each other as individuals, but cannot attenuate dialectal, accentual or other ingroup speech markers enough to avoid being perceived as divergently marking the situation in intergroup terms. Hence, it should be possible to use code-elaboration vs. code-restriction, a nonspecific marker of the "groupness" of a situation, in various combinations with other speech markers specific to particular groups. The implications of the variations possible here would be fascinating to explore. In so doing, it might even yet prove possible to approach a clearer understanding of the relation, if any, between social milieu, language, and educability, consideration of which has been plagued by confusion between code-restriction and dialect or sociolect markers.

## CONCLUSIONS

We have concentrated in this chapter on exloring some ways in which speech may vary in relation to the axis of person- vs. group-salience in social encounters. Obviously, we regard this as an important dimension on which encounters are perceived to differ by participants. We are thereby hypothesizing that ordinary people commonly employ this dimension in their informal theorizing about everyday situations and that, as they conduct their conversations, they tacitly (perhaps unconsciously) assess the group-salience of the encounter. A number of investigators have made it their aim to isolate major subjective dimensions of social encounters by inductive means, using multidimensional scaling techniques (Forgas, 1979; Wish, Deutsch & Kaplan, 1976), but they have not reported a dimension corresponding closely to the person- vs. group-salience one. This is probably because their selection of stimulus materials did not manipulate this variable vigorously, so that their studies may have been less inductive than they appear. It is interesting to note, though, that from their studies cooperation-competition, which we suggest may be identified with the internal disposition control factor of favourability in the cusp-modelling of speech accommodation, is reflected as a major situational dimension in these researches.

A question about the catastrophe theory model which should be faced squarely concerns the extent to which it is merely descriptive, and perhaps less economically descriptive than other possible formulations of Speech Accommodation Theory. Do the catastrophe theory mathematics really imply anything extra of an explanatory nature? The question cannot be answered yet and is in a sense premature, although important. Further consideration of the model's implications is still needed to establish whether it is consistent with already known speech accommodation processes. Even if it is not, the observed discrepancies may be conceptualized in catastrophe theory terms and lead to an alternative catastrophe model. If any catastrophe model proves consistent with the speech accommodation data, then the question of the peculiar value of such a model must be addressed. Part of the answer would lie in further empirical considerations, such as whether a psychologically meaningful dynamic can be identified and whether other catastrophe-theoretic phenomena, like a *bias factor* (cf. Ball et al, 1984) or elaboration of the cusp into a higher-order catastrophe under certain conditions, are observed. If so, there would be grounds for arguing that catastrophe theory provided a more *elegant* account than various alternatives, including perhaps mathematical alternatives. Even so, it would be like debating the merits of geometric and trigonometric proofs of Pythagoras's Theorum. The modest claim we presently suggest for the model is that it points in a useful direction for the social psychology of language, as well as for other social scientific endeavours; that is, we should be actively seeking theoretical models in the newer branches of mathematics. Psychology's posture towards mathematics has been one of self-enslavement to the twin masters of Newtonian mathematics and parametric statistics, as though scientific prediction was like prophecy and quantification of "error" was the appropriate response to prophetic failure. Some modern mathematics, by contrast, concerns itself with precision about structural qualities which remain largely unaffected by distortions of various kinds. In our opinion, these sorts of mathematics need consideration from social psychology as possibly offering the prospect of real scientific progress; speech accommodation is where we have chosen to try them out.

We have said nothing so far in this chapter about goals. As Giles and Hewstone (1983) have noted, the dimensional approach of Forgas (1979) and Wish et al. (1976) to social situations is only one way of looking at them, another being the goal structure analysis of Argyle, Furnham and Graham (1979). However, both these perspectives can be comfortably accommodated with the help of the quasi-motor skill framework developed some time ago for describing social interaction (see Argyle, 1978). That approach assumed that people set themselves situational goals in terms of target values on general dimensions such as intimacy. In terms of the general framework we adopted at the beginning of this chapter, we see people using these dimensions to *analyse* social events as necessary for them to select target values. Coincidentally, the subjective validity of the Intimacy dimension has, in fact, been attested by the aforementioned multidimensional scaling studies of Forgas and Wish.

What this naturally suggests for the person- vs. group-salience dimension and speech is that this subjective dimension itself is probably one of those used like Argyle's Intimacy dimension, i.e., among their situational goals, speakers probably define target levels of person- vs. group-salience. To pursue these targets, speakers may employ accommodative speech convergence or divergence tactics and degree of code-elaboration as active speech markers, which brings this chapter back to more or less where it began.

## REFERENCES

Applegate, J. L., & Delia, J. G. Person-centred speech, psychological development, and the contexts of language usage. In R. St Clair & H. Giles (Eds.), *The social and psychological contexts of language*. Hillsdale, N.J.: Lawrence Erlbaum Associates, 1980.

Argyle, M. *The psychology of interpersonal behaviour* (3rd ed.). Harmondsworth: Penguin, 1978.

Argyle, M., Furnham, A., & Graham J. A. *Social situations*. Cambridge: Cambridge University Press, 1979.

Austin, W. C., & Worchel, S. (Eds.) *The social psychology of intergroup relations.* Monterey, California: Brooks-Cole, 1979.

Ball, P., Giles, H., & Hewstone, M. Second language acquisition: The intergroup model with catastrophic dimensions. In H. Tajfel (Ed.), *The social dimension.* Cambridge: Cambridge University Press, 1984.

Bernstein, B. Codes, modalities and the process of cultural reproduction: a model. *Language in Society,* 1981, *10,* 327-363.

Bernstein, B. Social class, language and socialisation. In P. P. Giglioli (Ed.), *Language and social context: Selected readings.* Harmondsworth: Penguin, 1972.

Bernstein, B. A sociolinguistic approach to social learning. In J. Gould (Ed.), *Penguin social science survey.* Harmondsworth: Penguin, 1965.

Bernstein, B. Some sociological determinants of perception. *British Journal of Sociology,* 1958, *9,* 159-174.

Bourhis, R. Y., Giles, H., Leyens, J-P., & Tajfel, H. Psycholinguistic distinctiveness: Language divergence in Belgium. In H. Giles & R. N. St Clair (Eds.), *Language and social psychology.* Oxford: Blackwell, 1979.

Brehm, J. W. *Responses to loss of freedom: A theory of psychological reactance.* Morristown, N.J.: General Learning Press, 1972.

Brehm, J. W. *A theory of psychological reactance.* New York: Academic Press, 1966.

Coulthard, M. A discussion of elaborated and restricted codes. *Educational Review,* 1969, *22,* 38-50.

Coupland, N. Linguistic variation and interpersonal accommodation theory: Some phonological data and their implications. *International Journal of the Sociology of Language,* 1984, *46,* 49-70.

Doise, W., Sinclair, A., & Bourhis, R.Y. Evaluation of accent convergence and divergence in cooperative and competitive intergroup situations. *British Journal of Social and Clinical Psychology,* 1976, *15,* 247-252.

Festinger, L. A theory of social comparison processes. *Human Relations,* 1954, *7,* 117-140.

Festinger, L. *A theory of cognitive dissonance.* New York: Row, Peterson, 1957.

Flay, B. R. Catastrophe theory in social psychology: Some applications to attitudes and social behaviour. *Behavioural Science,* 1978, *23,* 335-350.

Forgas, J. P. Language, goals and situations. *Journal of Language and Social Psychology,* 1983, *2,* 267-293.

Forgas, J. P. *Social episodes: A study of interaction routines.* London: Academic Press, 1979.

Garfinkel, H. *Studies in ethnomethodology.* Englewood Cliffs, N.J.: Prentice-Hall, 1967.

Gergen, K. N. Social psychology as history. *Journal of Personality and Social Psychology,* 1973, *26,* 309-320.

Giles, H. (Ed.), The dynamics of speech accommodation. *International Journal of the Sociology of Language,* 1984, *46.*

Giles, H., & Byrne, J. L. The intergroup model of second language acquisition. *Journal of Multilingual and Multicultural Development,* 1982, *3,* 17-60.

Giles, H., & Hewstone, M Cognitive structures, speech and social situations: two integrative models. *Language Sciences,* 1982, *4,* 187-219.

Giles, H., & Johnson, P. The role of language in ethnic group relations. In J. C. Turner & H. Giles (Eds.). *Intergroup behaviour.* Oxford: Blackwell, 1981.

Giles, H., & Powesland, P. F. *Speech style and social evaluation.* London: Academic Press, 1975.

Giles, H., & Ryan, E. B. Prolegomena for developing a social psychological theory of language attitudes. In E. B. Ryan & H. Giles (Eds.), *Attitudes towards language variation: Social and applied contexts.* London: Edward Arnold, 1982.

Giles, H., Taylor, D. M., & Bourhis, R. Y. Towards a theory of interpersonal accommodation through speech: Some Canadian data. *Language in Society,* 1973, *2,* 177-192.
Gudykunst, W. B. (Ed.). *Intergroup communication.* London: Edward Arnold, in press.
Harré, R., & Secord, P. F. *The explanation of social behaviour.* Oxford: Blackwell, 1972.
Heider, F. *The psychology of interpersonal relations.* New York: Wiley, 1958.
Hymes, D. Models of the interaction of language and social setting *Journal of Social Issues,* 1967, *23,* 8-28.
Jones, E. E., & Davis, K. E. From acts to dispositions: The attribution process in person perception. *Advances in Experimental Social Psychology,* 1965, *2,* 220-267
Kelley, H. H. Attribution theory in social psychology. *Nebraska Symposium on Motivation,* 1965, *15,* 192-238
Kelley, H. H. The process of causal attribution. *American Psychologist,* 1973, *28,* 107-128.
Kelly, G. A. *The psychology of personal constructs.* New York: Norton, 1955.
Labov, W. The logic of nonstandard English, *Georgetown Monographs on Language and Linguistics,* 1969, *22,* 1-31.
Lambert, W. E. A social psychology of bilingualism. *Journal of Social Issues,* 1965, *23,* 91-109.
Moscovici, S. On social representations. In J. P. Forgas (Ed.), *Social cognition: Perspectives on everyday understanding.* London: Academic Press, 1981.
Moscovici, S., & Hewstone, M. Social representations and social attributions: From the 'naive' to the 'amateur' scientist. In M. Hewstone (Ed.), *Attribution theory: Social and functional extensions.* Oxford: Blackwell, 1983.
Osgood, C. E., Suci, G. J., & Tannenbaum, P. H. *The measurement of meaning.* Urbana Illinois. University of Illinois Press, 1957.
Platt, J. & Weber, H. Speech convergence miscarried: an investigation into inappropriate accommodation strategies. *International Journal of the Sociology of Language,* 1984, *46,* 131-146.
Robinson, W. P. *Language management in education: The Australian experience.* Sydney: Angus & Robertson, 1978.
Ryan, E. B. & Giles, H. (Eds.), *Attitudes towards language variation: Social and applied contexts.* London: Edward Arnold, 1982.
Ryan, E. B., Giles, H., & Sebastian, R. J. An integrative perspective for the study of attitudes towards language variation. In E. B. Ryan & H. Giles (Eds.), *Attitudes towards language variation: Social and applied contexts* London: Edward Arnold, 1982.
Scotton, C. M. Strategies of neutrality: Language choice in uncertain situations. *Language,* 1976, *52,* 919-941.
Shotter, J., & Burton, M. *Common sense accounts of human action: The descriptive formulations of Heider, Smedslund and Ossorio.* British Psychological Society December London Conference, 1982.
Simard, L. Social categorization, identity and discrimination: Their role in intergroup communication. *Journal of Language and Social Psychology,* 1983, *2, 183-205.*
Stephenson, G. M. Intergroup bargaining and negotiation. In J. C. Turner., & H. Giles (Eds.), *Intergroup behaviour.* Oxford: Blackwell, 1981.
Street, R. L., & Giles, H. Speech accommodation theory: A social cognitive approach to language and speech behaviour. In M. Roloff & C. Berger, (Eds.), *Social cognition and communication.* Beverley Hills, California. Sage, 1982.
Tajfel, H. The psychological structure of intergroup relations. In H. Tajfel (Ed.), *Differentiation between groups: Studies in the social psychology of intergroup relations.* London: Academic Press, 1978.
Tajfel, H., & Turner, J. C. An integrative theory of group conflict. In W. C. Austin & S. Worchel (Eds.), *The social psychology of intergroup relations.* Monterey, Cal. Brooks-Cole, 1979.

Taylor, D. M., Bassili, J., & Aboud, F. E. Dimensions of ethnic identity: an example from Quebec. *Journal of Social Psychology*, 1973, *89*, 185–192.

Tesser, A. When individual dispositions and social pressure conflict: A catastrophe. *Human Relations*, 1980, *33*, 393–407.

Thakerar, J. N., Giles, H., & Cheshire, J. Psychological and linguistic parameters of speech accommodation theory. In C. Fraser & K. R. Scherer (Eds.), *Advances in the social psychology of language*. Cambridge: Cambridge University Press, 1982.

Thom, R. *Structural stability and morphogenesis*. Reading, Mass.: Benjamin, 1975.

Turner, J. C., & Giles, H. (Eds.), *Intergroup behaviour*. Oxford: Blackwell, 1981.

Wicker, A. W. Attitudes versus actions: The relationship of verbal and overt behavioural responses to attitude objects. *Journal of Social Issues*, 1969, *25*, 41–78.

Wish, M., Deutsch, M., & Kaplan, S. J. Perceived dimensions of interpersonal relations. *Journal of Personality and Social Psychology*, 1976, *33*, 409–420.

Woodcock, A., & Davis, M. *Catastrophe theory*. Harmondsworth: Penguin, 1978.

Zeeman, E. C. Catastrophe theory *Scientific American*, 1976, *234*, 65–83.

# Author Index

Abbott, A. R., 134, 142
Abelson, R., 64, 85
Aboud, F. E., 117, 139, 268, 286
Ackerman, N. W., 17, 37
Addington, D. W., 158-61, 178
Adorno, T. W., 121, 139
Alkire, A., 23, 39
Allen, D. E., 195, 197
Allison, P. D., 239, 246, 261
Allport, G. W., 114-5, 129, 139, 151, 153-4, 156, 158, 178
Alve, S., 31, 36, 39
Alvy, K., 96, 108
Andersen, E., 101, 108
Apple, W., 133, 135, 139, 157, 166, 178
Applegate, J. L., 41, 69, 70-2, 75, 79, 81, 281, 283
Arendt, H., 183, 197
Argyle, M., 27, 37, 264, 283
Aronovitch, C. D., 157, 178
Arthur, B., 119, 139
Athanassiades, J. C., 23, 37
Austin, J. L., 235, 240, 261
Austin, W. C., 267, 284

Ayres, B., 189, 197
Azrin, N. H., 233, 261

Baer, D. M., 231, 234, 236, 238, 245, 262
Bales, R. F., 184, 197
Ball, P., 276, 278, 282, 284
Bamm, R. M., 92, 108
Baseheart, J. R., 206, 207, 210, 212, 226, 227, 228
Bassili, J., 268, 286
Bateson, G., 17, 19, 37, 40
Bauman, R., 51, 81
Bayton, J. A., 116, 143
Beach, R. I., 204, 226
Beatman, F. L., 17, 37
Beavin, J. H., 23, 40
Beier, E. G., 157, 175-6, 178
Bellinger, D., 89-90, 108
Bem, D. J., 209, 226
Bem, S. L., 209, 226
Benedict, H., 101, 109
Bengston, V. L., 136, 140
Bennett, R., 132, 134, 140
Berkowitz, L., 205, 226

287

Bernstein, B., 101, 108, 263, 278–9, 284
Berscheid, E., 112, 140
Biller, H. B., 92, 108
Blakar, R. M., 2, 8, 12–20, 22, 24–36, 38–40
Blank, A., 183, 198
Blumer, H., 49–50, 63, 81
Bock, J. K., 100, 108
Boersma, R. F., 90, 109
Bonvillian, J. D., 101, 110
Borden, A. W., 71, 81
Bostrom, R. N., 212, 227
Botkin, P. T., 69, 83
Bourhis, R. Y., 270, 275, 284, 285
Bowen, D. E., 173, 178
Bowerman, M., 43, 81, 234, 261
Bowers, J. W., 207–8, 210, 217, 226–7
Bradac, J. J., 117, 140, 226–7
Bradford, G., 119, 139
Braly, K. W., 112, 141
Brehm, J. W., 273, 284
Brennan, E. M., 114–5, 140
Brennan, J. S., 114–5, 140
Brewer, W. F., 43, 81, 234, 261
Brock, T. C., 221, 228
Broen, P., 88, 108
Broman, S., 93, 110
Bromley, D. B., 61, 84
Brooks, R. D., 200, 208, 217, 227
Brown, B. L., 133, 140, 144, 147–50, 153, 156–7, 163–6, 168, 173, 176, 178–9, 181
Brown, I. D. R., 137, 142
Brown, P., 73, 81
Brown, R., 43, 57, 81
Brown, T. J., 112, 143
Bruner, J. S., 45, 81
Bulik, C. M., 120, 142
Burgoon, M., 200–1, 208, 210–7, 219–24, 227–8
Burke, J. A., 69, 72, 81
Burleson, B. R., 61, 69, 71–2, 75, 80–2
Burton, M., 264, 279, 285
Buss, A. H., 130, 140

Buttino, A. J., 130, 140
Byrne, D., 112, 116, 124, 131, 140, 141
Byrne, J. L., 278, 284

Campbell, D. T., 129, 142
Cantor, N., 56, 82, 115, 140
Cantril, H., 151, 153–4, 156, 158, 178
Capadano, H. L., 132, 142
Carlsmith, L., 92, 108
Carmichael, C. W., 211–2, 227
Carranza, M. A., 114–5, 122, 140, 142
Carskaddon, G., 101, 110
Casagrande, J. B., 88, 108
Cazden, C., 97, 108
Ceropski, J. M., 70, 72, 84
Chandler, M. J., 58, 82
Chanowitz, B., 183, 198
Chase, L. J., 200, 208, 217, 219, 227
Cheshire, J., 268, 270, 286
Chomsky, N., 13, 15, 38, 42, 82, 88, 108, 233, 261
Cicourel, A. V., 63, 82
Clark, R. A., 43, 55, 69, 80, 82–3
Clément, R., 117, 139
Clore, G. L., 124, 140
Coffman, T. L., 112, 141
Cohen, B. D., 67, 82
Cohen, J., 187, 197
Cohen, M., 220–2, 224, 227
Cohen, S. B., 55, 59, 85
Cole, M., 99, 109
Cole, P., 45, 82
Colette-Pratt, C., 134, 140
Cook, M., 14, 40
Cornelison, A., 19, 39
Corso, L., 120, 123–4, 143
Cottingham, D. R., 205, 226
Coulthard, M., 279, 284
Coupland, M., 274, 284
Courtright, J. A., 117, 140, 226–7
Cowgill, O., 134, 140
Crawford, J. M., 88, 108
Crelin, S., 185, 198
Crockett, W. H., 56, 61, 82, 135, 140
Crockett, W. J., 60, 85

Cronkhite, G., 211-2, 227
Cross, T., 89, 110

Dabbs, J. M., Jr., 193, 195-8
Damon, W., 61, 82
Davies, E. E., 117, 141
Davies, R. A., 117, 140
Davis, E. E., 117, 143
Davis, K. E., 264, 285
Davis, M., 270, 276, 286
Davitz, J. R., 170-1, 178
Davitz, L. J., 170-1, 178
Dawson, W. E., 115, 140
Day, J., 19, 40
De la Zerda, N., 116, 140
De Wolfe, A. S., 203, 227
Delia, J. G., 41, 48, 55-6, 61-4, 69-72, 78, 80-4, 281, 283
DeNike, L. D., 234, 262
Denzin, N. K., 49, 60, 82, 84
Deutsch, M., 282, 283, 286
Devin, J., 96, 110
DeVito, J., 42, 82
Dicks, R. H., 150, 176, 178
Diehl, C. F., 144, 178
Dienstbier, R. A., 116, 140
Dion, K. K., 112, 140
Doane, J. A., 19, 39
Doise, W., 270, 284
Donnerstein, E., 112, 131, 140
Donnerstein, M., 112, 131, 140
Dore, J., 45, 83
Dowd, J. J., 136, 140
Dunn, J., 96, 109

Eckman, J., 132, 134, 140
Edwards, J., 97, 109
Edwards, J. D., 200, 228
Ehrlich, H. J., 115, 140
Eisenberg, P., 152, 154, 179
Elkind, D., 60, 83
Ellis, J., 94, 110
Ellsworth, P. C., 123, 142, 189, 198
Emery, J., 211, 227
Engle, M., 91, 92, 109
Erickson, B., 124, 141
Ervin-Tripp, S. M., 15, 39, 98, 109, 232, 261

Evans, M. S., 193, 197, 198
Exline, R. V., 189, 198

Fairbanks, G., 169, 170, 179
Fallot, R. D., 184, 198
Farr, R., 1, 8
Farrar, D., 119, 139
Farwell, C., 88, 109
Faunce, E. E., 17-20, 23, 40
Fay, P. J., 152-3, 179
Feldstein, S., 169, 179, 182, 189, 192, 195, 197-8
Ferguson, C., 88, 110
Ferguson, C. A., 137, 141, 143
Ferreira, A. J., 23, 39
Feshbach, S., 203, 205, 208, 210, 227
Festinger, L., 203, 215, 221, 227, 264, 277, 284
Fiedler, F. E., 184, 198
Fillmore, C. J., 44, 83
Fingarette, H., 176, 179
Fischer, J., 98, 109
Flavell, J. H., 69, 83, 96, 109
Flay, B. R., 270, 272, 284
Fleck, S., 19, 39
Fodor, F. A., 14, 39
Forgas, J. P., 263, 282-4
Fraser, B., 123, 141
Fraser, C., 2-4, 8
Frenkel-Brunswik, E., 121, 139
Fry, C. L., 69, 83
Furnham, A., 283
Furrow, D., 101, 109

Gaarder, S., 30, 40
Gamson, W. A., 183, 198
Gardner, R. C., 1, 8
Garfinkel, H., 26, 39, 264, 284
Gelman, R., 96, 110
Genthner, R. W., 131, 141
Gergen, K. N., 265, 284
Giattino, J., 90, 109
Giles, H., 1-3, 8-9, 95, 110, 112-6, 120-1, 123, 137, 141-3, 153, 164-5, 179, 260-1, 263, 266-8, 270, 275, 277-8, 282-6
Gill, J., 169, 180

Glass, D. C., 125, 141
Gleason, J. B., 90–1, 96, 103–4, 108–10
Gleitman, H., 101, 110
Gleitman, L., 101, 110
Goffman, E., 51, 59, 65, 67, 72, 83
Gold, A., 222, 229
Goldstein, M., 117, 141
Goldstein, M. J., 23, 39
Görlitz, D. D., 154, 179
Gouaux, C., 125, 141
Gould, E., 23, 39
Governale, C. N., 203, 227
Graham, J. A., 283
Greenbaum, P., 260, 262
Greenberg, B. S., 214, 217, 227–8
Greenfield, P. M., 43, 83
Greenspoon, J., 233, 261
Greif, E. B., 90–1, 104, 109
Grice, P., 63, 83
Griffith, W., 125, 141
Gross, E., 73, 83
Grossberg, L., 48, 82–3
Gudykunst, W. B., 263, 285
Gur, R. C., 154, 176, 180
Gurwitz, S., 222, 229
Guy, R. F., 195, 197

Haley, J., 17–20, 32, 37, 39
Hall, W., 99, 109
Halliday, M. A. K., 45, 83, 183, 198
Hamblin, D. L., 173, 178
Hamilton, D. L., 184, 198
Hardyck, J. A., 117, 143
Harkness, S., 92, 109
Harré, R., 3, 8, 264–5, 285
Hastorf, A. H., 123, 142
Hathway, S. R., 154, 180
Havelka, N., 14, 40
Hayes, J. R., 43, 83
Heider, F., 31, 33, 39, 56, 83, 203, 227, 264, 285
Helfrich, H., 132, 137, 141, 153, 179
Helmersen, P., 19, 39
Henry, P., 14, 40
Herkner, W., 14, 40
Herzog, H., 151, 179

Hewgill, M. A., 204, 207, 209–10, 228
Hewstone, M., 263, 265, 267, 277, 279, 282–5
Hirsch, S., 19, 40
Hoaglin, L. W., 169, 179
Hockett, C., 101, 109
Hogan, J. G., 90, 109
Holmes, L. C., 134, 140
Holz, W. C., 233, 261
Hooper, C. H., 193, 198
Hopper, R., 116, 140
Hornsby, M. R., 100, 108
Hultberg, M., 31, 36, 39
Husband, R. L., 70–2, 83
Hymes, D., 44–5, 83, 87, 109, 267, 285

Ichheiser, G., 26, 39

Jackson, D. D., 19, 23, 37, 40
Jacob, T., 19–20, 39
Jacobs, C. S., 65, 83
Jacobson, J. L., 90, 109
Jaffe, J., 182, 189, 198
Janis, I. L., 203, 205, 208, 210, 227
Jarvis, P. E., 69, 83
Johnson, B. C., 124, 141
Johnson, G. A., 125, 128, 141
Johnson, P., 2, 8, 263, 268, 284
Jones, E. E., 264, 285
Jones, J., 80, 83
Jones, S. B., 211–2, 216, 227
Judd, L. L., 23, 39

Kalin, R., 2, 8, 121, 141
Kanfer, F. H., 233, 261
Kaplan, B., 55, 59, 85
Kaplan, S. J., 282–3, 286
Karlins, M., 112, 141
Kasch, C. R., 72, 83
Katz, D., 112, 141
Katz, J. J., 14, 39
Kelley, H. H., 264, 285
Kelley, K., 131, 141
Kelly, G. A., 55–6, 83, 264, 285
Kelman, H. C., 72, 83

Kendrick, C., 96, 109
Kenrick, D. T., 125, 128, 141
Kent, D. P., 136, 141
Keogh, T., 125, 143
Kiesler, S. B., 222-3, 228
King, L. B., 219, 227
Kjeldergaard, P. M., 153, 161-2, 179
Kline, S. L., 61, 69-70, 72, 74-5, 80-4
Kogan, N., 135, 141
Kramer, E., 144, 171-2, 179
Krauss, R. M., 133, 135, 139, 157, 166, 178
Krumboltz, J., 211, 227
Kuhn, T. S., 18, 39

Labov, W., 97-8, 109, 279, 285
Lagerløv, T., 36, 40
Lakoff, R., 98, 109
Lambert, W. E., 113-5, 142-3, 153, 178, 277, 285
Landers, A. D., 211, 228
Langer, E., 183, 198
Laver, J., 144-5, 149, 155, 174, 179
Lenney, E., 209, 226
Leventhal, H., 203, 205, 228
Levin, L. A., 117, 143
LeVine, R. A., 129, 142
Levinson, D. J., 121, 139
Levinson, S., 73, 81
Lewis, M., 45, 84
Leyens, J-P., 275, 284
Lidz, T., 19, 39
Lieberman, A. M., 185, 198
Liker, J. K., 239, 246, 261
Lind, E. A., 124, 141
Lindesmith, A. R., 60, 84
Livesley, W. J., 61, 84
Lobe, J., 205, 208-10, 228
Lock, A., 45, 84
Loh, W. D., 117, 143
Lomax, R., 156, 179
Looft, W. R., 60, 84
Lott, A. J., 124, 142
Lott, B. E., 124, 142
Love, N., 121, 141
Ludwig, L. M., 189, 198

Lundy, R. M., 211, 228-9
Luria, A., 99, 110
Lyman, S. M., 73, 85
Lyons, J., 107, 110

Macaulay, J. R., 217, 229
McCarthy, D., 93, 110
McCauley, M. E., 189, 198
Maccoby, N., 221, 227
MacCorquodale, K., 233, 262
McDevitt, T., 91, 110
McEwen, W. J., 217, 228
McGrath, J. J., 189, 198
McGuire, W. J., 217, 222, 228
McKirnan, D., 4, 8
MacLachlan, J., 163, 180
McLaughlin, B., 91, 110
McNulty, J., 211, 228
McPeek, R. W., 200, 228
McPherson, S., 23, 39
McReynolds, M., 210, 228
McTavish, D. G., 132, 134, 142
Mahl, G. F., 144, 180
Mallory, P., 156, 180
Manton, K., 136-7, 142
Manuel, R., 137, 142
Markova, I., 2, 8
Masur, E., 90-1, 110
Mathog, R. B., 222-3, 228
Mattingly, I. G., 184-5, 198
Mead, G. H., 28, 33, 39, 49, 84
Meares, R., 89, 110
Meehl, P. E., 154, 180
Meltzer, B. N., 49, 84
Meltzoff, A. N., 191, 198
Mezei, L., 117, 142
Middleton, W. C., 152-3, 179
Milgrom-Friedman, J., 89, 110
Miller, G. R., 201, 204-10, 213-5, 220-1, 227-8
Miller, M. D., 220-4, 227-8
Miller, V. A., 156, 180
Mischel, W., 56, 82, 115, 140, 154, 180
Mishler, E. G., 19, 39
Moerk, E., 88, 110
Moffie, R. W., 114-5, 142

Montgomery, C. L., 220–2, 224, 227
Moore, M. K., 191, 198
Moore, T. E., 43, 84
Morgan, J. L., 45, 82
Moriarty, A. E., 156, 180
Moscovici, S., 27, 39, 202, 228, 264–5, 285
Moses, P., 156, 180
Mossige, S., 29, 36, 39
Mulac, A., 212, 228

Nafstad, H. E., 17, 19, 30, 34, 36, 38, 40
Nelson, K. E., 101, 109, 110
Newcomb, T. M., 203, 228
Newport, E., 101, 110
Nichols, P., 93, 110
Niles, P., 203, 205, 228
Nisbett, R. E., 127, 142
Norris, E. L., 217, 229

O'Barr, W. M., 124, 141
Ochs, E., 92, 110
O'Hanlon, J. F., 189, 198
O'Keefe, B. J., 41, 53, 55–6, 62–4, 69–70, 76, 78–9, 82, 84
O'Keefe, D. J., 41, 61–4, 82, 84
Olson, K. L., 90, 109
Opie, A., 93, 110
Opie, I., 93, 110
Osgood, C. E., 203, 214, 228, 264, 285
Osterhouse, R. A., 221, 228
Osterkamp, M., 135, 140
Ostwald, P. F., 156–7, 180

Palmore, E. B., 136–7, 142
Paulsen, O. G., 29, 38
Pawlovich, K. J., 212, 228
Pear, T. H., 150–1, 180
Pecheux, M., 14, 40
Pedersen, T. B., 27, 38
Peery, J. C., 194, 198
Penman, R., 89, 110
Peters, G., 14, 40
Petras, J. W., 49, 84
Pettersen, R. B., 29, 36, 39

Piaget, J., 28, 33, 40, 60, 84
Platt, J., 277, 285
Plitnik, G. R., 174, 181
Polanyi, M., 173, 180
Posner, M. I., 188, 198
Powell, F. A., 204–6, 228
Powesland, P. F., 112–6, 137, 141, 268, 284
Press, A. N., 61, 85, 135, 140
Price-Williams, D., 67, 85
Pronovost, W., 169–70, 179
Ptacek, P. H., 153, 180
Purvis, J. A., 193, 198

Raskin, R., 91, 110
Ray, E., 211, 229
Rayko, D. S., 121, 141
Remick, L., 88, 110
Rencher, A. C., 133, 135, 140, 144, 148–9, 156–7, 163–4, 178, 181
Rey, A., 116, 142
Reynolds, L. T., 49, 84
Riskin, J., 17–20, 23, 40
Robinson, W. P., 3, 8, 153, 180, 183, 198, 279, 285
Rochester, S. R., 169, 180
Rodnick, E. H., 23, 39
Rokeach, M., 116–7, 142, 205, 229
Rommetveit, R., 2, 8, 13–5, 23, 25–6, 28–30, 33, 38, 40, 44, 65, 85
Rondal, J. A., 90, 110
Rosenbach, D., 60, 85
Rosenblum, L. A., 45, 84
Rosenfeld, H. M., 231, 234, 236, 238, 245, 260, 262
Rosenthal, 97, 110
Rossiter, C. M., 212, 227
Rousey, C. L., 156, 180
Rubin, K. H., 137, 142
Ruesch, J., 17, 40
Ryan, E. B., 112, 114–7, 120, 122–5, 132, 134–5, 139–40, 142–3, 153, 180, 263, 268, 284–5
Ryan, J., 45, 85
Rykoff, I., 19, 40

Sabsay, S., 67, 85

Sachs, J., 90, 96, 98, 110
Sackeim, H. A., 154, 176, 180
St. Clair, R. N., 2, 8, 112, 141
Samter, W., 71, 82
Sandell, R., 202, 229
Sander, E. K., 153, 180
Sanford, R. N., 121, 139
Sartre, J. P., 176, 180
Sassoon, C., 120, 141
Scarlett, H. H., 61, 85
Schank, R., 64, 85
Scheflen, A. E., 191, 198
Scheidel, T. M., 210, 229
Scherer, K. R., 2-4, 8-9, 95, 110, 112, 141, 144-5, 149-50, 155-6, 163, 167, 169, 174, 180, 202, 229
Schmidt, A., 125, 143
Schmidt, G., 117, 140
Schneider, D. J., 123, 142
Schulze, G., 144, 180
Scott, M. B., 73, 85
Scotton, C. M., 275, 285
Searle, J. R., 240, 258, 262
Sebastian, R. J., 116-7, 120, 123-5, 130, 134, 140, 142-3, 268, 285
Secord, P. F., 3, 8, 264-5, 285
Shantz, C. U., 61, 85
Shatz, M., 67, 85, 96, 110
Shea, M., 260, 262
Shepherd, G. J., 76, 79, 84
Sherman, J. A., 234, 262
Sherman, S. N., 17, 37
Sherzer, J., 51, 81
Shotter, J., 264, 279, 285
Shuntich, R. J., 131, 143
Shuy, R. W., 114, 143
Siegman, A. W., 144, 169, 180
Silverstein, M., 46, 85
Simard, L., 263, 285
Simonson, N. R., 211, 228-9
Simpson, G. E., 136, 143
Sinclair, A., 270, 284
Sinclair-de-Zwart, H., 43, 85
Singer, J. E., 125, 141
Singer, R. P., 203, 229
Skinner, B. F., 175, 181, 232, 234, 240, 258, 262

Slobin, D., 15, 39
Smedley, J. W., 116, 143
Smedslund, J., 21, 40
Smith, B. L., 156, 163, 181
Smith, C. S., 43, 85
Smith, J. H., 43, 83
Smith, M., 117, 143
Smith, P. M., 3, 8, 153, 181, 260-1
Snow, C. E., 88, 110-1, 137, 143
Snyder, M., 193, 198, 222, 229
Solomon, R. C., 175, 181
Solvberg, H. A., 20, 29, 33-4, 36, 38, 40
Spielberger, C. D., 234, 262
Stagner, R., 158, 181
Staples, F., 211, 229
Stein, D. D., 117, 143
Stephenson, G. M., 267, 285
Stern, D. N., 194, 198
Stevens, K. N., 170-1, 181
Stewart, D., 200, 210, 227
Stewart, M. A., 120, 135, 143, 157, 163, 166, 181
Stewart, S., 157, 163, 166, 181
Stewart, W., 101, 110
Stokstad, S. J., 36, 40
Stone, G. P., 73, 83
Strauss, A. L., 49, 60, 72, 84-5
Street, R. L., 266, 285
Streeter, L. A., 133, 135, 139, 157, 166, 178
Strodtbeck, F. L., 184, 197
Strong, W. J., 133, 135, 140, 144, 147-9, 156, 163-4, 174, 178, 181
Suci, G. J., 264, 285
Sussman, N. M., 260, 262
Sypher, H. E., 61, 84
Szasz, T. S., 178, 181

Tajfel, H., 2, 9, 129, 143, 263, 267-8, 275, 284-5
Talkin, D. T., 149, 181
Tannenbaum, P. H., 203, 214, 217, 227-9, 264, 285
Taylor, C., 154, 173, 181
Taylor, D. M., 4, 9, 112, 117, 123, 139, 141, 143, 268, 275, 285-6

## Author Index

Taylor, H. C., 151-2, 181
Taylor, S. P., 131, 141
Terry, O., 19, 39
Terwilliger, R., 203, 227
Tesser, A., 270, 272, 286
Thakerar, J. N., 164-5, 179, 268, 270, 286
Thom, R., 270, 286
Thomas, J., 222, 229
Titze, I. R., 145, 149, 181
Triandis, H. C., 116-7, 143
Triandis, L. M., 116, 143
Trimboli, F., 156, 181
Trudgill, P., 98, 110, 144, 179
Tucker, G. R., 114, 143
Turner, J. C., 2, 9, 263, 267-8, 285-6
Tyler, L. E., 153, 181

Uhlenbeck, E. M., 14, 40
Ure, E., 94, 110

Veitch, R., 125, 141
Vine, I., 189, 198

Walker, E. G., 214, 228
Walster, E. E., 112, 140
Walters, G., 112, 141
Walters, R. H., 211, 228-9
Wapner, S., 55, 59-60, 85
Ward, R. A., 132, 143
Warner, C. T., 157, 176, 181
Waterson, N., 88, 111
Watzlawick, P., 23, 40

Waxler, N. E., 19, 39
Weakland, J. H., 18-9, 37, 40
Weber, H., 277, 285
Weinstein, E. A., 46, 72, 85
Weintraub, S., 99, 103, 109, 111
Welkowitz, J., 169, 179, 192, 195, 198
Wells, G., 43, 85
Wells, M. G., 150, 176, 178
Werner, H., 55, 59, 85
West, S. G., 112, 143
White, B., 91, 110
Wicker, A. W., 273, 286
Wilhite, M., 105, 111
Williams, C. E., 170-1, 181
Williams, F., 97, 111, 114, 116, 143
Wilson, T. D., 127, 142
Winther, W. D., 23, 39
Wish, M., 282-3, 286
Wittgenstein, L., 13, 40
Wold, A. H., 14, 40
Woodcock, A., 270, 276, 286
Worchel, S., 267, 284
Wright, J. W., 69, 83
Wynne, L., 19, 40

Yinger, J. M., 136, 143

Zajonc, R. B., 190, 198, 224, 229
Zalowitz, E., 152, 154, 179
Zeeman, E. C., 270, 276, 286
Zimbardo, P., 222, 229

# Subject Index

Abstract symbols, 185
Accent, 101
  Spanish, 113-31 *passim*
Acceptance, conveying, 76-7
Accommodation, interpersonal: and
  Situational construals, 7, 260,
  263-86
  Catastrophe theory, 270-8
  Social psychology
    And language, 267-70
    And social situations, 264-7
  Within-group communication and
  code-elaboration, 278-81
Accommodation, verbal:
experimental:
  Analysis of, 6-7, 230-62
  Behaviour, verbal, 232-4
  "Double agent" research, 236-44
  Empirical evidence, 244-58
  Mands and illocutionary acts,
  234-6, 240, 242, 258
Accuracy studies of vocal patterns:
  And emotion, 170-8
  And personality, 146, 148, 150-4
Acquisition of language *see* Children

Action:
  Language as mode of, 45
  Modes in conflict situation, 77-9
  Situated and emergent nature of,
  62-3
  Social and communicative, 68
Active participation paradigm, 201,
213-6
Age estimates and inferences, 113,
132-5
  And ethnicity, 136-8
Aggression and ethnicity, 129-32
Analytical procedures, 3
Anger *see* Aggression
Anxiety *see* Fear
Approval-dependence, 207
Arguing posture, 77-8
Arousal in conversation, 190-1
Articulation, 156-7
Assertion weakening, 217
Attribution, 33
  Studies of personality and vocal
  patterns, 146-50, 157-67
  And temporal, 167-9
Avoidance and ethnicity, 129-32

# Subject Index

Awareness of experimenters' intentions, 233-4, 236-7

Babies *see* Children
Behaviour:
  In catastrophe model, 271-8
  Communication perspective, 15-6
  Communication synonymous with, 23
  Ethnicity's effect on, 129-32
  In groups:
    Different, 267-78
    Same, 278-81
  And language, 3
  Modification as aim of message, 70-2
  And perception, 55
  Verbal, perspectives on, 232-4
Behavioural:
  Expressions of prejudice, 129-30
  Learning explanations, 231
  Strategies for interpersonal goals, 47-8
Belief:
  About functions of talk, 51
  Similarity, 121
Bifurcation in catastrophe model, 273, 275
Bimodality in catastrophe model, 272, 274-5
Black English, 114
Breakdown in communication *see* Schizophrenia

Catastrophe theory formalization, 270-8
  Need for dynamic, 276-8
Chicago School *see* Symbolic interactionism
Children:
  Competence, acquisition of, 94-6
  Egocentrism, 26
  Politeness routines, acquisition of, 102-6
  Speech to, 5, 57, 87-94
  Variation in language, 96-102
  *See also* Psychological and Interactional
Class:
  And children's speech, 93, 97
  Inferences, 114-24
  *See also* Speech cues
Codes, linguistic, 28, 42
  Elaboration of and within-group communication, 278-81
  Messages, 70-2
Cognitive:
  Development and acquisition of language, 43
  Egocentrism of children, 96
  Explanation of behaviour, 231
  Level and stress and emotion, 60
  Stress, 214-6
  *See also* Thought
Colour recognition studies, 125-8
Comfortableness rating, 125
Comforting communication, 70, 71
Commonality of constructs, 7, 56-8
Communication:
  Definition of, 22, 23-5
  *See also* Accommodation; Expectancy Interpretation; Psychological and interactional dimensions; Speech; Temporal patterns; Theory of communication; Voice variations
Communication-conflict situation, 32-6
Communication-oriented research, 10-1, 21-37
  On schizophrenia, 16-21, 32-7
Communicative competence, 42-8
Competence, linguistic, 42-8
  Acquisition of, 94-6
Complementarity role, 92
Compliance as aim of message, 70-2
Concept boosting, 217
Conceptual framework:
  Need for, 22
  Outline and explication of, 25-30
Conditioning, operant and verbal, 233-4, 237-8, 241-2, 245-58 *passim*
Conflict:
  Acknowledgement of, 77-9

Communication-, 32-6
Consistency of speech-accommodative behaviour, 277-8
Construals, social, 58-61
  See also Accommodation, interpersonal
Constructivist:
  Analysis of interpretive processes, 54-68
  Research on interpersonal processes and communication behaviour, 68-80
  See also Symbolic interactionism
Constructs:
  Commonality of, 7, 56-8
  Differentiation, 79
  Interpersonal, 56-61, 69-72
  Personal, theory of, 55
Contracts of behaviour, endorsed, 30-1, 33
Contractual aspect of communication, 30-1
Convergence (style-shifts), 268-70, 273-4, 276, 278
Conversation:
  Form of, 188-96
  Social and intellectual:
    Forms, difference between, 190-6
    Functions, 182-6
    "Look" of, 186-90
  See also Accommodation; Communication; Speech
Cooperation, 63
Coordination, interactional, 63
Copying in conversation, 191
Counterattitudinal message, 213, 223
  And cognitive stress, 214-6
Credibility of messages see Expectancy
Cross-cultural comparisons of children's speech, 92-3
Cusp catastrophe model see Catastrophe

Death, negative attitudes to, 134
Decentration, 27-30, 33

Decoding, anticipated, 28
  See also Codes
Developmental analysis of social construal process, 59-61
Deviant communication see Schizophrenia
Dialect, 44, 97, 101
Different groups, behaviour in, 267-78
Differentiation construct, 79
Directional act, communication as, 24, 30
Discontinuity of behaviour in catastrophe model, 273, 275
Discrimination and ethnicity, 129-32
Disfluency, 245-58 passim
Dissimilar perspectives, 122
Divergence (style-shifts), 268-70, 273-4, 276, 278
  See also Bifurcation
Diversity, linguistic see Dialect
"Double agent" research revisited, 236-44
  Functional differentiation of requests, 239-41
  Reconception of situation, 241-4, 259
Double jeopardy, 136-7
Double-bind theory, 18-19
Downgrading from speech cues, 115-39 passim

Egocentrism, 27-8, 31
  Of children, 26, 96
  Cognitive, 96
  In family, 29
  -Perspectivism, 60-1

Elderly see Age
Emergent nature of action, 62-3
Emotion and vocal patterns, 169-78
Emotional involvement and cognitive level, 60
Empirical evidence of accommodation, 244-58
  Complex repertoire, 249-53
  Improved analysis, 253-8

Simple repertoire, 245-9
Empiricism, 19, 22
Encoding, 28
  See also Codes
Environment, 124
  See also Situation
Ethnicity:
  Inferences about, 114-24
  And old age, 136-8
  See also Speech cues
Evaluation, social see Speech cues
Evaluative responses, Reinforcement-affect model of, 124
"Exercitives", 240
Expectancy interpretation of language and persuasion, 6, 199-229
  Active participation paradigm, 201, 213-6
  Passive message reception paradigm, 201, 203-13
  Resistance to persuasion paradigm, 201, 216-25
Experiments, 3
  Accommodation, 244-58
  Conversation, 186-7, 193
  Hallowe'en, 103-4
  Maps, 26-7, 33-6
  Requests, 244-58
  Speech cues, 117-35 passim
  Verbal conditioning, 237-8, 241-58 passim
"Explanation" mode of behaviour, 77
Explanatory value of current theory of communication, 15-21
  Schizophrenia research, 16-21, 32-7
Exposure to adult language, 88
  See also Children
Externalization studies of vocal patterns:
  And emotion, 169-70
  And personality, 146, 148, 154-7
    Articulation and timbre, 156-7
    Fundamental frequency, 155-6

Face, protection of, 72-6
Face-threatening action (FTA), 73

Facial expressions, 187
"Facts", situational, 266
Family:
  Communication in, 17, 22, 33
    And schizophrenia, 17, 19-20, 29, 32-6
    See also Children
  Egocentrism in, 29
  Position and children's speech, 93
  Size and children's speech, 93
  See also Children; Parents
Fathers, speech to children, 90-4
Fear:
  -Arousing appeals, 203-5, 208, 212
  Irrelevant, messages of, 211-3
Fluency, 245-58 passim
Forms:
  Of conversations, 188-96
  Of requests, 240
Frames for social encounters, 58-9
Frequency, 155-6
Functional differentiation of requests, 239-41
Functions of conversations, 182-6
Future research on speech cues, 136-8

Games and children's speech, 93-5
Gaze, 190-1
Goals, 283
  Interpersonal, behavioural strategies for, 47-8
Grammar, world of, 185
Grammatical knowledge, 42-3
"Grammaticalization" of utterances, 46
Group-salience/person-salience, 263, 268, 270, 276-7
Groups see Accommodation, interpersonal

Hallowe'en study, 103-4
Health, poor, negative attitude to, 134
Hierarchic ordering of message structure, 69-72
Historical perspectives, 11-12
Hysteresis in catastrophe model, 273, 275

Identity, 52
  Ethnic, inferences concerning, 114–24
  Of participants in social situation, 72–4
  Sex-role, 92
  Social, 2, 268, 277
  See also Individual; self
Illocutionary acts, 234–6, 240, 242, 258
Imperatives, fathers' use of, 90–1
"Implicit communication theory", 51
Inaccessibility behaviour in catastrophe model, 272, 275
Individual/s:
  Consistency in social constructs, 58–9
  Perspectives on, 11–2
  Speech with, 281
  See also Identity; Self
Individuality and commonality of constructs, 56–8
Inferences:
  Age-related, 132–5
  Class and ethnic identity, 114–24
"Information, flow of", 23
Ingroup:
  -Ingroup conversation, 278–9, 281
  -Outgroup conversation, 279
Innatists, 88
Inoculation viewpoint of resistance to persuasion, 216–25
Input, language, 89–90
Intellectual traits and respect, 184
  See also Conversation
Intensity see Language intensity
Intentionality, 24
Interaction, 20
  And communication, 62–8
    Constructivist conception of, 62–85
    Framework for analysis, 65–8
  Rules, 44
  Situation, 47
  Social see Conversation
Interactional aims, subsidiary, 72–9
Interactional coordination, 63

Interactionism see Symbolic interactionism
Interindividual speech, 281
Internal disposition in catastrophe model, 271
Interpersonal:
  Constructs and perceptions, 56–61, 69–72
  Goals, behavioural strategies for, 47–8
  See also Accommodation, interpersonal
Interpretations of language and persuasion see Expectancy
Interpretive:
  Concept of communication and symbolic interactionism, 48–55
  Processes, 46–53
    Constructivist analysis of, 53, 55–68
  "Schemes", 56–62, 64
Intimacy dimension, 283
Intragroup see Within-group
Irrelevant fear, messages, 211–3

Kipsigis tribe, children's speech in, 92–3
Knowledge, 42, 44–5

Language:
  Intensity of persuasive appeal:
    Active participation, 213–6, 219
    Passive message reception, 207–12, 220
    Resistance to persuasion, 216–26
  Study of, 12–5
  See also Communication
Learning process, 231
  See also Accommodation
Linguistics see Communication; Competence; Sociolinguistics
Listener-adapted message choices, 69
Logical relationship between prerequisites and communication, 29
"Look" of conversation, 186–90

Man see Individual

Mands, 234–6, 240, 258
Markers, speech, 263–4, 266
　*See also* Speech shifts
Meaning *see* Psychological and interactional
Message(s):
　Hierarchic ordering of, 69–72
　Reception, passive, 201, 203–13
　Strategies, 69–72, 203–13
　*See also* Expectancy interpretation; Persuasion
Methodological domain of social psychology of language, 2–3
Mimicking in conversation, 191
Minority groups *see* Speech cues
Modification, 96–102
Mothers, speech to children, 57, 88–90
　Compared with fathers', 90–2
　Receiver-focused strategies, 80
　*See also* Women
Musicality in speech, 89, 90

Negative-affect arousal and evaluative reactions, 124–9, 138
Noise, 125–8
Non-verbal communication, 191
Nonstandard speech, effect on social evaluation and behaviour, 114–32
　Ethnic identity and class, 114–24
　Ethnicity, effects on behaviour, 129–32
　Negative-affect arousal and evaluative reactions, 124–9, 138

Obscene language, 212
Old age *see* Age
Operant conditioning, 232–4, 258
Opinionated language message, 205–8, 212
Organismic-developmental theory, 55
"Organizing scheme", 63–4
Orthogenetic Principle, 59–61

Pace of conversation, 191
Paradigm:
　Active participation, 201, 213–6
　Conflict, 236
　Emerging, of person, 265
　*See also* Person-salience
　Passive message reception, 201, 203–13
　Resistance to persuasion, 201, 216–25
　Shift, 18
Parameters, vocal, 189
Parents: speech to children, 33, 80, 88–94
　Politeness routines, 105
Participation, active, 201, 213–6
Passive message reception paradigm, 201, 203–13
Pathological communication *see* Schizophrenia
Pauses in conversation, 189
Peers and children's speech, 93
Perceptions, 46, 55–61
"Performance factors", 42
Person-salience *see* Group-salience
Personal constructs theory, 55
Personality:
　And Children's speech, 95
　From speech cues, 118
　And vocal patterns, 5–6, 145–69
Perspective(s):
　On communication studies, 11–7
　Shift in, 17–8
　On Man, 11–2
　Socio-psychological, on children's speech, 94–5
　-Taking, 55, 69
Perspectivism, egocentrism-, 60–1
Persuasion, 69, 72
　Expectancy interpretation of language, 6, 199–229
　Resistance to, 201, 216–25
　Messages, 163–4
Pitch of parents' speech, 89, 90
Politeness:
　And face-saving, 73
　Routines, children's acquisition of, 102–6
Pragmatic usage of requests, 239, 241–2

Preconditions *see* Prerequisites
Prediction of unpredictability, 272
Prejudice, 129-30, 136
Prerequisites for successful communication, 25-6, 29
Pretreatment strategies, 216-25
Psychopathology *see* Schizophrenia
Psychological and interactional dimensions of communicative development, 4-5, 41-85
   Constructivist analysis, 54-68
   Constructivist research, 68-80
   Linguistic competence, communicative competence and resources of communication, 42-8
   Symbolic interactionism and interpretive concept of communication, 48-55
Psychology *see* Social psychology
Psychotherapy, 17
Punishment, 124, 233

Reality, social, 48, 57
   Construction of, 52-3
   "Shared", 26
Re-analysis of old data, 17, 231
   *See also* "Double agent"
Receiver, 24, 42
Receiver-focused strategies, 80
   Communication and social context of development, 79-80
   Communication strategies, 69-72
   "Reflexive self", 49-50
   *See also* Identity; Individual; Self
Refutational pretreatment strategy, 216-25 *passim*
Registers and children's speech, 93-5
Regulative communication, 70-2
Reinforcement, 233-4, 236-7, 242-58 *passim*, 260-1
Reinforcement-affect model of evaluative responses, 124
Reinterpretation, *see* Re-analysis
Rejection, conveying, 76-7
"Relational rules", 52
Requests, 69, 259
   Empirical evidence, 244-58

Functional differentiation of, 239-41
Pragmatic usage of, 239, 241-2
Resistance to persuasion paradigm, 201, 216-25
Resources, 42-8
Rewarding stimuli, 124
Rhythm in conversation, 192
Role:
   Acting, 101
   Awareness in children, 98
   Of children, 92, 101
   Complementarity, 92
   Delineated by speech, 92
   Sex, 92, 209
   "Taking", 50, 53-5
   *See also* Counterattitudinal message
Rules, interaction, 44

Schizophrenia, 67
   Communication-oriented research on, 16-21, 32-7
Scientific revolution, 18
Second language learning, 276
Self, "reflexive", 49-50
   *See also* Identity; Individual
Self-esteem, 277
Setting *see* Situation
Sex:
   Of child:
      And parents' speech, 91
      And speech differences, 98, 104-5
   Roles, 92, 209
"Sign stimuli", 184
Silence, pattern of, 182
Situated activity/action, 44, 62
Situations, 14
   And children's speech, 98-101
   Definition of and subsidiary interactional aims, 72-9
   Interaction, 47
   Social identity of participants in, 72-4
   Symbolic working models of, 265-6
Situational:
   Consistency in social constructs,

## Subject Index

58–9
Construals *see* Accommodation, interpersonal
"Facts", 266
Social:
  Act, communication as, 24, 30
  Action, communicative action as part of, 68
  Arousal, 190–1
  Behaviour in catastrophe model, 271
  Class *see* Class
  Construals:
    Developmental; analysis of, 59–61
    Individual and situational consistency in, 58–9
  Construction of reality, issues in, 52–3
  Context of development and receiver-focused communication, 79–80
  Conversation *see* Conversation
  Developmental approach, 29–30
  Distance from speech cues, 118–21
  Evaluation *see* Speech cues
  Frame for encounters, 58–9
  Identity, 2, 268, 277
  Interaction *see* Conversation
  Perception process, 46
  Perspective of communication studies, 13–4, 16
  Pressure in catastrophe model, 271
  Processes, 3
    Symbolic interactionist perspective, 49–53
  Reality *see* Reality
  Routines and politeness, 102–4
  Situation *see* Situation
  Traits and liking, 184
Social-development framework of communication-oriented research, 10–1, 21–31
  Conceptual framework, 25–30
  Definition of communication, 23–5
Social-individual model, 30
Social psychology, 230
  And language, 1–3, 267–70
    Intergroup relations, 267–8
    Speech accommodation theory, 268–70
  And social situations, 264–7
  *See also* Communication
Socialization, 48, 57, 90
"Socio-centric", child, 60
"Socioeconomic status *see* Class
Sociolinguistics, 1, 232
  Criticisms of linguistic competence, 43–6
Socio-psychological:
  Constructs, 1
  Perspectives, 94–5
Solidarity ratings from speech cues, 116, 118–21
Sounds, 185
Spanish-accented English, 113–31 *passim*
Spectral techniques, 190, 192, 195
Speech:
  Acquiring social variation in, 86–111
    Child language, variation in, 96–102
    To children, 5, 87–94
    Competence, acquisition of, 94–6
    Politeness routines, 102–6
  Acts, 45, 46
  Cues and social evaluation, 5, 112–43
    Age estimates and inferences, 132–5
    Future research directions, 136–8
    Nonstandard speech, 114–32
  Events, 45
  Markers, 112–13
    *See also* Speech cues
  Shifts, 268–70, 273–4, 276, 278
    *See also* Communication; Conversation; Temporal patterns
  Status *see* Class
  Stereotypes, 101, 114–39 *passim*
    *See also* Roles
Strategic:
  Control over communication, 46–53

Position of communication studies, 15
Strategies:
  Face-saving, 72–6
  Message, and expectancy interpretations, 203–13
  Receiver-focused, 69–72
  Message, 69–72
Stress, cognitive, 60, 214–16
Style-shifts *see* Speech shifts
Subsidiary interactional aims and definition of situation, 72–9
Symbolic interactionism, 48–55
  *See also* Constructivist
Symbolic working models of situations, 265–6
Symbols, abstract, 185
Synchrony in conversation, 191–2

Teachers' evaluation of children by speech, 97
Temporal:
  And attribution studies of personality and vocal patterns, 167–9
  Patterns of speech and gaze in social and intellectual conversation, 6, 182–98
    Differences between, 190–6
    Functions, 182–6
    "Look" of conversation, 186–90
Theoretical domain of social psychology of language, 2–3
Theory of communication, 4, 10–40
  Explanatory value of current, 15–21
  Perspective on Man, fundamental, 11–12
  Social-developmental framework of research 10–11, 21–31
  And study of language, 12–15
Thought, 53–4, 183
  *See also* Cognitive
Timbre of voice, 156–7
Time, changes over, 89
  *See also* Temporal
Turn-taking in conversation, 189
Twins, speech of, 93

Understandability, 125
Unpredictability, prediction of, 272
Use of language, 13–4

Value-judgements and children's speech, 97
Variations in children's language, 96–102
Verbal accommodation *see* Accommodation
Verbal conditioning, 233–4, 237–8, 241–2, 245–58 *passim*
Vocal features, 145
Vocal patterns *see* Voice Variations
Voice variations, social psychology of, 144–81
  And emotion, 169–78
  And personality, 5–6, 145–69

White noise, 125–6
Within-group communication and code elaboration, 278–81
  General and special theories of, 280–1
Women
  Expectancy interpretation, 209–11, 212
  Face-saving, 75
  Speakers, 132–3
  *See also* Mothers

For Product Safety Concerns and Information please contact our EU representative GPSR@taylorandfrancis.com
Taylor & Francis Verlag GmbH, Kaufingerstraße 24, 80331 München, Germany

www.ingramcontent.com/pod-product-compliance
Lightning Source LLC
Chambersburg PA
CBHW070723020526
44116CB00031B/1197